Dedication

[illegible], who says he doesn't need another dedication. Sorry, you get one anyway. Thanks for reading the manuscript of this book, for providing honest criticism, and for putting up with me.

1995 Update for *Hawaii Trails*

General. To see some of your hikes in advance as well as to read about them here, get the video trail guide *Pathways in Paradise: Hawaii*. If your outdoor or travel store doesn't carry the video, you can find its publisher, Purple Dragon Ventures, at Box 164, Virginia City, NV 89440, 702-847-9088.

Page 36, para. 2, line 3, "All" should be "Most of."

Page 44, Hiking Table, delete entries for Trips 40 and 41 (more on this below).

Page 46, para. 3, line 1: Add between "and" and "turn": a junction where you

Page 47, para. 1, line 2: Add after the dash: Milu,

Page 49, Driving instructions: Add the parking information now on page 262.

Pages 49–51, Trip 2: A reader reports trouble with rats, mice, and cockroaches at Waimanu.

Page 66, para. 2, note that road rebuilding may have changed the mile markers bracketing this trailhead.

Page 84, add at end of 3rd para.: Dehydration is a serious problem on these hikes. Especially if you normally sweat heavily when exercising, drink *lots* of water—as much as or more than you normally would.

Page 106, Driving instructions, line 2: Change "turn left" to "turn right."

Page 178, para. 3: Note that a reader reports finding few bugs while camping in this area during the winter. Might be worth a try!

Pages 182–186, Trips 40 and 41: Delete these trips. A reader writes, and Hawaii Volcanoes National Park confirms, that Lae Apuki and Kamoamoa beach have been overrun by lava.

Page 216, last para., lines 3 and 4: "park Pervice Brochure" should be "Park Service brochure."

Page 236, 1st para.: Note that the petroglyphs set up in the "small area on your left" are reproductions, not originals, and that the area is especially designed for those who are mobility-impaired.

Page 262, next-to-last para.: Delete. The Kona Lodge and Hostel is defunct.

Page 266, add to Hawaii Volcanoes National Park: Lae Apuki and Kamoamoa Black Sand Beach. Lava recently overran these attractions; they are no more. Formerly Trips 40 and 41 in this book.

Page 266, next-to-last paragraph: A reader reports that the Park Service now recommends this trail as the preferred route to Keauhou.

HAWAII TRAILS

Walks, Strolls and Treks on the Big Island

Kathy Morey

WILDERNESS PRESS
BERKELEY

FIRST EDITION May 1992
Second printing June 1995

Photos and maps by the author
Design by Thomas Winnett
Cover design by Larry Van Dyke

Library of Congress Card number 92-15130
ISBN 0-89997-134-2

Manufactured in the United States of America
Published by Wilderness Press
2440 Bancroft Way
Berkeley, CA 94704
(510) 843-8080

Write or call for free catalog

Library of Congress Cataloging-in-Publication Data

Morey, Kathy.
Hawaii trails : walks, strolls, and treks on the big island / Kathy Morey.
p. cm.
Includes bibliographical references (p.) and index.
ISBN 0-89997-134-2
1. Hiking--Hawaii--Hawaii Island--Guidebooks. 2. Hawaii Island (Hawaii)--Guidebooks. I. Title.
GV199.42.H32H386 1992
919.69'04'4--dc20 92-15130
CIP

Table of Contents

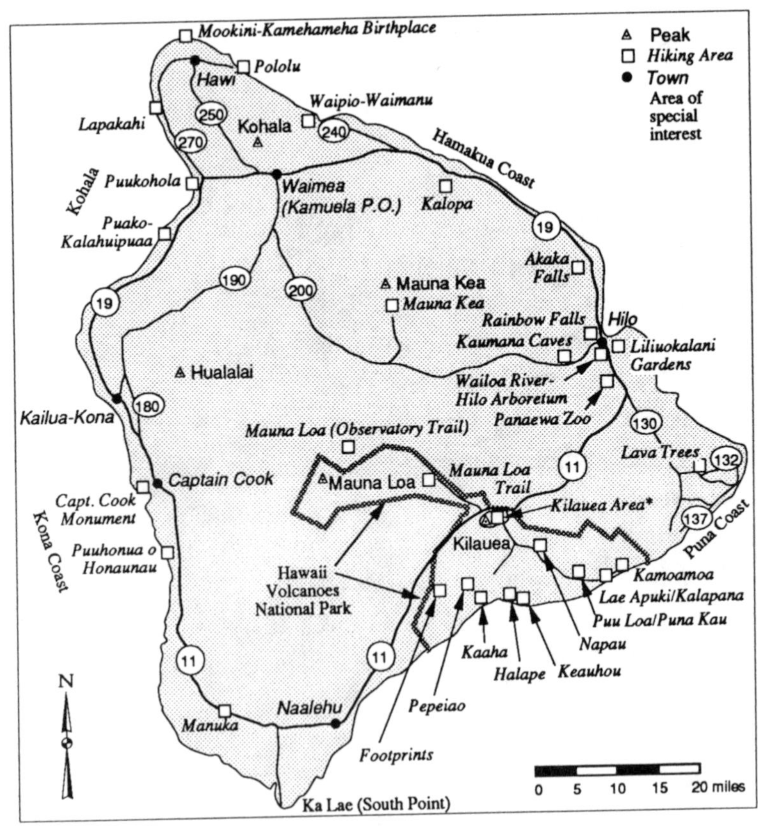

The Big Island of Hawaii: Overview of the Principal Hiking Areas

Introduction

Can you name this place? On its west, vast fields of forbidding lava stretch from mountains nearly 14,000 feet high to a coast that's dotted with shimmering blue bays and luxurious resorts. At its northern end, a remote valley, its steep walls richly clothed in rain-forest greenery and streaked by waterfalls, protects a way of life that harkens back to the 1900s. On its east, Earth's most active volcano destroys famous black-sand beaches and creates new ones just a few miles away. If you jumped into the roiling sea at its desolate southern tip—*don't do it!*—you wouldn't touch land again until you reached Antarctica. What can this contradictory place be? What else but the Big Island of Hawaii!

Some will say you can see the Big Island adequately from the air. Others will say you can drive around it and see everything in a day. Still others would park you in a resort and tell you *that's* Hawaii. Don't believe it! The best of the Big Island is outside, along the trails, where there are no barriers of metal, glass, or concrete to separate you from its lush rainforests, flower-filled parks, steaming volcanoes, and acres of lava "moonscapes." You don't have to walk far: a worthwhile hike on Hawaii can be as short as a quarter-mile stroll suitable for anyone who's ambulatory, or it can be as long as a five-day backpack to the top of its second-highest peak, Mauna Loa. How do I know? I walked every trail that's used as a trip in this book at least once in the spring, summer, and fall of 1991.

The shape of things. The Big Island of Hawaii is shaped almost like a square, tipped onto one corner—except that the thumb-shaped Kohala Peninsula juts northwest out of the square. The Big Island is made up of five or six volcanoes (more on this in the section on Geology and History). The island's center is dominated by the two largest volcanoes: 13,796-foot Mauna Kea, which hasn't erupted for at least 4,500 years, and 13,679-foot Mauna Loa, which last erupted in 1984, menacing the Big Island's main city, Hilo. Kilauea volcano on the east is the world's most active volcano. Its most recent eruption began in 1983 and continues as I write this. Kilauea is the centerpiece of Hawaii Volcanoes National Park, which also includes the summit of Mauna Loa. Hawaii grows each time fresh lava from

Kilauea reaches the sea, cools to become new land, and extends the state just a little farther eastward. It's the fastest-growing state in the nation!

Take time for the island of Hawaii. It really is *the* Big Island! If you have only a day or two on the island of Hawaii, stay put and enjoy what's nearby. There's probably a short hike or two in this book that will be very near you. The idea that you can drive around the Big Island and see it all in one day is laughable. Come back for a longer visit when you can.

If possible, stay a week or more on the island of Hawaii. The road that encircles most of the island is over 220 miles long—and it doesn't get you to the best of the scenery and hiking trails. Give yourself time to move around to different lodgings in order to more fully explore different hiking areas. You could easily spend a month on the island of Hawaii. *That's* how big and how spectacular the Big Island is!

Be a good visitor. Along the waterfront in Kailua on the Kona Coast (often called "Kailua-Kona"), the rental cars creep along bumper to bumper. Horns honk. Tourist drivers scream at tourist pedestrians. *What the hell kind of tropical paradise is this?!* you may think if you're caught in Kailua-Kona traffic. *Where's that aloha spirit?* Fortunately, there are plenty of less crowded, less frantic places on the Big Island.

Still, Hawaii is not Paradise. Paradise is infinite and self-renewing. Hawaii is a real place of finite space and resources, where real people live real lives with jobs, families, budgets, and bills. Hawaii needs loving care from its visitors as well as from its natives. As the number of tourists increases, I think it becomes important that we visitors actively contribute to the *aloha* spirit instead of just passively expecting to receive it. Bring your best manners and your patience with you to the Big Island. Be the first to smile and wave. Be the first to pull your car over so that someone else can pass. Be scrupulous in observing the rules of the trail in order to help preserve what's left of Hawaii's vanishing wild places. NO TRESPASSING, KEEP OUT, or KAPU ("forbidden") signs mean, "You stay out." Please respect those signs.

Terms. When I refer to the Hawaiian archipelago in general, and particularly to the inhabited islands, I'll say "Hawaii." When I refer to the island of Hawaii itself, I'll say "the island of Hawaii" or "the Big Island."

Getting Information About the Big Island of Hawaii

The search for the perfect trail guide. I wish I could be certain this was a flawless book. However, some things limit an author's ability to produce a perfect, error-free, always up-to-date book. Here are some of the factors, and what you can do to help yourself (and me).

Nature makes constant revisions; so do agencies. Nature constantly reshapes the landscape across which we plan to trek. That's usually a gradual process, but once in a while she makes drastic changes overnight. A landslide or a volcanic eruption can erase a trail in seconds. Erosion can undercut a cliff edge and make last year's safe hike an extremely dangerous one, so that the local authorities close a trail you'd hoped to ramble on. And Hawaii's fragile volcanic terrain erodes quite rapidly.

Agencies in charge of hiking areas may close an area because they've realized it's environmentally too sensitive to withstand more human visits. An area once open to overnight camping may become a day-use-only area. Trails become impassable from lack of maintenance. Happily, agencies may open new areas because they've been able to acquire new acreage or complete a trail-building project.

Change is the only thing that's constant in this world, so that guidebook authors and publishers always play "catch up" with Nature and with agencies. We want to keep the guidebooks up to date, but we are always at least one step behind the latest changes. The day when you'll have constantly revised books on-line at your wristwatch/computer terminal isn't here yet. So it's possible that a few trail descriptions are becoming obsolete even as this book goes to press.

Write for the latest information. It's a good idea to use this book in conjunction with the latest information from the agency in charge of the areas you plan to hike in. Unfortunately, the recreation map of Hawaii published by the Hawaii District of the divisions of Forestry and Wildlife and of State Parks lacks trail information for hikers. The information it does have is quite out of date. There isn't a better map available from those agencies. This book gives you a far more complete and detailed picture of Hawaii's principal hiking and backcountry camping opportunities than the current recreation map does. And it describes those opportunities from a hiker's perspective.

Still, it's a good idea to write to these agencies as soon as you've read this book and decided where you want to hike and camp on Hawaii. Ask them for their latest trail and camping maps, regulations, and permit-issuing procedures. Except for Hawaii Volcanoes National Park, enclose a stamped, self-addressed envelope for your convenience in getting the information you need as soon as possible. (National parks almost always use the franking privilege of Federal agencies, so you'd be wasting a stamp.) Their addresses and telephone numbers are in "Getting Permits or Permission."

Prepare yourself with general information, too. A generous source of a wide variety of useful information about Hawaii is the Hawaii Visitors Bureau. Here are the addresses of their offices on the mainland:

Canada: 4915 Cedar Crescent, Delta, B.C. V4M 1J9, Canada
Chicago: Suite 1031, 180 North Michigan Avenue, Chicago, IL 60601
Los Angeles: Room 502, Central Plaza, 3440 Wilshire Boulevard, Los Angeles, CA 90010
New York: Room 1407, 441 Lexington Avenue, New York, NY 10017
San Francisco: Suite 450, 50 California Street, San Francisco, CA 94111
Washington, D.C.: Suite 519, 1511 K Street N.W., Washington, D.C., 20005

A letter to them will get you a fat packet full of all kinds of handy information.

Let me know what you think and what you find. I hope this book helps make your visit to Hawaii even more enjoyable than it would have been. I plan to update it regularly, and you can help me. Let me know what you think of it. Did you find it helpful when you visited Hawaii? Was it accurate and complete enough that you enjoyed the walks and hikes you took based on the book? Did you notice any significant discrepancies between this book and what you found when you visited Hawaii, discrepancies that you judge are not just the result of two different perceptions of the same thing? What were they? The publisher and I are very concerned about accuracy. We'd appreciate your comments. I'd also like to know about it if you think there are ways in which the book can be improved. Write to me in care of Wilderness Press, 2440 Bancroft Way, Berkeley, CA 94704.

Spoken Hawaiian: An Incomplete and Unauthoritative Guide

What, only 12 letters?! Nineteenth-century American missionaries used only 12 letters to create a written version of the spoken Hawaiian language. Superficially, that might make Hawaiian seem simple. But Hawaiian is a much more complex and subtle language than 12 letters can do justice to. However, we're stuck with those 12 letters—the five English vowels (a, e, i, o, u) and seven of the consonants (h, k, l, m, n, p, w).

Consonants. The consonants have the same sound in Hawaiian as they do in your everyday English except for "w." "W" is sometimes pronounced as "v" when it follows "a," always pronounced as "v" when it follows "e" or "i."

Vowels. The vowels are generally pronounced as they are in Italian, with each vowel sounded separately. Authentic Hawaiian makes further distinctions, but those are of more interest to scholars than to hikers.[1] The following is a simplified system. Vowel sounds in general are:

a	like "ah" in "*Ah*!"
e	like "ay" in "d*ay*."
i	like "ee" as in "wh*ee*!"
o	like "o" in "g*o*."
u	like "oo" in "f*oo*d" (or "u" in "r*u*de").

[1]Remember that Hawaiian evolved as a spoken, not a written, language. Authentic *written* Hawaiian uses two special marks to indicate other variations on pronouncing vowels in *spoken* Hawaiian. Those variations change the meaning of a word. One is the glottal stop, indicated by a single quotation mark ('). It indicates that you should make a complete break in your voice before sounding the vowel that follows it. There really isn't an English equivalent, though the break in "uh-oh!" is close. Another is the macron mark, which is a straight line over a vowel. It indicates that you should pronounce a vowel as a long sound instead of a short sound. For example, the Hawaiian long-a sound is "ah," and the Hawaiian short-a sound is "uh." We have the same sounds in English but don't use special marks to distinguish between them except in dictionaries. Road signs, topographic maps, and this book don't use glottal stops or macron marks.

Notice that that means that when you see two or more of the same letter in a row, you pronounce each of them separately:

"Honokaa" is Ho-no-ka-a.
"Pepeekeo" is Pe-pe-e-ke-o.
"Milolii" is Mi-lo-li-i.
"Ookala" is O-o-ka-la.
"Puu" is Pu-u.

That seems *too* simple, and it is. If you tried to pronounce every vowel, speaking Hawaiian would turn into a nightmare. You wouldn't live long enough to pronounce some words. Fortunately, several pairs of vowels often—but not always—form merged sounds.

Vowel Pairs Whose Sounds Merge. Like every other language, Hawaiian has vowel pairs whose sounds naturally "smooth" into each other. They're similar to Italian or English diphthongs. The degree to which the two sounds are merged in Hawaiian is officially less than occurs in English, but most Hawaiian people I've talked with merge them fully. Vowel-pair pronunciation is approximately:

ae often smoothed to "eye" as in "*eye*ful" or "i" in "*i*ce." It's the English long-i sound.
ai often smoothed as for "ae," above.
ao often smoothed to sound like "ow" in "c*ow*."
au often smoothed to "ow" in "c*ow*", too.
ei sometimes smoothed to "ay" as in "d*ay*." It's the English long-a sound.
eu smooth the sounds together a *little*, like "ayoo."
oi usually like "oi" in "*oi*l"—in other words, just what you're used to.

Syllables. Every Hawaiian syllable ends in a vowel sound. A Hawaiian syllable never contains more than one consonant. That means every consonant goes with the vowel that *follows* it. Every vowel not preceded by a consonant stands alone when you break a *written* word into syllables (you may smooth some of them together when you *speak*). For example:

"Aa" consists of the two syllables a-a (it's a kind of lava flow that's very rough and jagged).
"Kapoho" consists of the three syllables Ka-po-ho (a village destroyed by Kilauea's 1960 eruption).
"Naalehu" consists of the four syllables Na-a-le-hu (not just the southernmost town on the Big Island but the southernmost town in the fifty states).
"Pahoehoe" consists of the five syllables pa-ho-e-ho-e (except that it's usually pronounced "pa-hoi-hoi"; it's another kind of lava flow, much smoother than aa).
"Kealakekua" consists of the six syllables Ke-a-la-ke-ku-a (the bay on the Big Island where Captain Cook was slain).
"Liliuokalani" consists of the seven syllables Li-li-u-o-ka-la-ni

(Hawaii's last monarch and writer of the beloved song "Aloha Oe").

Accent. In general, the accent falls on the next-to-last syllable for words with three or more syllables and on the first syllable for words of two syllables. For words of more than three syllables, you put a little stress on every other syllable preceding the accented one. Don't worry about this; it seems to come naturally.

There are common-usage exceptions, such as *makai* (ma-KAI, with the accent on the last syllable). When you see exceptions such as those, chances are that what has happened is that European usage has fully merged two sounds into one. Proper Hawaiian pronunciation of *makai* would be closer to "ma-KA-i," a three-syllable word with the last two syllables almost merging.

Hint for Longer Words: Repetition and Rhythm. Have you noticed the tendency in long Hawaiian words for groups of letters to repeat? That kind of repetition is fairly common. When you see a long Hawaiian word, don't panic. Identify its repeating letter groups, figure out how to pronounce them individually, then put the whole word together. Chances are you'll come pretty close to getting it correct.

For example, *Mokuaweoweo* might throw you (it's the huge caldera at the summit of Mauna Loa, one of the five volcanoes that make up the Big Island). But look at the repeating letter group *weo* (way-o). See the word as "Mokua/weo/weo." So, two "weo"s prefixed with a "Mokua"—that makes "Mo-ku-a-way-o-way-o." Once you've identified the repeating groups, the rhythm of the word comes naturally. Try this approach for longer words, including the state fish: *humuhumunukunukuapuaa:* two "hu-mu"s, two "nu-ku"s, and an "a-pu-a-a." Now try it: "hu-mu/hu-mu/nu-ku/nu-ku/a-pu-a-a." . . . Very good!

***Makai* and *mauka*.** In Hawaii, local people often give directions or describe the location of a place as *makai* (merge the *ai*), which means "toward the sea," or *mauka* (merge the *au*), which means "toward the mountains; inland." I had a terrible time remembering which was which until I came up with this mnemonic:

Go *makai*
Where sea meets sky,

and Tom Winnett came up with:

Mauka is toward the MAUntains.

However, I still think in terms of left, right, north, south, east, and west. I don't often use *mauka* and *makai* in this book.

Do your best, with respect. Approach the language with respect, and give it your best shot. Then be prepared to hear local people pronounce it differently. Learn from them. Maybe it's part of our jobs as visitors to inadvertently provide a little comic relief for those living and working here as opposed to just vacationing here.

Instant Hawaiian (see Bibliography) is a useful booklet that's a lot less frivolous than its title implies. It begins, "So you'd like to learn to speak Hawaiian—you should live so long!" I felt I'd come to the right place. Look for it when you get to Hawaii.

Lapakahi State Historical Park

Geology and History, Natural and Human

First, the earth

According to the theory of *plate tectonics,* the earth consists of:

A rigid, rocky outer shell, the *lithosphere* ("rocky zone").

Beneath the lithosphere, a hot, semifluid layer, the *asthenosphere* ("weak zone").

A core that doesn't play a part in this oversimplified discussion.

The lithosphere is broken into *plates* that move with respect to one another. Hot, fluid material, possibly from the asthenosphere or melted by contact with the asthenosphere, penetrates up through the lithosphere at three kinds of places:

Mid-oceanic ridges, where plates spread apart.

Subduction zones, where plates collide and one dives under the other (subducts).

Hot spots, where a plume of molten material appears in the middle of a plate.

Next, the land

It's believed that the Hawaiian Islands exist where the Pacific Plate, on which they ride, is moving northwest across a hot spot. An undersea volcano is built at the place where the plate is over the hot spot. If the volcano gets big enough, it breaks the ocean's surface to become an island. Eventually, the plate's movement carries the island far enough away from the hot spot that volcanism ceases on that island. Erosion, which begins the moment the new island appears above the sea, tears the land down.

The Hawaiian Islands are successively older toward the northwest and younger toward the southeast. Northwestern islands, like Necker, are hardly more than bits of volcanic rock now. Southeastern islands, including the major Hawaiian Islands, are still significant chunks of land. Kauai and Niihau are the oldest and the farthest northwest of the major islands. The Big Island of Hawaii is the youngest and the farthest southeast of the major islands. Southeast of the Big Island, Loihi Seamount is a growing volcano far beneath the ocean. In a few thousand years, Loihi may be the newest Hawaiian island.

The molten material—lava—characteristic of Hawaiian volcanoes is relatively fluid. The fluidity of the lava allows it to spread widely, and repeated eruptions produce broad-based, rounded volcanoes called shield volcanoes. The volcano expels not only flowing lava but volcanic fragments such as cinder and ash. Alternating layers of these materials build up during periods of volcanic activity.

Erosion has sculpted the exotic landscapes we associate with volcanic tropical islands. Waves pound the volcano's edges, undercutting them and, where the volcano slopes more steeply, forming cliffs. Streams take material from higher on the volcano, cutting valleys into its flanks and depositing the material they carry as alluvium. Alluvial deposits form the floors of valleys like Waipio and Waimanu. New episodes of volcanism wholly or partly fill in those landscapes, and erosional forces immediately begin sculpting the new surface as well as the remaining older surface.

The Big Island is geologically an infant on an Earth more than four billion years old. Potassium-argon dating of rocks suggests that lava welled forth to build Kohala, the oldest of the island's five or six volcanoes, beginning a little more than half a million years ago. Kohala is now extinct and is deeply eroded into spectacular valleys. Mauna Kea's rocks overlie Kohala's. Mauna Kea is old enough and

A crater on the flank of Mauna Kea

high enough to bear the scars of glaciation during the height of the last ice age. Mauna Kea's youngest-known lava flows are about 4,500 years old. Earthquakes still occur beneath Mauna Kea, so it's considered dormant, not extinct. Hualalai volcano, on the west side of the Big Island, last erupted in 1800–1801 and is only dormant. Ke-Ahole Airport on the Kona coast is built on Hualalai lavas. Mauna Loa is still very active, having last erupted in 1984. Its lava came within four miles of Hilo on that occasion. Some scholars believe that an extinct volcano, Ninole, lies buried under the huge mass of Mauna Loa. On the east side of the island, Kilauea, the world's most active volcano, continues an eruption that began in 1983. Written records of Kilauea's eruptions reach back to 1824, but Hawaiian traditions assure us that it has been active ever since people first settled the Big Island. Only on Kohala can we say that erosion prevails, changing the landscape constantly. Elsewhere on the Big Island, volcanism may rework the landscape at any time.

Life arrives

Living organisms colonize new land rapidly. In Hawaii, plants established themselves once there was a little soil for them. Seeds arrived on the air currents, or floated in on the sea, or hitched a ride on the feathers or in the guts of birds. Insects and spiders also took advantage of the air currents. Birds were certainly among the first visitors. Living things found little competition and quickly adapted to their new home, evolving into an astonishing variety of species many of which occur naturally only on the Hawaiian Islands ("endemic to Hawaii"). The only mammals to arrive were the bat and the seal. Some birds became flightless—a fairly common adaptation on isolated islands with no ground predators.

The Big Island is a virtual laboratory where scientists can study how life establishes itself on new lava flows. Hikers can see this process at work, especially in the Kilauea area.

People arrive

It's unlikely that the site of the very first human colony in the Hawaiian Islands will ever be found. Too much time has passed; too many destructive forces have been at work. However, recent archaeological work has established that people had settled in Hawaii by 300–400 A.D., earlier than had previously been thought. Linguistic studies and cultural artifacts recovered from sites of early colonization point to the Marquesas Islands as the colonizers' home; the Marquesas themselves seem to have been colonized as early as 200 B.C.

The colonizers of Hawaii had to adapt the Marquesan technology to their new home. For example, the Marquesans made distinctive large, one-piece fishhooks from the large, strong pearl shells that abounded in Marquesan waters. There are no such large shells in Hawaiian waters, so the colonists developed two-piece fishhooks made of the weaker materials that were available in Hawaii (such as bone and wood). Over time, a uniquely Hawaiian material culture developed.

At one time, scholars believed that, as related in Hawaii's oral traditions and genealogies, a later wave of colonizers from Tahiti swept in and conquered the earlier Hawaiians. Research does not support that theory. Instead, research has revealed that before European contact, Hawaiian material culture evolved steadily in patterns that suggest gradual and local, not abrupt and external, influences. The archaeological record hints that there may have been some Hawaiian-Tahitian contact in the twelfth century, but its influence was slight.

The Hawaiians profoundly altered the environment of the islands. They had brought with them the plants they had found most useful in the Marquesas Islands: taro, ti, the trees from which they made a bark cloth (tapa), sugar cane, ginger, gourd plants, yams, bamboo, turmeric, arrowroot, and the breadfruit tree. They also brought the small pigs of Polynesia, dogs, jungle fowl, and, probably as stowaways, rats. They used slash-and-burn techniques to clear the native lowland forests for the crops they had brought. Habitat loss together with competition for food with and predation by the newly introduced animals wrought havoc with the native animals, particularly birds. Many species of birds had already become extinct long before Europeans arrived.

On the eve of the Europeans' accidental stumbling across Hawaii, the major Hawaiian islands held substantial numbers of people of Polynesian descent. They had no written language, but their oral and musical traditions were ancient and rich. Their social system was highly stratified and very rigid. Commoners, or *makaainana,* lived in self-sufficient family groups and villages, farming and fishing for most necessities and trading for necessities they could not otherwise obtain. The land was divided among hereditary chiefs of the noble class (*alii*). Commoners paid part of their crops or catches as taxes to the chief who ruled the land-division they lived on; commoners served their chief as soldiers. Higher chiefs ruled over lower chiefs, receiving from them taxes and also commoners to serve as soldiers. People especially gifted in healing, divination, or important crafts served the populace in those capacities (for example, as priests). There was also a class of untouchables, the *kauwa.* Most people were at death what they had been at birth.

Strict laws defined what was forbidden, or *kapu,* and governed the conduct of *kauwa* toward everyone else, of commoners toward *alii,* of *alii* of a lower rank toward *alii* of higher rank, and of men and women toward each other. Some of the laws seem irrationally harsh. For example, a commoner could be put to death if his shadow fell on an *alii.*

Chiefs frequently made war on one another. If the chiefs of one island were united under a high chief or a king, often that island would make war on the other islands. Those unions could be shaky. For example, when the young chief Kamehameha thought he had made his rule of the Big Island secure enough that he could turn to conquering the other islands, his "ally" on the Big Island rebelled. Putting down Chief Keoua's rebellion and restoring his control over the Big Island took Kamehameha several years.

The Hawaiians worshipped many gods and goddesses. The principal ones were Ku, Kane, Kanaloa, and Lono. Ku represented the male aspect of the natural world. Ku was also the god of war, and he demanded human sacrifice. Kane was the god of life, a benevolent god who was regarded as the Creator and the ancestor of all Hawaiians. Kanaloa ruled the dead and the dark aspects of life, and he was often linked with Kane in worship.

Lono was another benevolent god; he ruled clouds, rain, and harvests. The annual winter festival in Lono's honor, *Makahiki,* ran from October to February. *Makahiki* was a time of harvest, celebration, fewer *kapu,* and sporting events. Images of Lono were carried around each island atop tall poles with crosspieces from which banners of white tapa flew. (Legend said Lono had sailed away from Hawaii long ago and would return in a floating *heiau* (temple) decked with poles flying long white banners from their crosspieces.) Chiefs and chiefesses met the image of Lono with ceremonies and gifts, and commoners came forward to pay their taxes.

Systems like that can last for hundreds and even thousands of years in the absence of compelling internal problems or changes and of external forces, as the Hawaiian system did. But change eventually comes.

The Europeans arrive by accident

Christopher Columbus had sailed from Spain to what he thought was the Orient, hoping to find a sea route to replace the long, hazardous land route. But in fact he discovered an obstacle now called North America. With a direct sea route between Europe and the Orient blocked, people sought other sea routes. The southern routes around the Cape of Good Hope at the tip of Africa and Cape Horn at the tip of South America proved to be very long and very treacherous. Still, the trade was lucrative. The European demand for Oriental goods such as spices, Chinese porcelain, and silk was insatiable. By trading their way around the world, a captain, his crew, and the government or the tradesmen that financed them might become very wealthy in just one voyage.

All over Europe, people came to believe that a good, navigable route *must* exist in northern waters that would allow them to sail west from Europe around the northern end of North America to the Orient. (It doesn't exist.) Captain James Cook sailed from England on July 12, 1776, to try to find the Northwest Passage from the Pacific side.

In December of 1777, Cook left Tahiti sailing northeast, not expecting to see land again until he reached North America. Instead, he sighted land on January 18, 1778, and reached the southeast shore of Kauai on January 19th. In Hawaii, it was the time of *Makahiki,* the festival honoring the god Lono. The Hawaiians mistook the masts

The Captain Cook Monument

and sails of Cook's ships for the poles and tapa banners of the floating *heiau* on which Lono was to return and received Cook as if he were Lono.

Cook was an intelligent and compassionate man who respected the native societies he found and who tried to deal with their people fairly and decently. He tried to keep crewmen who he knew had venereal diseases from infecting the natives, but he failed. Cook did not stay long in Hawaii. He spent most of 1778 searching for the Northwest Passage; unsuccessful, he returned to Hawaii in early 1779 to make repairs and resupply. He found sutitable anchorage at Kealakekua Bay on the Big Island. It was *Makahiki* again. All went well at first, but the Hawaiians stole an auxiliary boat from one of his ships. When he tried to retrieve it, there was a brief skirmish, in which Cook and four of his crew were killed.

Cook's ships survived a second futile search for the Northwest Passage, after which the crew sailed westward for England, stopping in China. There the crew learned the astonishing value of another of the expedition's great discoveries: the furs of the sea otters and seals of the Pacific Northwest. Trade with the Orient suddenly became even more profitable, and Hawaii was to become not an isolated curiosity but an important point on a major world trade route.

On the Big Island, Kamehameha began his conquest of the islands in 1790. Kamehameha actively sought Western allies, weapons, and advice; he conquered all the islands but Kauai and Niihau.

Kamehameha's wars, Western diseases, and the sandalwood trade decimated the native Hawaiians. Chiefs indebted themselves to foreign merchants for weapons and other goods. New England merchants discovered that Hawaii had abundant sandalwood, for which the Chinese would pay huge prices. Merchants demanded payment from the chiefs in sandalwood; the chiefs ordered the commoners into the mountains to get the precious wood. The heartwood nearest the roots was the best part; the whole tree had to be destroyed to get it. The mountains were stripped of their sandalwood trees. Many of those ordered into the mountains died of exposure and starvation. Communities that had depended on their labor for food also starved.

Kamehameha I died in 1819, leaving the monarchy to his son Liholiho and a regency in Liholiho's behalf to his favorite wife, Kaahumanu. Liholiho was an amiable, weak-willed alcoholic. Kaahumanu was strong-willed, intelligent, capable, and ambitious. She believed that the old Hawaiian *kapu* system was obsolete: no gods struck down the Westerners, who daily did things that were *kapu* for Hawaiians. Six months after Kamehameha I's death, she persuaded Liholiho to join her in breaking several ancient *kapu*. The *kapu* system, having been discredited, crumbled; the old order was dead.

The missionaries arrive

Congregationalist missionaries from New England reached Hawaii in 1820; Liholiho grudgingly gave them a year's trial. The end of the *kapu* system had left a religious vacuum into which the missionaries moved remarkably easily. To their credit, they came with a sincere desire to commit their lives to bettering those of the people of Hawaii. Liholiho's mother converted to Christianity and made it acceptable for other *alii* to follow her example. Kaahumanu became a convert, too, and set about remodeling Hawaii socially and politically, based on the Ten Commandments.

An ecosystem passes

Cook and those who came after him gave cattle, goats, and large European pigs as gifts to the Hawaiian chiefs, and the animals overran the islands. They ate everything. Rainwater sluiced off the now-bare hillsides without replenishing the aquifers. Areas that had been blessed with an abundance of water suffered drought now. Native plants could not reestablish themselves because the unrestrained animals ate them as soon as they sent up a shoot. People wrongly concluded that native plants were inherently unable to reestablish themselves, and they imported non-native trees like the eucalyptuses and ironwoods that you see so often today.

The native habitat area and diversity shrank still more before the new sugar plantations. Planters drained wetlands for the commercially valuable crop and erected dams, ditches, and sluices to divert the natural water supply into a controllable water supply. What they did was not so very different from what the Polynesians had done when they had cleared the native lowland forests in order to plant their taro, but the scale was far vaster. In one particularly terrible mistake, growers imported the mongoose to prey on the rats that damaged their crops. But the rat forages at night, while the mongoose hunts by day: they seldom met. What the mongooses preyed on instead were the eggs of native ground-nesting birds.

Few of Hawaii's native plants put forth showy flowers or set palatable fruit, so the new settlers imported ornamental and fruiting plants to brighten their gardens and tables. Many shrubs and trees did so well in Hawaii's favorable climate that they escaped into the wild to become pest plants, crowding out native species and interrupting the food chain.

Birds brought over as pets escaped to compete with native species. More species of native birds have become extinct in Hawaii than anywhere else in the world, and most of the birds you see will be introduced species like the zebra dove and the myna.

It is tragic but true that when you visit Hawaii, you will probably see very few of its native plants and animals. Hawaii Volcanoes National Park is one of the few places that offer you a chance to see remnants of native Hawaiian plant communities.

A culture passes

Literacy replaced the rich Hawaiian oral tradition, and many legends and stories were forgotten before someone thought to write them down. The significance of many place names, apart from their literal meaning, has been lost forever. Zealous missionaries and converts believed that the native traditions were evil, and they nearly succeeded in eradicating all traces of the native culture.

A nation passes

Hawaiians saw that their only hope of surviving as an independent nation in the modern world was to secure the protection and guarantees of freedom of one of the major powers. The Hawaiian monarchs would have preferred the British, but British influence was ultimately inadequate to withstand American influence. American missionaries doled out God's grace. American entrepreneurs established plantations and businesses. American ships filled the harbors. Economic and cultural domination of Hawaii eventually passed into American hands, particularly after the new land laws of 1850 made it possible for foreigners to own land in Hawaii. The Hawaiian monarchy lasted until 1893, but most of its economic and therefore its political power was gone. Hawaii as an independent nation disappeared soon after.

A race passes

The native Hawaiian people lost much of their importance in the changing, Westernized economy early in the nineteenth century. The burgeoning sugar and pineapple plantations needed laborers, and the Hawaiians were diligent, capable hired hands when they wanted to be. But they did not comprehend the idea of hiring themselves out as day laborers for wages. Planters began to import laborers from other parts of the world: China, Japan, the Philippines, Portugal. Many imported laborers stayed, married, raised families, and went on to establish their own successful businesses. The Hawaiians were soon a minority in their own land.

The numbers of full-blooded Hawaiians declined precipitously throughout the nineteenth century. Beginning with the tragic introduction of venereal disease by Cook's men, venereal diseases swept through the native population who, particularly at *Makahiki*, exchanged partners freely. Venereal disease often leaves its victims sterile, and many who had survived Western diseases, wars, and the sandalwood trade were unable to reproduce. Others married foreigners, so their children were only part Hawaiian. Today most authorities believe that there are no full-blooded Hawaiians left, not even on Niihau, the only island where Hawaiian is still the language of everyday life.

Hawaii becomes American

In the late nineteenth century, the Hawaiian monarchy seemed to some powerful businessmen and civic leaders of American descent to get in the way of the smooth conduct of business. They thought Hawaii would be better off as an American territory. Queen Liliuokalani did not agree. She wanted to assert Hawaii's independence and the authority of its monarchs. The business community plotted a coup, deposed Liliuokalani in 1893, formed a new government, and petitioned the United States for territorial status. The United States formally annexed Hawaii in 1898.

Military projects and mass travel brought mainland Americans flooding into Hawaii. Many stayed, and so the majority of people in Hawaii came to see themselves as Americans, though a minority disagreed (some still do). After many years as a territory, Hawaii became the fiftieth state in 1959.

Things to come

The huge tourist industry is both a blessing and a curse. Massive development pushes the Hawaii-born off the land to make way for hotels. Displaced Hawaiians, whatever their ethnic background, find themselves having to survive as waiters, chambermaids, clerks—in essence, as the servants of those who have displaced them. Many also fear that tourism will result in the Hawaiian paradise being paved over and lost forever; others feel that it already has been. The story of Hawaii's evolution is far from over.

Lyman Museum

The Lyman Museum, on the southwest corner of Kapiolani and Haili streets in Hilo, is a must-see. On the first floor, you'll find a well-laid-out series of exhibits of Hawaiian artifacts with historical notes. Wandering among these outstanding exhibits is almost like taking a walking tour through Hawaiian history. Imagine seeing a missionary wife's diary and reading in her own hand her account of that terrible day—April 2, 1868—of the greatest recorded earthquake in Hawaiian history!

Upstairs, there are wonderful collections of minerals, of shells, and of artifacts (clothes, tools, musical instruments) typical of the many different ethnic groups that settled in Hawaii. Next door, you can tour the nineteenth-century home and missionary school of Rev. and Mrs. David Belden Lyman. Tours are given on the half-hour in the morning and on the hour in the afternoon (no noontime tour) by the museum's docents.

The museum does not allow you to take large purses, daypacks, etc., into the exhibit areas. They're worried about the glass cases getting broken. The docents can store your bags safely while you're enjoying the exhibits. As of this writing, hours are Monday through Saturday, 9 a.m. to 5 p.m., and admission is $4.50 for adults and $2.50 for children 18 and under. It's worth it.

Hilo has a lot to offer besides the Lyman Museum; see Trips 14 through 17, for example. I hope you'll spend some time there.

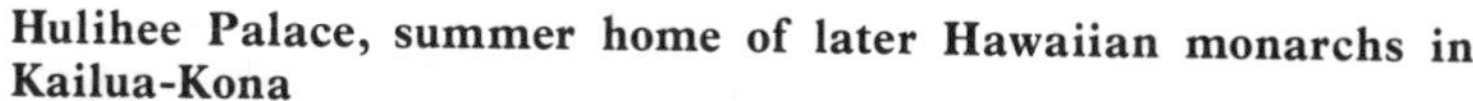

Hulihee Palace, summer home of later Hawaiian monarchs in Kailua-Kona

Getting Around on Hawaii and Finding Maps to Help You

The Big Island of Hawaii has a public transportation system, the Hele-On Bus, that is reported to be able to take you around the island for very modest rates. For more information, write or call the Mass Transportation System at 25 Apuni Street, Hilo, HI 96720, 808-935-8241. Whether it can get a hiker to and from a particular trailhead at reasonable times is another question (and one I didn't investigate).

Chances are that you'll be getting around in a rental car, which you should arrange for well in advance of your visit. Ask for a modest vehicle in a drab color so it's inconspicuous when parked at trailheads. Get a road map of Hawaii in advance, perhaps from one of the national automobile clubs if you belong to one. Even better, get the excellent "Map of Hawaii" published by the University of Hawaii Press. It's good to be able to study the map in advance and have some notion of the island's roads before you tackle them. Some of the maps provided by tourist bureaus are so cute they're useless.

Driving conditions on Hawaii vary widely, and driving time can make serious inroads on your hiking time. The sheer size of the island and the layout of its roads makes it unreasonable, for example, to stay in Kona and to hike in Hawaii Volcanoes National Park. Plan to stay in or near the areas you want to hike in. This may mean changing lodgings. It's worth the trouble.

Forget the silly notion that you can see the Big Island (or any of the other major islands, for that matter) by driving around it for a day. (It's a great way to see asphalt, though.)

Hawaii Belt Road. Highway 19 arcs northwest from Hilo, and Highway 11 arcs south from Hilo. The highways circle the island to meet again on the west side at Kailua-Kona. They form the 221-mile Hawaii Belt Road. The Hawaii Belt Road is the island's major highway. However, it is rarely more than a two-lane road. Your speed, nominally the 55-miles-per-hour limit outside of the towns, is frequently reduced to 45, 35, or even 25 miles per hour through the island's many little villages. You also have to slow down on mountain curves as the road winds around the south side of the island. Slow-moving trucks and stops for road work further impede progress on the Hawaii Belt Road. And the island's best scenery isn't along the Hawaii Belt Road—though lovely Hilo and the spectacular Hamakua coast are exceptions.

Secondary roads. Other, secondary roads link the Hawaii Belt Road with some of the island's finest scenery and hiking areas, particularly the Kohala Peninsula and Hawaii Volcanoes National Park. Don't miss Highway 250 over the Kohala Mountains and the special hikes it leads to. The Chain of Craters Road arcs through the Kilauea area of Hawaii Volcanoes National Park, sometimes allowing drivers to bypass a section of the Hawaii Belt Road in favor of a scenic drive through the park. At other times—and 1992 is one of them—lava from Kilauea has overrun the Chain of Craters Road. You can't shovel lava off the road like snow, as a volunteer ranger explained to us. When lava has blocked the Chain of Craters Road, drivers must return to the Hawaii Belt Road where they left it. The Saddle Road links Hilo with the west side of the island by crossing the 7,000-foot saddle between Mauna Kea and Mauna Loa. It's fully paved but narrow and, at times, potholed and winding. It's *not* a shortcut! Many rental-car contracts explicitly forbid driving on the Saddle Road. The other often-forbidden road is the road to South Point, the southernmost point in the United States. It, too, is paved but it is a one-lane road with lines of sight that are sometimes very short.

Rental car prohibitions. As noted above, rental-car contracts may forbid you to drive the car on the Saddle Road or on the road to the southernmost tip of the island, Ka Lae. Neither road is *that* bad. You will have to decide for yourself whether to risk the drive.

What to leave in the car. Nothing. Never leave valuables in your car, even in a locked trunk. "Valuables" include not only jewelry, money, checks, and credit cards but things you can't readily replace: glasses, prescription medication, identification, keys, snapshots of loved ones, etc.

Hiking. Road maps are useless for hiking trails. For trail maps, I recommend the maps in this book and the United States Geological Survey (USGS) 7½′ series of topographic ("topo") maps for Hawaii. Topos show elevation details as well as roads and trails. However, topos are not updated as often as you'd like. That's why you should use them in conjunction with the maps in this book and information from the agencies in charge of the island's hiking areas—the Division of State Parks, Hawaii District, and the Division of Forestry and Wildlife, Hawaii District (I can't recommend their map). If you do not write for these in advance, you will need to go into Hilo to get them. See their addresses in "Getting Permits or Permission" in this book.

Hawaii is covered by 98 topos, as shown in the illustration below. Fortunately, you won't need all of them. As of this writing, you can buy Hawaii topos (as well as lots of interesting books) on the Big Island at Basically Books at their new location, 46 Waianueue Avenue in Hilo (808-961-0144). There may be other stores on the Big Island that stock topos, but I don't know of them. If your mainland backpacking store does not carry the Hawaii topos, you can also get them in person or by mail from:

Western Distribution Branch
U.S. Geological Survey
Box 25286, Federal Center
Denver, CO 80225

or

Western Mapping Center
U.S. Geological Survey
345 Middlefield Road
Menlo Park, CA 94025

Write first for catalogs and prices. When you order the maps, enclose your check for the required amount, made out to the U.S. Geological Survey.

Or there may be a store near you that specializes in maps. Look in your telephone directory under "Maps." For example, the store where I get my topos isn't a backpacking store; it's a mining-supplies store (Allied Services, 966 N. Main St., Orange, CA 92667, 714-637-8824). Its stock of maps, including topos, puts any backpacking store in my area to shame ten times over.

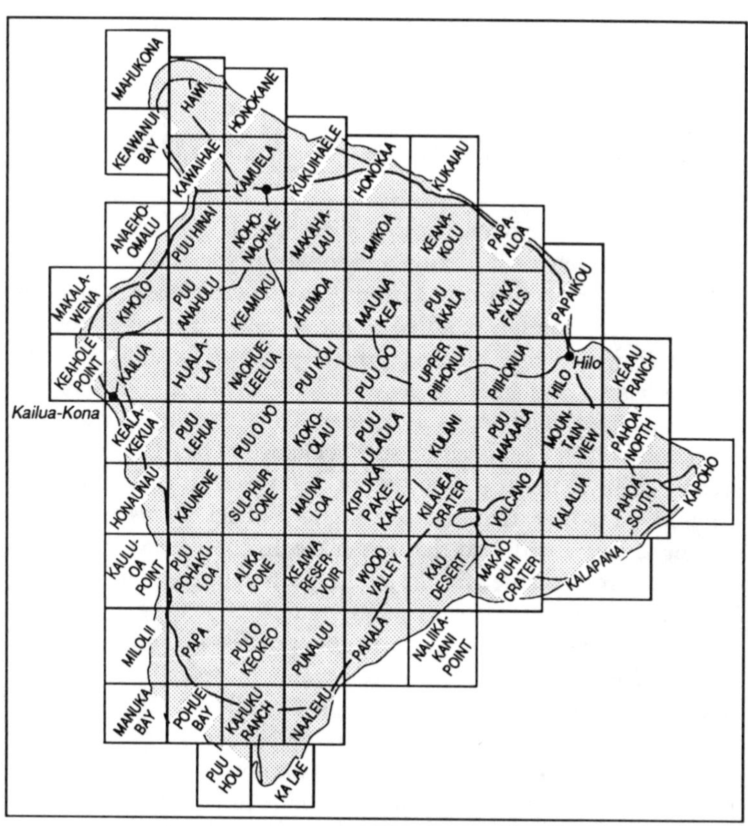

U.S.G.S. 7½' Topographic Maps of the Big Island of Hawaii

Getting Permits or Permission

The trip descriptions in this book include information about what permits you need (if any) and to whom you should apply for them. In this book, there are currently no *dayhikes* on private property for which you are required to get a permit from the property owner. However, any hike on private property is subject to the owner's wishes, and an owner may decide at any time to require permits or even to deny access altogether. To be absolutely sure your hiking plans won't be foiled by such a change of heart, call ahead if possible. Check the trip descriptions for whom to call, if anyone. Note in particular that the Kona and Kohala coasts are being developed very rapidly, so that any hikes on those coasts that have not already been secured for the public (such as by the National Park Service) are subject to closure at any time.

As of this writing, the government agencies—federal, state, and county—don't require you to have permits in order to *dayhike* on Hawaii in areas under their jurisdiction. Permits are required for all the *backpacking* trips in this book. For completeness, I also include the addresses and telephone numbers of the government agencies, as you may want to write or call them for more information. Appendix A in this book gives you detailed information about *camping*—car camping, tent camping, and cabins—including permit requirements, fees, etc.

Waipio Valley camping (Hamakua Sugar Company)

You must get a permit *in person* from the Hamakua Sugar Company, 808-776-1211, in order to camp in Waipio Valley. See Appendix A for their location and a description of the amenity-free camping area.

Waimanu Valley camping (Division of Forestry and Wildlife)

In March of 1991, the Division of Forestry and Wildlife began strictly controlling camping in Waimanu Valley, which is now protected as the Waimanu National Estuarine Research Reserve. You *must* have a permit from them to camp in Waimanu. The Division of Forestry and Wildlife's address and telephone number are below under **Division of Forestry and Wildlife.** See Appendix A for more on the camping area.

Hawaii Volcanoes National Park

No permits are required to dayhike in Hawaii Volcanoes National Park. Car camping and backpacking, including tent camping or use of the backcountry shelters and cabins, requires permits. See Appendix A in this book. For more information, write or call:

Hawaii Volcanoes National Park
P.O. Box 52
Hawaii 96718-0052
808-967-7311

Division of State Parks

Car camping or use of the cabins in a state park does require a permit and sometimes a fee; one park's cabins are run by a concessionaire. See Appendix A in this book. For more information, write or call:

Department of Land and Natural Resources
Division of State Parks, Hawaii District
P.O. Box 936
Hilo, Hawaii, HI 96721–0936
808-961-7200

If you need to see them in person, they are currently in Hilo in the State Office Building at 75 Apuni Street, just inland of the visitor center and tsunami memorial in Wailoa River State Park. Their office is on the second floor.

Division of Forestry and Wildlife

This agency controls Waimanu Valley (above) and also controls several cabins along a 4WD road that arcs around Mauna Kea. For information from this agency, write or call:

Department of Land and Natural Resources
Division of Forestry and Wildlife, Hawaii District
1643 Kilauea Avenue
Hilo, Hawaii 96720
808-933-4221

The office of the Division of Forestry and Wildlife is *not* co-located with the office of the Division of State Parks. Instead, the Division of Forestry and Wildlife is co-located with Hilo Arboretum (Trip 16) on the seaward side of Kilauea Avenue between Lanikaula and Kawili streets (the office itself is near the corner of Kilauea and Kawili).

Weather

The short of it. The Big Island is:

—Rainiest on its north side, which boasts rainforests. Waipio and Waimanu valleys have rainforest conditions, though agriculture has displaced most of the native rainforest vegetation on the valleys' floors.

—Less rainy on its east side, but still rainy enough to support lush tropical growth. Hilo's streets, parks, and yards are bursting with flowers. A rainforest flourishes on the northeast slope of Kilauea volcano. Just think how much rain it must take to nourish a rainforest on the rim of the world's most active volcano!

—Driest and hottest on the south and west. These areas lie in the rain shadows of the island's volcanoes. While a rainforest grows on Kilauea's northeast slope, a desert stretches down its southwest slope.

—Rainier in the mountains on any side of the island. However, the summits of Mauna Loa and Mauna Kea are frigid alpine deserts. At nearly 14,000 feet, altitude, not latitude, governs the climate of those summits.

The dry Kona and north Kohala coasts attract the most visitors, have the principal resorts, and have the most popular beaches. The figure below summarizes the situation:

The long of it. Hawaii's *coastal* weather is temperate to a degree that puts the so-called "temperate" zones of the world to shame. The humidity is moderate, too: 50 to 60%, not the sweltering horror of some other tropical lands. It is warmer in the summer and cooler in the winter, but the "extremes" are only a few degrees apart—nothing like those on the mainland.[1]

Hawaii's mild climate is determined largely by its tropical location and also by the northeast trade winds that sweep across it. The

[1]Hawaii's mountainous interior, however, is quite another matter.

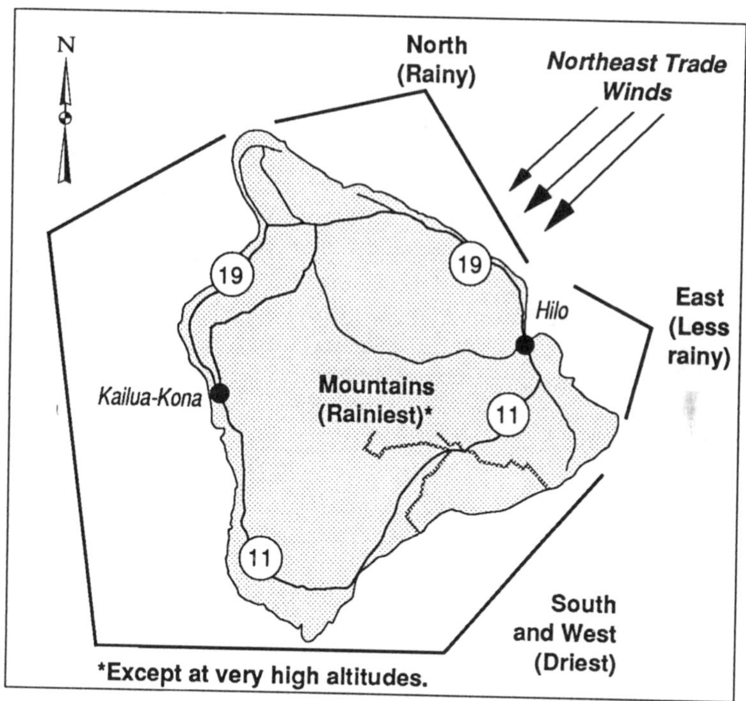

Big Island Weather

northeast trade winds—so-called because sea captains took advantage of them on their trade routes—are dependable, steady winds that blow from the northeast across the thousands of miles of open sea that separate the Hawaiian Islands from the continents. They are responsible for keeping the temperature and the humidity moderate. Since they are the prevailing winds in this area, the side of the island that faces them is called the "windward" side. The opposite side of the island is the opposite of windward; in nautical terms, "leeward."

Sometimes the trade winds fail and are replaced by "kona" winds coming from the south. "Kona" means "leeward," because it's the leeward side of the island that more or less faces these occasional winds. Kona winds bring hot, sticky air. Fortunately, they are rare in summer, when they would be really unpleasant, and occur mostly in winter, when the lower overall temperatures moderate their effect. Kona storms are subtropical low-pressure systems that occur in winter, move in from the south, and can cause serious damage. There is apparently no pattern to them; in some years, they do not occur at all, but in others they occur every few weeks.

On the island of Hawaii, average temperatures in Hilo range from highs of 79–82° F to lows of 61–70° F. In Kona, temperatures range from highs of 80–82° F to lows of 62–68° F. The "cooler" ones are winter temperatures, the warmer ones summer. It's rainier from November through March than it is the rest of the year. Hilo gets an average of 133 inches of rain per year, while coastal Kona may get as little as 15 inches of rain per year. Expect cooler temperatures, more wind, and considerably more rain if you are in a mountainous region. For example, the uplands of south Kona are rainy enough to support the nation's only coffee plantations! The summits of Mauna Loa and Mauna Kea are often chilly, even by day, and can be bitterly cold at any time. Both are snow-covered in winter. Kilauea's northeast side can be very cold because of its high rainfall, though its summit is only 4,078 feet high.

Hapuna Beach is one of the best on the island

Equipment Suggestions and Miscellaneous Hints

This book isn't intended to teach you *how* to hike or backpack. If you can walk, you can hike, especially the "very easy" hikes. You can learn about backpacking in *Backpacking Basics* by Thomas Winnett and Melanie Findling (see Bibliography). Just be sure the trip you pick is within *your* hiking limits.

This book is intended specifically to let you know *where* you can hike on Hawaii, *what* to expect when you hike there, and *how* to get to the trailhead for each hike. And that, I hope, will help you decide *which* hikes to take.

This section contains suggestions which I hope will make your hikes even more pleasant, and perhaps better protect you and the environment. Of course, you're the only person who lives in your body, so you'll have to judge what's really appropriate for you. But there are a few things you might want to know before you go—things that may be very different from the hiking you've done at home on the mainland. (Maybe you already know them, but it's hard to shut me up when I think I have some good advice.)

It's up to you. No book can substitute for, or give you, five things only you can supply: physical fitness, preparation, experience, caution, and common sense. Don't leave the trailhead without them.

Don't spread pest plants. As I mentioned in the chapter on geology and history, Hawaii has been overrun by introduced plants. It's important to try to control the spread of these plants. One thing you can do to help is to wash the soil, and with it the seeds of any pest plants, you hope, off of your shoes or boots *before you leave* a hiking area. Note also that you, like any other animal, can carry pest-plant seeds in your digestive tract and deposit them, ready to sprout, in your solid wastes. Either hold it till you get to a toilet or dig your hole deep enough to make it impossible for the seeds to sprout (one foot deep, according to a pamphlet on the subject. I'm just passing this information on. I have no idea how to carry enough equipment to dig a hole that deep when hiking). Pest plants include all the guavas. For more information, call the Hawaii State Department of Agriculture, Weed Control Section, 808-548-7119.

Equipment for strolls and easy hikes. You don't need to make extensive preparations for a stroll along a beach or a half-mile nature trail as long as there's food, water, and shelter nearby—perhaps in your car. The things you must not go without are:

- Sunglasses
- Appropriate footwear
- Mosquito repellent
- Strong sunblock applied *before* you set out.

Your mosquito repellent should be "jungle juice"—that is, have a high percentage of DEET (diethyltoluamide). DEET is vile stuff, but it works.

Equipment for moderate and strenuous hikes. Carry at least the Ten Essentials Plus One as I've adapted them from the Sierra Club. They are:

- Pack (to put these good things in; could be a large fanny pack)
- Food and water (assume that all open water sources are unsafe to drink)
- Extra clothing (always take rain gear, as it can rain any time on Hawaii)
- Map (and compass if you can use it)
- Flashlight with extra bulbs and batteries
- Sunglasses and strong sunblock
- Means to dig a hole 6–8 inches deep and at least 200 feet from water, in order to bury solid body wastes; tissue that you will also bury (or pack out)—see also "Number 2 in the Lava," below
- Pocket knife
- First-aid kit
- Waterproof matches and something you can keep a flame going with (such as a candle) *only when necessary to start a fire in order to save a life*
- Mosquito repellent ("jungle juice")

Equipment for backpacks. The following is a minimal checklist for backpacking equipment.

Minimal Backpacking Equipment List

Backpack	Tent	Sleeping pad
Sleeping bag	Permit	"Ten Essentials Plus One"
Boots	Socks	Shirts
Shorts or long pants	Hat	Rain gear
Underwear	Personal medication	Toiletries
Cookware and clean-up stuff	Stove and fuel*	Eating utensils

*You cannot take stove fuel on a plane. You must buy it at your destination.

Tennis shoes? I've noted in the hike descriptions whether tennis shoes are okay to wear or whether I think you should wear boots. I base that recommendation on the length of the hike and the difficulty of the terrain. What tennis shoes may lack that boots can provide are ankle support and soles that grip. Only you can really decide how important those are to you.

Boot care. If you're going to hike a lot, be sure your boot seams are freshly sealed and you've freshly waterproofed the entire boot, including the cloth part, if any. Use a heavy-duty waterproofing compound like a wax, and bring some of it along in order to renew the coating if necessary. Chances are your boots will get wet, especially in the winter. And they'll stay wet, because things dry slowly in the tropical humidity. It's pretty tough on the boots and, together with the abrasion of mud particles, could cause boot seams to fail.

Hiking stick. Take your hiking stick if you usually hike with one. The flight attendants can put it in the closet where they hang the carry-on suits and dresses or in the overhead compartments. Hawaii's terrain can be very slippery when wet, and a hiking stick can be a big help in maintaining your footing. And it can double as a spider stick (see below).

Spider stick. There are a very few overgrown trails (for example, the Kalapana Trail) where you and some orb spiders may meet unexpectedly, head-on. You probably don't like collecting spiders with your face, but these critters make it hard not to do so. Here's one way to avoid them without killing them. Pick up and use a "spider stick"—a long, strong stick that you carefully wave up and down in front of you as you hike. You can feel the tug when the stick connects with a web. Detach the anchor strands that hold the web in your way, and lay them aside on the adjacent shrubbery. An orb spider normally rebuilds most or all of her web daily, so you've caused her only minor inconvenience. Your hiking stick can probably double as a spider stick.

Sleeping bag. It should be able to tolerate wet conditions. For example, it could have a Gore-Tex shell or it could have a synthetic fill. You are almost certain to get rained on a bit while camping.

Tent. You'll need one for protection from the rain and, along the coast, the bugs.

Clothes while backpacking. On the one hand, it's best to go as light as possible; on the other hand, almost nothing—not even synthetics—dries overnight in Hawaii's damp climate under backpacking conditions. Consider which things you can stand to wear damp and which you can't stand unless they're dry. Pack just one or two of the "okay if damp" things. Pack a set of the "gotta be dry!" things for each day plus one or more extras, just in case. (For me, it's socks.)

At the end of a soggy day of camping out. On those occasional rainy days, you may wonder how you're going to get reasonably clean without getting any wetter than you already are. The socks you've worn all day are "goners" for the time being, wet and muddy on the outside but relatively clean on the inside. While you're changing into dry clothes, turn your "used" socks inside out and mop yourself off with them.

Hypothermia? On Hawaii? It's possible if you go into the mountains. Remember that going higher is equivalent to going north into colder climates, and mountains are often very windy. Please be prepared as you would be for going into any mountainous region.

Biodegradable? Ha, ha, ha! The following things are popularly supposed to be biodegradable if you bury them: toilet tissue; facial tissue; sanitary napkins; tampons; disposable diapers. That must be a joke. They often last long enough for either running water to exhume them or animals to dig them up. It's actually pretty easy to carry them out if you put them in a heavy-duty self-sealing bag. (I use a couple of heavy-duty Ziploc bags, one inside the other.)

Extra hints for hiking in lava fields.

Boots and clothes. Lava is unbelievably sharp—even the smooth-looking *pahoehoe* (pronounced pa-hoi-hoi) flows are full of tiny, glassy, sharp edges. *Never* walk on lava barefoot or in sandals! With every step you take, the lava cuts your shoes, so be sure your shoes are in good shape before you start. Lava is tough on clothes, too. Every time you sit on it to catch your breath, it saws little holes in the seat of your pants.

Stay on the marked route! The rock of lava fields is too hard to make a beaten path through. Typically, you'll follow cairns through *pahoehoe* (the smoother form of lava), *aa* (the chunky, rough form), or (rarely) a beaten path through cinders. Cairns are big piles of rocks obviously made by people. The cairns mark out a safe route for you. Lava fields are dangerous places to go wandering around. Apparently solid lava can turn out to be nothing but a fragile shell over a lava tube, collapsing when you put your weight on it. You could be in for a nasty, even fatal, fall. The one time you need to get a *little* off-route is when you have to go to the bathroom; see below.

Routes on active volcanoes can change. Routes on Mauna Loa and Kilauea can change abruptly because of an eruption. That might make the cairn-marked route vary from its description in this book. Follow the cairns, not the description.

Number 2 in the lava. You can dig a hole in cinders, but digging a hole in *aa* or *pahoehoe* is impossible. As a result, too many people leave various gross objects sitting out on the lava: feces, tissues, tampons, etc. If possible, wait until you get to a toilet. Otherwise, look a little off-route for a small crevice in which to defecate (but be careful about going off-route). You may not be able to find a suitable crevice. With or without a crevice, *completely* cover your feces with rocks. It takes a lot of rocks; you'll have built quite a little rockpile by the time you're through, though not one big enough to be confused with a cairn. In *aa,* you can use the smaller chunks of lava. In *pahoehoe,* the crust is often easy to break into plates you can build with. Carry your tissues, tampons, etc., out.

Getting hiking and backpacking food. If you are planning to backpack on Hawaii, consider shopping for your hiking and backpacking chow on Hawaii. Food prices *are* higher in Hawaii, but you have enough stuff to put in your luggage without bringing your food, too. You'll find supermarkets in the larger towns: Kailua-Kona, Waimea, and Hilo. They have marginally adequate selections of long-lasting, lightweight, quick-cooking foods. I did not find any of the standard freeze-dried backpacking chow, however.

Companions. The standard advice is: never hike alone; never camp alone.

Water. Take your own drinking water for the day. Plan on treating water while backpacking. No open source of water anywhere in the U.S. is safe to drink untreated. Treat water chemically (iodine or chlorine preparations designed for the purpose) or by boiling (1–5 minutes at a rolling boil). It now seems that filtering may be ineffective against the bacterium that causes leptospirosis (below).

At the backcountry cabins and shelters in Hawaii Volcanoes National Park, the water is supplied by collecting rain from the roofs. It is presumed to be *unsafe* to drink without treatment. Treated or not, the water at the Mauna Loa Cabin is unpleasantly rusty. The backcountry water supply is at the mercy of the elements and of previous visitors, so be sure to ask when you get your permit whether there will be adequate water for *your* trip.

Avoiding leptospirosis. Fresh water on Hawaii may be contaminated with the bacterium that causes leptospirosis. A pamphlet about leptospirosis is available from the Epidemiology Branch of the Hawaii State Department of Health (on Hawaii, call 808-244-4288). The following summarizes some of its contents: Muddy and clear water are both suspect. The bacterium invades through broken skin or the nose, mouth, or eyes. It enters the bloodstream and infects different organs, particularly the kidneys. Precautions that would especially apply to you here are not to go into streams if you have open cuts or abrasions and not to drink (untreated) stream water. Treat water chemically or by boiling it.

If you do swim in fresh water on Hawaii, you should know that the incubation period of leptospirosis is 2–20 days. The onset is sudden, and the symptoms may resemble those of flu: fever, chills, sweating, severe headache, conjunctivitis (red eyes), muscle pains, weakness, vomiting, and diarrhea. You should see a physician immediately if you suspect leptospirosis. It's believed that administering certain antibiotics early in the course of the disease will shorten the disease and make symptoms less severe. The pamphlet says that most cases are mild and that people (with mild cases) recover in a week or two without treatment. However, severe leptospirosis infections may damage kidneys, liver, or heart or even cause death.

Families frolicking in Wailoa Stream

How This Book Organizes the Trips

Imagine the hour hand of a clock pinned to a point near the center of a rounded island. Think of it sweeping around clockwise from a 12-o'clock position that's due north. It's easy to envision the hour hand pointing to 3 o'clock (due east), 6 o'clock (due south), and 9 o'clock (due west) as it moves around.

You can think of Hawaii as a clock with its hour hand pinned to its middle, about halfway up the slope of Mauna Loa from the Saddle Road. A little before the twelve o'clock, the imaginary hour hand points at Waipio Valley. Near three o'clock, it points to Lava Tree State Monument, and at nine o'clock it points to Captain Cook's Monument. Here's the Hawaii clock pointing to Waipio Valley:

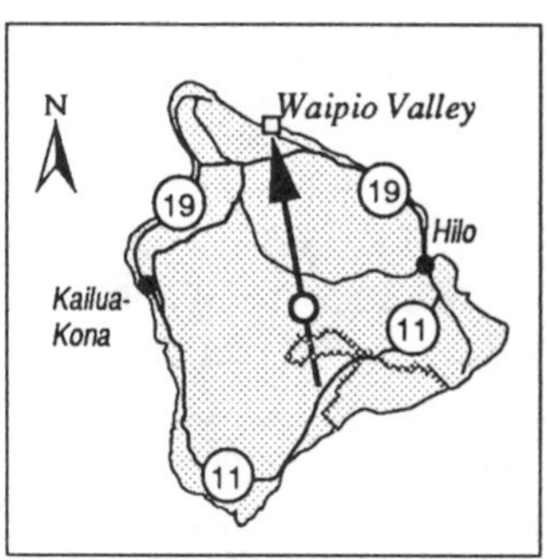

The trips start near twelve o'clock at Waipio Valley (Trip 1) and move clockwise around the island, ending near eleven o'clock at Pololu Valley (Trip 59). There are two *big* sets of exceptions to this order; I've described them below.

Hikes from the Saddle Road. The first set of exceptions to this organizational scheme are the seven hikes from the Saddle Road (Trips 7 through 13). You can get to the first two, Kaumana Caves and Puu Oo, by daytripping from Hilo. Kaumana Caves and Puu Oo appear first among the Saddle Road hikes and in that order (Trips 7 and 8). Then you jump past a couple of trailheads to the westernmost Saddle Road hike, the one at Mauna Kea State Park (Trip 9). You can do this one as a daytrip from Hilo, too. However, I judge that you should stay at Mauna Kea State Park in order to take the last four Saddle Road hikes (see Appendix A for information on renting a cabin at the park). Staying at Mauna Kea State Park will allow you to get a little bit acclimated and will cut your driving time significantly for the last four Saddle Road hikes (Trips 10 through 13). They are very strenuous, high-altitude trips, one to the top of Mauna Kea and three on the slopes of Mauna Loa.

Hikes in Hawaii Volcanoes National Park. No other area on the Big Island offers anything approaching the number and variety of trails you will find in Hawaii Volcanoes National Park. All the Big Island backpacking trips that appear in this book are in the park. Kilauea's latest eruption has severed the park's road system from the Puna District's Highway 130. Most of the park's roads, and therefore most of the hikes in the park, are accessible only from the main entrance off Highway 11, 28 miles southwest of Hilo. Thirty-one of the thirty-four Hawaii Volcanoes National Park trips in this book originate southwest of Hilo. They are Trips 20 through 51.

A left turn from Highway 11 brings you to the toll booths of the entrance station. Just past the entrance station, a right turn brings you to the park's remaining visitor center, Kilauea Visitor Center.[1] This is an excellent place to stop, take advantage of the restrooms and water fountains, stretch your legs, enjoy the interpretive displays, perhaps buy some books and maps, and get information from the rangers at the front desk. A number of outstanding park trails begin just across the street from Kilauea Visitor Center, near Volcano House (which sits on the rim of Kilauea Crater but is well-hidden from the visitor center by a charming grove of *ohia* trees and tree ferns). Hikes from Kilauea Visitor Center appear first of those park hikes that originate southwest of Hilo.[2] They are Trips 20 through 27.

---

[1]Wahaula Visitor Center on the Puna coast fell to advancing lava in June, 1989. David Zurick, author of *Hawaii, Naturally,* was among those who watched helplessly as it burned to the ground.

[2]But they're not, strictly speaking, the first hikes in Hawaii Volcanoes National Park in this book. The hikes up Mauna Loa that originate at the end of the Observatory Road (Trips 11 through 13), off the Saddle Road, cross into the park at about 12,000 feet.

The street in front of Kilauea Visitor Center is Crater Rim Road. It allows you to drive completely around Kilauea and Kilauea Iki craters (if it's not interrupted by road work or volcanic activity). The next set of hikes in this book are those that start somewhere on Crater Rim Road other than Kilauea Visitor Center. They're in the order you'd find them as you drove away from the visitor center toward Thurston Lava Tube for a clockwise trip around the road. They are Trips 28 through 31.

A few miles down Crater Rim Road, just at the turnoff for the Devastation Trail, you'll reach the turnoff for the Chain of Craters Road. This road winds down from the Kilauea area of the park, through terrain often drastically altered by the volcano, for more than 20 miles to its end on the Puna coast at the glossy black lavas of 1989. The next set of hikes in this book are those that start on the Chain of Craters Road, roughly in the order they appear as the road descends. They are Trips 32 through 41.

On your way down the Chain of Craters Road, you pass the turnoff for Hilina Pali Road. The next set of hikes in this book are those that start on Hilina Pali Road. They are Trips 42 through 47.

The next set of hikes for Hawaii Volcanoes National Park originates outside the Kilauea area, along the Mauna Loa Road. (Sometimes it's called the Mauna Loa Strip Road.) You get to this road by staying on Highway 11 for just over two miles past the turnoff to the visitor center. The most important foot trail up Mauna Loa begins—no surprise—at the end of the Mauna Loa Road. Trips 48 through 50 start from the Mauna Loa Road.

There's one more park hike still farther southwest on Highway 11. That's the last Hawaii Volcanoes National Park hike in this book, Trip 51, the Footprints Trail.

How to Read the Trip Descriptions

The trip descriptions are in the following format, and here is what the information in each description means. Items marked "(icon)" are shown in the trips by icons (small pictures) arranged in a box at the beginning of each trip and defined below.

Title (pretty self-explanatory).

Type (icon): There are four types of trips described:

Loop trips: You follow trails that form a closed loop; you don't retrace your steps, or you retrace them for only a proportionally short distance.

Semiloop trips: The trip consists of a loop part and an out-and-back part.

Out-and-back trips: This is by far the most common type of trip in this book. You follow trails to a destination and then retrace your steps to your starting point.

Shuttle trips: You start at one trailhead and finish at another, "destination" trailhead. They are far enough apart (or walking between them is sufficiently impractical) that you need to have a car waiting for you at your "destination" trailhead or to have someone pick you up there.

Difficulty (icon): A trip's difficulty is based first on total distance and second on cumulative elevation gain and rate of gain. Let's say that the elevation gain is negligible to moderate (it's never steeper than about 500 feet/mile for any significant distance). In that case:

V A very easy trip is 1 mile or less.

E An easy trip is 1–2 miles.

M A moderate trip is 2–5 miles.

S A strenuous trip is more than 5 miles.

If the trip has a section of, say, a half-mile or more where it's steeper than 500 feet/mile, or if the trail is hard to follow, I've given it the next higher difficulty rating.

Shoes (icon): Some trips just aren't safe if you're not wearing boots which have soles that grip and which will give you some ankle support. However, only you live in your body, so you will have to be the final judge of what you can safely wear.

 Tennis shoes are okay.

 Boots recommended.

 Boots necessary, as terrain is rough.

Coastal or inland (icon): General type of area this hike is in. For those hikes that include both coastal and inland segments, this is a judgment call.

 Hike is along the coast, possibly on a beach or on cliffs above the ocean.

 Hike is inland, possibly in the hills or mountains.

Distance: The distance is the total distance you have to walk.

Elevation gain: This figure is the approximate cumulative elevation gain; it counts all the significant "ups" you have to walk, not just the simple elevation difference between the trailhead and the destination. It's the cumulative gain that your muscles will complain about. Some trips are *upside-down:* you go downhill on your way out to the destination, uphill on your return.

Average hiking time: This is based on my normal hiking speed, which is a blazing 2 miles/hour.

Location (icon defined in previous section): The Hawaii clock shows the hike's approximate location relative to the rest of the Big Island.

Topos: The topo or topos listed here are the ones that cover the area you'll be hiking in on this particular trip. Topos are strictly optional for the very easy and easy trips but are strongly recommended for the other trips.

Trail map: This tells you where this book's trail map for this trip is (usually at the end of the trip or of another trip in the same area). As explained in Appendix C, the trail maps are based on the topos wherever possible. However, a number of trails on Hawaii do not appear on any official agency map or on the topos. I have approximated their routes based on field notes and sketches and labeled them "(route approximated)." Some maps are too big for one page and are continued on another page, sometimes at the end of another trip, as noted on the edges of those maps. I've allowed a little overlap between those maps to help you follow them from one page to another. The following figure shows the trail map legend:

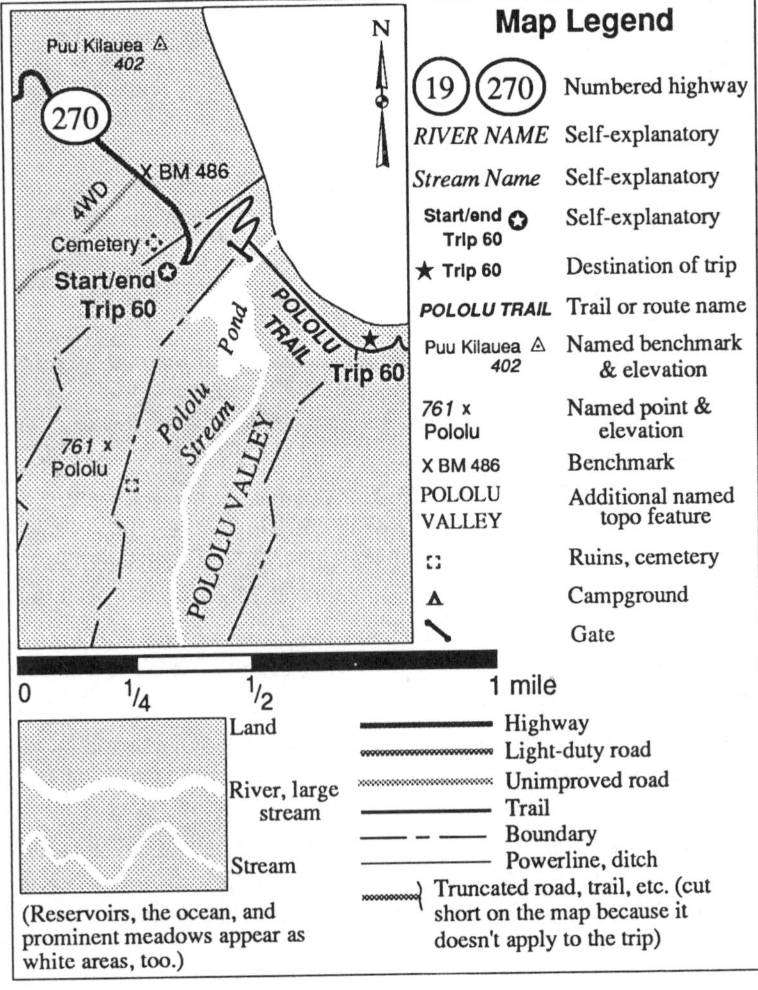

Highlights: This gives you an idea of what I think the best features of the trip are. Usually, it's the scenery—that's one of the principal things you came to Hawaii for!

Driving instructions: This gives you instructions for driving to the trailhead, usually in terms of driving from Hilo, the county seat. You may be staying anywhere on the Big Island, but Hilo is a convenient reference point. The starting point in Hilo is the junction of Highways 11 and 19; it's mile zero for those highways, which form the island-circling Hawaii Belt Road.

Some trips simply aren't feasible unless you're staying nearer to them than Hilo. Trips like that include:

—Longer trips from the Saddle Road (Trips 10 through 13). Stay in Mauna Kea State Park.

—Those on the west side of the Big Island (Trips 53 through 60). Stay somewhere on the Kona Coast or in the Kohala area.

Those trips are treated as *side trips* from a place where I think it's practical for you to stay.

To savor an extended visit to Hawaii Volcanoes National Park, stay in Volcano village or in the park itself if possible. But Hilo is close enough to the park if those places are booked or are priced out of your range.

Be sure you have a good road map of Hawaii to supplement these instructions.

Permit/permission required: Some trips require you to have someone's permission to camp. This section will tell you what you need permission for, if anything, and whom to apply to. See Getting Permits or Permission and Appendix A in this book for addresses and telephone numbers.

Description. This is the detailed description of the trip as I perceived it. I've tried to give you an idea of the more obvious plants and other features you'll find, where the rough spots are, when you'll be ascending and when descending, where viewpoints are, and what you'll see from those viewpoints.

On some trips, the trail is faint to nonexistent, and the agency in charge has attempted to mark the route by tying tags of colored plastic ribbon to plants along the route. You navigate by moving from tag to tag. I found route-tagging on the island of Hawaii to be largely unreliable, I'm sorry to say. Don't count on tags to get you in and out of an area. Always keep track of where you've been by map and compass or by landmarks, as the tags can be misleading or can just peter out.

In Hawaii Volcanoes National Park, routes across lava fields are marked by cairns—piles of rocks, obviously manmade and sometimes quite elaborate, even playful. You'll also find cairns marking a few of the trails outside of the park. I found the cairns to be reliable guides. However, it can be hard to tell a cairn from the rest of the rocks in a field of *aa,* the rough, chunky kind of lava. Be sure you have the next cairn in sight before you move from the present cairn. Once you've moved on, check behind yourself occasionally to keep track of the cairns you've left. If you discover that you've gotten off track—you've missed the real cairns and have been following odd heaps of *aa*—you'll be prepared to retrace your steps to the last real cairn. It happened to me more than once! Cairns can be hard to follow in rain, fog, or snow; avoid cairn-marked routes when the weather is poor or the route is under snow.

Supplemental information.... At the bottom of most of the trips, there's some extra information about the historical significance of places you'll see along the route. Or maybe there's a story—a myth, for example—related to the trip which I hope will add to your enjoyment of the trip. Perhaps there'll be a bit more information about the plants in or the geology of the area. I put most of the supplemental information at the end so that it wouldn't interfere too much with the description of the trip itself. I think safety dictates that you give your attention first to the trip and only secondarily to the supplemental information. That is not a problem with easy and very easy hikes, so the supplemental information is often part of the main description in those hikes.

Hiking table. The following table summarizes the trips and also indicates whether the trips are backpacks or dayhikes. Some trips are suitable for dayhikes or backpacks. Dayhikes listed as "ST" are treated as *side trips* from a point that you must drive to or backpack to and at which you stay overnight. Backpacks show, under "Backpack," the number of hiking days for the least strenuous trip. A dash under "Dist." (which stands for "total distance") means the total distance is negligible.

HIKING TABLE

#	Name or Description	Best As		Type				Difficulty				Dist. (miles)
		Day-hike	Back-pack	Loop	Semi-loop	Out& Back	Shut-tle	V	E	M	S	
1	Waipio Valley	x				x					x	3
2	Waimanu Valley		4			x					x	17
3	Side Trip to Falls	ST				x					x	2 1/4
4	Kalopa Nature Tr.	x		x				x				3/4
5	Kalopa Jeep Trail	x				x				x		2 1/2
6	Akaka Falls	x		x				x				1/2
7	Kaumana Caves	x				x			x			—
8	Puu Oo	x		x							x	8
9	Mauna Kea State Park	x				x				x		2 1/2
10	Mauna Kea	ST		x							x	15
11	Observatory Trail to North Pit	ST				x					x	7 2/3
12	Observatory Trail to Mauna Loa Cabin	ST	2			x					x	11 3/4
13	Mauna Loa Cabin to True Summit	ST				x					x	9 1/2
14	Rainbow Falls	x		x				x				—
15	Wailoa River	x				x			x			*
16	Hilo Arboretum	x				x			x			*
17	Liliuokalani Gardens	x			x			x				*
18	Panaewa Zoo	x			x			x				<1
19	Lava Tree	x		x				x				2/3
20	Crater Rim Loop	x		x							x	10
21	Halemaumau	x				x				x		5
22	Crater Rim-Halemaumau	x		x							x	6 1/2
23	Halemaumau-Byron	x			x						x	6
24	Sandalwood Trail	x		x				x				1 1/3
25	Sulphur Bank	x				x		x				1/2
26	Sulphur Bank-Sandalwood	x		x					x			1 1/2
27	Waldron-Byron-Halemaumau	x		x						x		2 1/2
28	Kilauea Iki	x		x						x		3 1/3
29	Thurston Lava Tube	x		x				x				1/3
30	Devastation	x				x	x	x				1/2-1
31	Crater Rim Dr. to Halemaumau	x				x		x				2/3
32	Puu Huluhulu	x				x				x		2 2/3

HIKING TABLE (Continued)

#	Name or Description	Best As		Type				Difficulty				Dist. (miles)
		Day-hike	Back-pack	Loop	Semi-loop	Out& Back	Shut-tle	V	E	M	S	
33	Makaopuhi Crater	x				x					x	9
34	Napau Crater	x				x					x	12 1/2
35	Naulu-Kalapana	x					x				x	10
36	Puu Loa Petros.	x			x				x			1 1/3
37	Apua Point.	x				x					x	12
38	Ch. Crs. Rd. to Keauhou		2			x					x	18
39	Ch. Crs. Rd. to Halape		4				x				x	21 1/3
40	Lae Apuki	x				x		x				1/2
41	Kamoamoa	x				x		x				*
42	Pit Craters	x				x					x	5 1/2
43	Kipuka Nene to Halape		2			x					x	14 1/2
44	Kipuka Nene to Keauhou via Halape		4			x					x	17 3/4
45	Kipuka Nene to Ch. Crs. Rd.		3				x					18
46	Hilina Pali to Pepeiao	x	2			x				x	x	9
47	Hilina Pali to Kaaha via Pepeiao		4			x					x	21
48	Bird Park	x		x					x			1
49	Red Hill Cabin		2			x					x	15
50	Mauna Loa Tr to Mauna Loa Cabin		4			x					x	38 1/4
51	Footprints	x				x			x			1 3/4
52	Manuka Nature Tr	x		x						x		2 1/4
53	Puuhonua o Honaunau	ST		x				x				≥1/2
54	Capt. Cook Mon.	ST				x				x		4
55	Kalahuipuaa	ST			x			x				≤1
56	Puako	ST				x			x			3/4
57	Puukohola	ST				x			x			2/3
58	Lapakahi	ST		x				x				≤1
59	Mookini-Kamehameha Birthplace	ST				x			x			1
60	Pololu	ST				x				x		1 1/2

*Either no trails or paths to speak of or so many different routes to choose from that I can't specify just *one* for you.

The Trips

Trip 1. Waipio Valley

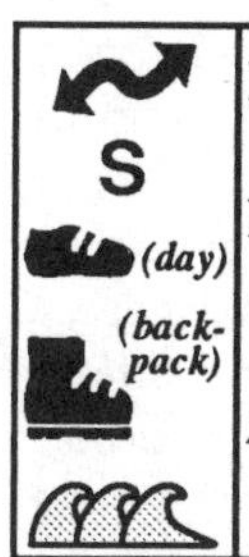

Distance: 3 miles to/from mouth of Wailoa Stream.
Elevation gain: 960 feet (upside-down trip), all in the first ¾ mile to valley floor!
Average hiking time: 2 hours (allows for extreme steepness).

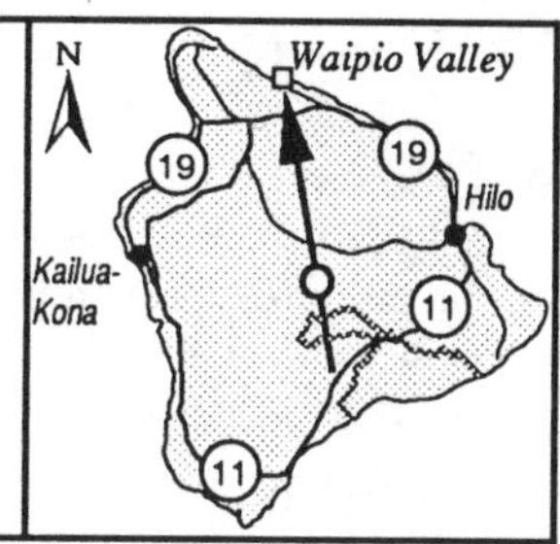

Topos: Optional: *Kukuihaele* 7½

Trail map: At the end of this trip.

Highlights: When you were dreaming of visiting Hawaii, did you linger over photographs of a broad, Eden-like green valley sealed off from the outside world by sheer, thousand-foot-high walls? Chances are that valley was Waipio Valley. This is your chance to spend some time in it.

Driving instructions: From Hilo, drive northwest along the Hamakua Coast on Highway 19 for 40 miles to the turnoff to Honokaa (Highway 240). Allow plenty of time for this drive, as the Hamakua Coast is very lovely. After turning right (north) onto Highway 240, follow it through Honokaa and several smaller towns to the end of the road, 9⅓ more miles (49⅓ miles total), just above Waipio Overlook. *Under no circumstances should you even consider driving down into Waipio Valley!* The 4WD-only road is extraordinarily steep, narrow, and a trial even for drivers who know it well.

Permit/permission required: No permission is required for dayhiking. Permission is required from the Hamakua Sugar Company to camp overnight; see Appendix A.

Description: Take a few minutes to walk down to Waipio Overlook to enjoy the view of the valley. Rain-drenched, dazzlingly green Waipio Valley is one of the Big Island's most famous beauty spots. However, some of the waterfalls may be dry: their streams are tapped "topside" for irrigation, so there's little water left to cascade down into the valley. The overlook offers the best views you're going to get unless you decide to tackle the switchbacks you'll see zigzagging up the west wall of Waipio Valley. This is an excellent place to take your photos of Waipio, too.

Back at the top of the road, you'll see a sign with a black diamond on it. You're probably familiar with the use of the black-diamond symbol to indicate the most difficult runs at skiing areas. Well, the road that you hike down into Waipio Valley is a black-diamond road—though the warning is for cars rather than hikers. Watch out for the loose gravel on the shoulders; it's easy to lose your footing on it and fall. Ignore side roads (they're driveways to private property.)

In ¾ mile you reach the valley floor and turn right, toward the beach. As you approach the coast, you enter a grove of ironwoods and curve left through the grove (which also happens to be the camping area). The grove ends on the banks of the major stream through Waipio Valley, Wailoa Stream, 1½ miles from your start. Most of Waipio's gray-sand beach is on the other side of Wailoa Stream, so ford the stream as best you can—no bridge, no rocks, no logs. Especially on weekends, you'll find families frolicking in the stream, so you can watch them to get an idea of where it's safe to cross. Some innovative people float their picnic gear across the stream on boogie boards. (At its deepest, the water was almost armpit-deep on me.)

Once across Wailoa Stream, you can wander across sand and cobbles as far as the opposite wall of the valley. Waipio's waters are too rough for swimming, but don't let that ruin your day. Pick your spot, spread out your towel, get out your picnic lunch, and enjoy the scenery. Much of Waipio Valley is privately owned, so you're not free to wander through the valley. However, you can ascend the switchbacks on the west wall of the valley partway for some different but equally spectacular views of the valley. (The extra mileage and elevation gain/loss are not included in this trip.) See Trip 2 for directions to the switchbacks.

Save some energy for that monumental climb back up the road, as you must eventually return the way you came.

Waipio stories. . . . Waipio Valley's fertile and beautiful acres are the site of many old Hawaiian legends and the home of many of Hawaii's heroes. The god Lono found his earthly bride here. Kane and Kanaloa once dwelt here. According to one story, the entrance from the Big Island to the underworld—where the spirits of the dead went after they were banished from the land of the living—was in Waipio Valley. It's said that this entrance could still be found until this century, when a sugar company plowed it over while planting part of the valley in cane.

Waipio Valley was famous for its agricultural productivity. Reportedly, the output of Waipio Valley could sustain the entire population of the Big Island even if the crops and livestock failed everywhere else. Yet over the past half-century, Waipio has gradually been deserted. Probably the greatest single blow to Waipio's once-self-sufficient lifestyle was the great *tsunami* (tidal wave) of 1946. No one was killed in Waipio, but the *tsunami*, which also devastated Hilo, destroyed buildings and fields and terrified many people into leaving. Most of them never returned.

A few old-timers, as well as a few newcomers looking for Eden, still live in Waipio Valley. Waipio has no electricity, so people who want a modern lifestyle must move away, even if it's just "topside" to the villages on the cliffs above the valley. Finally, even with modern 4WD vehicles, getting in and out of Waipio is an adventure—one that draws visitors but discourages dwellers. What will become of Waipio Valley in the twenty-first century? We'll know soon enough.

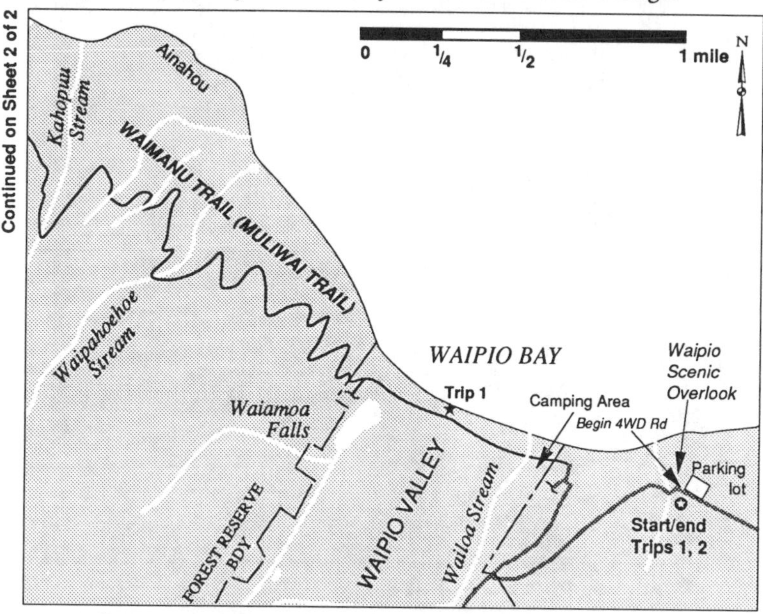

Trips 1 through 3. Waipio and Waimanu Valleys and Waiilikahi Falls (Sheet 1 of 2)

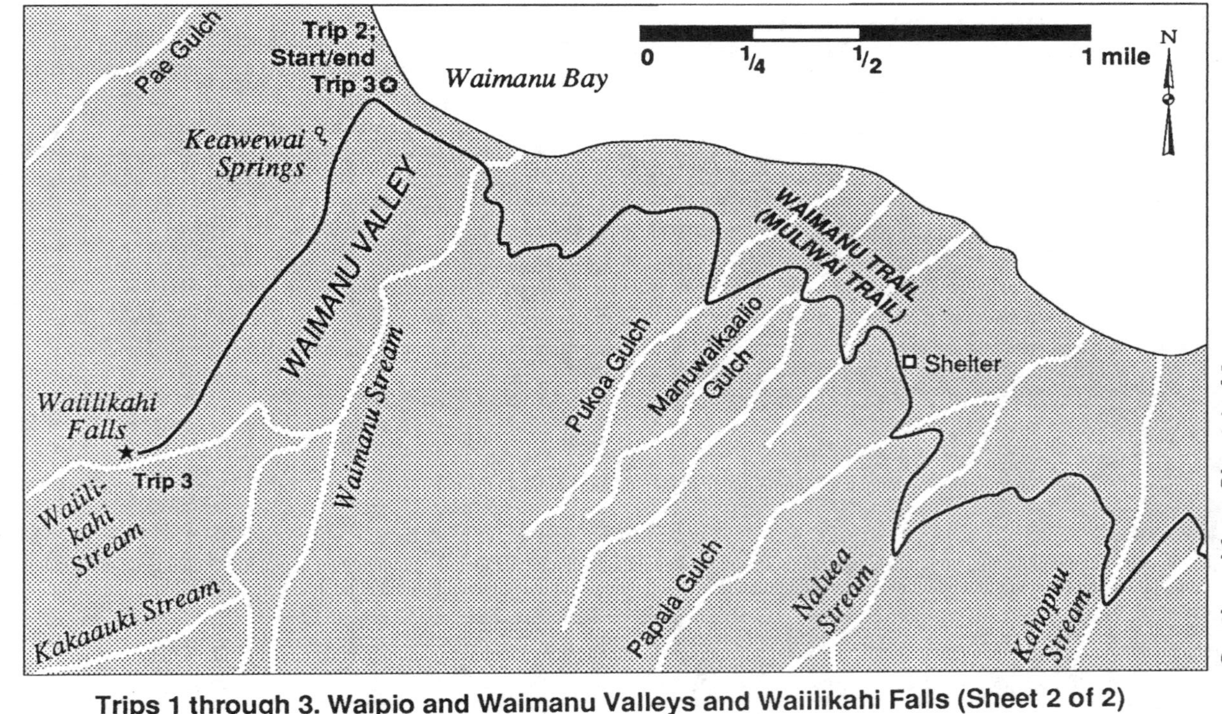

Continued from Sheet 1 of 2

Trips 1 through 3. Waipio and Waimanu Valleys and Waiilikahi Falls (Sheet 2 of 2)

Trip 2. Waimanu Valley Backpack

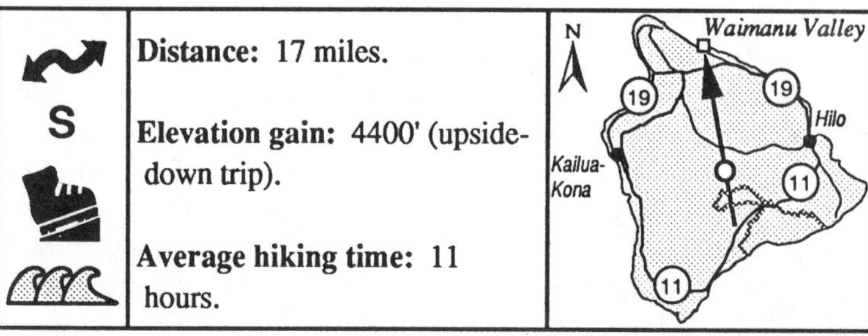

Distance: 17 miles.

Elevation gain: 4400' (upside-down trip).

Average hiking time: 11 hours.

Topos: *Kukuihaele, Honokane* 7½.

Trail map: At the end of Trip 1.

Highlights: Waimanu Valley is famed for much of the same kind of beauty as is Waipio Valley. Smaller Waimanu Valley was once well-populated and fertile, too. But Waimanu is now utterly uninhabited and wild. It's preserved as the Waimanu National Estuarine Research Reserve. *Take this trip only during the "dry" season (roughly May through October) because of the large number of potentially dangerous stream crossings involved.*

Driving instructions: Follow the driving instructions of Trip 1.

Permit/permission required: Dayhiking into Waimanu does not require permission—no wonder: Waimanu is so remote and so difficult to reach that there is no practical way to treat it as a dayhiking destination. You should backpack into Waimanu and camp there. Camping in Waimanu is very strictly regulated by the Division of Forestry and Wildlife as of March 1, 1991; you must have a permit from them and may camp only at the site assigned to you. Your stay is limited to 4 days and 3 nights. See Appendix A.

Description ("easier" trip): Even in the dry season, you must ford at least two good-sized streams on this trip: Wailoa Stream in Waipio Valley (nearly armpit-deep on me) and Waimanu Stream in Waimanu Valley (waist-deep on me). Be sure you and your backpack are prepared to get wet. Also be sure you have a rainproof tent: it will almost certainly rain at night in Waimanu. *Caution:* This trip is *not* for beginning backpackers.

Day 1 (1½ miles). Follow the directions of Trip 1 and camp in Waipio Valley or, if it's still operating, stay at Mr. Araki's hotel (also see Appendix A).

Day 2 (7 miles). From the east bank of Wailoa Stream, cautiously ford the stream and follow the beach until you are almost at the valley's west wall—just below a small rise with a rather flat but steeply pitched, grassy top. A very faint path leads away from the beach, through the cobblestones, and into the forest about 200 feet east of (before) the small rise. Even if you cannot pick out the path at this point, head through the cobbles into the forest, keeping your eyes peeled for a well-trampled path. It's currently used for horseback tours of Waipio, so it's not only well-trampled but full of hoofprints and dung. You may smell it before you see it. Pick it up and head west, toward the valley's west wall. You shortly reach a junction with a trail that goes right, toward the valley wall. The junction may have a sign, but don't count on it.

Turn right at this junction to begin climbing the steep switchbacks up the thousand-foot sheer west wall of Waipio Valley. At first you're still in dense forest. Soon you emerge into sunlight and to unsurpassed views of Waipio. The trail is generally well dug into the sheer cliff, so it's not quite as scary as it may have seemed from the overlook on the east wall—Waipio Overlook. But it is every bit as steep as you'd feared when you were scanning it from Waipio Overlook.

As you near the top, the trail enters a dry forest of ironwoods, silk oaks, paperbark eucalyptuses, and Norfolk pines. Your long-range views are gone (gone until you reach the beach at Waimanu, in fact). The trail levels out amid spindly ironwood seedlings and wanders over the soft, slippery carpet of fallen ironwood needles as it rounds the nose of a ridge. Plants more typical of the rainforest replace the dry-forest trees as you dip into the first of the many gullies you must traverse between Waipio and Waimanu. The mosquito-y gullies can be very muddy, so watch your footing. Streams run through most of these gullies, and the second stream you cross has some pretty cascades and a small, deep pool in a fern-lined nook just upstream of the trail.

This pattern of dry-forest ridge "noses" alternating with rain-forest gullies continues all the way to Waimanu. At some points, the trail has been hacked through dense thickets of Koster's curse (*Clidemia hirta*), one of Hawaii's most troubling pest plants. At 4⅔ miles you reach a trail shelter and an outhouse, both of them battered, dirty, and uninviting. The nearest water—possibly just stagnant pools—is in the next gulch from here toward Waimanu. (See below for another idea if you must make camp before you reach Waimanu.)

At last you negotiate the final ridge nose and begin your descent to Waimanu—hard to tell for sure because of the heavy growth. Take your time here, as the trail not only pitches very steeply down but becomes much worse: narrow, exposed, and debris-filled. (It would be almost impassable when wet.) Small landslides cut across it at inconvenient spots. Lower down, the track is also filled with slippery *hala* leaves. Arrival at the valley floor comes as a relief. Bear right, toward the beach and toward one of the two composting toilets for campers in Waimanu. There is a campsite here on the east side of Waimanu Stream, but it is for use only in an emergency, such as when the stream is unfordable.

Carefully ford Waimanu Stream and, once across, pause to take in the view of the valley from here. It's one of the best viewpoints of this deep, dramatic valley, which has more waterfalls plunging over its sides than Waipio has. Most of the "beach" at Waimanu is boulders, so you veer away from the boulders and follow a path under ironwoods past the first few campsites as far as the other composting toilet. Your campsite is assigned to you when you get your permit. Not all of the campsites are marked with their numbers, but the map you get with your permit will help you identify your site. If your campsite is farther on, turn seaward and continue on the boulders, and eventually on the sand, to your site. Water is available from a stream, fed by Keawewai Springs, on the west side of the valley: follow a muddy track from the end of the beach back into the valley to a running stream. Be sure to purify the water before drinking it.

Even with a stop at Waipio Valley, the trip to Waimanu—especially that last drop down into the valley—is exhausting. Plan to spend at least a day relaxing and enjoying Waimanu! Under sunny skies, the gray-sand beach at Waimanu is a lovely place to stretch out. Unfortunately, the bay is too dangerous for swimming. Need anything more to do? The next trip, Trip 3, is a side trip to the nearest of Waimanu's many waterfalls.

Day 3 (8½ miles). Retrace your steps.

Camping midway to/from Waimanu. . . . What can you do if you can't make it all the way to or from Waimanu in one day? The shelter at 4⅔ miles is, as I said, uninviting. Possible campsites between Waipio and Waimanu valleys are the flat areas under the dry forests of the ridge noses. Just be certain you observe this caution: *don't have any kind of open flame while you're camped there!* The ironwood needles that thickly carpet these flat spots are extremely flammable. I wouldn't even light a match or use a backpacker's stove there.

Trip 3. Waiilikahi Falls Side Trip from Waimanu Valley

Distance: Just over 2¼ miles as the crow flies, but circuitous.

Elevation gain: 200'.

Average hiking time: 2⅔ hours (following tags is slow!).

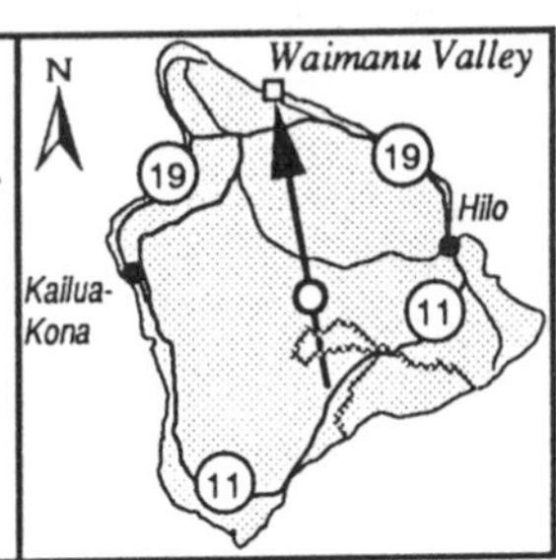

Topos: Optional: *Honokane* 7½.

Trail map (route approximated): At the end of Trip 1.

Highlights: Waterfalls are enchanting! Too often, Hawaiian waterfalls are inacessible unless you can afford a helicopter flight—and even then, you can only look but not touch. One of Waimanu Valley's thundering waterfalls is accessible on foot—with a little patience and navigating skill.

(Of course, for *viewing* it, rather than splashing in it, this waterfall, like waterfalls anywhere, is much more impressive when seen at a distance, where its long, silky white plumes of water are fully revealed to our admiring eyes. In other words, the best *view* of this waterfall is not from its base but from the ford of Waimanu Stream.)

Warning: Wild pigs live in Waimanu Valley, and you may encounter one on your way to these falls, as I did. It's reported that wild pigs can be dangerous if they are surprised and are unable to find a safe escape route. Make some noise as you go to warn the pigs to get away. (I whack the shrubbery and rocks with my hiking stick.)

Driving instructions: Not applicable.

Permit/permission required: See Trip 2 for permission required to camp in Waimanu Valley.

Description: Waiilikahi Falls in Waimanu Valley is accessible if you're patient and look carefully for tags—colored plastic ribbon tied to trees or shrubs—and follow them on this route. There is no trail—not even a beaten path.

Start as if you were heading for the drinking-water source I described in Trip 2. Continue, generally south, beyond the water source, by following the tags. You cross several dry waterways right after the spring-fed courses. Your route is in the rainforest, and it's very circuitous, though you generally stick to the valley's west wall. You pass a number of ruins—the fine stone walls so typical of Hawaii before European contact. You weave through guava, *kukui,* and coffee, trying to avoid falling into ponds. A difficult section early in the hike forces you to climb slippery rocks and tree roots up and around a large pond.

About halfway, the route is apparently hacked through a *hau* thicket. Conflicting, confusing tags may have you wondering which way to go. In the spring of 1991, I found that the route that ran closer to the edges of the *hau* thicket connected better with the rest of the route.

You finally stumble upon a third, "wet" watercourse—possibly marked by a metal rod painted red and white. Turn upstream along this third "wet" watercourse without crossing it (if that is how the tags still direct you). With the help of the tags, you'll soon pick your way through drenching spray to the base of the fall, where the pool is said to be swimmable. The din of falling water is deafening, and the fog of spray may conceal the true size of this waterfall. There's plenty of broken rock around the pool. Beware of falling rocks at this or any other waterfall!

Waterfalls at work. . . . In Hawaii, the terrain tends to consist of alternating layers of resistant lava and less-resistant material such as consolidated ash or clinker. A stream wears down through the softer layer and cascades over the harder layer. The force of the falling water wears away the rock at the base of the falls, forming a lovely pool. Undercut by that process, the rock above the pool succumbs to gravity and falls away, shattering at the base of the falls. This process wears the stream's channel farther and farther back into the slope. Over eons, the stream cuts its gorge back toward its headwaters. Because harder and softer layers alternate, streams often form a chain of waterfalls on their long descent to the sea.

Trip 4. Kalopa State Park—Nature Loop

V

Distance: Just under ¾ mile; in poor condition but worth it.

Elevation gain: 30'.

Average hiking time: 1 hour (allows time to read brochure).

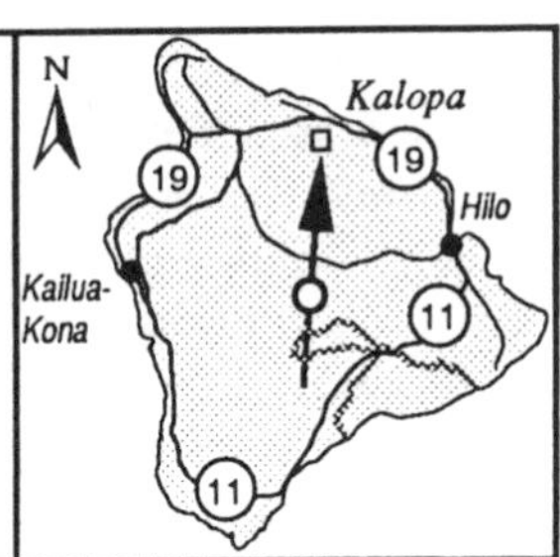

Topos: Optional: *Honokaa* 7½.

Trail map (route approximated): At the end of this trip.

Highlights: Kalopa's Nature Loop offers an excellent opportunity to see native Hawaiian plants in their natural setting. The attractive day-use pavilion should tempt you to stay for a picnic in spite of the area's raininess.

Driving instructions: From Hilo, drive northwest on Highway 19 for 37½ miles—not quite as far as the turnoff to Honokaa. At the signed turnoff for Kalopa State Park, turn inland and follow country roads according to a series of signs for a zigzagging 3⅓ more miles to the entrance of Kalopa. Follow the road through Kalopa another ⅓ mile, past the caretaker's cabin. At a fork, curve right, passing a handsome day-use pavilion, to the parking area near Kalopa's cabins, 41½ miles. (See Appendix A for information on renting the cabins or camping at Kalopa.) Park here (or, if there isn't room, park back down the road at the day-use pavilion and walk back to this parking lot).

Permit/permission required: None.

Description: Across the parking lot, opposite the cabins, you'll find an information sign about Kalopa and a self-service dispenser of brochures about the park. It's well worth your time to read the information sign and well worth the small fee for a brochure. However, most of Kalopa's trails are no longer worth hiking (or safe for hiking); see below.

The beginning of the nature trail isn't obvious from the parking lot. Head away from the parking lot and information sign toward a little shed that was on your right as you were facing the information sign. Keep the shed on your left as you skirt a row of trees and pass the ends of what are labeled as the Arboretum Rainforest Trail and the Arboretum Dryland Forest Trail (neither is worth bothering with). Keep left at a sign that says ENJOY THE TRAIL. PLEASE WALK WITH CARE. In about ten steps from that sign, you can stop to pick up a guide to the Nature Loop from a self-service dispenser. Continue ahead to a fork, where you bear left, just before a small gully. Innumerable insect voices sing throughout the forest; rainforest roots writhe across the muddy trail. At last you reach the fork at the beginning of the loop portion of the Nature Loop. Turn right at this fork to follow the stations as they're laid out in the brochure. It's time to devote your attention to the brochure, the rainforest, and the trail.

As you approach the halfway point, you climb gently toward the fenced edge of the mostly native rainforest this trail loops through. Not long ago, this forest reserve was planted with non-native species. The glimpses of cropped fields and non-native plants on the other side of the fence remind you that this native rainforest exists only because it was deliberately replanted and has been protected from encroaching non-native plants and from animals like wild pigs. Your trail curves left, past a fallen log, as you turn away from the fence and continue following the trail according to the brochure.

The trail is sometimes hard to follow, particularly where the giant roots of a strangler fig spread across it near the ½-mile point. You need to climb over the roots of this bizarre and unwelcome intruder and then go around the left side of the fig (and the *ohia* it's strangling) to regain the trail. You soon close the loop, and turn right to return to the parking lot. Be sure to return the brochure or pay for it at the information sign!

Hiking at Kalopa. . . . Although Kalopa State Park once had a trail system, most of its trails are in such bad shape from lack of maintenance that I can recommend only this Nature Loop and the Jeep Road (Trip 5). Plants in a rainforest—which is where Kalopa is—can grow right back over a trail in no time at all. The current full-time staff of one person at Kalopa has time to maintain only the day-use and cabin areas. The overgrown, rutted, muddy remnants of some of the trails are tagged, but the tagging is inadequate. The slippery remains of the Gulch Rim Trail expose you to a nasty fall and are so overgrown you have almost no views of the gulch that's supposed to be the attraction. One Big Island resident told me he likes to ride his mountain bike as fast as he can down the Gulch Rim Trail—another good reason to stay off it.

Are the trails really that bad? Someone at Kalopa suggested that

I would have no trouble with the overgrown trails if I just turned back toward the Jeep Road when I wanted to escape the rainforest. Following this advice, and with map and compass, I attempted the "tagged" Perimeter Horse Trail. When the badly spaced tags petered out altogether, I turned back to the Jeep Road—I thought. After thrashing through tangled plants and sliding down a muddy slope on my fanny, I stumbled out of the rainforest into somebody's back yard, on the wrong side of a NO TRESPASSING sign. There was no one around to chase me off—or to give me directions back to Kalopa. I eventually found my way back to the entrance of Kalopa via country lanes, ditches, and fields. I wish you better luck.

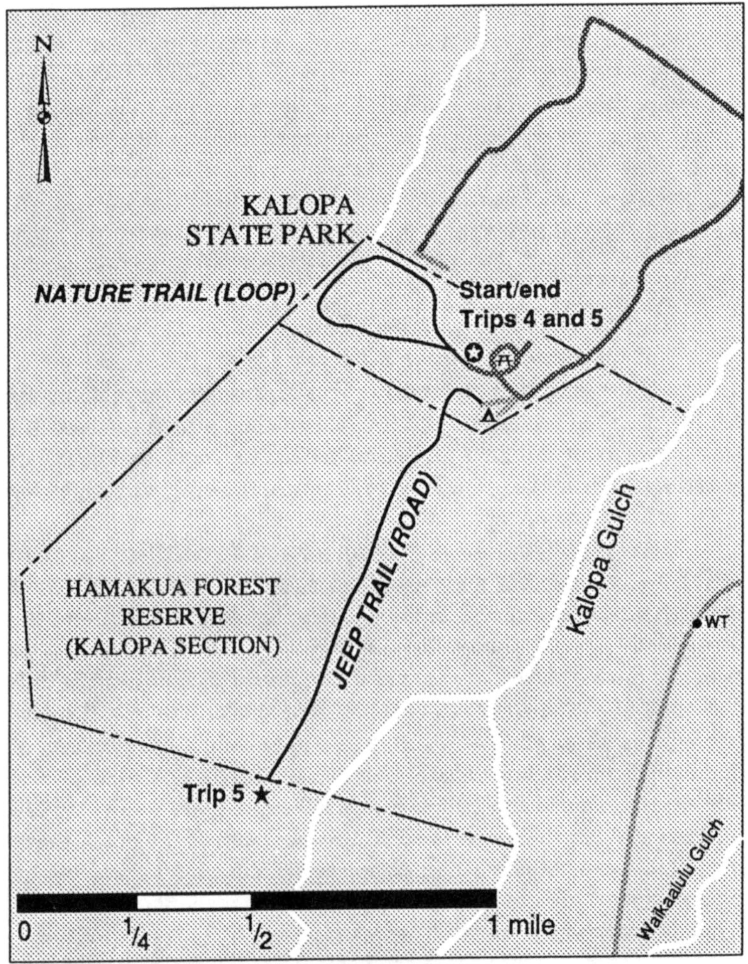

Trips 4 and 5. Kalopa—Nature Loop and Jeep Trail *(Trail sketched from Hamakua District Development Council map)*

Trip 5. Kalopa State Park—Jeep Road

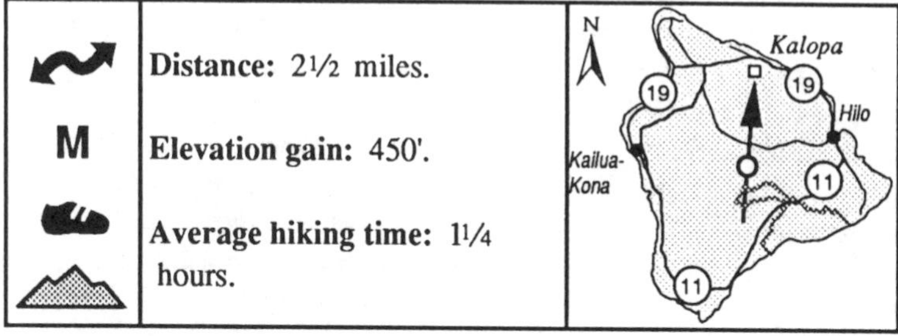

Distance: 2½ miles.

Elevation gain: 450′.

Average hiking time: 1¼ hours.

Topos: Optional: *Honokaa* 7½.

Trail map (route approximated): At the end of Trip 4.

Highlights: The Jeep Road offers a straightforward and pleasant ramble through Kalopa State Park's largely non-native forest.

Driving instructions: Follow the instructions of Trip 4.

Permit/permission required: None.

Description: From the parking lot by the cabins, you can retrace your steps down the road past the day-use area to the fork and take that fork to the right through the uninviting tent-camping area (this is the beginning of the Jeep Road). Or you can simply cut through the trees next to the information sign at the parking lot for a few yards and pick up the Jeep Road on the other side of the trees.

Starting from the fork, the unpaved Jeep Road curves through the camping area and toward the cabins at first, but soon it straightens and goes generally south and gradually uphill. Shrub-sized cayenne vervain, waving its spikes of blue flowers, crowds the understory. Strawberry guavas elbow in on either side; some have fallen across the road. Behind them rise the tall, spicy-smelling swamp mahogany and paperbark trees, both of them types of eucalyptus. The bark of the paperbark, which is constantly peeling off, looks papery from a distance. Up close, a sheet of damp, shed bark looks more like a cross between cork and sponge.

As the road wanders, it is usually wider than a trail. But the forest sometimes moves in on it so closely that it's hardly wider than a footpath. Intersecting trails are so overgrown it's hard to distinguish them from the rest of the forest—you wouldn't know they were there if a couple of them weren't still marked by signs. Watch your footing on a section near the top of the Jeep Road where it has eroded into a series of steep, narrow "steps" in the slippery clay.

The road has narrowed almost to invisibility by the time you reach the top of it at a wire fence that marks the forest boundary. Beyond it lie green fields constantly manicured by grazing cattle and broken by occasional spinneys of non-native trees. There's quite a contrast here between the dense forest and the open fields. One of them is that if you were to wander into the fields, you would find yourself wading into cow pies as well as trespassing. So, instead, you end your hike here and retrace your steps.

Kalopa State Park. . . . began as Kalopa Forest Reserve, according to a park brochure. The acreage was set aside for the reserve in 1903. As in other forest reserves, managers planted non-native trees, some for timber, some because they were faster-growing than native species. Five hundred fifteen of the reserve's 615 acres are still forested in non-native trees.

The other hundred acres of the reserve are now Kalopa State Park. In the early 1960s, Hamakua citizens realized that their forest reserves were being cleared. They formed a strong grassroots movement that persuaded the Division of Land and Natural Resources to set aside 100 acres of Kalopa's 615 acres as a state park in 1967. It was opened to the public in 1970. Volunteers built the trail system and replanted much of the state-park acreage in native species.

The Nature Loop is entirely within the state park. The Jeep Road is mostly in the remaining forest reserve and extends, as you just saw, all the way to one of the reserve's boundaries.

The jeep trail in Kalope State Park

Trip 6. Akaka Falls State Park

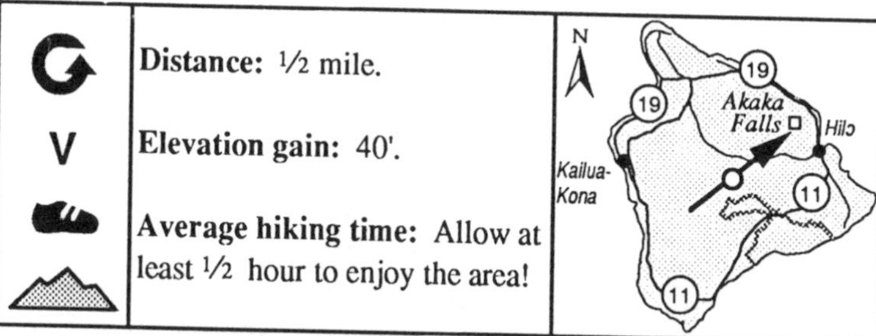

Topos: Optional: *Akaka Falls* 7½.

Trail map (route approximated): At the end of this trip.

Highlights: Akaka Falls State Park offers an easy walk on paved trail through a luxuriant rainforest to fine overlooks of not one but two beautiful waterfalls. It's a must-see!

Driving instructions: From Hilo, drive northwest on Highway 19 and follow it for 11½ miles to its junction with Highway 220. Turn inland on Highway 220 and follow signs to Akaka Falls State Park as the highway jogs through tiny Honomu village. You drive through cane fields and reach the small parking lot at the park 3¾ miles after turning off Highway 19 (15¼ miles from Hilo altogether).

Permit/permission required: None.

Description: Before you set out, note that neither waterfall is accessible from the park and that swimming is prohibited in the park. The trail can be quite slippery when it is wet, so watch your step.

With tangles of blackberry and the brilliant flowers of impatiens on either side, you descend a stairway from the parking lot and shortly reach the first junction, where you turn right. (Sure, you can turn left, too. However, turning right lets you enjoy Kahuna Falls as the salad and Akaka Falls as the main course.) You continue your gentle descent on a paved walkway through bamboo, ginger, ferns, and more impatiens. The setting is truly, as the *Hawaii Handbook* puts it, "everybody's idea of a pristine Hawaiian valley," except that almost none of the plants are native. But it *is* gorgeously tropical!

You presently cross a stream on a bridge and reach a second junction. Go right here on a short spur trail and descend a little more to a delightful viewpoint. Across the deep valley, hundred-foot Kahuna Falls dashes in long cascades down its narrow channel to meet Kolekole Stream.

Return to the second junction. With the spur to Kahuna Falls at your back, you turn right, climb a short flight of stairs and then descend a little to level out on a narrow ridge. The ridgetop is lined with trees draped in ephiphytes and philodendron, giving it a jungly feeling. A little more climbing and descending bring you to the viewpoint for Akaka Falls, where there is a rain shelter, too. Across the valley, Kolekole Stream makes a single dramatic leap 420 feet over a shelf of rock and down into an almost perfectly circular pool as Akaka Falls. Depending upon how much water is in Kolekole Stream, you may also notice other, far smaller cascades down the sides of the natural amphitheater that holds Akaka Falls. *This* is how we expect Hawaiian waterfalls to look!

Reluctantly, you turn away at last from Akaka Falls and, continuing around the loop, stroll past some lobster-claw heliconia plants. You cross a little stream on a bridge just below a small cascade, then cross a larger stream on another bridge, this one strategically placed between several handsome cascades. You pass a rock wall from which springs seep and climb a little to return to the first junction. You turn right and climb the stairs back to the parking lot to end the hike. The lot boasts restrooms and a picnic table, so why not enjoy a picnic here instead of hurrying away from this lovely area?

An interesting family. . . . A delightful discovery you can make in Hawaii is of the many different kinds of bananas (as opposed to the standard mainland supermarket variety). In the islands, more than fifty species of bananas once grew. They're not native to Hawaii; they were introduced originally by the Polynesians. The best bananas I've ever tasted came from a place near Waipio Valley: small, white-fleshed till you bit into them, they had a delicate orange tint inside and were wonderfully fragrant as well as delicious.

Why talk about bananas at Akaka Falls? The banana family isn't just long on fruit. You should see the flowers! In fact, you've just walked past some banana relatives famed not for their fruit but for their flowers: the lobster-claw heliconias. Those boiled-lobster-red "flowers" aren't really flowers, though. As with all the heliconias, they're the bracts around the inconspicuous true flowers.

The banana family doesn't stop there: the birds-of-paradise are banana relatives, too. The vivid orange-and-blue petals of the bird-of-paradise, poised atop a purplish sheath as if ready to leap into the air, really are part of its flower. So are the white petals of the white (or "giant") bird-of-paradise.

Akaka Falls

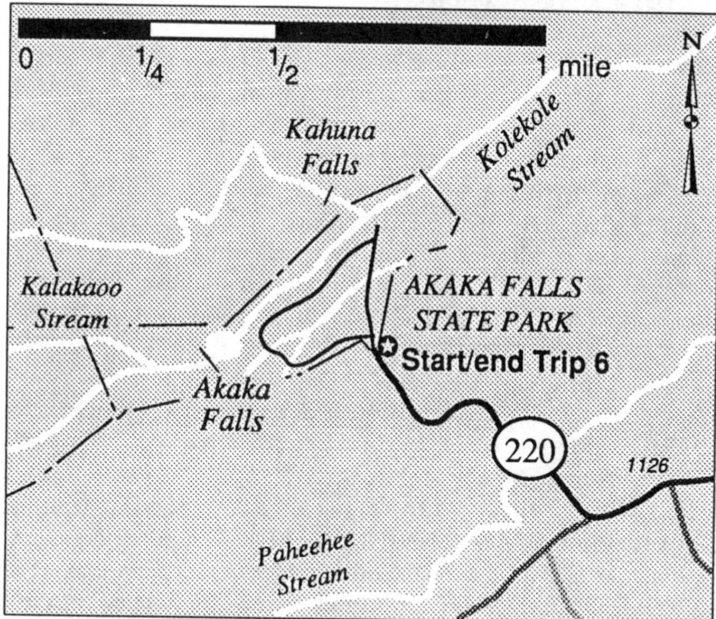

Trip 6. Akaka Falls *(Trail sketched from DNLR brochure; not to scale. Small streams within park do not appear on topo and are not shown extending outside park.)*

Trip 7. Kaumana Caves

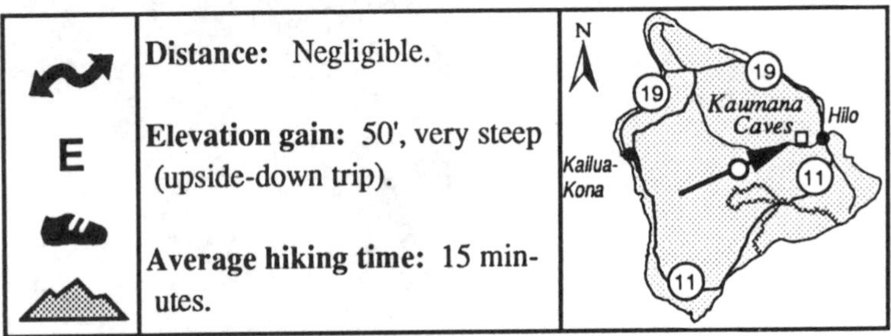

Topos: Optional: *Piihonua* 7½.

Trail map (route approximated): At the end of this trip.

Highlights: A pretty roadside rest along the Saddle Road offers you a chance to briefly descend into a lava tube whose ends then proceed who-knows-how-far into the cool darkness. It's such a contrast to the warmth of Hilo. Be sure to bring a flashlight if you wish to peer farther into the caves than their openings.

Driving instructions: At the fork just after Highway 19 crosses over the Wailoa River, bear left into downtown Hilo on Kamehameha Avenue. In just under 1⅔ miles, turn left (inland) at the light at one-way Waianuenue Avenue and follow it uphill past Hilo High School. Where it forks, take the *left* fork; it's Kaumana Drive, also Highway 200 and the beginning of the Saddle Road. Drive cautiously as you wind through the outskirts of Hilo and into its suburbs: you may find children playing in the road. The unpaved parking lot is on the left side of the road, while Kaumana Caves County Park is on the right side, a little past the mile-4 marker, 6 miles from Hilo. Park here and carefully cross the road to the park.

Permit/permission required: None.

Description: A few yards across some old *pahoehoe,* you'll find a steep staircase leading 50 feet down a philodendron-draped maw into a pit from which spring full-grown trees. The ceiling of a lava tube fell in here—obviously many years ago. At the bottom, dark caverns—the lava tube—lead off to right and left; the one to your left drips with groundwater. Above, it may have been hot and steamy; down here in this collapsed lava tube, it's cool, damp, and ferny. You can make short forays into the horizontal tube from here, but there are no lights and no trails. My backpacker's flashlight was barely enough to illuminate a few feet into each of them.

How far do these tubes go? Perhaps to Milu, now that the entrance from Waipio Valley is gone (see Trip 1). You, of course, won't go that far. Further exploration would be unsafe without large, heavy-duty flashlights and some experience exploring lava tubes or, better yet, an experienced guide.

But this is an experience in contrasts, so you retrace your steps up the staircase. The park also offers a picnic pavilion, benches, restrooms, and water. Enjoy a picnic or at least a snack stop here as you reflect on the heat of Hilo and the cool depths of the lava tube. Maybe you'll be tempted to descend for a second look after your snack!

Lava tubes. . . . form when a *pahoehoe* flow is confined in a gully or a valley. The flow's outer layers cool and solidify while molten lava continues flowing in an inner, pipe-like zone. Sooner or later, the source of fresh lava moves away. The volume of the active flow dwindles, and the flow comes to occupy the lower part of the tube. Gases from the flowing lava may be hot enough to melt the ceiling of the tube, and the melted ceiling material may drip to form lava "stalactites" hanging down into the tube. Eventually, lava ceases to flow through the tube, and the material remaining in the tube can then solidify, giving the tube a flat floor.

Some lava tubes channel still-molten lava underground to a place where it emerges (surprise!) many miles away. As of this writing, lava tubes are conducting a river of fire from Kilauea's current eruption under a shelly new surface to a steaming, sometimes explosive, exit into the ocean along the Puna coast. Lava tubes may lurk under surfaces that look safe to walk on, and their ceilings have been known to crumble underfoot, leaving hikers hanging in midair or falling. The caves you're visiting here exist because a lava tube's ceiling broke and revealed the tube. It's never safe to strike out across a lava field at random.

The Big Island's best-known lava tube, Thurston Lava Tube, is in Hawaii Volcanoes National Park. *Everyone* goes there, but it's still well worth a visit when you get to the park (see Trip 29). Thurston Lava Tube is illuminated so that you can walk through it. In the meantime, few people visit Kaumana Caves County Park. Here, you can visit and admire a lava tube in a much more leisurely way.

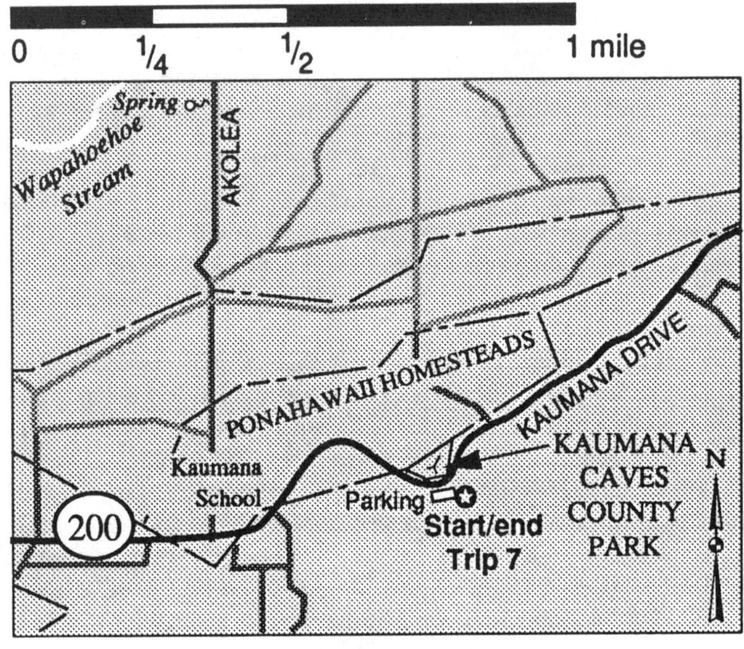

Trip 7. Kaumana Caves County Park

Trip 8. Puu Oo

Distance: 8 miles.

Elevation gain: 200'.

Average hiking time: 4 hours.

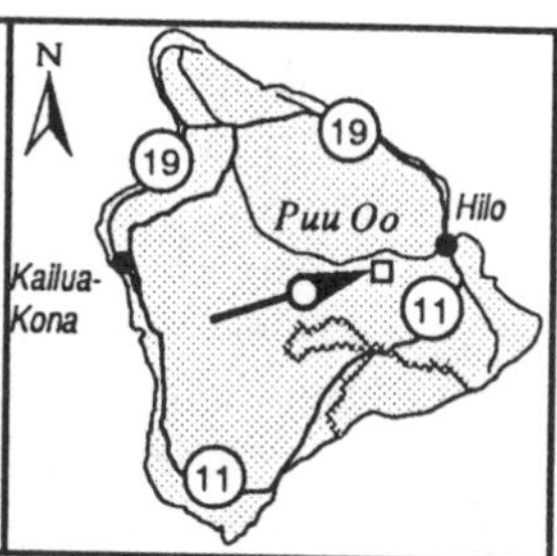

Topos: Optional: *Puu Oo, Upper Piihonua* 7½.

Trail map: At the end of this trip.

Highlights: The Puu Oo Trail offers a variety of scenery: open woods, broad meadows, and stark intrusions of barren lava. One of its most beloved features is the amount of bird life along it. It's an outstanding trail for birders. Even if you don't feel up to the entire trip, I hope you'll go at least as far as the first meadow.

Driving instructions: *Note that some rental car companies forbid you to drive their cars on the Saddle Road. You will have to decide for yourself whether to drive on the Saddle Road in spite of such cautions. I think their fears are largely unwarranted: the Saddle Road, though narrow, winding, and potholed in some places, is completely paved. One problem is that some may drive the road far faster than is safe, considering its narrowness, its ups and downs, its occasional lack of shoulders, and its sudden zigs and zags. Drive very carefully and pull over to let others pass when you can do so safely (if they want to drive at breakneck speed on the Saddle Road, that's their problem).*

At the fork just after Highway 19 crosses over the Wailoa River, bear left into downtown Hilo on Kamehameha Avenue. In just under 1⅔ miles, turn left (inland) at the light at one-way Waianuenue Avenue and follow it uphill past Hilo High School. Where it forks, take the *left* fork; it's Kaumana Drive, also Highway 200 and the beginning of the Saddle Road. Drive cautiously as you wind through the outskirts of Hilo and into its suburbs: you may find children playing in the road. You pass Kaumana Caves County Park (Trip 7).

The "objectionable" part of the road begins after you pass the next community and a turnoff to a golf course. The County of Hawaii has been improving the Saddle Road, and you are likely to be held up for road work on your way. This work is turning the Saddle

Road into a respectable two-lane road and may, when completed, overcome the rental car companies' objections.

Keep an eye on the mile markers. Between markers 21 and 22, you'll pass a small, shot-up sign on the Mauna Loa (left) side that says PLR POWER LINE ROAD. This is where you'll rejoin the Saddle Road near the end of this hike. Continuing, you then crest a small hill and see a grassy pullout on the Mauna Kea (right) side just a little down the slope. Park here, just under 26 miles from Hilo, without blocking the gate. This isn't the official trailhead. The official trailhead is a short distance up the road and very hard to spot unless you've been there before. So we'll start here at a spot that's easier to find and offers better parking.

Permit/permission required: None.

Description: Carefully walk west on the shoulder of the Saddle Road toward the crest of the next hill. I recommend that when you're walking on a road, you assume that anyone operating a vehicle on that road is deaf, blind, and insane. As you approach the crest of this little hill, look for an old road on the south-southwest (left) side of the Saddle Road. About 100 feet down that road you'll see a small wooden trailhead sign and, below it, a yellow sign with a big hole in it. Take the old road past those signs; it's the Puu Oo Trail. It quickly becomes a rough track that heads south through *aa* toward an *ohia* forest.

At the forest's edge, alien weeds give way to native *kukaenene, pukiawe, ohia,* and ferns. The track then crests a hump of lava. Once you're over this hump, the road noise behind you vanishes, and you are alone with the rustling forest and the chattering birds. Climbing a little, you pass through an old fence and descend into a grassy meadow, passing a crumbling sign that says UPPER WAIAKOA FOREST RESERVE. The trail is a bit faint here but heads southwest by some *koa* trees. Pockets of stagnant water—okay for the wildlife but not for you—have accumulated along the trail where old *pahoehoe* is exposed. The rusty-hinge calls of *iiwi* and the red flashes of *iiwi* and *apapane* on the wing enliven the tranquil scene. Mauna Loa looms ahead until you veer briefly into the woods, just over 1 mile from your start.

Back on the grass, you follow the faint track over *pahoehoe* and then veer south-southeast through thimbleberry and *koa.* Soon you emerge at another meadow. On the other side of this meadow, you wind down into a pleasant *koa* forest where the trail is faint enough that the help offered by a couple of plastic-ribbon tags is welcome. You come out of the woods at an *aa* field. On this segment, your route through the lava field is marked by cairns. The lava here is covered with a thick shag of gray-white lichens.

Leaving the *aa* field, you twine down into another *ohia* forest—proof that a *kipuka* (an area not overrun by lava) can be lower than its surrounding, newer lava field. Past this *kipuka,* you cross a *pahoehoe* flow and then plunge back into the forest heading east and southeast. Repeating this pattern, you cross another lava flow and then another *ohia* wood. Look for the orange berries of *pilo* in this *kipuka.*

Crossing the next lava field brings you to a *kipuka* with very tall *ohia* trees and tree ferns. The track is hard to follow at first, but the air is full of the songs and the branches full of the scarlet glow of those living *ohia* blossoms, the *iiwi* and *apapane.* In these last few *kipuka,* look for a low plant with a blossom very like that of the mainland self-heal but with scentless foliage. You reluctantly leave this *kipuka* to follow cairns and tags across a long stretch of *pahoehoe* to a low mound of lava at the edge of the next *kipuka.* The beaten path through the *kipuka* picks up just on the other side of that lava mound. Your stay in this *kipuka* is brief, and you're soon out on a lava field again.

Nearing 3¾ miles now, the next *kipuka* has you rolling up and down through its forest. At a fork, the tags direct you to go uphill to the right. At the top of the hill, you cross some *pahoehoe,* slip through the next *kipuka* (which has a narrow lava intrusion), and soon see the brown stump of a sawed-off power pole ahead of you. The track seems to end here, so head for the stump to meet the Power Line Road, 4 miles from your start.

Turn left (north-northwest) onto the Power Line Road and follow it, beginning with an easy ascent through the forest. It soon descends and establishes its general pattern: up and down, generally through lava fields. Sawed-off pole stumps stand along the road, and shattered pieces of ceramic insulators lie along it. Nearing the end of the Power Line Road, you top a moderate rise, pass a couple of rusted-open gates, and curve left at the junction just north of the "Boulder" benchmark, near a pole that's still in service. You can begin to hear traffic on the Saddle Road now. In a few yards, you curve right and meet the Saddle Road. Turn left (west) along its shoulder to walk back to your car.

Dropping mainland defenses. . . . is a common adaptation among plants on isolated islands like the Hawaiian archipelago. The strong scents of mainland herbs, such as the mints, and the thorns of mainland shrubs and trees, such as the raspberries and blackberries, are defenses intended to deter mainland predators like insects and grazing animals. Here on Hawaii, members of these families that are native to these islands have largely dropped their defenses. Before people arrived, there were few insect predators and no grazing animals at all. Producing scented oils or growing thorns costs the plant energy, energy it could better use for adapting to other environmental demands. And so, over the millennia, most of these plants lost defenses they no longer needed and became increasingly adapted to the islands' demands, such as dense rainforests and limited light. For example, in order to thrive in a rainforest, a plant species might gradually come to be dominated by those members that put their energy not into growing thorns but into producing larger seeds with more food for the young plant to live on until it was large enough to compete for a little space and light. The Hawaiian Islands' native flora includes scentless mints, perhaps like the one you saw on this trip, and a nearly thornless raspberry, the *akala.*

Then came the Polynesians and, later and worse, the Europeans with their grazing animals. The cattle, sheep, and goats were happy to snack on the defenseless native plants. The *akala,* for example, had no time to adapt to this predator. It is now very rare. Several native mints are now extinct.

Keep these distinctions in mind as you wander through forests, botanical gardens, and arboretums. Which plants might have evolved on isolated islands and which on the continents, with their hordes of predators? As a rule of thumb, the thornier a plant is, or the stronger-smelling its foliage or bark is, the better the chances are that it's a continental species.

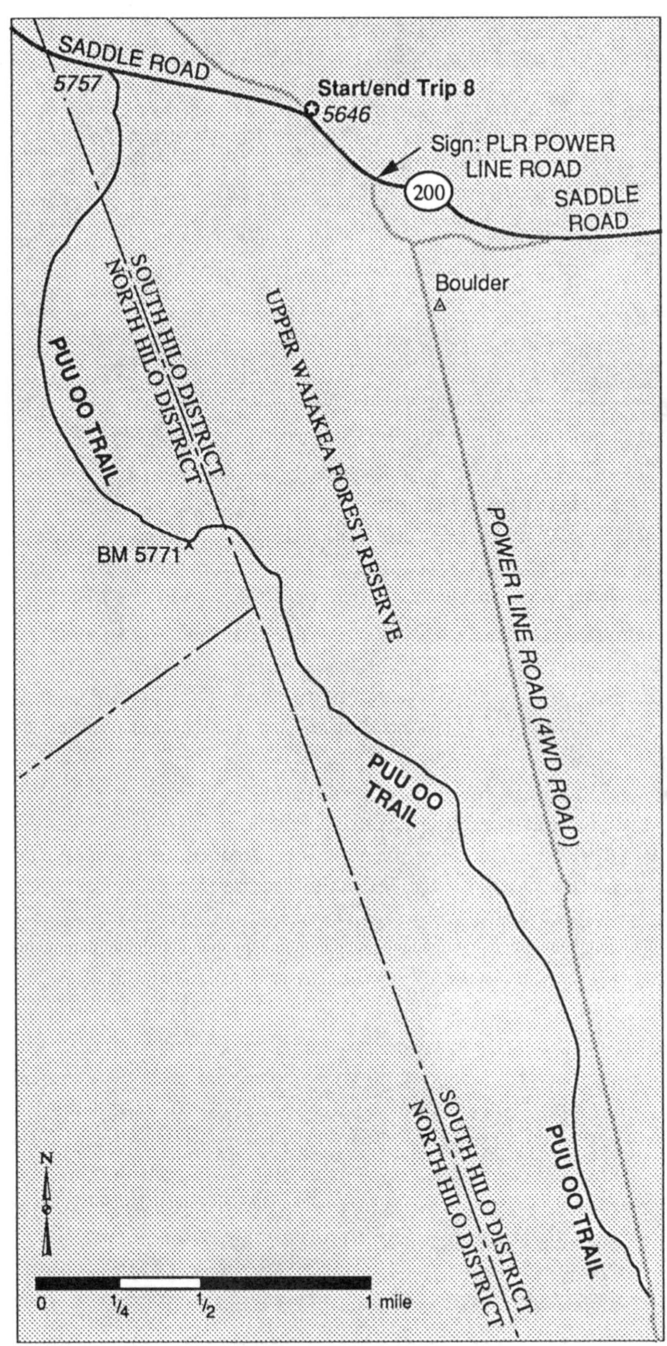
SADDLE ROAD
5757
Start/end Trip 8
5646
Sign: PLR POWER LINE ROAD
200
SADDLE ROAD
Boulder
SOUTH HILO DISTRICT
NORTH HILO DISTRICT
UPPER WAIAKEA FOREST RESERVE
PUU OO TRAIL
POWER LINE ROAD (4WD ROAD)
BM 5771
PUU OO TRAIL
SOUTH HILO DISTRICT
NORTH HILO DISTRICT
PUU OO TRAIL
N
0
1/4
1/2
1 mile

Trip 8. Puu Oo

Trip 9. Mauna Kea State Park—Hill 7154

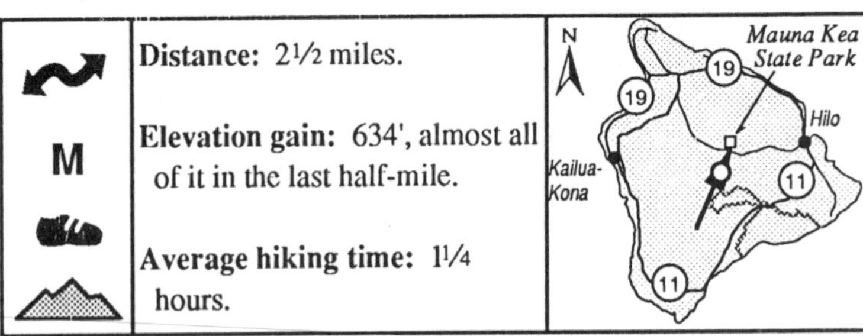

Topos: Optional: *Ahumoa* 7½.

Trail map (route approximated): At the end of this trip.

Highlights: Mauna Kea State Park, high on the saddle between Mauna Kea and Mauna Loa, offers picnicking and cabins set among native *naio* and *mamane* trees and non-native eucalyptuses and pines. An inconspicuous bump north of the park, Hill 7154, provides splendid views of the saddle region. What's special about the saddle? Here, you are on a tropical island—*and on a mountain saddle at 6511 feet!* The saddle region ranges from 6000 to 7000 feet high. And it's flanked by mountains that are twice that high. Some saddle! Some island!

Mauna Kea State Park is most tranquil on weekdays. That's the best time for tourists to visit. On weekends, it's apt to be full of local people enjoying their mountain park. Exercises at adjacent Pohakuloa Military Training Area may shatter the tranquility at any time of day or night—sometimes with spectacular flashes of artillery fire.

Driving instructions: Follow the driving instructions of Trip 8 past the Puu Oo trailhead. Continue west on the Saddle Road. About halfway between mile-markers 27 and 28, you pass a small cinder cone that's covered with trees that give it a shaggy look—unusual among the cones along this road. It's called Puu Huluhulu ("very hairy hill") because of its shaggy appearance, and it's a convenient landmark along this road. You pass Puu Huluhulu and continue west. The road presently zigs almost 90° north and then, near the 35-mile marker, zags 90° west. The entrance to Mauna Kea State Park is just at the point where the road zags west, 49⅓ miles from Hilo. Turn right into the park. The day-use area is to the right of the park headquarters building (which has a flagpole in front of it). Park here to have your picnic and start your hike. If you've rented a cabin and are staying here, the individual cabins are a little farther to the right down this same road. Group cabins are to the left of the headquarters building.

I mentioned that Puu Huluhulu was a convenient landmark. On its east side, the unmarked Observatory Road leads south (left), uphill to the Mauna Loa Weather Observatory and the trailhead for Trips 11 through 13. Across the road and a few hundred yards west is the unmarked road that leads north up Mauna Kea to the trailhead for Trip 10. Puu Huluhulu's west side is scarred by a cinder quarry. There's also a decrepit building—a hunters' check station—on its west side. There is a trail on Puu Huluhulu, but I don't recommend it; see Appendix B.

Permit/permission required: None.

Description: This is best as a morning hike. Dense, soggy clouds often move in over the saddle region in the afternoon, obscuring views and sending you rummaging through your pack for your rain gear.

From the picnic area, follow the paved road past park headquarters and the group cabins. Beyond the cabins, the road is unpaved. At first, it looks as if you're heading for the water tanks north of the park and shown on the *Ahumoa* topo. From the end of the paved road, the 4WD track (not shown on the topo) up Hill 7154 is visible as a steep squiggle ahead and upslope. The hill itself is so inconspicuous that it's difficult to separate it from the rest of the scrub-covered slopes. Just in this short distance, numerous side roads intrude. You stick to the "main" road for now, crossing a shallow wash. At a three-way junction just past the wash, take the center road. At an indistinct junction near a cinderblock building, take the left fork. A fenced area on your left sports signs announcing NO ENTRY, OFF LIMITS, KEEP OUT, FEDERAL SPORT FISH & WILDLIFE RESTORATION AREA. Okay, you get the idea. Take the right fork at the next two junctions.

Soon you're just below the newer water tanks, the ones shown on the topo. A couple of older, wooden water tanks (not shown on the topo) share the slope with them. Where a road peels off left toward the water tanks, you go right, passing a 4WD road that's been blocked off with boulders. The grade has been almost imperceptible so far, but in a few steps, the road begins its extremely steep climb up Hill 7154. Near the top, the road curves east to the hill's broad summit, where there are superb views of the saddle region—vast, lonely, and dotted with cinder cones. Mauna Loa rises to the south and Hualalai to the west-southwest. To the west is Pohakuloa Airfield, part of the military installation. To the east is the scar of Pohakuloa Gulch, through which Lake Waiau, at 13,020 feet on Mauna Kea, drains when it overflows. Turning around, you can see surprisingly far up the slopes of Mauna Kea itself. There are numerous little piles of rocks up here—perhaps casual shrines, so don't disturb them. It's hard to leave this viewpoint, but when you're ready to do so, retrace your steps to the picnic area.

The sheep, the *mamane* forests, and the *palila*. . . . Back at the picnic area, look around a little. Mauna Kea State Park hosts a number of native and non-native plants and animals. Aliens include various grasses, yellow-flowered evening primroses, tall and unattractive yellow-flowered forms of wild lettuce, white-flowered horseweeds with their limp leaves, garden geraniums, eucalyptuses, pines, firs, and junipers. On a quiet day, you may come upon a covey of California quail foraging on the lawns. They were introduced before 1855 for sport hunting.

Conspicuous among the native plants are the *naio* (also called false sandalwood) and the yellow-flowered *mamane*. The *palila* bird, a yellow and gray honeycreeper native to these slopes, is particularly dependent for food upon the buds and fruit of the *mamane*. It also nests in *mamane* trees. *Mamane* forests are critical to the *palila*'s survival. However, the *mamane* forests have been all but destroyed by feral sheep, which overgraze the young trees. Sheep were first introduced by Captain George Vancouver in 1790. He wanted a source of fresh meat for his ships. Merino sheep were introduced later for their wool. As happened with so many other introduced species, the sheep flourished and were soon out of control.

On Hawaii, sheep are hunted for food as well as for sport, so the idea of eliminating them entirely is unpopular. However, hunting does not effectively control the numbers of sheep. Most sheep move about in herds, causing considerable devastation. One attempt at solving the problem was to introduce Mouflon sheep, which live in small family groups instead of herds. It was thought that the smaller Mouflon groups would cause less damage and still provide for hunting. Unfortunately, there's no evidence that Mouflon sheep do less damage than other feral sheep. Worse yet, hunters reportedly do not care for the taste of Mouflon sheep and prefer not to hunt them.

Under a law passed in 1979, Hawaiians have fenced some the *mamane* forests on Mauna Kea and are removing the feral sheep from them so that the *mamane* forests can regenerate and the *palila* can survive. Domestic animals are artificial in a sense: they are deliberate human creations. Experiments like this one dramatically demonstrate the fact that domestic animals (or their escaped, feral descendants) and native ecosystems cannot coexist.

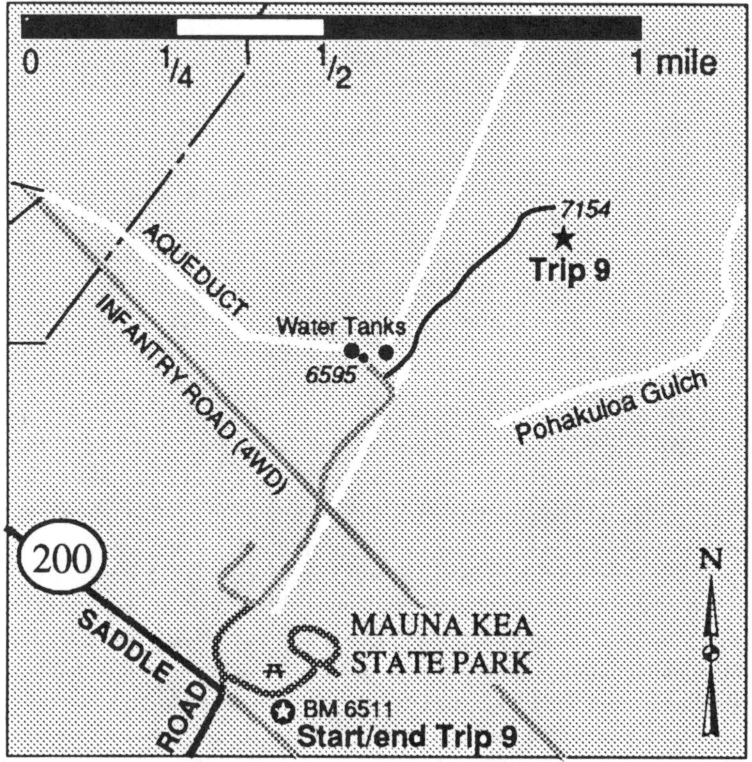

Trip 9. Mauna Kea State Park.

Trip 10. Mauna Kea Summit Side Trip from Mauna Kea State Park

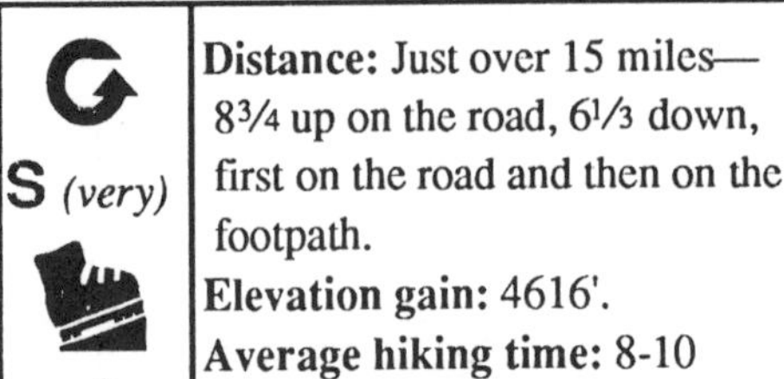

Distance: Just over 15 miles—8¾ up on the road, 6⅓ down, first on the road and then on the footpath.
Elevation gain: 4616'.
Average hiking time: 8-10 hours.

N
19
19
Mauna Kea
Hilo
Kailua-Kona
11
11

Topos: *Mauna Kea* 7½.

Trail map: At the end of this trip.

Highlights: There are fine views of Mauna Loa and of the saddle area from the first part of this hike. Weather permitting, you'll see colorful cinder cones on Mauna Kea's upper slopes. You'll also enjoy the science-fiction setting of the telescopes near the summit. Views of Mauna Loa from the summit are outstanding. On your way down the foot trail, you have a chance to visit one of the rarest features in all of Hawaii: a natural, year-round lake, Lake Waiau—tiny but, at 13,020 feet, one of the nation's highest! Farther down the path, you pass an ancient quarry whose hard, dense, blue-black rock was prized for adzes (tools for shaping wood). *Feathered Gods and Fishhooks* calls this quarry "probably the best single source of adz rock in the archipelago."

Driving instructions: From Mauna Kea State Park, drive south and then east-southeast on the Saddle Road as if you were going to Hilo. Keep your eyes peeled for Puu Huluhulu and the hunters' check station just west of it, as described in the driving instructions of Trip 9. Turn left (north) onto the unmarked, paved road across from the check station, 7½ miles from Mauna Kea State Park, and follow it uphill for 6¼ miles through open rangeland. Cattle graze the unfenced acres you drive through, and they often wander onto the road. Be alert for them and give them time to amble off the pavement. Hitting a cow can be as damaging to you and the car as it is to the cow. Park at the Ellison Onizuka Visitor Center, 13¾ miles from Mauna Kea State Park, to start your hike. Ellison Onizuka, a native of the Big Island, was one of the astronauts who died in the *Challenger* tragedy.

Don't even *think* about driving an ordinary passenger car all the way up Mauna Kea, even in the best of weather. The road's surface isn't the problem. Ascending isn't the problem. Descending is. You can't gear an ordinary passenger car down far enough to descend the steep road safely without riding the brakes. You'd almost certainly burn out the brakes, lose control of the car, and join the ghosts of others who've lost it on that road. It is possible to drive up and back if you rent a suitable 4WD vehicle.

Permit/permission required: None.

Description: A few more preliminary words: Get a *very* early start for this long and extremely demanding hike—surely the most difficult dayhike in this book! Do not attempt it in marginal or poor weather or in the cold season; see the cautions at the end of Trip 11. As I've described this trip, you ascend the more gradual road and descend the steep, rocky foot trail. If the weather deteriorates or if you are running late and will be hiking in the dark, I suggest you return on the road, as the foot trail may be impossible to follow in the rain or the fog or the dark. Remember to be wary of vehicular traffic when you are hiking on a road. Support personnel commute up to the observatories in the morning, astronomers in the evening. The observatories don't want drop-in visitors. This means you will not find food, water, restrooms, or shelter around the summit in spite of the many buildings there. See the supplemental information below for other ways to visit the summit and the observatories.

From the Visitor Center parking lot at 9300 feet, head back to the road and turn right (north) up it, passing Hale Pohaku. There's a big red cone across the road from the Visitor Center; it's a useful landmark on your way back. Just before the pavement ends, you'll see a dirt road coming in on the left (west) on the north side of the cone. You'll be on that road for the very last part of your hike if you descend on the foot trail. For now, you enjoy wonderful views as you follow the main road, well-graded though unpaved, as it climbs and swings east. *Mamane* trees flourish along the first part of the road, but they soon give way to scrub: *pukiawe*; a compact, white-flowered native shrub geranium; alpine grasses; and common mullein, a yellow-flowered alien that has thoroughly invaded the saddle region. Those green rosettes along the road aren't relatives of the silverswords. They're the first-year form of mullein. In their second year, these biennials throw up phallic green stalks several feet high to bloom and die, leaving the blackened spikes you also see.

Near the 1-mile point, a very steep, rough "road" (not shown on the topo or the map accompanying this trip) intersects the road you're walking on; stay on the main road. Below 11,000 feet, the stony landscape is almost entirely dominated by grays and browns, but there are occasional dashes of cream, soft gold, and even orange. Some of the cinder cones are a rich brick-red, and the green pastures far below provide a pleasant visual contrast. As seen from Mauna Kea, Mauna Loa's summit caldera is a rectangular nip right out of the top of the mountain, as neat as a cross-sectional drawing in a textbook.

The road climbs in big switchbacks at first and then goes more or less north-northwest. The landscape becomes increasingly colorful above 11,000 feet as you leave your saddle views behind for a world of cinder cones. Look for cinders, lava "bombs," and sand in red, gold, pink, purplish-red, cream, and ochre against the gray-brown background. The upper part of the road—roughly the last 2000 feet of your climb—is now paved to reduce dust at the summit. How the pavement will hold up to a few Mauna Kea winters remains to be seen.

Near the 6-mile point and 12,700 feet, a 4WD side road leads slightly downhill to the left to a parking lot from which you can see a path extending roughly west. That path meets the foot trail on Mauna Kea near the foot trail's junction with a spur trail to Lake Waiau. You will reach those junctions on your return. For now, you continue on the main road toward the summit. You may be puffing in the thin air by now, and a parking lot a little farther along, on your right, offers some decent "sitting" rocks for a welcome break, perhaps for lunch.

As you approach 13,300 feet and the first hairpin turn for some miles, some of the observatories at last come into view. This area is referred to as "Millimeter Valley" because the observatories here are dedicated to studying the universe not in the optical wavelengths but in the high end of the radio band—millimeter and submillimeter wavelengths. One of the observatories looks just like a silver version of the EVA pods from the film *2001: A Space Odyssey.* Remember that drop-in visitors are unwelcome at the observatories, so don't knock on their doors. On the left side of the hairpin turn, boulders block vehicle access to an ex-4WD road that leads downhill and can be regarded as the upper end of the foot trail. Ahead rises Puu Poliahu, a cone whose east flank is beautifully splashed with pink cinders. Poliahu is the Hawaiian goddess of the snows and lives here on Mauna Kea. She is the icy rival of her sister Pele, the Hawaiian goddess of volcanic fires.

You follow the road uphill and east, away from Puu Poliahu and Millimeter Valley and the paved spur road that leads to its

Looking across Millimeter Valley to the other telescopes

observatories. On the main road, you negotiate another hairpin turn, traverse below Puu Wekiu, and, as the grade eases, approach the highest of the observatories. At the next junction, you take the right fork toward the square support building and prominent dome of the University of Hawaii observatory, which is on the left side of the road. Across the road from it, a trail of use drops steeply downslope. Pause for a moment to enjoy the panorama of colorful cinder cones to the northeast. Then carefully climb over the railing, follow the trail of use down and across a saddle, and climb steeply to Mauna Kea's true summit on Puu Wekiu. Here, at 13,796 feet, the summit benchmark protrudes from the cinders.

If time permits, you may wish to stroll around some more up here to enjoy the surreal landscape. When you're ready, retrace your steps back to the road and then down the road to Millimeter Valley.

Near the hairpin turn in Millimeter Valley, pick your way over the boulders that block off the ex-4WD road and follow it south around Puu Hau Kea. At a fuzzy **Y** junction on the saddle between Puu Hau Kea and Puu Waiau, take the right fork to an overlook of lonely little Lake Waiau, ½ mile from your turnoff onto the 4WD road. The ancient Hawaiians believed that Lake Waiau was bottomless, but in fact it's quite shallow. It's easy to understand how awed they must have been by finding one of Hawaii's rare permanent lakes in this high, utterly desolate, and unearthly place. Return to the **Y** junction and continue downhill; in a few steps you meet the path from the parking lot at 12,700 (as described a few paragraphs above). If the weather is deteriorating, you can take this path back to the main road. Otherwise, curve right (south-southeast) on the foot trail, where a row of slender iron poles marks the increasingly steep path.

Along with the poles, cairns, some splashed with yellow paint, irregularly mark the foot trail. At 12,400 feet, you pass a tall heap of blue-black chips: flakes of the basalt quarried here at Keanakakoi, the adz quarry. The quarry was well-developed by the fifteenth century and worked until European contact, according to *Feathered Gods and Fishhooks*. This particularly dense basalt is the product of a lava flow that emerged under an ice cap when Mauna Kea had glaciers during the last great ice age. The flow cooled very rapidly under the ice, thus becoming extremely dense. Half-finished adzes sit out on boulders for you to look at, but don't remove anything—not even the tiniest chip. This site, like all archaeological sites, is protected by law.

Leaving Keanakakoi, you twine down into a broad, shallow valley, heading toward a large reddish cone. The trail traces an indistinct course around the lower slopes of this cone and then heads south-southeast toward a smaller cone with a deep crater. You veer west of that cone on poor footing, level out briefly, and then veer left around a mound of rocks. Slipping and sliding, you descend the loose cinders into the zone where shrubs reappear—at last! If your view is not blocked by clouds, you can see downslope to distant green pastures and red cinder cones.

At a confusing junction, the main foot trail curves right toward a white pole, but a red pole sits off to your left, marking a faint track leading toward the road. If the weather is deteriorating, take this opportunity to return to the road. Otherwise, stay on the main foot trail and head for the white pole. It's the last pole along the trail; from here on, you must follow a beaten track or footprints. The trail curves around a small ridge, heads south-southwest down a steep, dusty slope, and then curves back toward the big red cone that's opposite the Visitor Center. You soon pass another spur trail to the road. Staying on the "main" trail, you continue down the extremely steep and dusty track, which levels out to cross an *aa* field. You cross a runoff channel and then, about 100 feet beyond the runoff channel, turn steeply downhill again before crossing a ridge of *aa*.

You presently pass a trio of brown posts and meet a dirt road. Follow it downhill as it curves briefly to the right and then to the left. At a fork, turn left (east). You meet the main road in ⅓ mile more, opposite the service road into Hale Pohaku. Turn right for a few yards to the Visitor Center to end an exhausting but satisfying trip.

More on Mauna Kea. . . . I found Mauna Kea to be a far more interesting and scenic peak than Mauna Loa. If possible, treat yourself to Dale P. Cruikshank's booklet *Mauna Kea: A Guide to the Upper Slopes and Observatories*. It's full of fascinating information about the observatories (a little out of date but still useful), the geology, the archaeology, and the mythology (past and—believe it or not—present) of Mauna Kea.

"The Mighty Keck," currently the world's largest optical telescope, is on Mauna Kea. It's the 10-meter multiple-mirror telescope of the new W. M. Keck Observatory. Rarely does anyone actually *look* through the telescopes up here. The observational data are instead gathered by electronic devices far more sensitive than the human eye, particularly at wavelengths outside the visible spectrum, and recorded for later analysis. People go up the mountain to care for the equipment, to set up and monitor the observing sessions, and to take the collected data down the hill. If you wish to see inside the observatories, check well in advance with Mauna Kea Support Services in Hilo (808-935-3371 or 808-961-3392) or at the Ellison Onizuka Visitor Center (808-935-7606) to learn what opportunities, if any, currently exist to visit them.

Are you wondering about the areas labeled "Mauna Kea Ice Age Natural Area Reserve"? Mauna Kea is the only place in the Hawaiian Islands that is known to have had glaciers during the great ice ages (see *Volcanoes in the Sea*). The glaciers, though tiny by continental standards, left typical scars on Mauna Kea: moraines, *roches moutonnées,* and small areas of glacial polish and striation. Meltwater from the last of the glaciers carved Pohakuloa Gulch. Perhaps the most curious legacy of the ice ages is the permafrost—in this case, a mix of cinders and ice—that forms a layer under the cinders of some of the highest cones. It's believed that the overlying cinders insulate and preserve the permafrost, which is 35 feet thick in some places. The permafrost may be responsible for the observation that Mauna Kea "breathes": if a hole is drilled into the permafrost, dry air is rapidly "inhaled" into the hole and later "exhaled," saturated with moisture, in a daily cycle.

Mauna Loa may have had glaciers, too, but its frequent eruptions have plastered the mountain with fresh lava again and again, erasing any glacial traces there may once have been.

If hiking this entire route is out of the question for you, it is possible to drive the road in a 4WD vehicle. As described above, Mauna Kea's true summit is a very short hike from the University of Hawaii telescope, though at almost 14,000 feet, it may be more of a wheeze than a hike. However, casual visitors aren't encouraged to drive up, as there is enough traffic already. There are guided 4WD tours to the summit. Check John Penisten's *Hawai'i: The Big Island: A Paradise Guide* or J. D. Bisignani's *Hawaii Handbook* for them.

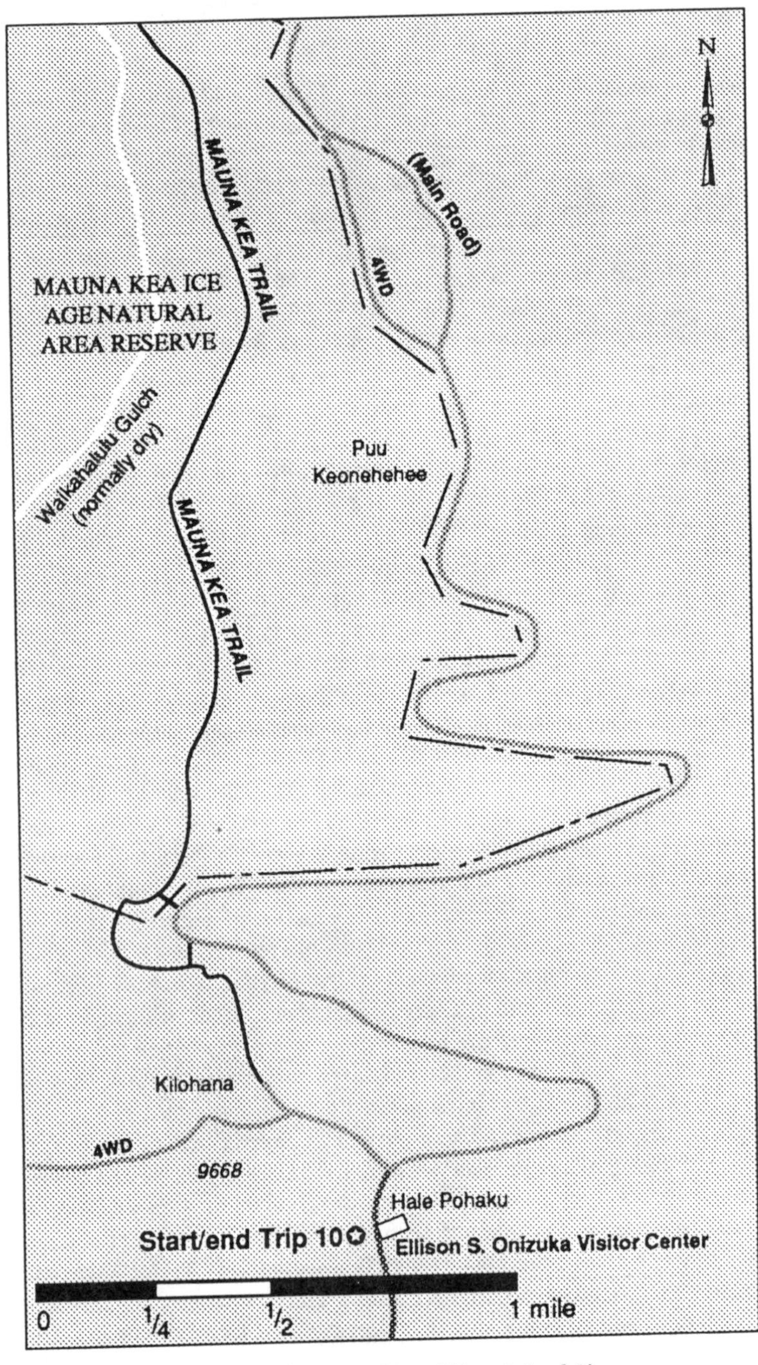

Trip 10. Mauna Kea (Sheet 1 of 2)

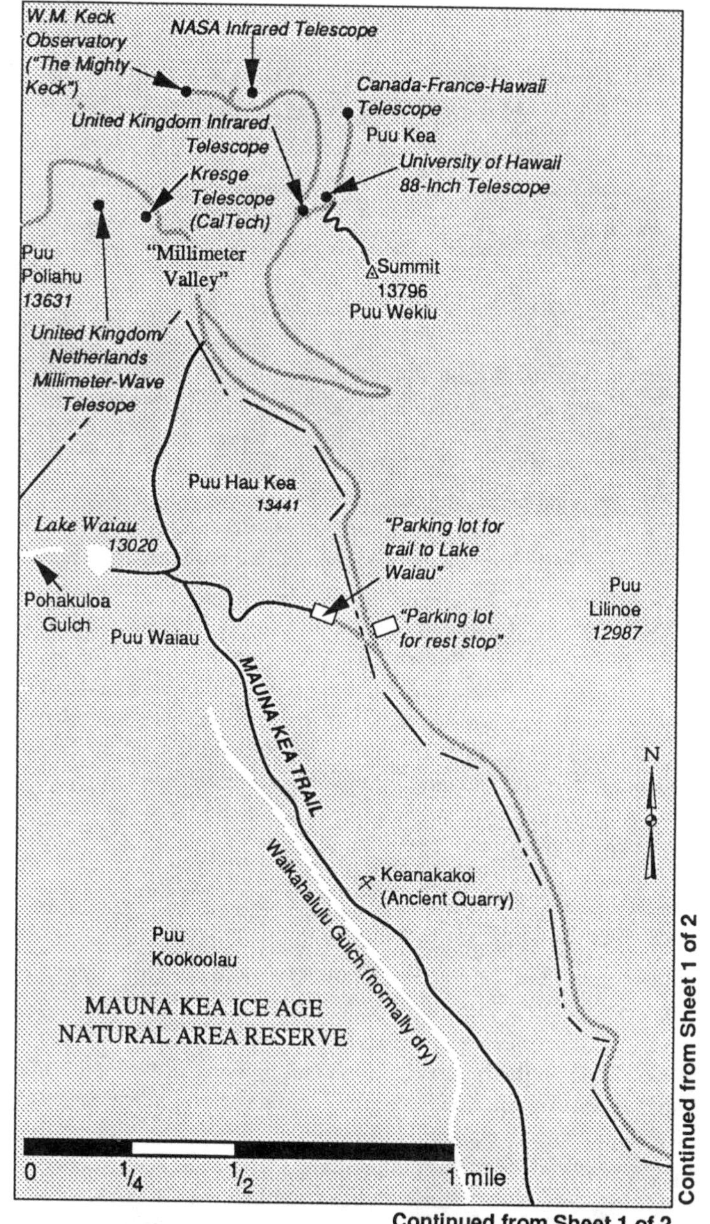

Continued from Sheet 1 of 2

Trip 10. Mauna Kea (Sheet 2 of 2) *(Telescope locations and names are from Cruikshank's* Mauna Kea: A Guide to the Upper Slopes and Observatories, *dated 1986. There are more telescopes up there now and smaller ones that I haven't shown.)*

Trip 11. Observatory Trail to North Pit Side Trip from Mauna Kea State Park

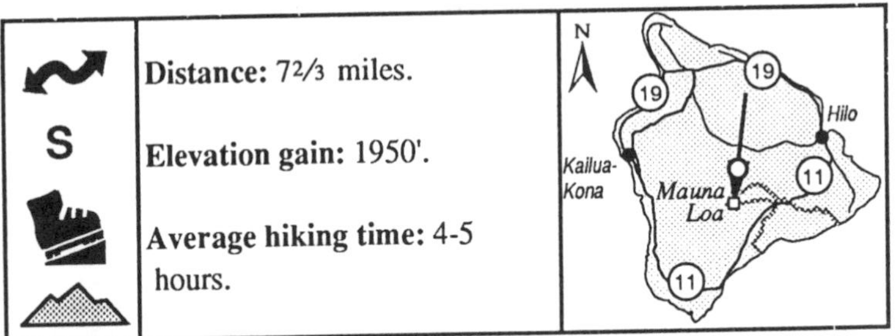

Topos: *Kokoolau, Mauna Loa* 7½.

Trail map: At the end of this trip. Preceding it, there's an overview of Mauna Loa to help you visualize its major trails and its relationship to Hawaii Volcanoes National Park.

Highlights: This trip allows the visitor to see and enjoy virtually every kind of volcanic feature on Mauna Loa on a relatively short dayhike instead of a grueling, multi-day backpack. In the morning, before the daily clouds move in, there are fine views of Mauna Kea and the saddle region from your starting point. Be sure to get an early start: the altitude will slow you down. You begin at 11,150 feet and have your lunch at just over 13,000 feet at the edge of North Pit, the north bay of Mauna Loa's huge caldera, Mokuaweoweo!

Driving instructions: Allow the better part of an hour for this drive. From Mauna Kea State Park, drive south and then east-southeast on the Saddle Road as if you were going to Hilo. Keep your eyes peeled for Puu Huluhulu and the hunters' check station just west of it (as described in the driving instructions for Trip 9). Turn right (south) onto the narrow, paved road just *east* of Puu Huluhulu, 7¾ miles from Mauna Kea State Park. This is a one-lane road whose lines of sight are occasionally very short. Scorched, shot-up signs along the road proclaim DANGER DRIVE SLOWLY KEEP TO RIGHT, but it is hard to keep to the right on a road so narrow that it hardly has a left or right lane! Proceed carefully south and then southwest for 17¾ slow miles to the public parking lot below the Mauna Loa Weather Observatory. Park here. The signed trailhead is on your right (west) as you face the observatory.

The Mauna Loa Weather Observatory, at 11,150 feet, monitors the atmosphere. Visitors are *not* welcome. The Observatory Road is always open, although there is a piece of Park Service literature that says (erroneously) that it's closed during the work-week.

Permit/permission required: None.

Description: Take a moment to enjoy the view from the trailhead: Mauna Kea towers across the saddle, and huge, irregular patches of lava of different textures and tints plaster Mauna Loa's slopes like pieces of a giant jigsaw puzzle. Remember that you are hiking on an active volcano, so the following trail description could be made obsolete by Mauna Loa's next eruption. In case of conflict, follow the Park Service's cairns, not the description below. Be sure visibility is adequate before you undertake this or any other trip where you must follow cairns across lava.

The trail begins as an unpaved 4WD road that's a continuation of the road you just drove up. Ignore the side roads to the observatory. In a little less than ½ mile, a sign on your left directs you south-southeast off the road past a huge cairn and into the lava fields. Follow the cairns up the slope, sometimes rather steeply. It's more like boulder-hopping than walking. Nearing 1½ miles, you pass west of a brown cinder cone and soon curve between a pair of very large cairns, avoiding a collapsed but colorful lava tube. Around here, be sure you distinguish between the human-built cairns and small spires of lava in order to stay on the route. At a distance, they may look similar; when you're closer to them, the cairns are obviously manmade.

As you near 2½ miles and 12,400 feet, the trail curves east and presently meets the 4WD road again. Turn right and follow the 4WD road for ⅓ mile. After the road passes a curious lava dome delicately webbed with fine ribbons of lava, the trail jogs to the right off the road at a huge cairn. You step off into golden-brown cinders, just opposite a striking red-and-black vent. The beaten path through these iridescent cinders is a pleasant change for a while. The cinders come to an end at a *pahoehoe* field. Here you cross the 4WD road and climb through *pahoehoe* and reddish *aa* to intersect a rather tidy aa-bordered path. Turn left onto this path for a few yards to reach the junction of the Observatory Trails with the trails to Mauna Loa Cabin and the true summit.

Turn left, as if you were going to the cabin. In another few yards, you pass Jaggars Cave and arrive at the rim of North Pit at a junction with the Mauna Loa Trail. Jaggars Cave, a large, sandy-floored pit, was used as a shelter in historic times. A few steps away and a few feet down, North Pit is a seemingly flat plate of cracked black *pahoehoe* across which a line of cairns stretches southward, marking the route to the cabin. The walls of Mokuaweoweo rise on either side beyond North Pit. Mauna Loa Cabin is 2 rough miles away from here, atop the east wall. The true summit is 2½ miles away, atop the west wall (on your right). You can't single out the summit from here; it's indistinguishable because of the continual gentle curvature of this immense volcano. One source asserts that Mauna Loa's volume from sea floor to summit is greater than that of California's entire Sierra Nevada!

This is the north edge of Mokuaweoweo, Mauna Loa's caldera, and it is as unearthly and barren a landscape as any the park offers. Settle down for lunch here before retracing your steps back to your car.

Hiking Mauna Loa and Mauna Kea. . . . Do not take these mountains lightly just because they are in the tropics. Going higher is equivalent to going northward. Their *bases* are in the tropics, but their *summits* might as well be in Alaska. Snow, rain, high winds, poor visibility (for example, fog), and icy conditions are possible at any time of year on Mauna Loa (13,677 feet) and Mauna Kea (13,796 feet). Snow is almost certain between November and April. *Be prepared for weather extremes!* Hikes on Mauna Kea and Mauna Loa are serious, strenuous undertakings.

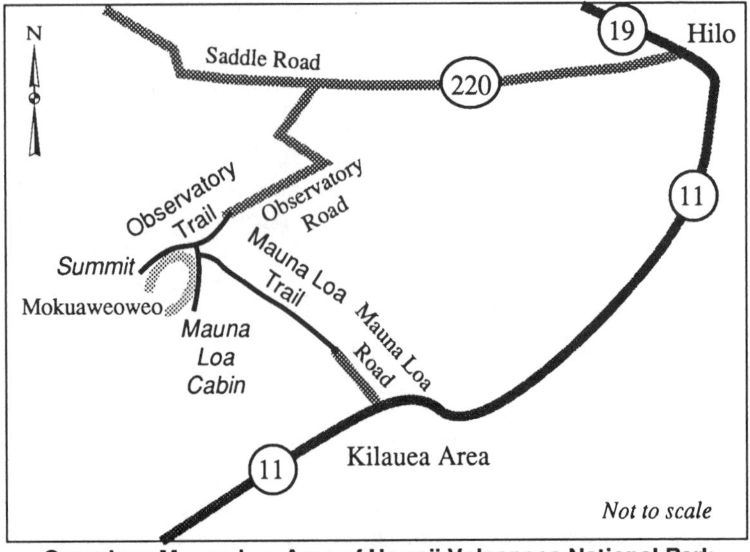

Overview: Mauna Loa Area of Hawaii Volcanoes National Park

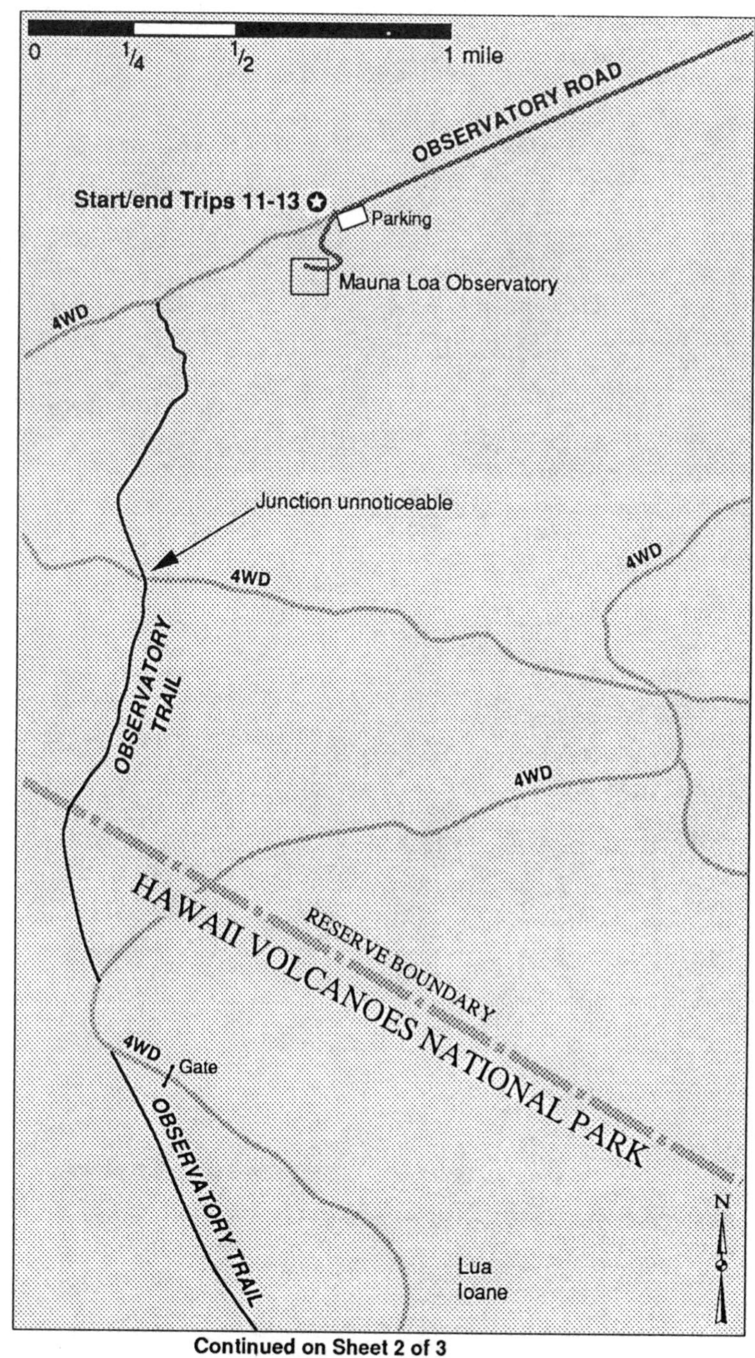

Continued on Sheet 2 of 3

Trips 11 through 13. Observatory Trail to North Pit, Cabin, and True Summit (Sheet 1 of 3)

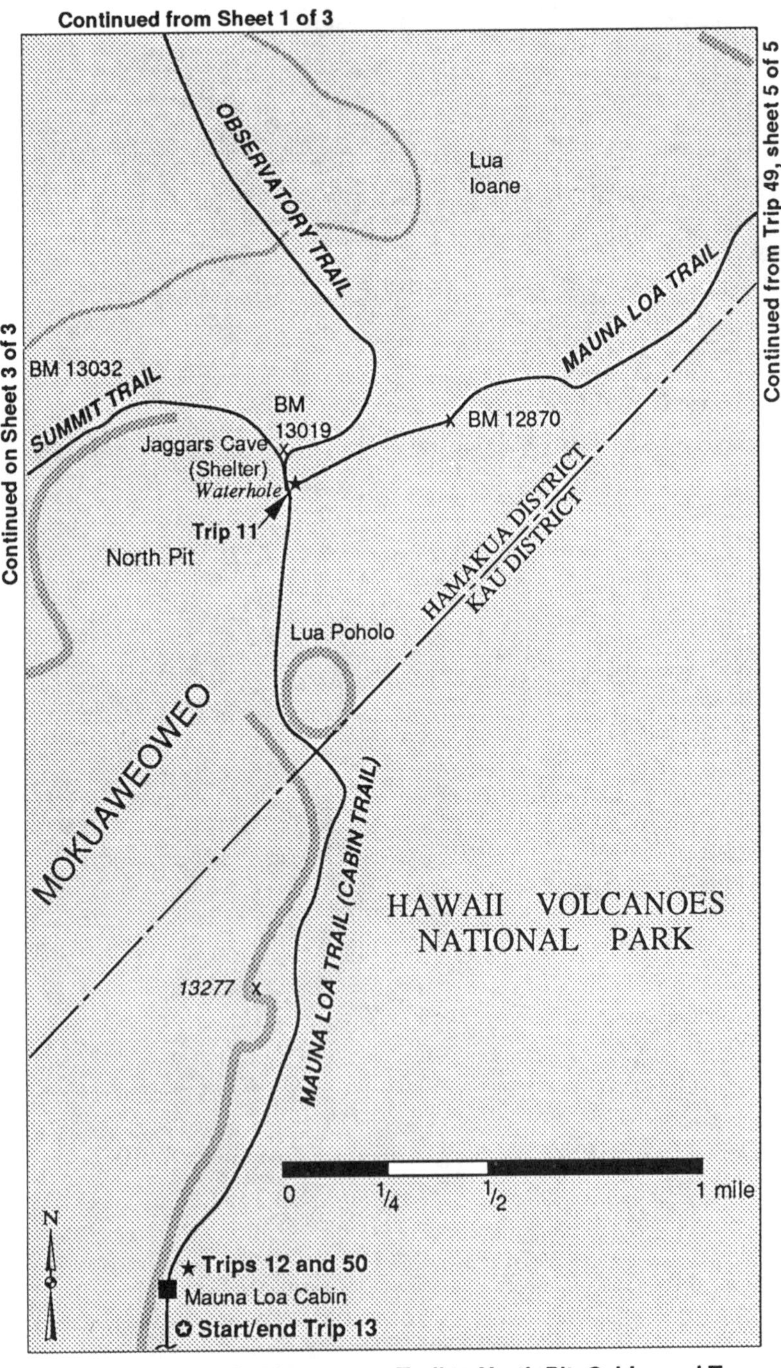

Trips 11 through 13. Observatory Trail to North Pit, Cabin, and True Summit (Sheet 2 of 3) *(Wide line (▒▒▒) roughly indicates cliffs around Mokuaweoweo, including North Pit and Lua Poholo.)*

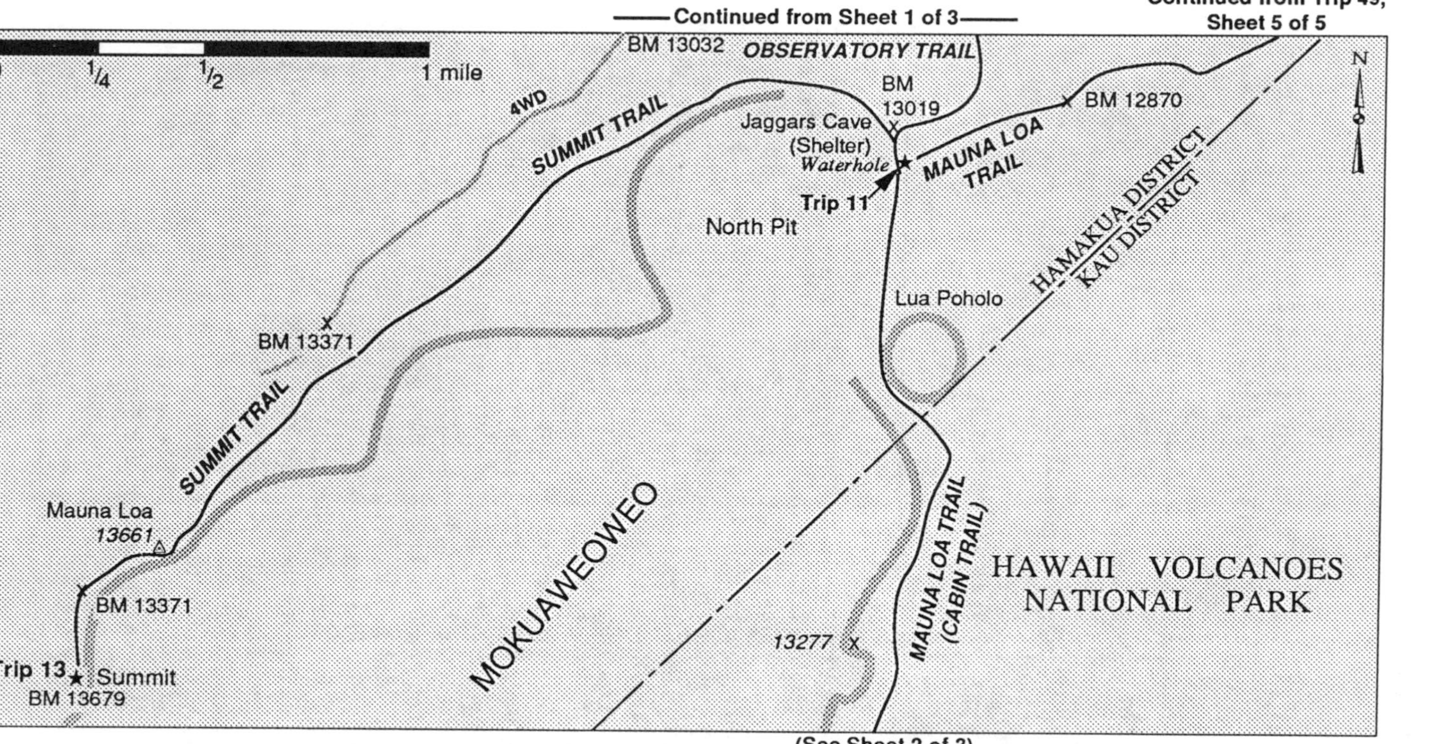

Trips 11 through 13. Observatory Trail to North Pit, Cabin, and True Summit (Sheet 3 of 3) *(Wide line (▒▒▒) roughly indicates cliffs around Mokuaweoweo, including North Pit and Lua Poholo.)*

Trip 12. Mauna Loa Cabin via Observatory Trail Side Trip from Mauna Kea State Park

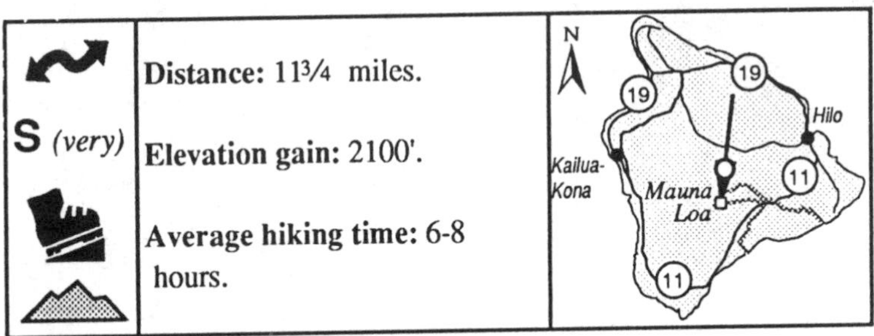

Topos: *Kokoolau, Mauna Loa* 7½.

Trail map: At the end of Trip 11.

Highlights: For those in a hurry but still determined to see more of Mauna Loa than Trip 11, the Observatory Trail offers a shorter route to Mauna Loa Cabin[1] than the Mauna Loa Trail but with a greater risk of altitude sickness, especially if you stay overnight. That's because you start higher and gain elevation faster. Also see **As a dayhike,** below.

Driving instructions: Follow the driving instructions of Trip 11.

Permit/permission required: None, unless you plan to stay overnight at Mauna Loa Cabin. You must have a valid permit from Hawaii Volcanoes National Park, available only by applying in person at the Kilauea Visitor Center, to stay overnight in the park's backcountry. This is true whether you stay in the cabins or at the three-sided shelters dotting the backcountry (all of which are on a first-come, first-served basis) or camp out near a cabin or shelter. Unless you carry all your own water, you're going to have to stay near a cabin or a shelter: water is available only at the cabins and the shelters. Their roofs catch dew and rain and funnel the water into an adjacent tank. However, a combination of no precipitation and lots of visitors can drain the tank. When you pick up your permit at Kilauea Visitor Center (see Trip 20), be sure to check on the water supply at the cabins and the shelters you'll visit on your trip.

[1]But not to Red Hill Cabin. From the junction near Jaggars Cave, it's 9½ miles down the other trail—the Mauna Loa Trail—to Red Hill Cabin.

Description (as a backpack, which requires a permit).

Day 1 (Just under 6 miles). Follow Trip 11 to the junction with the Mauna Loa Summit Trail on the edge of North Pit. From here, descend a few feet into North Pit and follow the cairns across its black *pahoehoe* surface south toward Lua Poholo. North Pit's surface, which seemed so flat when you were looking at it from its rim, turns out to be far from level. It's cracked into huge, irregular slabs, and each slab lies at an angle with respect to its neighbors. The surface you walk on is always tilted, though the tilt is not pronounced at first. But as you near Lua Poholo, the tilt of the black slabs you must traverse becomes much steeper. It would be easy to slip and fall here—be careful! In a few more steps, you're back in very rough *aa,* skirting Lua Poholo—a very deep pit crater of dark rock with dashes of reds and whites. As you continue, the rugged route leads alternately over *pahoehoe* and then *aa.*

Take it slowly; you're climbing at over 13,000 feet here. Altitude not only impairs your physical performance but can insidiously undermine your judgment. The cairns can be particularly hard to distinguish from the rest of the rubble when you are traversing the *aa* fields up here. Examples of intellectual impairment, in the form of some of the visitors' entries, drivel on and on *ad nauseam* in the register at the cabin.

Take plenty of water with you for this trip. The air is very dry at these altitudes, and you will lose a lot of water as you perspire and breathe. My friend Ray Brouillard reports from personal and unpleasant experience that dehydration can lead straight to altitude sickness up here (and he runs marathons in his home state of Georgia). A number of "water holes" are marked on the *Mauna Loa* topo, but your chances of finding any of them are almost nil, except for the one at Jaggars Cave on the edge of North Pit. They're tiny caves in the lava where snow or ice still lingers, yielding dirty water drop by grudging drop. Even if you find a water hole, it may be dry: I found the water hole by Jaggars Cave snow-filled in May but dry by September.

On your way to the cabin, you may notice some cairns that appear to lead west-southwest toward the rim of the caldera, Mokuaweoweo. Don't follow them. Instead, continue south-southwest toward the cabin, which is at last visible when you are a little less than half a mile from it. You pass an outhouse about 100 yards from the cabin. It's tied down to the surrounding lava with cables to keep it from blowing over in the strong, cold winds that are the rule up here. What a haven of comfort the spartan cabin seems after your trying hike! It provides bunks, tables, chairs, and a separate kitchen area with counters and a sink. There's no bedding, no stoves, no lanterns (bring candles), and no eating or cooking utensils. Water is available from a tank on the other side of the cabin. It's unpleasantly rusty-tasting, but it will do the job as long as you purify it before drinking it. There are excellent views of Mokuaweoweo from the vicinity of the cabin.

A layover day here will allow you to dayhike to the true summit, which is on the other side of Mokuaweoweo, almost directly opposite the cabin. Follow the directions of Trip 13 to get to the summit.

Day 2 (Just under 6 miles). Retrace your steps to your car.

As a dayhike. . . . This trip can be done as an extremely strenuous 11¾-mile dayhike *if* you are physically able to cope with the demands of the high altitude and if you get an early start. Make no mistake about it: at these altitudes, the hike will take longer than an equivalent hike would take down by park headquarters—quite possibly twice as long. A Park Service handout says, "It will take you a good 4–6 hours to hike from the Mauna Loa Weather Observatory to the Mauna Loa Cabin. *[Note that that's just one way.]* DO NOT leave from the Observatory after 10 A.M." Good advice!

If you can bag Mauna Kea the hard way (Trip 10), you can bag Mauna Loa by dayhiking the Observatory Trail. But remember that it gets dark sooner in Hawaii at any time of year than it does on a summer night on the mainland, that twilight is very brief in Hawaii, and that you will not have a trail to follow on Mauna Loa. You can't expect to safely follow cairns by flashlight.

About Mauna Loa. . . . In his fascinating book *The Control of Nature,* John McPhee lets examples of human attempts to control nature speak for themselves. This lesson is well-learned on the Big Island. Hilo, the principal city, and its priceless harbor lie at one end of a natural channel for Mauna Loa's lava: the Mauna Loa-Mauna Kea saddle. Losing Hilo is unthinkable—and yet it is always a possibility. In 1881, lava flowed through what is now part of the city and came within a mile of Hilo Bay. Lava came within a dozen miles of Hilo in 1852, 1855, 1942, and 1984—in the last case, within four miles.

Various schemes have been proposed, and some even tried, to control the liquid fire: diversion barriers, bombing the flow, inundating the advancing lava with water in the hope that solidifying the front of the flow would form a barrier to divert the molten material behind it, a huge dam on the saddle to provide the water for that inundation. However, it is impossible to stop an eruption. If the lava is stopped *here,* it must go *there.* If the lava is diverted to save your house, it will probably gobble up your neighbor's house. During an eruption on Sicily's Mt. Etna in 1669, McPhee reports, the citizens of the city of Catania tried to break the crust on one side of the lava flow and divert the lava from Catania toward the city of Paterno. The citizens of Paterno, says McPhee, "came out shooting."

So what is the Hawaiian answer to the question, "What do you do when the lava flows?" According to McPhee, "Nothing." Or, rather, get who and what you can out of the way, and let 'er rip. The schemes for diverting the Hawaiian flows were dreamed up by non-Hawaiians. Hawaiians have lived for centuries with two of the most active volcanoes in the world. They know better than to try to stop the flows from Kilauea and Mauna Loa. The fire department makes no attempt to stop the lava but stands by to try to keep the fires it may cause from getting out of control. If your house is in the path of the flow, it's history. Grab your stuff and run for it. Rebuild when the rock cools.

Hawaii is not without a sense of humor about building on this new land. A photo in the *National Geographic* of March 1975 shows a house lot staked out in nearly barren *aa.* In the lifeless rock of the front-yard-to-be is a sign proclaiming KEEP OFF THE GRASS.

What happens when people do try to stop the lava? More on this after the next trip. . . .

Mauna Loa cabin

Trip 13. Side Trip from Mauna Loa Cabin to True Summit

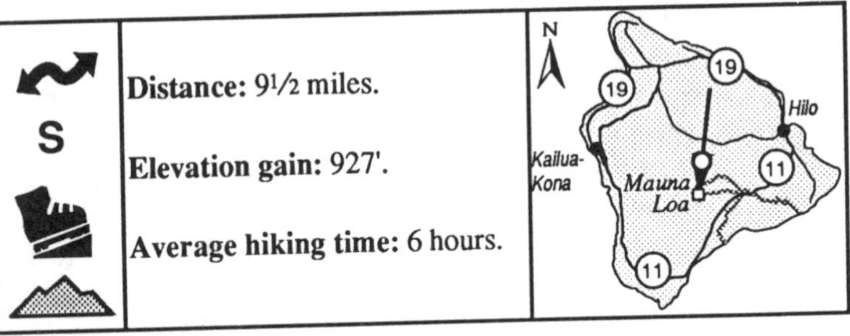

Topos: *Mauna Loa 7½*.

Trail map: At the end of Trip 10.

Highlights: If you make it to Mauna Loa Cabin, you probably won't be able to resist the temptation to bag the true summit, which is on the opposite side of Mokuaweoweo. Although not particularly scenic, this hike is an memorable demonstration of the immense scale of Mokuaweoweo and of Mauna Loa.

Driving instructions: Not applicable.

Permit/permission required: You need a valid permit to stay overnight at the Mauna Loa summit cabin (refer to Trip 12 or Appendix A).

Description (as a side trip). The "low point" on this trip is 13,000 feet, so the side trip to the summit is an all-day trip, even from the cabin, because the altitude will slow you down. From Mauna Loa Cabin, retrace your steps 2 miles to the trail junction on the edge of North Pit. Turn left (northwest) on the Summit Trail and pass the deep shelter hole called Jaggars Cave on your left. You soon pass an even deeper ice pit on your right, and presently step over a crack from whose torn edges red and yellow lavas hang like draperies.

Soon you're curving west and then southwest around North Pit on a rough but fairly well marked trail. You cross another, larger crack on a bridge of debris. Near ⅔ mile from the junction, you find yourself in an *aa* field where the going gets much rougher and the route less distinct. As of this writing, the correct line of cairns heads up a ridge west-southwest. From the top of this ridge, you begin traversing a series of small ridges and gullies. You pass the labeled KSUMMIT SEISMOGRAPH, which you are careful not to disturb.

As you near the summit, you'll notice some gray boulders with a greenish tint, an interesting variation on the predominant brown of this landscape. As you finally approach the summit, the line of cairns veers southeast toward the caldera rim for a dizzying view over its barren, cracked, black floor. You can barely make out the cabin to the southeast across the caldera. To the south are the 1940 and half-hidden 1949 cinder cones, as well as the gap in the caldera wall that marks the beginning of South Pit. Resuming your summit trek west-southwest, you reach the summit cairn with its benchmark and register in a few hundred yards, 4¾ miles from your start. To the northeast, shattered rock, tinted with reds, slumps into the caldera. If weather permits, you can see Mauna Kea over Mauna Loa's immense shoulder to the north-northeast. To the south, a field of greenish cinders forms a streak westward from the 1949 cone.

In the spring of 1991, the summit register box was broken, so handle it with care. A note on the box itself asked, "Is this the summit?" It's hard to tell. Other rock heaps around it seem to be as high, maybe a little higher. You'll find that if you visit these other heaps and look back at the heap with the register, the latter seems to be a little higher. I'm inclined to accept the benchmark and the summit register as proof that this is the summit. It's also a good spot to enjoy your lunch before retracing your steps back to Mauna Loa Cabin.

As a dayhike.... It is possible to dayhike from the Observatory Road trailhead to the true summit. It's an out-and-back trip; extremely strenuous; requires boots because the terrain is so rough; 12¾ miles; 2527′ elevation gain; and 7–9 hours. Follow the directions for Trip 11 to the junction on the edge of North Pit; then turn right on the Summit Trail and follow the directions for this trip to the true summit.

Now I'll repeat what I said for Trip 12: I strongly recommend you dayhike this trip *only* if you are staying at Mauna Kea State Park. Get a very early start from there. Make no mistake about it: at these altitudes, the 12¾ miles to and from the true summit will certainly take longer than they would down by park headquarters. And since you must navigate by following cairns, you must have enough visibility to safely follow them. That means you need daylight and good weather.

What happens when people try to stop the lava?... In *The Control of Nature,* John McPhee tells of a number of human attempts to divert lava flows.

In 1935 and 1942, lava tubes of Mauna Loa eruptions were bombed from the air in the hope of breaking them open and diverting their contents. The 1935 bombing results were inconclusive: debris did clog the tube, and the lava spilled to one side, but the eruption happened to stop. The 1942 bombing also caused the lava to spill sideways for a short distance, after which it rejoined the main flow. Not a big success.

The heart of McPhee's account of making war on lava is the story of a 1973 eruption in Iceland. Like Hawaii, Iceland sits atop a hot spot—this one on the Mid-Atlantic Ridge. In late January 1973, a new volcano was born in the back yard of the town of Heimaey. Iceland's principal industry is fishing. A lobe of the Heimaey flow headed for Heimaey's harbor, threatening to overrun it and fill it. Heimaey's harbor was the only harbor along the 300 miles of Iceland's south coast. Could Heimaey's harbor be saved by pouring immense quantities of seawater on the lobe moving toward it?

Over the next five and a half months, those who remained in Heimaey undertook heroic efforts to save the harbor, and in the end, they saved it. On the other hand, it's probable that saving the harbor diverted the flow into the town, where it destroyed hundreds of homes and buildings.

Was the effort successful and worthwhile? McPhee was told that much of the apparent success was due to luck. The flow that had threatened Heimaey's harbor was a small lobe of the overall flow. Elsewhere, the lava had buried a whole village 300 feet deep. The lava was relatively slow-moving and cool—only 2000° F, the kind Hawaiians call an *aa* flow. If that lobe had been just a little more voluminous, a little faster, or a little hotter.... So the answer is, "Maybe. Who knows?"

Would Hawaii undertake such a vast (by human standards) and puny (by volcanic standards) effort if lava threatened to destroy Hilo's harbor? Hawaiians have another weapon in their armory, anyway: they still make offerings to Pele. Flowers, fruit, and, most important, bottles of gin sit on and around a large altar-like stone at the rim of Halemaumau, the most active part of Kilauea caldera. Even tourists get into the act. I know a visiting hiker who left an offering of M&Ms up here at Mauna Loa's summit. Maybe it helps. Who knows?

Trip 14. Rainbow Falls

V

Distance: Almost negligible.

Elevation gain: 50'.

Average hiking time: 5 minutes (but allow more to enjoy).

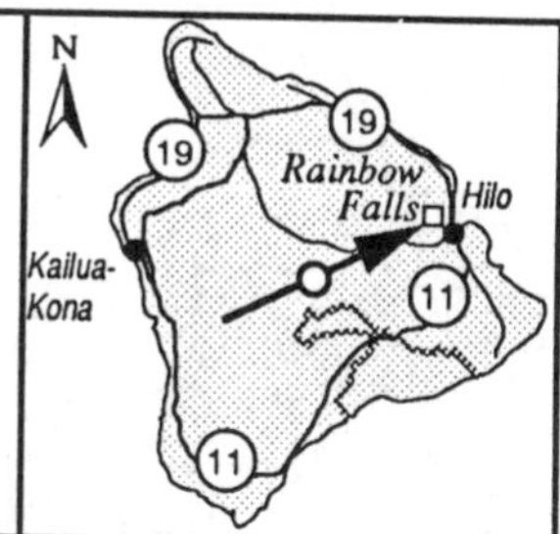

Topos: Optional: *Hilo* 7½.

Trail map (route approximated): At the end of this trip.

Highlights: Rainbow Falls is a broad, beautiful waterfall on the Wailuku River near the northern outskirts of Hilo. The falls are so named because you'll often see rainbows in the mist that rises from where the falling water strikes the large pool. (This viewpoint does not offer access to the river or to the falls, so don't plan on a swim.)

Driving instructions: At the fork just after Highway 19 crosses over the Wailoa River, bear left into downtown Hilo on Kamehameha Avenue. In just under 1⅔ miles, turn left (inland) at the light at one-way Waianuenue Avenue and follow it uphill past Hilo High School. Where it forks, take the right fork, which remains Waianuenue Avenue (the left fork becomes the Saddle Road). In ¼ mile, signs for Rainbow Falls direct you to turn right onto a one-way side road, Rainbow Drive, which leads into the parking lot for Rainbow Falls, 3⅓ miles from your start.

Permit/permission required: None.

Description: Rainbow Falls is part of Wailuku River State Park. Here at Rainbow Falls, the park provides a lush tropical scene for visitors' enjoyment: tall mango trees draped in philodendron; *kukui*; Aftrican tulip trees; banana plants; and clumps of split-leaf philodendron. You need do no more than walk across the parking lot to the railings in order to enjoy a fine view of impressive Rainbow Falls.

For another perspective on Rainbow Falls, try this very short loop that includes an excellent viewpoint above the falls: To your left as you stand at the railing facing the falls, there's a flight of stairs that

Rainbow Falls

guides you away from the parking lot and 50 feet up to the viewpoint. After taking in the view, continue on the walkway as it curves back toward the parking lot under the deep shade of big old banyan trees. Watch your footing; the path gets a little faint here and can be slippery when wet.

Back at the parking lot, you'll probably want to return to the railing to enjoy the falls for another few moments before hopping back into your car.

Rainbow Falls, Boiling Pots, and the goddess Hina. . . . According to *Hilo Legends,* the Wailuku River was once infamous for its violent floods, and myths explained some of its more interesting features as well as its treacherous behavior. The goddess Hina, mother of the demigod Maui, lived in a large cave behind the watery curtain of Rainbow Falls. Moo Kuna, a huge dragon, lived upriver from the falls. Moo Kuna hated Hina and tried to kill her many times with great floods or by rolling boulders downstream onto her.

On one occasion, when a storm had swelled the river's flow, Moo Kuna seized the opportunity to block the river downstream of Rainbow Falls with a huge boulder. He hoped the rising water would trap and drown Hina. She was asleep until the cold water invaded her home, waking her. She cried for help, and Maui, who was fishing out in Hilo Bay, heard her and turned back to shore immediately. Just two mighty paddle strokes brought his canoe to the river's mouth. He jumped out, rushed to his mother's aid, and split the boulder with his magic club. The river flowed freely again, and Hina was saved.

But Maui was terribly angry and vowed revenge. Moo Kuna fled and tried to hide in a deep pool in the river. Maui cornered him there and summoned Pele's help. Pele sent red-hot rocks and fiery lava for Maui to throw into Moo Kuna's hiding place. They were so hot that the water boiled when Maui cast them at Moo Kuna. Scalded, Moo Kuna tried to slip away, but Maui pursued him with floods of boiling water that killed him at last. The place is called the Boiling Pots today.

The Boiling Pots are another 1⅔ miles up Waianuenue Avenue from Rainbow Falls; you may wish to see them. They're part of Wailuku River State Park, too. To get there, return to Waianuenue Avenue, turn right (uphill), and follow it to Peepee Falls Street. Turn right here to the parking and viewing area for the Boiling Pots. The "pots" are actually large pools connected by cascades through which the river swirls and tumbles vigorously, giving it the appearance of being at a rolling boil. If you look upstream you can glimpse Peepee (pay-ay-pay-ay) Falls. There's no hiking at the Boiling Pots, but it's certainly a pretty spot. Maybe you should conclude your explorations with a picnic on the lawn here!

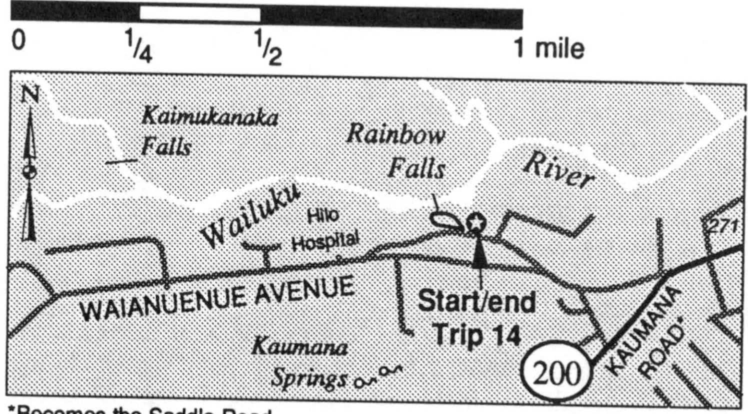

Trip 14. Rainbow Falls *(Trail not to scale)*

Trip 15. Wailoa River State Park

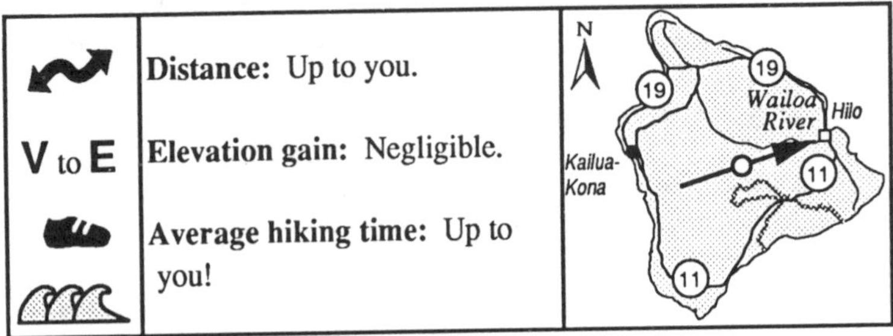

Topos: Optional: *Hilo* 7½.

Trail map (route approximated): At the end of this trip.

Highlights: Here, near the harbor's edge in a bustling city, are acres of enchanting emerald lawns, a mirror-like lagoon spanned by high-arched footbridges, and many wandering footpaths and grassy routes to choose from. You can picnic, walk, jog, fish (regulated), and bicycle here. Setting aside this much acreage in what would appear to be a highly desirable business or industrial area is wisdom, not just civic generosity, as you will read below.

Driving instructions: Go west from the intersection of Highways 19 and 11 and cross the Wailoa River. The park stretches inland from here. When the road forks just on the other side of the river, take the left fork (Kamehameha Avenue) to Pauahi Street. Turn left onto Pauahi Street. In a few hundred yards, turn left onto little Piopio Street, which extends southeast into Wailoa River State Park. (The imposing buildings on the inland side of Piopio Street are the county and state office buildings, which front on the next street inland, Apuni Street.) Follow Piopio Street to its end and park in one of the small lots near the circular Visitor Center Building to start your walk, 1⅓ miles from the intersection of Highways 11 and 19.

Permit/permission required: None.

Description: You'll find memorials to Hilo's Vietnam War veterans and tsunami victims near the Visitor Center; you may want to pay your respects at each. The memorial to the tsunami victims is a handsome work of art. The Visitor Center is operated by volunteers; I haven't yet found it open after several tries.

But not to worry. You came here to saunter across the lawns and stroll along the lagoon. It isn't possible simply to circle the lagoon, as a number of office buildings abut its southern end and cut off access. Northward, a path leads to a footbridge that arches across one arm of the lagoon. There's no connecting path on the other side, but you can doodle along on the grass, possibly walking back to Pauahi Street and closing a loop by following Pauahi Street uphill to Piopio Street, then taking Piopio Street back to your car. Eastward, a double-arched footbridge crosses another arm of the lagoon, touching down on an islet in the middle of the lagoon. The path on the other side extends north and south along the lagoon, passing some picnic pavilions and benches. Southward, it extends almost to the office buildings. It does not provide practical opportunities for a loop, so you will need to retrace your steps. And you can walk on the grass along the west side of the lagoon for a short way south or north along the lagoon and then west along little Alenaio Stream toward Pauahi Street. (The park also extends on the west side of Pauahi Street, where it includes an archery range. Stay away from target ranges whether there's anyone visible on them or not. You never can tell.)

You see the dilemma: how can I tell you to follow a particular route when there are so many good choices? And how can I predict how long your choice will take? You will just have to enjoy this lovely place as best you can.

The lagoon itself is for pleasure fishing, and there are usually a number of boats bobbing on its surface, their relaxed occupants dangling a line in the water. Besides you and the fishermen, the park attracts a fair number of walkers, joggers, and bicyclists. Watch your footing at the islet touch-down point of the double-arched footbridge, or you may collect a skinned knee. Believe me, this is harder than you think if it is raining gently and you are absorbed in watching rainbows play over the lagoon. By the way, the arm of the lagoon that elbows east and north into Hilo Bay is the Wailoa River; the bulk of the lagoon is called Waiakea Pond.

Come to think of it, you don't even have to *walk* here to enjoy the sights. You can just pick a spot near the lagoon under one of the trees, lean against the trunk with your picnic lunch, and let the human parade move past *you!*

Tsunami . . . , according to *Volcanoes in the Sea,* is Japanese for "long wave in a harbor." It's a more accurate description than "tidal wave," as a tsunami has nothing to do with the tides. Tsunamis are caused by large earthquakes on seacoasts or under the sea. Hawaii is particularly vulnerable to tsunamis. Earthquakes along the so-called Rim of Fire surrounding the Pacific Basin can generate tsunamis that radiate out into the Pacific, where there is little between Hawaii and their origins to help absorb some of their enormous energy. Volcanic Hawaii itself is the source of many earthquakes, some of which have generated devastating tsunamis on its own shores.

A tsunami is actually a *series* of waves. The speed of the waves is proportional to the depth of the water. At sea, they are small waves very far apart and traveling very fast. Ships on the open, deep ocean will not even notice the waves. But as they approach a coast, the ocean abruptly becomes very shallow. The waves slow down considerably, and much of their immense energy is transformed from speed to height. The waves of a tsunami usually strike at intervals of 12 to 20 minutes. Never assume a tsunami has passed after the first giant wave! Typically, they strike the exposed headlands harder than the sheltered bays, but Hilo Bay's configuration unfortunately focuses tsunamis along its waterfront.

In 1946 a 7.5 earthquake in the Aleutian Islands triggered a tsunami that struck Hawaii six hours later. It is still on record as the most devastating in Hawaii's history. It pounded Hilo's waterfront, reaching farthest inland across the acres that are now Wailoa River State Park, according to a chart in *Volcanoes in the Sea*. A photograph shows part of Hilo's business section looking like "pick-up sticks" afterward. It's also the tsunami that scared many people into abandoning Waipio Valley; see Trip 1.

In 1960 a huge earthquake off Chile spawned a tsunami that first devastated Chile's own coast. It struck Hawaii about 15 hours later and went on to strike Japan, too. At Hilo, it inundated even more of the area of Wailoa River State Park than had the 1946 tsunami. The maximum wave height was recorded just seaward of Wailoa River State Park at 35 feet. The force of the tsunami was so great, says *Volcanoes in the Sea*, "that the pipes supporting parking meters along the waterfront were bent over parallel to the ground." The people of Hilo had learned some lessons from the 1946 tsunami, and losses were smaller in 1960 than in 1946 even though the area flooded was larger. Tragically, they had built extensively in the Waiakea area, because the 1946 tsunami had spared it. People thought it was safe from tsunamis. The 1960 tsunami did not spare it, and many died here.

So this beautiful park testifies to a hard lesson: there's no point in building on these acres. Will another tsunami even more powerful than the 1960 tsunami teach that lesson to the people around the park's current boundaries? Let us hope not.

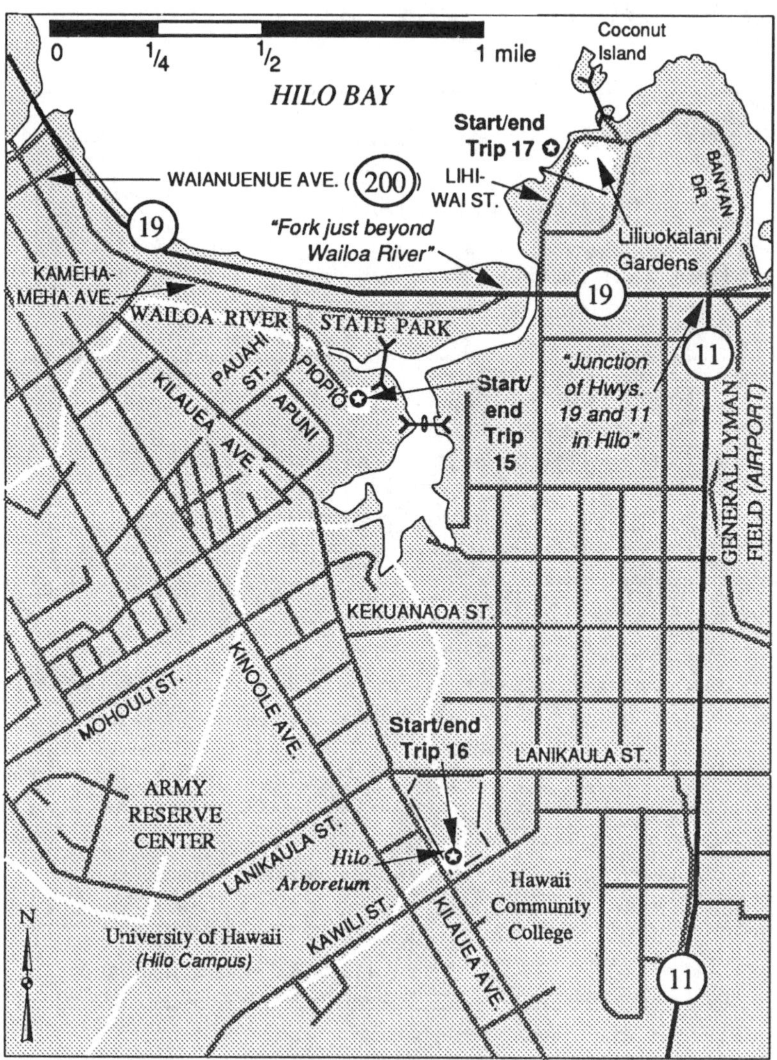

Trips 15 through 17. Wailoa River State Park, Hilo Arboretum, and Liliuokalani Gardens.

Trip 16. Hilo Arboretum

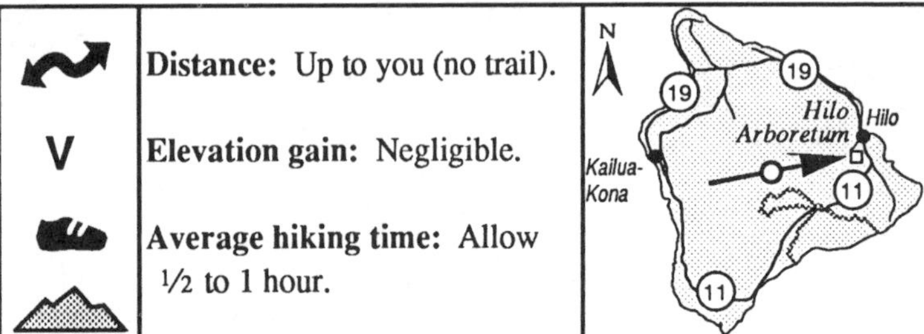

Topos: Optional: *Hilo* 7½.

Trail map: At the end of Trip 15. (It just shows where the Hilo Arboretum is. There is no trail at all through the arboretum, and none is needed.)

Highlights: If you like trees, you will enjoy Hilo Arboretum. Hilo Arboretum's broad lawns stretch out under a wide variety of non-native trees that, in years past, were being evaluated for their usefulness to Hawaii. It's a good spot for the solo visitor or for a very small group but not for a large group or for a picnic. The arboretum is open from 7:45 A.M. to 4:30 P.M. Monday through Friday and is closed Saturdays, Sundays, and holidays.

Driving instructions: Hilo Arboretum is located with the Division of Forestry and Wildlife's office. The entrance to both is a few yards northeast of the northeast corner of Kilauea Avemue and Kawili Street. It isn't well-marked, so keep your eyes peeled. If you are coming from the intersection of Highways 11 and 19 in Hilo, a possible route is to take Highway 11 south, turn right onto Lanikaula Street, and then left onto Kilauea Avenue. Turn left into the parking lot just before the intersection of Kilauea and Kawili; it's just over 2 miles from the intersection of Highways 11 and 19. There are other ways to get there; just consult your road map.

Permit/permission required: None.

Description: The arboretum occupies much of the block along the northeast side of Kilauea Avenue between Kawili and Lanikaula streets, but the only entrance you're allowed to use is opposite the Division of Forestry and Wildlife's office. If you're interested in identifying the trees, stop in the office to pick up the laminated pages of the tree listing. Most of the trees are missing the number tags that correspond to the tree listing, but with the help of the little map that's included, you can make some educated guesses at a tree's identity.

Walk across the parking lot to the arboretum entrance. Here, you'll see at once that there's no path to follow. You wade across the lawn in ankle-deep grass, perhaps pausing to identify a tree or perhaps looking for a tree that you particularly want to see. No matter how hot it may be in Hilo the day you visit, there's plenty of restful shade here. This is a true arboretum: it's overwhelmingly devoted to trees. If it also displayed a significant number of shrubs, perennials, and annuals, it would more properly be called a botanical garden. The handsome house for the chief forester is set in this lovely spot, and you will probably wish as I did that you could live there.

Most of these trees are likely to be new to you. Few of them have found wide application in Hawaii. You won't see most of them on the mainland, and you will see few of them elsewhere in Hawaii. That makes the arboretum especially interesting—perhaps even frustrating if you can't find a particular tree on the list you got from the office!

Your time here will be some of the most pleasant and tranquil you'll enjoy anywhere in Hilo. Be sure to return the tree list to the office before you go.

Chief Forester's residence in Hilo Arboretum

Trip 17. Liliuokalani Gardens and Coconut Island Beach Park

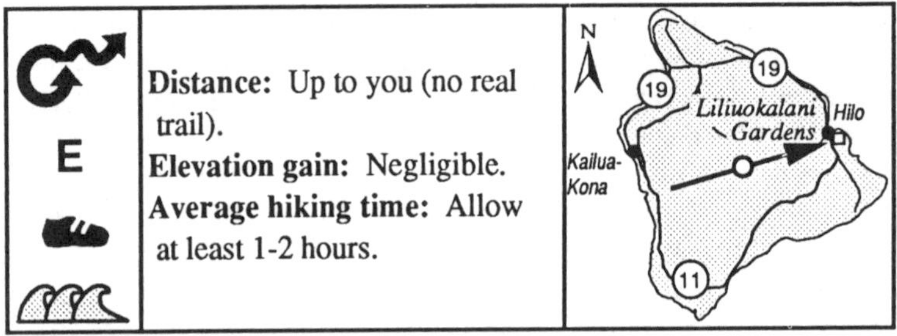

Topos: Optional: *Hilo* 7½.

Trail map: At the end of Trip 15.

Highlights: Liliuokalani Gardens' Oriental look is beautifully set off by the bright blue waters of Hilo Bay. It's a lovely place to stroll. And while you're at it, why not stroll across the street and over the pedestrian bridge to Coconut (spelled "Cocoanut" on the topo) Island Beach Park? It's a tiny island of lava and coconut palms, accessible only to those of us traveling on the Ankle Express!

Driving instructions: From the intersection of Highways 11 and 19, go west on Highway 19. Drive one block west to Lihiwai Street and turn right. You pass the southwest end of Banyan Drive—Hilo's "hotel row"—in a couple of hundred yards; stay on Lihiwai Street. Liliuokalani Gardens lies here within the loop formed by Lihiwai and Banyan, ¾ mile from the intersection of Highways 11 and 19, and there are numerous parking places on the seaward and garden sides. Park where convenient.

Permit/permission required: None.

Description: As with other Hilo area park walks, there is no fixed route you "should" follow in Liliuokalani Gardens. Pause at the edge of the gardens to look over the broad lawns, small footpaths, ponds and streams, Oriental bridges, and shady pavilions. Where would *you* like to go first? Perhaps you'd like to stroll along the streams, watching children splashing in them for goodness-knows-what watery treasures. Or you can sit by one of the ponds, under the huge trees, watching small fish schooling, turtles swimming, and families fishing—a great spot for a picnic. Another pleasure is following the paths across all the interesting little bridges and to the pavilions, where people sit and chat. There are restrooms on the east side of the park and a teahouse, not open to the public, on the south side of the park.

Coconut Island is plainly visible out in the harbor to the north. With its many nodding coconut palms, it looks like everyone's ideal tropical islet. Little bits of rock dot the blue water between Liliuokalani Gardens and Coconut Island, some even sporting beach *naupaka*. Carefully cross Lihiwai Street at the north end of the park, stroll first across a bit of lawn and then a parking lot, and then cross a pedestrian bridge to grassy-rocky Coconut Island. There are wonderful views across the harbor to downtown Hilo. Although there is very little sand, families splash and play in the clear water at the island's edges. Older children dare to jump into the water from the mossy remains of a monument on the north edge of the island. There are restrooms here and grassy areas where you can stretch out to enjoy this tropical setting.

When you're ready, return to your car. Or, if you still feel like walking, you may enjoy strolling along Banyan Drive and "hotel row," admiring the many splendid banyan trees that give the street its name. ("Hotel row" is the northern arc of Banyan Drive, so called because many of Hilo's finest hotels line it.) The extra distance for this is not included in this trip. Retrace your steps when you're ready.

Coconut Island. . . . was once a Hawaiian place of refuge, according to *Hilo Legends*. Swimming around a certain rock in one of Coconut Island's inlets was believed to cure illnesses.

But that's not all. You may have heard of the demigod Maui's attempts to draw all the Hawaiian Islands together to form a single land mass. Each island has its own version of the Maui stories. On the Big Island, Maui tried to pull the islands together with the help of Hawaii's strongest chiefs and warriors. Maui told them that no matter how hard they had to pull or how long it took, they could not look back to see how the work was going until the islands were united.

The chiefs and warriors got into Maui's canoe. The demigod hooked the island of Maui with his magic fishhook so that he start could by pulling Hawaii and Maui together. The chiefs and warriors began paddling, and slowly the islands of Hawaii and Maui came together—almost. When they were just a few feet apart, one of the chiefs could no longer resist the temptation to look back. The charm was broken, and the islands drifted apart. Only the fragment of Maui in which the magic fishhook was embedded remained a part of Hawaii. And that fragment is Coconut Island.

Trip 18. Panaewa Rainforest Zoo

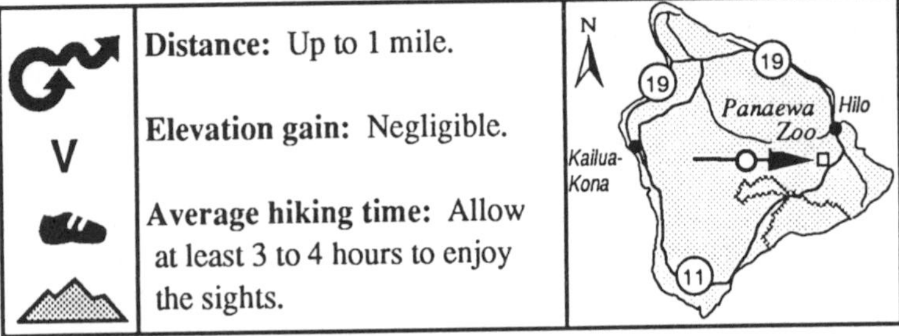

Distance: Up to 1 mile.

Elevation gain: Negligible.

Average hiking time: Allow at least 3 to 4 hours to enjoy the sights.

Topos: Optional: *Hilo* 7½.

Trail map (route approximated): At the end of this trip.

Highlights: Peacocks and lemurs and tigers, oh my! Not to mention the many other animals and marked plants. The Panaewa (pa-na-ay-va) Rainforest Zoo is fun no matter what the weather is. It's definitely a good family trip. Even if caged animals bother you, consider this trip for the botanical interest. There are dozens of interesting plants on the grounds, and many are identified for you. Zoo hours are 9:00 A.M. to 4:00 P.M.; it's closed only on Christmas Day and New Year's Day. Admission to the zoo is free, but voluntary contributions are encouraged. There are plenty of shady picnic tables, so bring your lunch and enjoy it here.

Driving instructions: Drive south on Highway 11. Shortly after Highway 11 becomes a divided road, turn left onto Stainback Highway (it's marked for the zoo; on some maps, it's labeled Mamaki Street). Follow Stainback Highway for just under 1 mile to the turnoff for Panaewa Equestrian Center and Zoo. Turn right here and follow the road past the Equestrian Center. The road ends at the parking lot for the zoo, a total of 7 miles from the start.

Permit/permission required: None.

Description: Just inside the zoo entrance, you'll find a little gift shop, some information signs, and a giant version of one of those charity coin-collectors that make the coin do some spinning before it vanishes forever into the black hole of the collection box. This one puts such a long and fancy spin on a quarter that the eyes of any small child watching it will be as big as quarters by the time it disappears with a buzz and a clatter.

Just outside the entrance building, there are several ways you can go. I suggest you head toward a wire-covered walkway that's more or less in the center of the paths here. The walkway is a sort of "cage" for the people while, outside but actually in a much larger enclosure, animals play, chatter, strut, quarrel, eat, and nap all around you. A herd of handsome Axis deer dominates one side of the enclosure. Squirrel monkeys in a *kukui* tree dominate the other side. The squirrel monkeys are anything but placid at times. Squirrel-monkey war breaks out: they scream, rush up and down the *kukui* tree yelling and making mock charges at each other, leap onto the wire mesh and climb all over it, then leap back into the *kukui*. It's hard to leave this part of the zoo.

Other sections here include lemurs and more monkeys, native Hawaiian animals, domestic animals, wild pigs, birds, and the showpiece, the tigers. Yes, real gold and black Bengal tigers in a huge, jungly enclosure of their own that has a pool—tigers like to swim. Multiple barriers keep you and the tigers farther apart than you realize. You are not in imminent danger of becoming a tiger's *hors d'oeuvre*. Sometimes the tigers are hard to see because they're lolling in the shrubbery. At other times, they may still be in their cages (in a small building at the back of the big enclosure). If you don't see them, ask the zoo personnel if the tigers are out and, if they aren't, when they will be let out. (On my first visit, I was terribly disappointed not to see them until after I went up onto the observation platform. The sounds from underneath the platform were unmistakably those of something higher on the food chain than I am. The tigers were snoozing and schmoozing there. Once I knew where they were, I was able to find a viewpoint from which I could watch them.)

Peafowl, mynas, jungle fowl (*moa*), and cardinals have the run of the place. What a spectacle it is to see three or four peacocks all displaying their magnificent tailfeathers to impress a peahen! She has seen this before and is not impressed, but *you* are. Picnic tables invite you to have your lunch here. Don't be surprised if a peacock swaggers up imperially as you're about to bite into your food: *Give that lunch to the King of All the Birds, peasant!* This you will not do, of course, as each species kept here has its own food especially formulated to meet its needs, and your lunch isn't on any of their menus. He is deeply offended by your refusal, furls his tailfeathers, turns his back on you—*peasant!*—and stalks off in the King of All the Huffs to sulk under a tree fern.

Though small and compact, the zoo has so much to offer that you should probably make a second pass through it on your first visit, just to be sure you haven't missed anything. Then, when you're ready, retrace your steps to the parking lot. Don't forget to drop some quarters in the kitty!

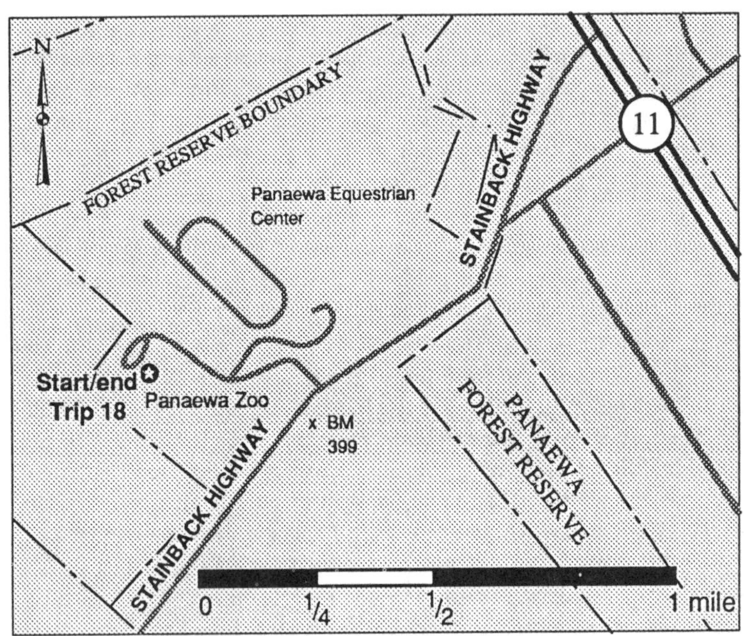

Trip 18. Panaewa Rainforest Zoo

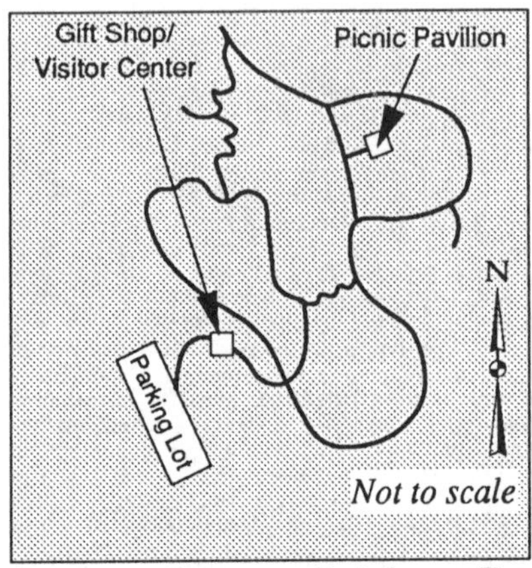

Close-up: Panaewa Rainforest Zoo

Trip 19. Lava Tree State Monument

V

Distance: ⅔ mile.

Elevation gain: Negligible.

Average hiking time: Allow at least 1 hour.

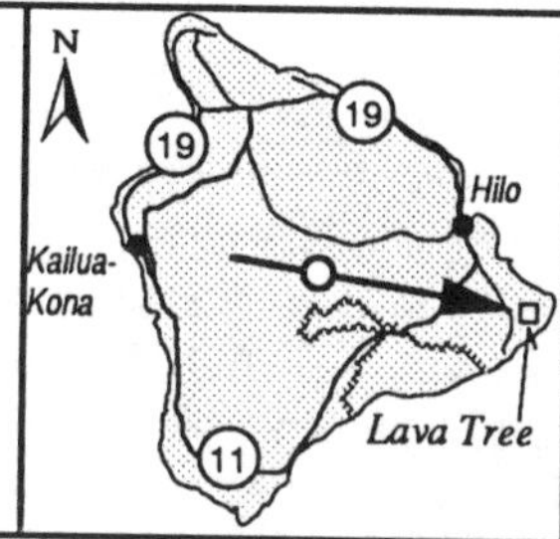

Topos: Optional: *Pahoa South* 7½.

Trail map (route approximated): At the end of this trip.

Highlights: An easy stroll in a beautiful, tranquil setting, with volcanic features that will be new to mainlanders. You can readily combine it with a leisurely visit to Panaewa Rainforest Zoo for a relaxing day of sightseeing. What more could you ask for?

Driving instructions: Drive south on Highway 11 to its junction with Highway 130 at Keaau. Turn left onto Highway 130 and follow it southeast through Pahoa to its junction with Highway 132. Turn left onto Highway 132 and follow it east 2½ miles to the entrance to Lava Tree State Monument, which will be on your left, 21¼ miles from the start. Turn into Lava Tree and park in the lot that's a few yards down the entrance road.

Permit/permission required: None.

Description: As this is a loop, you can start in either direction. This description assumes a start from the south end of the parking lot (away from the entrance road), past a large interpretive sign. Signs warn you to stay on the paths—there are dangerous cracks in the earth off-trail—and to watch out for falling branches. *Hau, ti,* and glory-bush (the one with the wide purple flowers) form a tropical understory to a lacy roof of immense monkeypod trees, some garlanded with pothos vines. *Hau* thickets form part of the backdrop, monstera another.

Farther along the trail, a new *ohia* forest has sprung up where the old one died long ago, leaving lumpy columns of lava fuzzy with moss. These are the lava trees. In about 1790, the earth trembled, cracks opened in it, and fast-moving *pahoehoe* flowed through the *ohia* forest here. It was several feet deep as it surrounded the trees. The trees caught fire, but lava in contact with the trees and their remaining moisture cooled rapidly, forming shells of rock around the trees. The rest of the lava flowed away, leaving the burning trees encased in their glassy jackets. When the trees burnt away, they left the shells hollow. It is these 200-year-old shells that are this park's lava trees.

Lush stands of *uluhe* and *amauu* ferns, schefflera, impatiens, banana, and ginger emphasize that this is a rainforest in spite of its fiery past. Tree roots twine dramatically down into the cracks in the earth. Two shelters along the way offer protection from sudden showers. A slight uphill stretch signals the end of the loop and brings you back to the parking lot, too soon.

You could zip around the loop in 20 minutes, but the interpretive sign at the trailhead suggests an hour. Good idea! Take your time; let the peace and beauty of Lava Tree soak in.

Lava trees and tree molds.... Here, you see the free-standing shells called lava trees. Elsewhere, you'll find pits called tree molds. The process that makes tree molds is similar to the one that makes lava trees. The difference is that tree molds are left when the surrounding lava does not drain away. The flow cools in place around the burning trees. When the trees are gone, they leave the pits that are called tree molds. The process is drawn-out enough that some lava trees and tree molds retain fossil-like impressions of the bark patterns of the trees that once stood there.

Lava trees and tree molds aren't unique to this corner of the island. Lava Tree State Monument is certainly the most easily accessible large assemblage of lava trees, but a turnout on a road in Hawaii Volcanoes National Park offers you a chance to visit some tree molds; see the supplementary information for Trip 47. You'll also see them along the Napau Crater Trail (Trips 32 through 34) and the Naulu Trail (Trip 35).

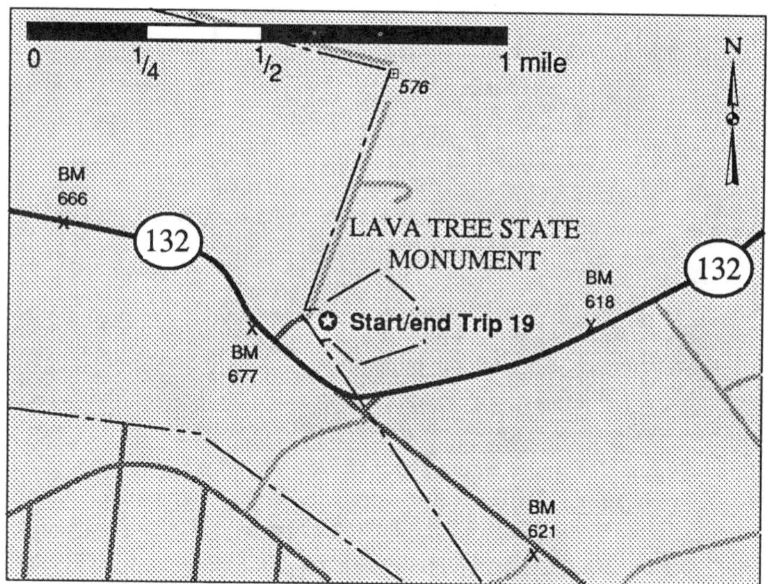

Trip 19. Lava Tree State Monument

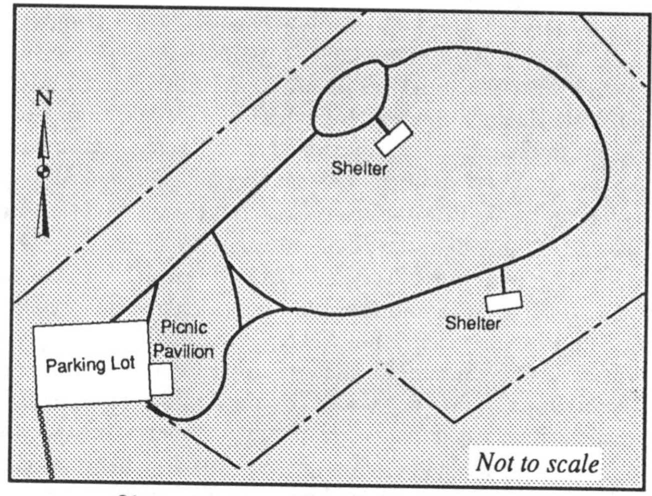

Close-up: Lava Tree State Monument

Trip 20. Crater Rim Trail Around Kilauea and Kilauea Iki

S

Distance: 10 miles.

Elevation gain: 700'.

Average hiking time: 5-6 hours of hiking, but give yourself a full day to savor this trip!

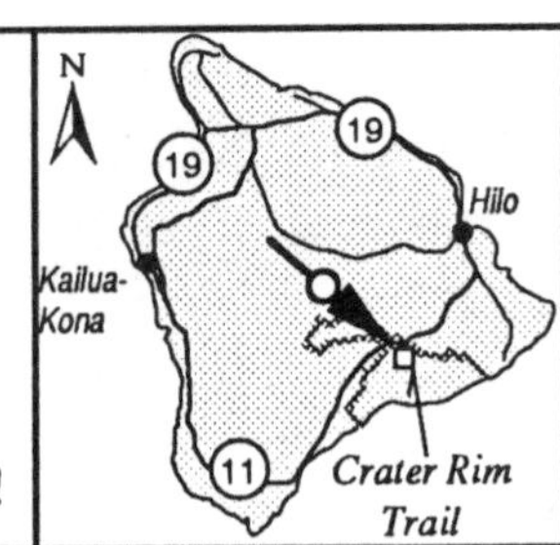

Topos: *Kilauea Crater, Volcano* 7½.

Trail map: At the end of this trip. Preceding the trail map, there's an overview of the Kilauea area of Hawaii Volcanoes National Park (including the Kau Desert and the Chain of Craters Road) to help orient you to the park, and a detailed close-up map of the many trails right around Kilauea Visitor Center.

Highlights: In reading about the Big Island, you undoubtedly have encountered descriptions of a long trail that completely encircles not only Kilauea caldera but Kilauea Iki pit crater. Well, this is *it*—the biggie, a spectacular trip that's unbeatable for its scenery and the sheer variety of its life zones. The Crater Rim Trail does not visit Halemaumau, historically the most active part of the caldera, but the latter is so easily visited from Crater Rim Road that you can pick it up on another hike (see Trips 21, 22, and 31).

Driving instructions: From Hilo, drive south and southwest on Highway 11 for 28 miles. The entrance to Hawaii Volcanoes National Park is well-marked on the highway; turn left into the park, and pay your fee or flash your receipt or pass. A few yards beyond the entrance station, turn right onto Crater Rim Road. Kilauea Visitor Center is on your right here. Park in its ample lot to begin your hike. The Crater Rim Trail is accessible from a number of other points along Crater Rim Road that offer parking (Kilauea Iki Overlook, Thurston Lava Tube, Jaggar Museum, a picnic area between Jaggar Museum and the Steam Vents, and the Steam Vents viewpoint). But Kilauea Visitor Center offers you the opportunity to stop in, buy maps, and get information from the rangers.

Permit/permission required: None.

Description: From the west end of the parking lot in front of

Kilauea Visitor Center (left end as you face the center), carefully cross Crater Rim Road and pick up a paved path marked only by the "hiking trail" symbol and a sign pointing you to Volcano House (which you will not pass until the very end of this hike). The path plunges west into fat banks of *uluhe* fern, passing ginger, tree ferns, and *ohia*. Keep an eye out for signs labeling the plants if you're interested in sharpening your plant-identifying skills.

You pass a steam vent and, at a marked junction, turn right toward Hawaii Volcano Observatory and Jaggar Museum. Soon you're descending moderately to steeply. At the next marked junction, go to the right again. The trail is no longer paved now, and the grade eases as you pass through an *ohia* forest. Curving northwest and then southwest, you reach the caldera rim for your first breathtaking view over Kilauea. Astonishing! You probably had no idea it was as huge as it really is. Below your viewpoint, great slabs of the caldera wall have broken free of the present rim and stand isolated, like a range of hills above the caldera floor, plush and green with a luxuriant rainforest. Far away on the caldera's edge to the west-southwest, you can make out the observatory tower; it looks very much like an air traffic control tower. Southwest and still farther away is the deep pit of Halemaumau (ha-lay-ma-oo-ma-oo), its walls faintly tinted with reds and pale yellows. Steam curls skyward from a hundred cracks in the flat brown floor of the caldera and from hundreds more in the sheer, layered walls. Precipitation seeps into these cracks, meets the hot volcanic rock that lies just below the surface, and oozes back out as plumes of steam. You can warm your hands in the steam (if it's not too hot) on a cold morning. The more rain, the better the steam display, unless the rain obscures the view altogether. An unforgettable treat is watching filmy gray tatters of rain sweep across the caldera and its rainforest hills, and then, in the clear space between the showers, seeing steam gush from a thousand cracks.

The trail curves to the right, and Mauna Loa's immense, deceptively gentle bulk looms in the west. On most days, clouds will begin gathering around it by midmorning, and by noon it will be quite hidden from Kilauea. If it's very clear, you may even glimpse Mauna Kea to the east of it over its lower slopes. However, the views along here are often obscured by scrubby *ohia* trees and sometimes by clouds of steam. Look for a native sedge, *uki*, as well as for a couple of non-natives: little purple Philippine orchids with lily-like foliage and small white bamboo orchids, their lower lips purple-stained, atop tall, stiff stems like miniature bamboo. Railings keep you from stepping off the edge and plunging to the caldera floor hundreds of feet below.

As you continue, the views open up again, and you pass a junction with the Sandalwood Trail. Continue ahead (southwest) on the Crater Rim Trail to the superb viewpoint at Steaming Bluff. Pause to enjoy the panorama and to take a few photos here. Continuing, you pass another splendid viewpoint, climb a little, level out past yet another viewpoint, and duck briefly into a small grove of *koa* trees. Near the 1-mile point, you pass an unmarked junction with a path that leads off to the right to Kilauea Military Camp (a rest and recreation camp for military personnel and their families stationed in the Hawaiian Islands). You continue ahead on the Crater Rim Trail and ascend gently to moderately toward Hawaii Volcano Observatory and Jaggar Museum. You're on Uwekahuna Bluff, and the earth is deeply cracked on both sides of the trail. Passing the picnic area, you stop to study the interpretive signs and to enjoy more wonderful views.

You reach the observatory and museum area in a little over 2 miles. The observatory is not open to the public, but the museum is. It's a worthwhile stop if you have the time; if not, come back when you can. Of course, there's an outstanding view here—this is, after all, the summit of Kilauea (4078 feet). The museum also offers water, restrooms, and a telephone. A half-mile-long trail connects the museum to Namakani Paio Campground (1 mile out-and-back, 158 feet of elevation gain; biggest challenges: crossing Highway 11 and Crater Rim Road).

The Crater Rim Trail currently resumes at the far edge of the parking lot, away from the caldera rim. Avoiding a marked-off, unstable area, the trail gradually makes its way back to the rim. You descend through increasingly dry, desert-like terrain and carefully cross Crater Rim Road. Here, on the southwest slope of Kilauea and in its rain shadow, you are in the Kau Desert. Acid fumes from Halemaumau, blown this way by the prevailing northeast winds, contribute to making the Kau Desert a hostile environment. Tough, twisted *ohia, aalii,* and *ohelo* are among the scrubby plants hardy enough to survive here. From here to Thurston Lava Tube, many miles ahead, you will have little company. The trail levels out and becomes quite eroded and occasionally hard to follow. It's soon little more than a shallow trace in the sand, and you need the help of the cairns that now mark your way.

Halemaumau, the most active place in Kilauea Caldera

At the marked junction with the Kau Desert Trail, you bear left (south) on the Crater Rim Trail and soon find yourself walking right next to Crater Rim Road. If you thought the landscape was barren before, check out *this* "moonscape"! The gently undulating lava-scape, a soft, dusty-rose color up close, brown or black at a distance, stretches all around you, becoming more and more lifeless as you go. Dry washes and collapsed lava tubes interrupt your progress; pick your way across them with the help of the cairns on either side. Recent lava flows make gray slashes across the dusty-rose face of the desert. Huge slabs of the newer lavas are heaved up into frozen pressure ridges; the tread of the trail where it crosses one of those slabs is worn down into reddish patches.

As you come abreast of Halemaumau, which is ½ to ⅔ mile north of this segment of the Crater Rim Trail, acid fumes begin to make your nose sting.[1] You descend a sandy hill very steeply to a recent lava flow, where cairns stretch far away across the shiny blackness. Broken slabs of *pahoehoe* surround you, their upturned edges showing pink, lavender, yellow, and silvery-black tints. The thin, glassy surface of these slabs shatters under your boots. It's unnerving: *is this really solid, or am I going to break through it and fall forever?* It's solid enough, as long as you stay on the marked route, but exploring off-route can be very dangerous because of hazards like thin-ceilinged lava tubes. Soon you arrive at the junction with the Halemaumau Trail, which goes north-northeast to that crater. From this junction, you continue east-southeast on the Crater Rim Trail over gray and orange cinders.

[1]It is true that the fumes can aggravate respiratory problems. If you have a respiratory problem, either avoid Halemaumau or keep your fastest-acting medication handy when you're anywhere near Halemaumau. I know of a person whose visit to Halemaumau—and his vacation—ended in an emergency room because of those fumes.

A great bowl of cracked, black *pahoehoe* lies to your left. After passing a many-mouthed spatter vent, you cross a couple of cracks in the bowl's edge through which the dark lava has spilled. Gradually, shrubs reappear as you traverse the transition zone between the Kau Desert on Kilauea's southwest slope and the rainforest on its east slope. The Crater Rim Trail grazes the south edge of a deep, dramatic pit crater called Keanakakoi (yes, the same name as that of the quarry on Mauna Kea). It crosses a *pahoehoe* field where you'll see some lava trees (see Trip 19), and abruptly enters an *ohia* forest. Suddenly, the trail is faint not because it's on sand or lava but because it's alive with grasses, orchids, and trees trying to grow over it.

In another half mile, you carefully walk across a paved road—the Chain of Craters Road—and pick up the Crater Rim Trail in the rainforest on the other side. In a little over a mile, you intersect a dirt road and turn left onto it. You pass through a fence, closing the gate behind you, and emerge into the auto-choked, tourist-filled precincts of Thurston Lava Tube. Water and restrooms are available here, and it will take you only a few minutes to join the crowd for the brief but worthwhile loop through Thurston Lava Tube (see Trip 29).

The Crater Rim Trail resumes across the parking lot from Thurston Lava Tube near Kilauea Iki crater, which is not visible through the dense growth. Leaving the parking lot behind, you climb steeply but briefly and level out in an *ohia* forest. You are on one of the most scenic parts of the Crater Rim Trail here, where breaks in the forest offer breathtaking views over Kilauea Iki crater. The views are particularly good at Kilauea Iki Overlook, a short way ahead. Kilauea caldera is visible to the west over the sill that separates them, Byron Ledge. Kilauea Iki crater's black *pahoehoe* floor, like Kilauea caldera's, has plenty of hot rock beneath it, as the steam smoking out of it testifies. The trail across the crater floor is visible as a gray line on the dark lava. A striking cone of red cinders rises from the crater floor and above the crater rim. This cone, Puu Puai, was formed during the 1959 eruption by a fountain of lava that spurted as much as 1900 feet into the air at times. Any time you watch a program about Hawaii's volcanoes, you're likely to see footage of that spectacular fire-fountain.

Beyond Kilauea Iki Overlook you bear left and descend a couple of steep staircases. Bamboo orchids flourish here, and the crater views are excellent from here to the junction with the trail to Byron

Ledge. At that junction, you take the right fork toward Kilauea Visitor Center, cross a disused auto turnout, and bear left onto an abandoned section of paved road. This was once part of Crater Rim Road, but cracks appeared in it, as you see. The road was rerouted, and this abandoned section became part of the foot trail. (The trail map at the end of this trip doesn't show these bits of abandoned road except as they happen to be part of the Crater Rim Trail now. Signs and fences make the foot route plain.)

You pass the old Waldron Ledge Lookout and soon meet a paved footpath that curves off to the left. Take it down to a shelter overlooking Kilauea caldera. From here, you follow a paved path that continues around the caldera between the rim and Volcano House. The caldera views here are some of the very best on the Crater Rim Trail and a fitting climax to this superb though taxing hike. A little beyond Volcano House, you meet the spur back to Kilauea Visitor Center (your first junction when you began this hike many hours ago). Turn right here to cross Crater Rim Road to your car at Kilauea Visitor Center.

About the weather here. . . . A lush rainforest grows on the east slope of Kilauea. It takes a lot of precipitation to nourish a rainforest on the rim of an active volcano! So what's the most likely weather condition around Kilauea Visitor Center? Right: rain. At around 4000 feet, it can get very cold, too, even during the summer. Lots of tourists are caught unprepared and stand around, surprised and shivering, in their soaked, flimsy resort wear. *Hawaii is not supposed to be like this,* their faces say. *Hawaii is supposed to be warm and sunny.*

Not entirely true. Areas where you can hike in Hawaii seldom have resort-quality weather. If they had resort weather, they would probably have resorts instead of hiking trails. You and I with our scruffy hiking gear would probably be quite out of place.

About the caldera rim. . . . As I write this, it is only a few weeks since a group of hikers walked up to the rim of Kilauea caldera at night. The lead hiker stepped right off the edge and fell to his death. Not funny. Easy to do. The Crater Rim Trail is seldom right on the very edge of the caldera because that edge is unstable, the caldera walls are extremely steep, and a hiker distracted by the scenery or traveling in conditions of poor visibility could get too close to the edge and be the next one to fall off it. So stick to the trail; watch where you're going.

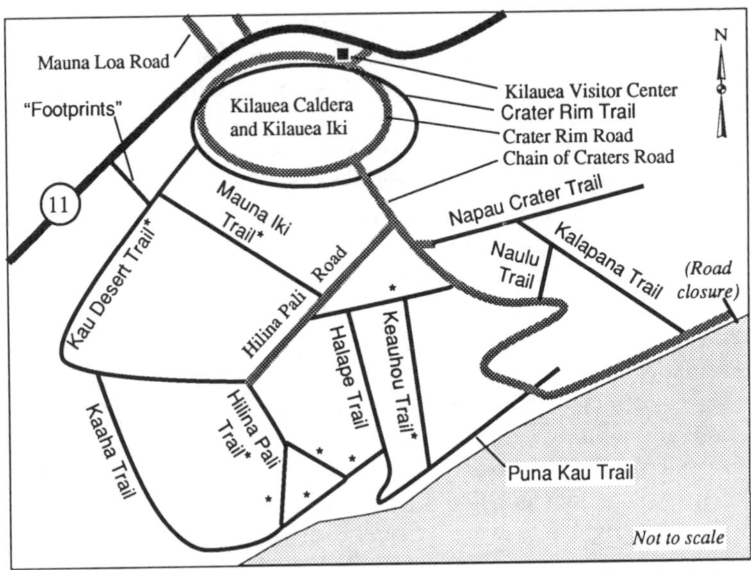

*Part or all of these trails not recommended: uninteresting or very unpleasant or both.

Overview: Kilauea Area of Hawaii Volcanoes National Park

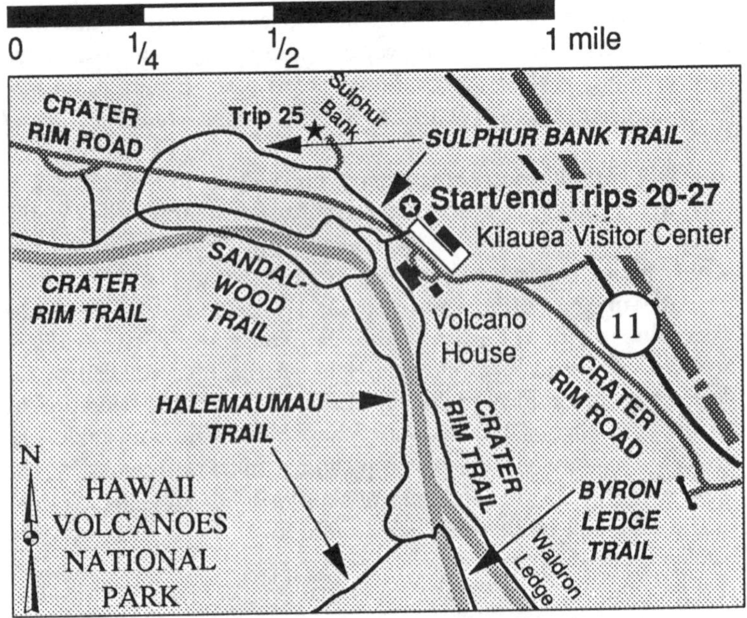

Close-up of Kilauea Visitor Center Area for Trips 20–27

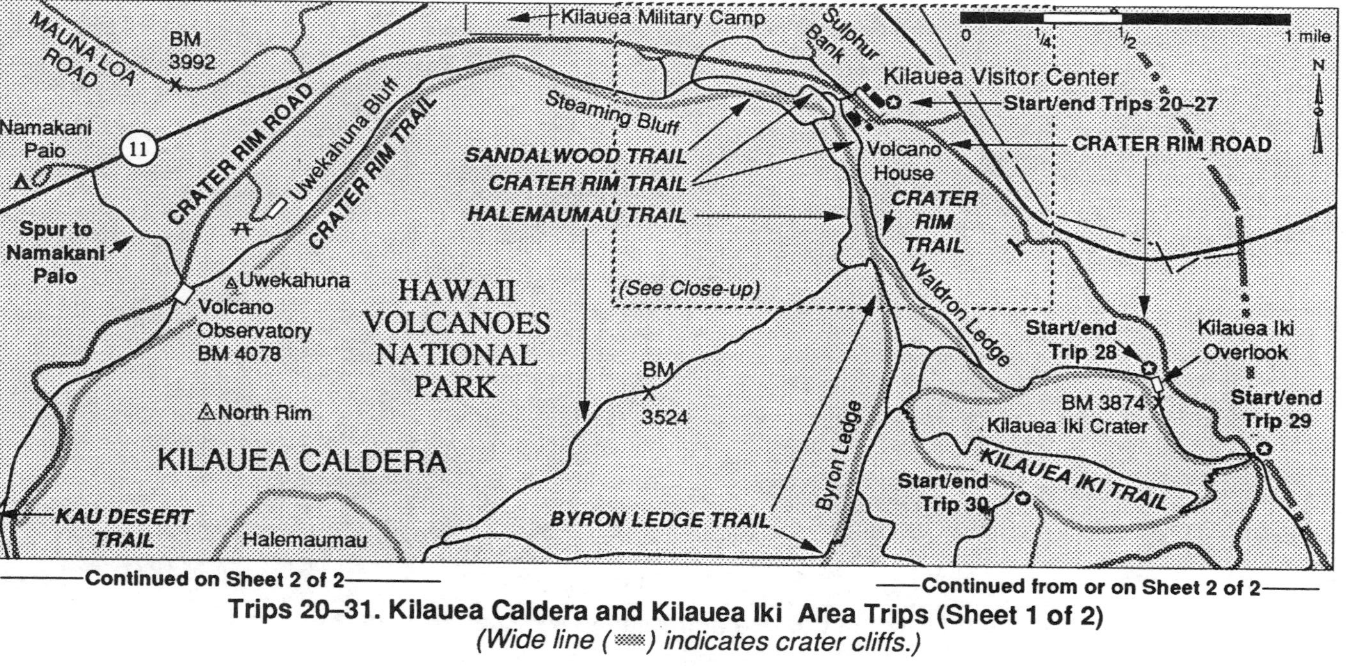

Trips 20–31. Kilauea Caldera and Kilauea Iki Area Trips (Sheet 1 of 2)

(Wide line (▒) indicates crater cliffs.)

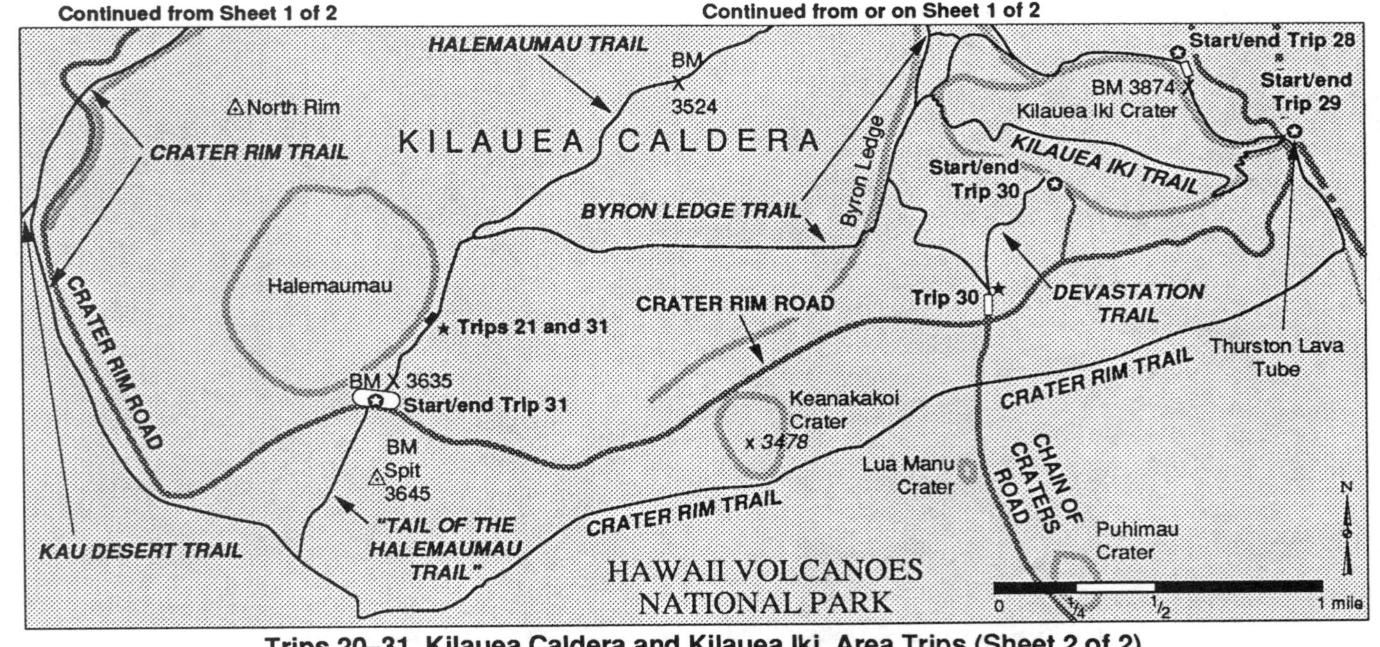

Trips 20–31. Kilauea Caldera and Kilauea Iki Area Trips (Sheet 2 of 2)

(Wide line ([swatch]) indicates caldera or crater cliffs.)

Trip 21. Halemaumau Trail

21 (Halemaumau Trail)

Distance: 5 miles.

Elevation gain: 400' (upside-down trip).

Average hiking time: 2½ hours.

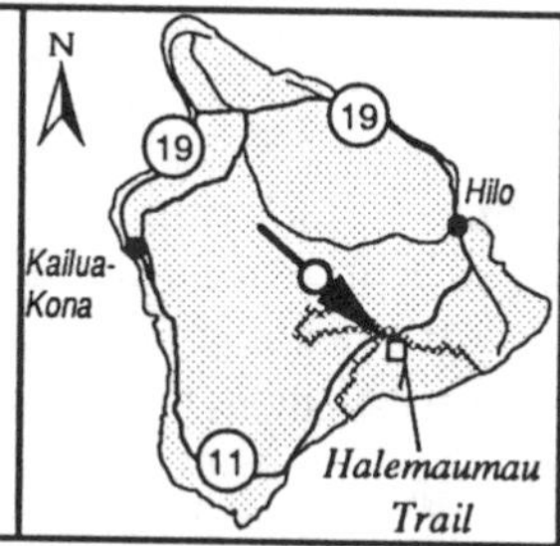

Topos: *Kilauea Crater 7½.*

Trail map: At the end Trip 20.

Highlights: After winding down through the "rainforest hills" below Volcano House (some fine birding opportunities here), you venture out onto the black *pahoehoe* floor of Kilauea Crater for a close-up view of Halemaumau Crater.

Driving instructions: Follow the driving instructions of Trip 20 to Kilauea Visitor Center and park there.

Permit/permission required: None.

Description: You begin this trip as you began Trip 20: From the west end of the parking lot in front of Kilauea Visitor Center (left end as you face the center), carefully cross Crater Rim Road and pick up a paved path marked only by the "hiking trail" symbol and a sign pointing you to Volcano House. You pass a steam vent and, at a marked junction, take the right fork toward Halemaumau and the observatory (this is part of the Crater Rim Trail). You descend and, in a few more steps, you're at another junction. Here, you turn left onto the Halemaumau Trail (and away from the Crater Rim Trail).

You continue to descend, sometimes steeply, through a delightful rainforest dominated by *amau*[1] and *hapuu* tree ferns, *ohia, uluhe,* and ginger. *Amau* stems terminate in a simple frond, while *hapuu* stems end in a compound frond. Happily, many of the plants are marked, so this stretch is educational as well as beautiful. The wiry

[1]You may find this fern called *amau* (a-ma-oo) in some places, *amaumau* (a-ma-oo-ma-oo) in others. According to *The Pocket Hawaiian Dictionary,* both names refer to the endemic Sadleria ferns. *Amau* is singular (one *Sadleria* fern) and *amaumau* is plural (many *Sadleria* ferns; sometimes used as an adjective meaning "ferny"). "Halemaumau" means "house of many *amau* ferns," as explained in the supplementary information for this trip.

stems of new *uluhe* ferns, ending in perfectly smooth, tight, blue-green curls, and the young fronds of *hapuu* ferns, closely furled and generously clad in ruddy down, are among the most elegant natural forms to be seen anywhere. "Stairsteps" cut into the trail ease your descent, and a bench offers a rest spot. At the junction with the Sandalwood Trail, you'll find another bench to rest on. To continue, take the left fork toward Byron Ledge. The trail is nearly level for a while. A little beyond ⅓ mile from your start, a spur trail on your right invites you to stroll some 50 feet to a shelter offering fine views over the rainforest and to Byron Ledge in the distance. This is a good spot for birding, too. (And if you go no farther on this hike, you will still have enjoyed a most worthwhile trip.)

Leaving the shelter, you rejoin the Halemaumau Trail and descend gradually. Soon the black cliffs of Waldron Ledge come plainly into view. You ascend past black boulders as you circumvent a rockfall. Now you descend again through a beautiful, dense rainforest. Views open up briefly as you pass a huge black boulder. Nearing the ⅔-mile point, a view of Kilauea's black floor with its cairn-marked trails opens up below you, and you curve right, descending, to the northern junction of the Halemaumau and Byron Ledge trails. The righthand fork here leads to Halemaumau, the left to Byron Ledge.

You bear right (southwest) into the firepit and are soon walking across its floor; ahead, distant Volcano Observatory seems precariously perched on the crater rim. Steam rises from numerous cracks in the floor around you as you follow the cairns toward the prominent spatter rampart left by the 1982 eruption. Pele's Kilauea home is very rainy, so new plants have already colonized these 1982 lavas: red-flowered *ohia; ohelo* with its plump red berries; *kupukupu* sword ferns; *pukiawe* with its tiny, dagger-shaped leaves and hard red or white berries; grasses; and, of course, the hardy *amau* fern, whose coppery-red young fronds are so stunning when set against the black lava.

You make your way over the spatter rampart, past the unmarked southern junction of the Halemaumau and Byron Ledge trails, and, 2½ miles from your start, gingerly approach Halemaumau crater. Keep back from its cracked, steep rim except where cairns indicate you may safely go. The fumes are distinctly sulfurous here, often causing problems for those with respiratory ailments (see the footnote in Trip 20). Walk up to the fenced overlook to read the interpretive sign and to enjoy a first-rate view of the crater, whose sheer, reddish-brown walls are in places yellow with caked-on sulfur. I think the most amazing sight here is not the fuming crater but the white-tailed tropicbirds wheeling through the fumes down in the crater. White-tailed tropicbirds like to nest in inaccessible places. If Halemaumau's walls aren't inaccessible, I don't know what is. There are plenty of offerings to Pele here: food (especially fruit), flowers (probably including some beautiful leis), and gin. Please don't disturb the offerings.

Retrace your steps from here.

The "tail" of the Halemaumau Trail. Purists may want to continue to the far end of the Halemaumau Trail, where it meets the Crater Rim Trail south of Halemaumau. It's ¾ mile farther south-southwest (adds 1½ miles to your trip). You pick your way through a steaming, sulfur-stained landscape to the parking lot, continue across the parking lot and across Crater Rim Road, and follow a sandy path along the edge of an iridescent *pahoehoe* flow, or cairns across it, to its junction with the Crater Rim Trail. Retrace your steps from here.

Pele. . . . Pele's favorite offering used to be *ohelo* berries, and it's still a good idea to share any *ohelo* berries you pick with her. You don't want Pele to get angry and spit fire at you. Or you can save yourself the trouble by not picking any in the first place. Raw *ohelo* berries, so appealing with their rosy color and seemingly bursting with juice, are almost tasteless. They are more enjoyable when they are used in drinks and desserts like those served at Volcano House. Even Pele has switched—to gin. Perhaps the bitter tang of juniper berries pleases her more. The *ohelo* is endemic to Hawaii (grows

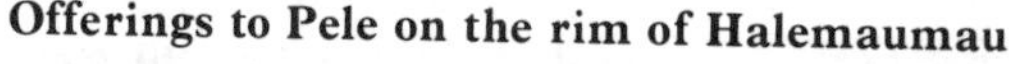

Offerings to Pele on the rim of Halemaumau

naturally only in Hawaii) and is related to the mainland blueberries, huckleberries, and cranberries.

Pele is often represented nowadays as a beautiful young woman. Her more common guise when she appears to people is as an old lady with a dog. Local legend has it that during the 1960 eruption on the Puna coast, an old lady appeared near Cape Kumakahi in Puna, the easternmost point of the Big Island. She went from door to door asking for food. Everyone but the lighthouse keeper turned her away. The lighthouse keeper treated her kindly. The subsequent lava flow destroyed most of the neighborhood but split as it went around the lighthouse, sparing it, and continued out to sea. Who do you think that old lady was?

Pele's favorite home was, of course, Halemaumau. Myth has it that in her young-woman form, she attracted the attentions of the *kupua* Kamapuaa. A *kupua* is a demigod; some *kupua* have the power to take on many different forms. Kamapuaa was half man, half pig (*puaa* means pig). Martha Beckwith, in her classic *Hawaiian Mythology,* reports that one of Kamapuaa's forms was that of a handsome man; another, that of a pig; at other times, that of the pig-nosed fish, the *humuhumunukunukuapuaa;* and that of a coarse grass called *kukae-puaa.*

Kamapuaa came to Halemaumau as a man to woo Pele. Her sisters saw him only as a handsome man, but Pele saw his pig form, too, and rebuffed him with taunts and insults. Kamapuaa, hurt and angry, insulted Pele in turn. At first they fought with insults. Then, when Kamapuaa attempted to approach her, Pele threw flames at him. Kamapuaa responded by deluging Halemaumau with water, hoping to put out its fires. Pele's allies kept the fires going, and again she assaulted Kamapuaa with fire. The contest raged until both Pele and Kamapuaa were exhausted. Some versions of this myth say the fight ended when, to fend off Pele's last attack, Kamapuaa surrounded Kilauea with *amau* ferns, which remain abundant in the Kilauea area to this day. And that is why the active crater in Kilauea caldera is called "the house of many *amau* ferns," Halemaumau.

Trip 22. Crater Rim-Halemaumau Loop

22 (Crater Rim-Halemaumau)

Distance: 6½ miles.

Elevation gain: 400' (upside-down trip).

Average hiking time: 3¼ hours.

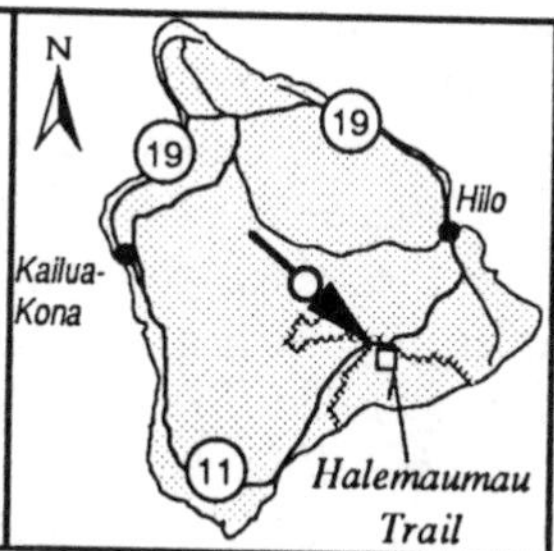

Topos: *Kilauea Crater* 7½.

Trail map: At the end of Trip 20.

Highlights: After sweeping around the Crater Rim Trail from Kilauea Visitor Center to the junction with the Halemaumau Trail, you close your loop on the Halemaumau Trail and take in one of Hawaii Volcanoes National Park's most riveting sights, the pit crater Halemaumau in Kilauea caldera's floor. For those who lack the time or energy to take the full Crater Rim Loop (Trip 20), this trip offers an exciting and wonderfully scenic alternative.

Driving instructions: Follow the driving instructions of Trip 20.

Permit/permission required: None.

Description: Follow the description of Trip 20 as far as the junction with the Halemaumau Trail south of Halemaumau. Instead of proceeding east-southeast on the Crater Rim Trail, turn left (north-northeast) onto the Halemaumau Trail and reverse the description of the "tail" of the Halemaumau Trail (a supplemental description at the end of Trip 21) to the pit crater. After taking in the wonders of Halemaumau and perhaps leaving your own offering for Pele, reverse the description of Trip 21 to return to Kilauea Visitor Center and close this fascinating loop.

Calderas and pit craters. . . . Calderas are huge, steep-sided pits that may occur at the summits of volcanoes. Pit craters are just that: deep, steep-sided pits associated with volcanoes. Calderas and pit craters are differentiated largely on the basis of size (calderas are much bigger) and location (calderas occur at a volcano's summit; pit craters may occur in calderas or on the volcano's flanks). No one has actually seen a caldera or a pit crater in the process of formation, but the evidence is that they are formed by similar processes and differ mainly in location and size.

According to *Volcanoes in the Sea*, the principal agent of caldera and pit crater formation is the swelling of the mountain as magma pushes up beneath it. The swelling weakens the overlying material, and the material cracks in arcs around the magma body. Eventually the cracks form a roughly circular or oval pattern of faults. When the magma withdraws, the weakened material within the circle or oval collapses along those faults. The remaining magma may then ooze over the collapsed material, forming a relatively flat floor, or subsequent eruption episodes may partly fill the caldera or the crater, leaving a flat floor.

It's also possible that the overlying material, which is relatively dense because it's solid, sinks along the established fault pattern into the underlying magma, which is lighter because it's fluid.

On the trips in this book, you've seen Mauna Loa's and Kilauea's calderas and the pit craters around them (Lua Poholo on Mauna Loa and Halemaumau and Kilauea Iki on Kilauea, for example). A question naturally arises: where is Mauna Kea's caldera? Not every volcano forms a caldera. However, there's a roughly circular pattern of cinder cones around Mauna Kea's summit. They may trace the boundary of a former caldera that has since been buried by all those cones and their cinders. All right, then, where is Hualalai's caldera? *Volcanoes in the Sea* says, "There is no direct evidence that a caldera ever existed on Hualalai. If it did, it has been completely buried by later lavas." And Kohala? *Volcanoes in the Sea* observes, "A series of curved faults [near the present summit of the mountain] suggests that a caldera probably was formed in the summit of the shield . . . , but it has been entirely buried. . . ."

Straying off the Big Island, what about the "crater" atop Haleakala on Maui? (Haleakala last erupted just a little before Hualalai's last eruption—about 1790 versus 1801.) It's not a caldera or a volcanic crater at all! It is, in fact, the product of stream cutting, as described following Trip 3 in this book, but on a very grand scale. The streams of Keanae and Kaupo valleys cut their heads back so far that they merged near Haleakala's summit, forming its "crater." Later volcanic activity partly filled the erosion-cut depression and produced the colorful cinder cones that Haleakala is so famous for.

Trip 23. Halemaumau-Byron Ledge Semiloop

Distance: 6 miles.

Elevation gain: 840' (upside-down trip).

Average hiking time: 3 hours.

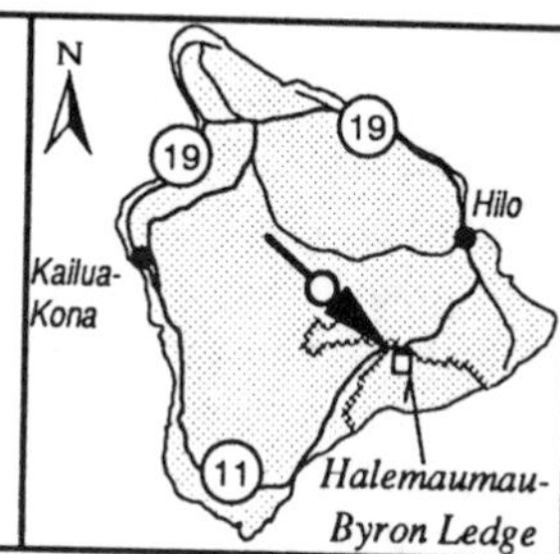

Topos: *Kilauea Crater 7½*.

Trail map: At the end of Trip 20.

Highlights: This trip adds the beauty of the forest on Byron Ledge to the fascination of the Halemaumau Trail.

Driving instructions: Follow the driving instructions of Trip 20.

Permit/permission required: None.

Description: Follow Trip 21 down into Kilauea caldera, passing the northern and southern junctions of the Halemaumau and Byron Ledge trails, to the fenced viewpoint at Halemaumau crater. Pick up the "tail" of the Halemaumau Trail as described in Trip 21 if you wish; its mileage is not included above. Retrace your steps as far as the southern junction with the Byron Ledge Trail. It was unsigned in the spring of 1991; look for an eastbound line of cairns diverging to the right (east) from the Halemaumau Trail just south of the spatter rampart. Those cairns mark the Byron Ledge Trail.

Turn right onto the Byron Ledge Trail and follow the cairns east to the foot of Byron Ledge. Byron Ledge is the sill that separates Kilauea caldera from Kilauea Iki crater. You ascend the ledge over black cinders. After the trail levels out, you settle down for a delightful forest ramble with rare, but excellent, views of Kilauea. At 1½ miles from the junction, you meet a spur trail to the Devastation Trail. This trip stays on the Byron Ledge Trail. (Optionally, you can make the half-mile out-and-back detour to and from the Devastation Trail; see its brief description below.)

Bearing north-northeast on the Byron Ledge Trail, you're likely to notice a tall, coarse-stemmed plant with broad, vaguely maple-like leaves in threes, and, in season, fat buds and handsome, three-inch-wide white flowers with green centers surrounded by yellow stamens. Rangers tell me this is an alien, a Japanese anemone. You soon pass through a fence, closing the gate behind you, and meet a spur trail that branches right for less than a tenth of a mile to meet the Kilauea Iki Trail near a little bench. You bear left here, staying on the Byron Ledge Trail, to a junction whose righthand branch the sign describes as going to Crater Rim Road. Well, it does—but only after you climb up Waldron Ledge to the Crater Rim Trail. You bear left here, again staying on the Byron Ledge Trail.

Just beyond that junction, there's a pleasant bench where, in spite of considerable plant growth, you can still enjoy views over Kilauea caldera while you rest. It's a good spot for a little birding, too. Leaving this bench, you make a steep, switchbacking descent back to Kilauea's floor. You follow cairns for a little more than a hundred yards across the caldera and reach the northern junction of the Halemaumau and Byron Ledge trails, closing the loop portion of this trip.

Now retrace your steps up the Halemaumau Trail to Kilauea Visitor Center.

Spur to Devastation Trail. . . . This out-and-back detour adds just under 1¼ miles and 90 feet of elevation gain to your trip. The Devastation Trail isn't nearly as devastated as you may think from looking at pictures of it. Plants have thoroughly regrown along most of it. After all, the eruption that laid the area waste happened over thirty years ago, in 1959. The only area that's really barren now—the one we all photograph—is a stretch just south of Puu Puai. This spur between the Byron Ledge and Devastation trails, part of which is on a section of the pre-eruption Crater Rim Road, looks more devastated than the Devastation Trail does now. After turning off the Byron Ledge Trail, you're still in the forest. Suddenly the forest ends, and you step out into a barren cinder field. The naked hump of Puu Puai, built by the 1959 eruption, rises ahead on your left. Dead branches mark your track through the bare cinders. Alien plants have taken advantage of the destruction, colonizing the cinder field: blackberries, a red-and-pink ground cover, and thistles. Fortunately, native *ohia* trees are making a comeback here. You make a lazy zigzag up the cindery ridge southwest of Puu Puai, pick up the fragment of the pre-eruption Crater Rim Road, and meet the boardwalk of the Devastation Trail at its parking lot. From here, retrace your steps to the Byron Ledge Trail.

Trip 24. Sandalwood Trail

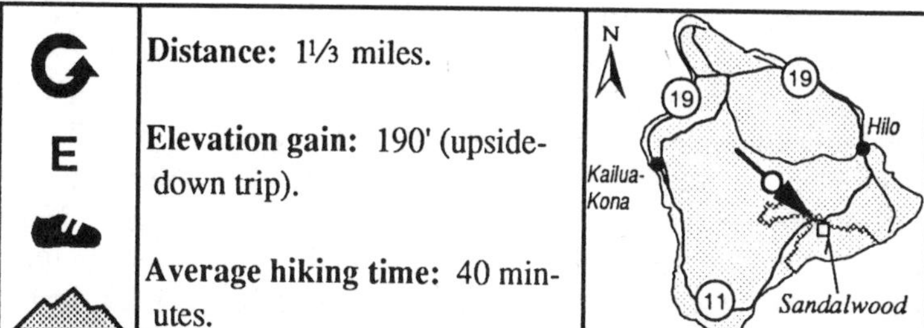

Distance: 1⅓ miles.

Elevation gain: 190' (upside-down trip).

Average hiking time: 40 minutes.

Topos: Optional: *Kilauea Crater* 7½.

Trail map: At the end of Trip 20.

Highlights: This short ramble offers spectacular caldera views as well as rainforest beauty. The upper end of the Sandalwood Trail is home to a few now-rare sandalwood trees—interesting if you can spot them.

Driving instructions: Follow the driving instructions of Trip 20.

Permit/permission required: None.

Description: Follow the description of Trip 20 along the Crater Rim Trail to the junction with the Sandalwood Trail, a little less than ⅔ mile. Turn left onto the Sandalwood Trail through puffs of steam—there are many steam vents around this junction. There are outstanding views of Kilauea Caldera as you curve east, back toward Kilauea Visitor Center and Volcano House (the latter visible on the rim). The *ohia* and *amau* forest and its *uluhe* understory become quite lush as you descend. A few sandalwood trees survive along here, but you'll need to be sharp-eyed to find them (I had to ask the rangers for help). You seem to be on a narrow ridge between Kilauea's abyss on your right and deep steam vents and cracks on your left. Birdsong fills the air.

Still descending, the trail curves left toward the cliffs below Volcano House. You meet the Halemaumau Trail at a junction where there's a bench. You'll want to rest here and enjoy the birds and the scenery for a while. When you're ready to move on, take the left fork (which is the Halemaumau Trail) back toward Volcano House and Kilauea Visitor Center. You climb now, rather steeply at first, but stairs help you negotiate this section. Soon you reach a bench shaded by *hapuu* tree ferns and surrounded by *ohia* and yellow ginger. Another rest is in order! Now the grade eases and the trail curves left. You pass some marked plants and catch glimpses of the black basalt cliffs beneath Volcano House.

You presently reach the junction with the Crater Rim Trail near Volcano House, closing the loop. Turn right here and retrace your steps back to Kilauea Visitor Center.

The sandalwood trade. . . . was a social disaster far beyond the human and plant losses discussed in the "Geology and History, Natural and Human" chapter in this book. Remember that the mountains were stripped of their sandalwood trees to pay off the chiefs' debts to foreign merchants, and that many of the common people who were forced into the mountains to do the work died of starvation and exposure. Some authorities believe that this drove a wedge between the common Hawaiians and their chiefs. Formerly, the commoners had trusted their chiefs to keep their demands reasonable. The chiefs understood that the commoners had to have time to make a living for themselves. Most chiefs realized that they were ultimately dependent upon the commoners, and respected these necessary limits. The chiefs in turn organized and led armies to protect the people. And the chiefs provided the link between their people and the gods. There was a mutual and necessary dependence and trust between chiefs and commoners.

But when the commoners slaved and even died to harvest the sandalwood, they received nothing at all, not even the amount of food and clothing they needed in order to survive in the chilly, rainy mountains. The sandalwood went to the foreign merchants; the chiefs got fancy china, satin robes, and European furniture; and the commoners were literally left out in the cold. Certainly, that must have eroded the trust between the chiefs and the commoners. Perhaps this was the experience that led the commoners to stop seeing the chiefs as their protectors and to begin regarding them as their oppressors.

The plantation system in Hawaii grew up against this background. Plantation owners, largely foreigners, tried to persuade the common people of Hawaii, often through their chiefs, to work for the plantations. As far as many of the Hawaiian commoners could see, it was just another arrangement in which commoners would slave and starve while foreigners and chiefs prospered. The commoners believed the owners would pay the chiefs for the commoners' labor and the chiefs would keep all the money. A person would have to be crazy to accept such an arrangement. The old religion had fallen, so the commoners no longer needed the chiefs to intercede with the gods. It was better to stay home and tend your taro patch and fishnets. At least you would eat!

Another factor was the absence of any precedent in Hawaiian society for hiring yourself out for wages. What a strange idea! If you could make a living with your own farming and fishing, why slave for wages?

Unable to hire Hawaiian natives, the plantation owners began importing non-Hawaiian day laborers—one of the many events that led to the Hawaiians' eventually becoming a powerless minority in their own land.

Along the Halemaumau Trail

Trip 25. Sulphur Bank Trail

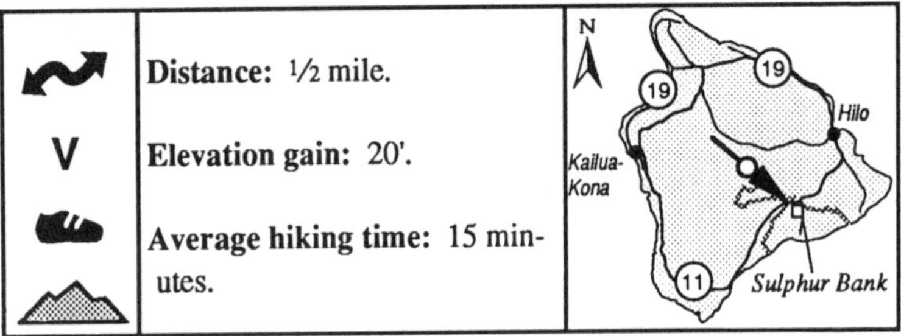

Topos: Optional: *Kilauea* 7½.

Trail map: At the end of Trip 20.

Highlights: Sulphur Bank is set like a little piece of hell in the middle of the cool, green rainforest of Kilauea. Most of Kilauea's steam vents lack the rotten-egg smell of hydrogen sulfide, which is so characteristic of many mainland hot springs. Sulphur Bank makes up for it.

Driving instructions: Follow the driving instructions of Trip 20.

Permit/permission required: None.

Description: From the end of the Kilauea Visitor Center parking lot, you *don't* cross Crater Rim Road. Instead, you pick up a path parallelling the road on the visitor-center side and follow it north-northwest, away from the visitor center and the adjacent art center. You pass *koa* trees and *hapuu* tree ferns. The trail remains fairly level as nearby Crater Rim Road begins to descend; a few roses and blackberries line the road's edge here. The stone Kahua Hula Platform, surrounded by *ti* plants, is on your right.

You very quickly reach an indistinct junction, fortunately marked, where you bear right (north) on the grassy Sulphur Bank Trail. Ginger lines the trail as it begins a gentle descent through *ohia* and *uluhe,* curving left toward the source of a rotten-egg smell. Heaps of yellow- and red-stained earth come into view, and the trees draw back from the sulphurous fumes. The trail hugs a bank of *uluhe* and then meets a spur road. Turn right on the spur road, toward Sulphur Bank, which is at the end of the road. Yellow, white, and greenish deposits, including clusters of yellow sulfur crystals, lie all around you and up on the otherwise-bare soil of the low bank. Pungent steam rises from numerous vents. Small heaps of rocks mark off active vents at the road's edge. One such vent is particularly pungent. It's best to stay off the delicate formations on the bank itself; study them from a distance.

When you're ready, retrace your steps back to Kilauea Visitor Center.

When humorist Mark Twain visited Kilauea. . . . In 1866, when Mark Twain visited Kilauea, the caldera held plenty of lava. Kilauea was putting on quite a show, complete with fountains and rivers of lava. It had been some years since there had been such a lively display in the caldera, so the visitors counted themselves very fortunate. From Volcano House, which was then a modest, thatched building, Twain and his party saw and heard the lava boil, hiss, fountain, and run like glowing creeks. Twain wrote, "The smell of sulphur is strong, but not unpleasant to a sinner."

One night, the group wished to hike across the cooled lava of the caldera in order to stand at the edge of the most active fire-lake. After descending a "crazy, thousand-foot pathway in a crevice fractured in the crater wall," the party found the apparently cooled black crust to be so hot they could not be sure their shoe soles would last long enough to cross it. A man named Marlette, not of Twain's party, believed he knew the caldera well enough to guide them safely across in the dark to a cooler section. And so, with little sense and much daring, they dashed some three hundred yards across the hottest part and reached the cooler part with their soles intact. From there, they began making their way toward the fiery lake by lantern light. Suddenly, Marlette called a halt and announced that they had lost the trail. They were in danger of falling "a thousand feet" through the thin crust! (Twain said he thought eight hundred feet would do for him.) Marlette did break through and fell up to his armpits. In the dim lantern light, they could not distinguish the trail from the rest of the blackened surface. Then Marlette remembered that he could hear and feel the grinding of fine "lava-needles" underfoot except on the trail, where they were worn away. Thus, the party made their way safely across the caldera at last, more or less by ear. They sat down on a great shelf overhanging the lava lake in order to enjoy the hellish spectacle, until a chunk of the shelf broke off and fell into the lake. ". . . that may have been intended for a hint, and may not. We did not wait to see," wrote Twain. They got lost again on the way back and finally reached Volcano House around two in the morning.[1]

[1]From *Roughing It* by Mark Twain (Hartford, Connecticut, American Publishing Company, 1872), excerpted as "A Visit to the Volcano" in *A Hawaiian Reader* (see Bibliography).

Twain doesn't say *exactly* what Marlette fell into up to his armpits. If he had fallen through into molten lava, I think the story would have been very different. My guess is that he broke through the ceiling of a small lava tube, cool and quite empty of fluid lava. His fall was arrested when his feet hit the floor of the tube. You'll probably see many such small tubes on your hikes in the park, their ceilings wholly or partly broken in.

Forbidding landscape of cracked lava

Trip 26. Sulphur Bank-Sandalwood Loop

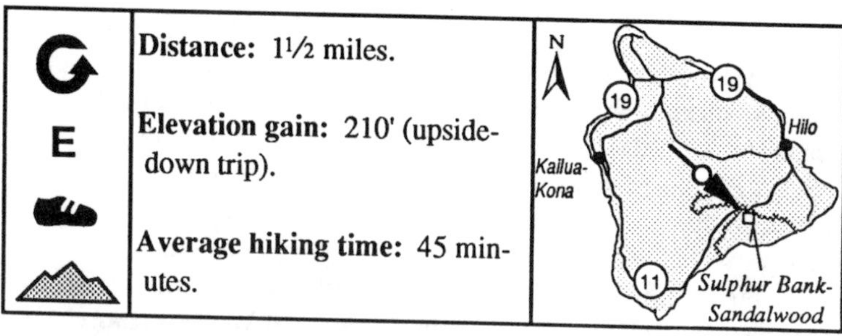

Distance: 1½ miles.

Elevation gain: 210' (upside-down trip).

Average hiking time: 45 minutes.

Topos: Optional: *Kilauea Crater* 7½.

Trail map: At the end of Trip 20.

Highlights: This loop offers an easy walk through some dramatically contrasting landscapes: the evil-smelling, mineral-crusted Sulphur Bank and the green, misty Sandalwood Trail.

Driving instructions: Follow the driving instructions of Trip 20.

Permit/permission required: None.

Description: Follow Trip 25 out to Sulphur Bank. You won't see a concentration of sulfurous fumaroles like this (called "solfataras") anywhere else in the Kilauea area except right around Halemaumau. From Sulphur Bank, go around the roadend's loop and pick up an extension of the Sulphur Bank Trail on the other side of the access road. Vents, some active and some not, spew steam across your route, which is more like an old dirt road than a trail. The amount of sulfurous gases in Hawaiian steam vents is usually negligible. See if your nose can tell you which of these vents, if any, has traces of sulfur compounds. As the vents grow farther apart, *uluhe* and *ohia* crowd in along the trail.

You presently curve away from Sulphur Bank, pass some large steam vents, and meet Crater Rim Road. Cross the road carefully, pick up the trail on the other side, and bear south through a field of bamboo orchids. You soon meet the Crater Rim Trail at its junction with the Sandalwood Trail.

From here, follow Trip 24 down the Sandalwood Trail and back to Kilauea Visitor Center to end a short but satisfying trip.

Volcano spirits. . . . Every visitor to Kilauea, even the most blasé, feels a sense of awe in the presence of the volcano's untamed power and unpredictable nature. Pele seems real here; offerings to her seem not just superstitious gestures.

With the very spirit of the earth itself alive and moving beneath your feet, what other spirits may be abroad in this strange and wonderful place? Volcano House, on the edge of Kilauea caldera, has a rich history. For many years, "Uncle" George Lycurgus operated Volcano House, where he sometimes lived. You'll see his picture around Volcano House. "Uncle" George is gone now—or is he? One person told me "Uncle" George still occupies his old room at Volcano House. At the moment, according to my informant, his old room happened to be our room. Our honeymoon room. With "Uncle" George perhaps still in it. We're glad we didn't see him.

Our friend Dan Masaki says he and his wife, who were born and raised in Hawaii, spent their honeymoon at Volcano House. Mrs. Masaki is very sensitive to spirit influences. As far as *she* was concerned, there were enough spirit goings-on at Volcano House that she couldn't sleep.

You've probably heard that taking rocks from Hawaii Volcanoes National Park brings bad luck. Some say that's mere superstition. Nevertheless, every week, unhappy pilferers return boxes of stolen rocks, praying that their bad luck will stop. What does Mrs. Masaki have to say about removing these rocks? Dan says that on their honeymoon trip, he picked up a crystal on the volcano—"a *crystal*," he emphasizes, "not a *rock*." He said nothing to his wife about it—it was just a *crystal*—and put it in the car's glove compartment. No big deal. A few minutes later, Mrs. Masaki opened the glove compartment and saw it. "She started screaming. She screamed and screamed and didn't stop until I put it back!"

Trip 27. Waldron Ledge Loop

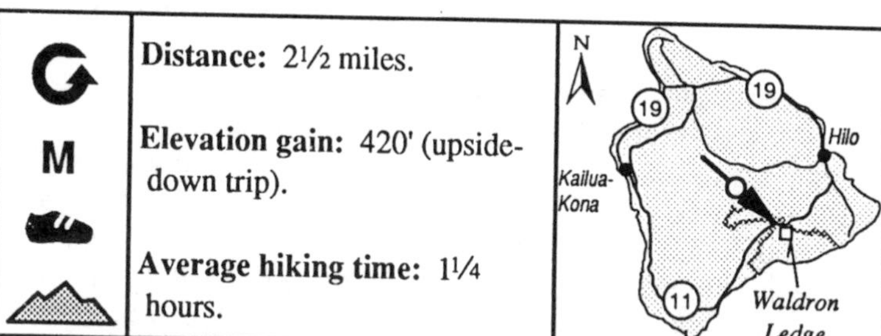

Topos: *Kilauea Crater* 7½.

Trail map: At the end of Trip 20. (Having trouble seeing it on the map? It looks less like a loop and more like a battered parallelogram that angles south-southeast from Kilauea Visitor Center, passes under the words "Waldron Ledge," angles sharply west at a junction with the Kilauea Iki Trail, bumps across a spur trail, and then returns north-northwest on the Byron Ledge and Halemaumau trails.)

Highlights: There are excellent views of Kilauea caldera from Waldron Ledge, as the clifftop on the northeast edge of the caldera is known. That's followed by a visit to the beautiful rainforest on Byron Ledge and along the Halemaumau Trail. This route lets you experience the best part of the Byron Ledge and Halemaumau trails along with one of the most scenic segments of the Crater Rim Trail!

But wait—there's more. This trip is a good choice for those who feel uneasy about walking across the caldera floor—after all, there is molten lava somewhere beneath that floor. The lava theoretically could burst forth at any time.[1] (It's very unlikely.) On the other hand, you don't want to go home and have to admit to your friends and family that you *didn't* walk on the caldera floor. They might ask why.

[1]Kilauea has historically been a fairly well-behaved volcano. Swelling of the mountain and swarms of small earthquakes help identify when and where the lava is moving. Sites all around Kilauea and Mauna Loa are monitored continuously for those symptoms. The scientists at Volcano Observatory use those data to locate potential eruption sites. I'm not saying there's *no* danger, but if no eruption is currently predicted, or if you're well away from the current eruption site, there's not much danger of an unexpected eruption under your feet. On the other hand, the scientists have on occasion been mistaken about where the lava would burst forth; see the end of Trip 28. There are no guarantees.

It could be embarrassing. So try this trip: you zip across barely a hundred yards of black lava floor before you're safely back on good old dirt.

Driving instructions: Follow the driving instructions of Trip 20.

Permit/permission required: None.

Description: From the far end of the Kilauea Visitor Center parking lot, you cross Crater Rim Road to pick up the spur to the Crater Rim Trail. At the first junction, you turn hard left toward Kilauea Iki and Thurston Lava Tube, passing Volcano House on the caldera side and the original site of Volcano Observatory. Interpretive signs, birdlife, yellow ginger, *ohia, uluhe,* and orange montbretia combine with the superb views over Kilauea caldera to fill this stretch with fascination and beauty. The edge of the caldera seems to slump away from you in narrow steps; thank goodness for the stone wall that keeps you safely up on the rim here.

Wire fencing soon replaces the stone wall as your trail curves left. After a short descent past a viewing shelter, the path curves left again, away from the caldera. You ascend to meet a disused road, and you turn right (southeast) onto it. This is an old segment of the Crater Rim Road, abandoned when cracks appeared in it. As you see, *uluhe* is gobbling up the old road fast! The path is soon restricted between wire fences. Where another old road comes in on your left (not shown on the map), you continue ahead, around the caldera. An old interpretive sign tells you you're on Waldron Ledge. An old automobile turnout arcs away on your right and will rejoin this old road soon. You can follow either route; if you take the old turnout or, rather, the path paralleling it, your way is presently interrupted by a fence that forces you to circumvent a section that's collapsed. Your attention is divided by watching out for holes in the pavement—they're why this is no longer part of Crater Rim Road—and enjoying the outstanding views over the caldera. Below, the Halemaumau Trail seems hardly more than a scratch stretching west-southwest across the caldera floor. A very short, faint scratch connects the Halemaumau Trail with Byron Ledge; this is the segment you'll follow across the caldera floor.

The fence guides you back to the old turnout, where you pass some big cracks. You meet the old Crater Rim Road again, but another fence soon directs you away from a destroyed road segment and briefly onto a forested path. You emerge from the forest, cross the old road, and pick up the next part of the Crater Rim Trail on the caldera's edge. Views here include Byron Ledge far below and, across

Car camping at Punaluu

Heiau at Puuhonua o Honaunau (see Trip 53)

New life on recent lava flow: ohia beside Naulu Trail

In Lava Trees State Monument (see Trip 19)

Petroglyphs at Puu Loa (see Trip 36)

Banyan-draped stairway at Rainbow Falls (see Trip 14)

Large fishpond at Kalahuipuaa (see Trip 55)

High Priest's hut at Mookini Heiau (see Trip 59)

Coconut Island at Queen Liliuokalani Gardens (see Trip 17)

Lava Dome on Mauna Iki Trail (see Trip 42)

Polulu Valley beach (see Trip 60)

In Wailoa River State Park (see Trip 15)

Kilauea Iki, the towering cinder cone of Puu Puai, built by the spectacular fire fountains of the 1959 eruption.

Now you descend to a junction with the Kilauea Iki Trails. Turn hard right (west-northwest) toward Kilauea Iki and Byron Ledge. You descend moderately to steeply on switchbacks, climb a little around some boulders, and then stroll through *amau, hapuu, uluhe, ohia,* yellow ginger, a tall white-flowered Japanese anemone, and a branched moss called lycopodium. Look for the red flash of *iiwi* and *apapane* here, and listen for the *iiwi*'s characteristic "rusty-hinge" call. You presently reach a junction; go right toward the Byron Ledge Trail. Climbing a little, you very soon reach that trail. Turn right onto it. In a few more steps, there's a bench set amid *ohia* and *pukiawe* offering views of Kilauea caldera and the distant observatory.

Now you begin descending to the caldera floor moderately to steeply on stony, weedy switchbacks. At the bottom of these switchbacks, a line of cairns directs you some 100 yards across the caldera floor to a junction with the Halemaumau Trail. You take a deep breath, march bravely across the caldera, and turn right (uphill) at the junction.

Follow the Halemaumau Trail uphill into the rainforest for a delightful climb back up the caldera walls as described in Trip 21 (but in reverse). Don't miss the opportunity to take the spur trail to the viewing shelter for a rest as well as some birding. At the junction with the Sandalwood Trail, where there's a nice bench, you bear right toward Kilauea Visitor Center. The going becomes a little steeper but soon levels out.

Faster than you'd think possible, you're at the junction of the Halemaumau and Crater Rim trails. Turn right here and then left onto the spur back to Crater Rim Road and Kilauea Visitor Center.

Where did Pele come from?... According to W. D. Westervelt's retelling of Hawaiian myths, most stories of Pele's origin say she came from a distant land, like the Polynesians themselves. Although she lived there happily with her parents and many brothers and sisters, she longed to travel. At last, her wanderlust drove her to ask her parents to let her leave. One of her brothers, who was a sea god, built a canoe with a sail for her. Her parents asked her to take along her little sister Hiiaka, who slept unborn in an egg. Pele tucked the egg carefully in her skirt, close to her body, to keep it warm.

Then she began her long voyage, carried in her canoe by her relatives The Whirlwind, The Strong Current, and The Moving Seas. After visiting many mysterious islands, she came at last to

Niihau, the northwesternmost of the major Hawaiian islands. From Niihau, she sent the boat back to her brother. It's said that eventually all of her brothers and sisters migrated to the Hawaiian Islands in this boat. In the meantime, the egg hatched and beautiful little Hiiaka was born.

Pele carried a magic stick with which she dug for the fire she needed to build a home. Taking Hiiaka with her, she went from one Hawaiian island to the next, searching for fire. On most of the islands, the pits she dug quickly filled with water, denying her a home. After many adventures, including her consuming passion for and pursuit of the handsome Kauai chief Lohiau, she reached the Big Island. She was looking forward to seeing Kilauea.

But Pele was not the first volcano deity to live on the Big Island. Before Pele came, Kilauea was home to the god Ai-Lauu, the insatiable forest-eater, who had devoured Hawaii's forests with fire again and again. Pele planned to move into Kilauea and make her home with Ai-Lauu. But when Ai-Lauu saw Pele coming to Kilauea, he was overcome by fear of her greater powers. He fled, never to return.

Pele found Kilauea to be everything she had wanted in a home. She dug up Ai-Lauu's house, built herself a new one, and moved into Kilauea. In myth, Pele sometimes traveled around the archipelago or lived in Mokuaweoweo, the great caldera at the summit of Mauna Loa. But wherever she may once have come from, her wanderlust is gone now. Her long journeys to distant lands are over, her sisters and brothers have joined her here, and they are at home in Hawaii, never to leave.

Trip 28. Kilauea Iki

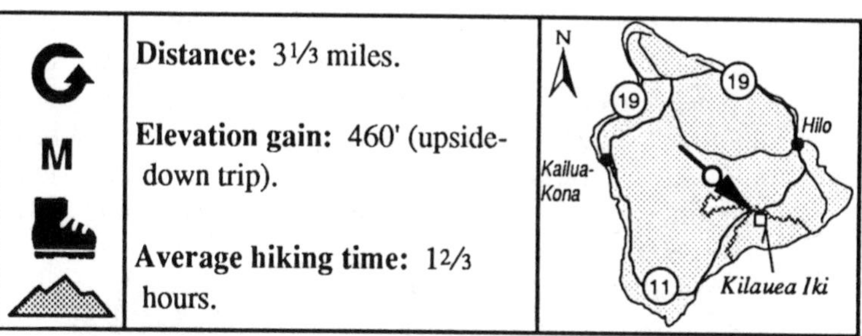

Topos: *Kilauea Crater, Volcano 7½.*

Trail map: At the end of Trip 20.

Highlights: What does this trip offer you? Fabulous rainforest and crater scenery; a thrilling walk across a crater floor; and a visit to the site from which spewed the highest and hottest lava fountain ever recorded in Hawaiian history. If you have time for only one hike in Hawaii Volcanoes National Park, this should be it. Perhaps the biggest challenge on this hike is keeping yourself moving, because every few steps will reveal yet another viewpoint where you just *have* to stop and take one more picture

Driving instructions: Follow the driving instructions of Trip 20 but instead of turning right to go to Kilauea Visitor Center, turn left and follow Crater Rim Road downhill through a lush, fern-and-*ohia* rainforest. You soon make a mandatory left turn and continue downhill to Kilauea Iki Overlook, a little less than 1½ miles from Kilauea Visitor Center and 29½ miles from Hilo. Park here to begin your hike. (I prefer to start here rather than at Thurston Lava Tube because the parking lot for the latter is often jammed with cars and buses by midday.)

Permit/permission required: None.

Description: Pause to take in the spectacle of Kilauea Iki pit crater from the overlook, which is on the east end of the crater. The rainforest trees line the rim thickly. Far below, the trail on the crater floor stretches away from you, seeming little more than a scratch on the floor's blackness. Near its west end is the great reddish cinder cone of Puu Puai. The crater is on two levels—the main, lower level below you here on the east and a slightly higher bay on the west end. Byron Ledge rises at the west end of the crater, separating it from Kilauea caldera. If the weather permits, you can see across Kilauea caldera and beyond Kilauea to the gently sloping mass of Mauna Loa. This trip stays on the crater rim for a while, then descend into the crater at the west end, via Byron Ledge.

Bear to your right as you face the crater and pick up the Crater Rim Trail at the end of the overlook area. It's paved at first. You descend a.couple of steep staircases, leave the paving behind, and settle down for a delicious ramble along the crater's edge in the birdsong-filled rainforest. Crater views soon open up, and you ascend a little. Spur trails tempt you nearer the crater's rim for even better views, but you continue ahead on the Crater Rim Trail, descending a little and then leveling out again.

At a magnificent viewpoint, you reach a fork. Take the left fork here toward Byron Ledge and Kilauea Iki (the right fork is the continuation of the Crater Rim Trail and will take you to Volcano House and Kilauea Visitor Center). You descend moderately through the forest, where *apapane* flit through the *ohia* crowns. You pass a dilapidated bench and begin switchbacking moderately to steeply down a black basalt cliff clothed in rainforest plants. The footing is loose, and you will want to watch your step here. Now you dip and then climb a little to circumvent a rockfall.

The descent eases, and you stroll through a delightful forest of ferns and *ohia*. At the next fork, you bear left (southwest) on the Kilauea Iki Trail (right goes to the Byron Ledge Trail). Ginger, lycopodium, bamboo orchid, and *uluhe* dominate the understory here along with Japanese anemone. The forest becomes drier as you approach another dilapidated bench. A spur trail takes off to the right here for the Byron Ledge Trail (the sign is hidden in the weeds just uphill of this junction), but you continue ahead on the Kilauea Iki Trail.

Soon you're cautiously descending weedy, rocky switchbacks down into the west end of Kilauea Iki. The going is very steep in places, and it's a good thing the trail has been constructed in stairsteps at these spots. At the bottom, cairns beckon you to begin picking your way eastward across the forbidding crater floor. You can see from here what is not apparent from above: the floor is not flat at all but has been heaved, buckled, and warped into a heap of great, shiny black slabs that lie jumbled against one another at shallow angles. *Amau* ferns, *ohelo* bushes, and *ohia* sprouts have ventured to colonize this alien landscape. You descend the rumpled edge of the lava flow and follow the cairns past pressure ridges of *pahoehoe,* some smooth-surfaced and others pulled out like taffy. Sometimes you must find your way over piles of rough *aa*, dull-colored at a distance but on closer examination brushed with pinks, soft oranges, lavenders, and golds and whitened by lichens.

You climb the orange-tinged *pahoehoe* mound that separates this higher bay at Kilauea Iki's west end from the rest of the crater floor. Steam curls from cracks in the *pahoehoe* on your left, and Puu Puai's vent gapes red on your right. In 1959, lava fountained from this vent to a record height of 1900 feet. An interpretive sign stops you near the vent, where broken red rock cascades into it. It's unsafe to go any closer, so you curve left, away from the vent, and descend to the lower, eastern part of the crater floor.

Here, the floor seems to be made up of of huge, fuming *pahoehoe* blisters, gray on the surface but often brick-red, orange, gold, and white at their broken edges. The going is rather easy now, and you're soon at the eastern end of the crater. You climb a bit to reach the forested edge above the crater floor and pick up the trail in the forest—no more cairns. Your switchbacking, forested ascent is—thank goodness—more gradual here on the eastern side of the crater than was your descent on the western side. Some of the plants along this section are labeled, adding further interest to your trip. A bench partway up offers a welcome rest stop.

You emerge through ferns to find yourself—*cough!*—engulfed by auto-exhaust fumes at the Kilauea Iki-Thurston Lava Tube parking lot. You turn left onto the paved Crater Rim Trail and scurry away from the parking lot as fast as you can. Now you ascend briefly and then descend gently past some terrific viewpoints to close your loop at Kilauea Iki Overlook.

The 1959 eruption. . . . Kilauea Iki had been inactive since 1868. When scientists at the Hawaiian Volcano Observatory detected swarms of earthquakes and a general swelling of Kilauea in late September of 1959, they suspected an eruption was imminent and that it would begin at Halemaumau. The number of earthquakes recorded daily rose; the amount of fume in Halemaumau increased.

On November 14, 1959, about 2200 earthquakes shook the volcano. The eruption would happen at any minute; scientists still expected it to be at Halemaumau. The harmonic tremor characteristic of the actual eruption appeared on the seismographs at 8:00 P.M. At 8:08 P.M. the lava burst forth—through the southwest wall of Kilauea Iki. The initial eruption must have been spectacular: it quickly grew to a line of fountains halfway between the crater floor and its rim, almost ⅔ mile long, spewing "golden cascades of lava," according to *Volcanoes in the Sea.* Fountaining was intermittent and finally focused on a single fountain. The episode that included the record-setting fountaining began on the night of November 25–26. By December of 1959, it was all over.

The eruption added 377 feet of new lava to Kilauea Iki's floor, which is probably why Puu Puai's vent is now at "floor level" instead of on the wall, where the eruptions began. As late as 1982, the remaining molten lava core in Kilauea Iki was still 16 feet thick. Don't think about that as you cross Kilauea Iki's floor.

Author in Kilauea Iki crater

Trip 29. Thurston Lava Tube

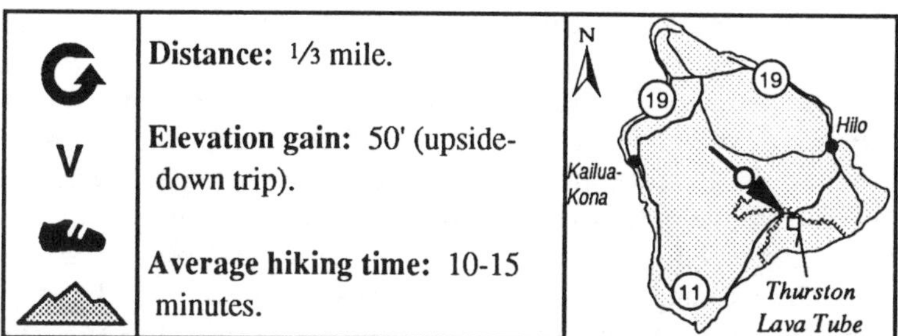

Topos: Optional: *Volcano* 7½.

Trail map: At the end of Trip 20.

Highlights: This mini-adventure through a huge lava tube and its surrounding rainforest is both pretty and geologically interesting. Better still, it's not much longer than its name.

Driving instructions: Follow the driving instructions of Trip 20 but instead of turning right to go to Kilauea Visitor Center, turn left and follow Crater Rim Road downhill through the rainforest. You soon make a mandatory left turn and continue downhill past Kilauea Iki Overlook to the Thurston Lava Tube parking lot, 2 miles from Kilauea Visitor Center and 30 miles from Hilo. Park here to begin your hike. An early start is best: Thurston Lava Tube is a very popular spot, and the lot is often full of cars and tour buses by midday.

Permit/permission required: None.

Description: The hike begins on the east side of the parking lot, away from Kilauea Iki. From the interpretive signs, you turn right as directed by the trail signs, climb a little to a walkway, and then descend moderately to steeply on the walkway to the lava tube. You cross a bridge just as you enter the mouth of the tube. Now you proceed across the tube's nearly level floor. Lights in the interior allow you to see how the lava left a sort of crude but rather smooth plastering on the tube's bumpy walls. Roots from trees growing far above dangle down through the ceiling, and water drips through hundreds of tiny cracks.

In a few minutes, you exit the tube at a stairway. If you look to your left as you leave the tube, you can see the remainder of the tube diving down into the darkness. You, however, ascend the stairway, pick up another walkway, and follow it back to your start. (The spur walkway on your right along this return segment leads to the restrooms, while you'll find a drinking fountain back at the trailhead.)

What is Thurston Lava Tube? .... It's a very large lava tube! The information at the end of Trip 7 explained how lava tubes form.

At Kaumana Caves, the destination of Trip 7, you visit a lava tube whose ceiling has fallen in at one place. There, you descend a "trail" to see the tube's halves leading off in opposite directions, but you don't actually walk *through* the tube. (You can walk a few steps into either half if you dare.) At Thurston Lava Tube, you visit a lava tube whose ceiling has caved in at two places. The trail at Thurston Lava Tube lets you enter the tube through one cave-in, walk through a short segment of the tube between the two cave-ins, and exit through the other cave-in.

Thurston Lava Tube once drained one of the Twin Craters, two small pit craters nearby (but hidden in the dense rainforest). These craters lie on Kilauea's east rift zone, along which lie most of the pit craters you will see along the Chain of Craters Road.

Finding lava tubes is not an exact science. Ceiling cave-ins seem to be one of the principal ways lava tubes are found, and they must be one of the most painful ways to find them. *Volcanoes in the Sea* tells of a bulldozer clearing land on the slopes of Kilauea. It broke through the ceiling of a lava tube and fell more than 30 feet. The book does not say what became of the bulldozer and its operator—but it's not hard to guess.

Trip 30. From Puu Puai Down the Devastation Trail

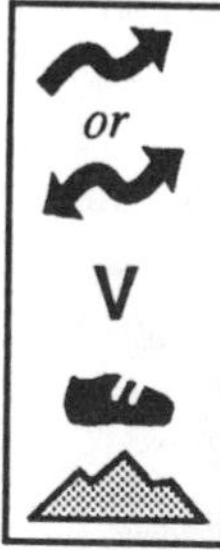

Distance: ½ to just under 1 mile (shuttle vs. out-and-back).
Elevation gain: 43' (upside-down trip—out-and-back only).
Average hiking time: 15-30 minutes.

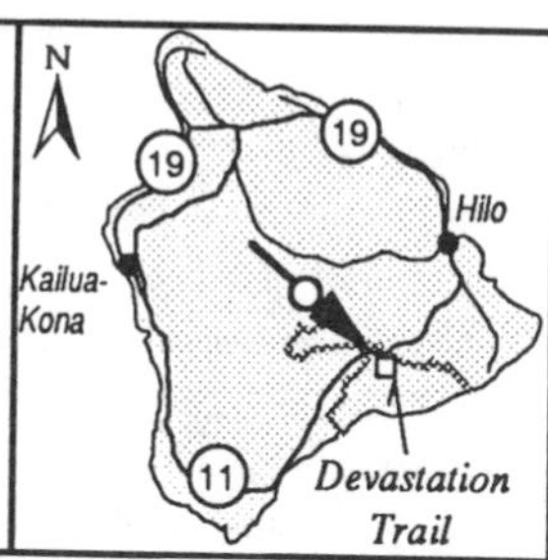

Topos: Optional: *Kilauea Crater* 7½.

Trail map: At the end of Trip 20.

Highlights: The 1959 eruption in Kilauea Iki that built Puu Puai with lava fountains up to 1900 feet high devastated the area south-southwest of Puu Puai. Since then, that area has been left to regenerate on its own—a sort of experiment. Hikers passing through the area on the famous Devastation Trail have been an ingredient in the experiment, too, but they are kept to a boardwalk in order to keep from trampling the new plants. You've probably seen photos of the Devastation Trail that make the area look as if it were nothing but a carpet of naked cinders with the bleached bones of dead trees poking through it. Now, most of the area is covered with new growth, but there's still a bare patch for you to photograph.

Driving instructions: Follow the driving instructions of Trip 20 but instead of turning right to go to Kilauea Visitor Center, turn left and follow Crater Rim Road downhill. You soon make a mandatory left turn and continue downhill past Kilauea Iki Overlook and the Thurston Lava Tube parking lot. Turn right at the sign for Puu Puai and follow this side road uphill to the Puu Puai parking lot, just over 3 miles from Kilauea Visitor Center and 31 miles from Hilo. Park here next to Puu Puai to begin your hike.

Or, to make a shuttle of this hike, have your shuttle driver drop you off at Puu Puai as described above and pick you up at the lower end of the Devastation Trail. The driver gets to the lower end of the Devastation Trail by returning to Crater Rim Road, turning right (away from Kilauea Visitor Center), going ⅓ mile more down Crater

Rim Road, and turning right into the Devastation Trail parking lot (opposite the junction with the Chain of Craters Road).

Permit/permission required: None.

Description: Walk across the parking lot toward the bare hump of Puu Puai to a superb viewpoint high on Kilauea Iki's south rim. (If you go no farther than this, it's still worthwhile!) Now backtrack a little to pick up the boardwalk of the Devastation Trail. On the boardwalk, you pass through a seemingly unscathed *ohia* forest and then abruptly enter a world of cinders. Where all was death and destruction over 30 years ago, a new forest now grows, and the dead-white remains of the old one lie on the ground, furred with moss. Descending gently, you pass through the still-bare area. It is distressing to see that aliens like blackberry and a red-and-pink ground cover have established themselves so firmly.

Soon you re-enter the new forest and reach the lower parking lot for the Devastation Trail. Here, you see a bit of the old Crater Rim Road leading off toward Byron Ledge. Retrace your steps from here or meet your shuttle ride here.

Or, if you're feeling sprightly, turn hard right onto that bit of old road and ramble down to Byron Ledge and back as described below (the mileage and elevation gain for this addition are not included in the icon box above).

Spur to Byron Ledge. . . . This spur adds just under 1¼ miles and 90 feet of elevation gain to your trip. Reverse the directions given at the end of Trip 23 and then retrace your steps all the way back to the parking lot at Puu Puai. Today, a stretch along this spur looks more devastated than does the Devastation Trail.

The Devastation Trail

Trip 31. Crater Rim Road to Halemaumau Overlook

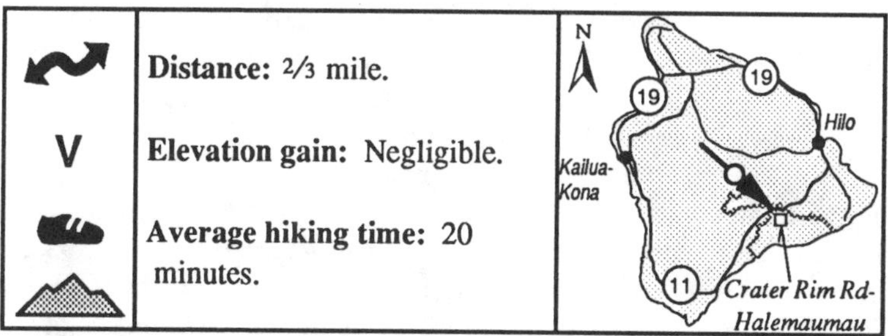

Topos: Optional: *Kilauea Crater* 7½.

Trail map: At the end of Trip 20.

Highlights: This is surely the easiest (but least interesting) way to approach Halemaumau and to get a look into its steaming depths. It's so short that where you find a parking spot in the huge parking lot can make a noticeable difference in the distance you walk.

Driving instructions: Follow the driving instructions of Trip 20 but instead of turning right to go to Kilauea Visitor Center, turn left and follow Crater Rim Road downhill, soon making a mandatory left turn. You continue downhill past Kilauea Iki Overlook, Thurston Lava Tube, the Puu Puai turnoff (to the upper end of the Devastation Trail), and the Devastation Trail parking lot (at the lower end of the Devastation Trail). At the junction with the Chain of Craters Road (opposite the Devastation Trail parking lot), you continue ahead on Crater Rim Road instead of turning left onto the Chain of Craters Road. There's a huge parking lot for Halemaumau Crater on the north side of Crater Rim Road 5⅓ miles from Kilauea Visitor Center and 33⅓ miles from Hilo. Park here to start your hike.

Permit/permission required: None.

Description: From the parking lot, you head generally north through the rubble of the 1924 steam eruption (more on that below) along a path marked by wire strung between wooden posts. You pass through an area stained with sulfur deposits, where steam oozes from dozens of little vents. The route is fairly level until you turn left and climb ever so slightly to a fenced overlook with an interpretive sign. Offerings to Pele—oranges, apples, grapes, pears, leis, bottles of gin, bouquets of flowers—lie on an altar-like boulder beyond the fence.

Please treat this site, and these offerings, with respect. Far below, Halemaumau huffs and puffs steam plumes through its sulfur-splashed, reddish walls and lava floor, while white-tailed tropicbirds soar through the hot mist.

After taking in this spectacle, retrace your steps to your car.

Halemaumau and its lava lake. . . . As *Volcanoes in the Sea* relates, Europeans first saw Kilauea caldera and Halemaumau crater in 1823. The Rev. William Ellis was the first such visitor to leave a record of what he saw. And what a sight it was! Throughout most of the nineteenth century and well into the twentieth century, parts of Kilauea caldera, particularly Halemaumau, were continuously filled with red-hot lava—fiery lakes on which floated black "islands" of cooled crust. Ellis did not see Halemaumau on that trip; Halemaumau apparently formed sometime around 1838. It was to such a lava lake that Mark Twain and his companions hiked one night in 1866 (see Trip 25). The level of the lakes fluctuated, but if they disappeared, it was only for a few days or weeks.

A lull between 1894 and 1907 was the first real interruption in Kilauea's activity. The volcano was active again almost continuously from 1907 to 1924. Molten lava overflowed Halemaumau's brim in 1919 and again in 1921.

In 1924, the Halemaumau lake was at a high level and very active. Then, in March, the lake's level dropped hundreds of feet. Swarms of earthquakes occurred on Kilauea's east rift zone in April, and cracks opened. One of them was big enough for a cow to fall into; then the crack closed, crushing the poor creature. The lava lake in Halemaumau continued to drop. Small steam explosions began in Halemaumau in May. It was the beginning of a series of increasingly violent steam explosions that climaxed on May 18 in—

> Great boiling cauliflower-like clouds of dust [that] rose 6.5 kilometers [over 4 miles] above the crater. Spectacular lightning bolts flashed through the cloud. . . . Blocks of rock weighing several tons were thrown as far as nearly a kilometer [0.62 mile] from the crater.

This explosion is the only one known to have caused a human fatality in historic times. A man determined to photograph the crater between explosions was caught by the falling debris from one of them. He had been warned that another explosion was imminent but went too close anyway. Ash burnt him, a falling block severed one leg, and he died on the way to the hospital. You walked through the debris of those explosions on your way to Halemaumau's rim.

Lava lakes have rarely been seen in Kilauea and Halemaumau since then. In fact, there was no eruption at all between 1934 and 1952. During that period, some said the volcano was dead. Volcanologists knew otherwise. They monitored earthquakes and the mountain's swelling in 1944, 1950, and 1951. The 1952–1953 eruption was the first of many recent Kilauea eruptions. The current eruption, which began in 1983, is the longest continuous eruption of Kilauea on record. Most of the activity, however, has been on the rift zones rather than in the caldera. When Mauna Loa erupted in 1984, it was the first time since 1919 that both volcanoes had been in eruption at the same time.

Curiously, traditional Hawaiian stories do not include records of eruptions, and eruptions rarely figure in Hawaiian legends. Some people think this means that the volcanoes were inactive in the long centuries between the Polynesians' and the Europeans' arrivals. However, as *Volcanoes in the Sea* observes,

> . . . [I]t seems too great a coincidence that activity should happen to resume just at the time of arrival of literate persons capable of keeping a record of events. More probably the Hawaiians took natural events such as volcanic eruptions very much as a matter of course, the more so as eruptions almost never took human lives and most of the property destroyed was of little permanent value. A grass house was easily replaced, and there was plenty of arable land for the relatively small population. Only rarely did an eruption make a sufficient impression on the people to find its way into tradition.

Trip 32. Napau Crater Trail to Puu Huluhulu

32 (Puu Huluhulu)

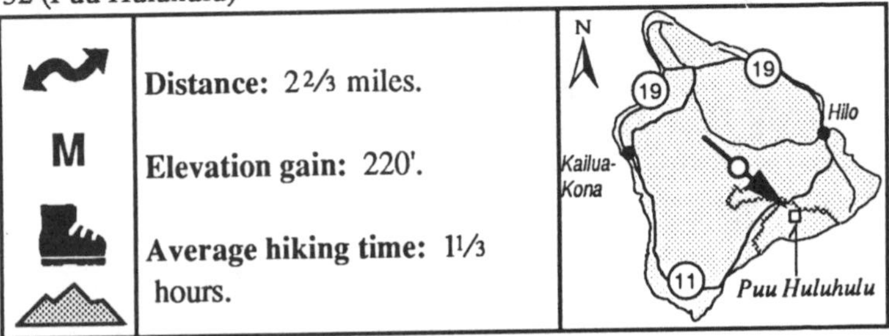

Topos: *Makaopuhi Crater, Volcano 7½.*

Trail map: At the end of this trip.

Highlights: This moderate jaunt takes you past lava trees and up a rainforest-clad cinder cone, Puu Huluhulu. At its top, there's an outstanding viewpoint over the eerie remains of the landscape ravaged during the 1969–1974 eruption. You can see Mauna Ulu (a small shield volcano built on Kilauea's east rift by that eruption) as well as the landscape the eruption spared.

Driving instructions: Follow the driving instructions of Trip 20 but instead of turning right to go to Kilauea Visitor Center, turn left and follow Crater Rim Road downhill, soon making a mandatory left turn. You continue downhill past Kilauea Iki Overlook, Thurston Lava Tube, the Puu Puai turnoff, and the Devastation Trail parking lot. At the junction with the Chain of Craters Road (opposite the Devastation Trail parking lot), turn left onto the Chain of Craters Road. Follow the Chain of Craters Road downhill past the turnoff for Hilina Pali Road to the turnoff for Mauna Ulu (7 miles from Kilauea Visitor Center). Turn left toward Mauna Ulu and follow this spur road ½ mile to the loop at its eastern extreme. Go around the loop to the parking area, 7½ miles from Kilauea Visitor Center and 35½ miles from Hilo. Park here to start your hike.

Permit/permission required: None.

Description: Your hike begins as you walk eastward on a stub of road, probably a remnant of the pre-1969 Chain of Craters Road. In a few steps, your route turns abruptly left (north) past some information signs. You follow cairns over black lava and presently curve through a remnant of forest. Soon you're on lava again. Looking around, you'll see "lava trees" as described in Trip 19. Some of them are bent over, twisted and warped, probably reflecting the violence done to the tree by the advancing lava that encased it.

Near the ⅔-mile point, you curve south below a well-vegetated hill, "very hairy" (*huluhulu*) by comparison to the bare, shiny *pahoehoe* around you. As you've probably guessed, this *huluhulu* hill is Puu Huluhulu. You turn left (east-northeast) on a spur trail and zigzag up to the top. There's a little observation platform at the top that offers great views of the fern-filled crater of Puu Huluhulu and the rainforest beyond it to the north. To the south and east, you'll see the smoking hulk of Mauna Ulu and the slag-heap of a landscape left by the 1969–1974 eruption. Even farther to the east, you may be able to make out the remaining rainforest and the steaming cone of Puu Oo. Puu Oo was built at the center of activity early in the current eruption, which began in 1983. (Since then, the center has moved farther east along Kilauea's east rift zone.)

When you're ready, retrace your steps to your car.

Pele's hair. . . . It's one of the contradictions of volcanism that all that untameable violence can produce some of Nature's most delicate structures. Perhaps you'll see them on the way to Puu Huluhulu: fine, shiny, golden threads called "Pele's hair." Pele's hair forms when lava is blown into the air and solidifies in midair in glassy drops called "Pele's tears." These glassy drops often draw out behind them viscous filaments of lava that also freeze in midair. They become Pele's hair. *Volcanoes in the Sea* reports that filaments of Pele's hair may be over three feet long and may drift on the wind for many miles. You will often find Pele's hair collected in sheltered locations downwind from recent eruptions. There's a surprising amount of it in the Kau Desert to the west and here in a few places along the Napau Crater Trail. Sometimes Pele's hair collects in the hollows on the irregular surface of a cooled lava flow. Another place Pele's hair may collect is between *pahoehoe* layers. *Pahoehoe*'s outer crust sometimes consists of layers separated by hollows, almost like layers in a giant puff pastry. Strands of Pele's hair from a later eruption, settling to earth at last, can collect between the layers when they are exposed. See if you can spot Pele's hair trapped like that along the Napau Crater and Naulu trails.

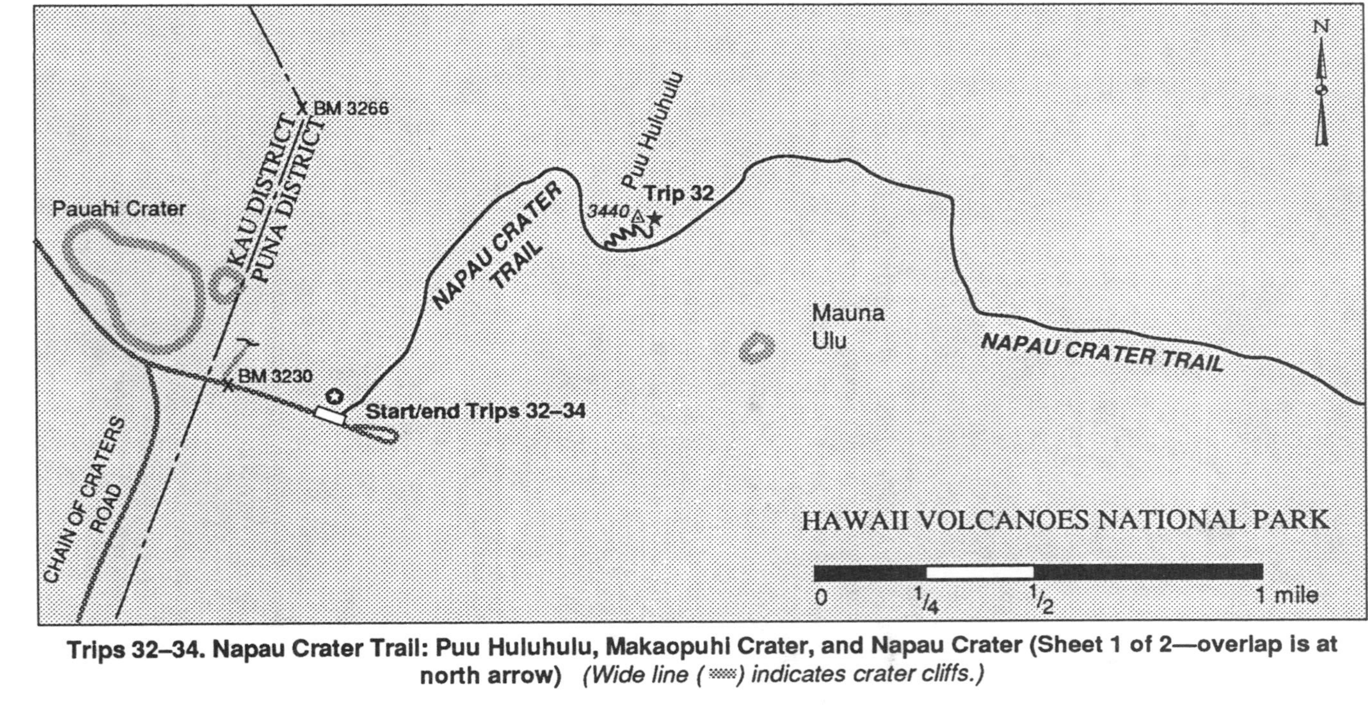

Trips 32–34. Napau Crater Trail: Puu Huluhulu, Makaopuhi Crater, and Napau Crater (Sheet 1 of 2—overlap is at north arrow) *(Wide line (▒) indicates crater cliffs.)*

Continued on Sheet 2 of 2

Continued from Sheet 1 of 2

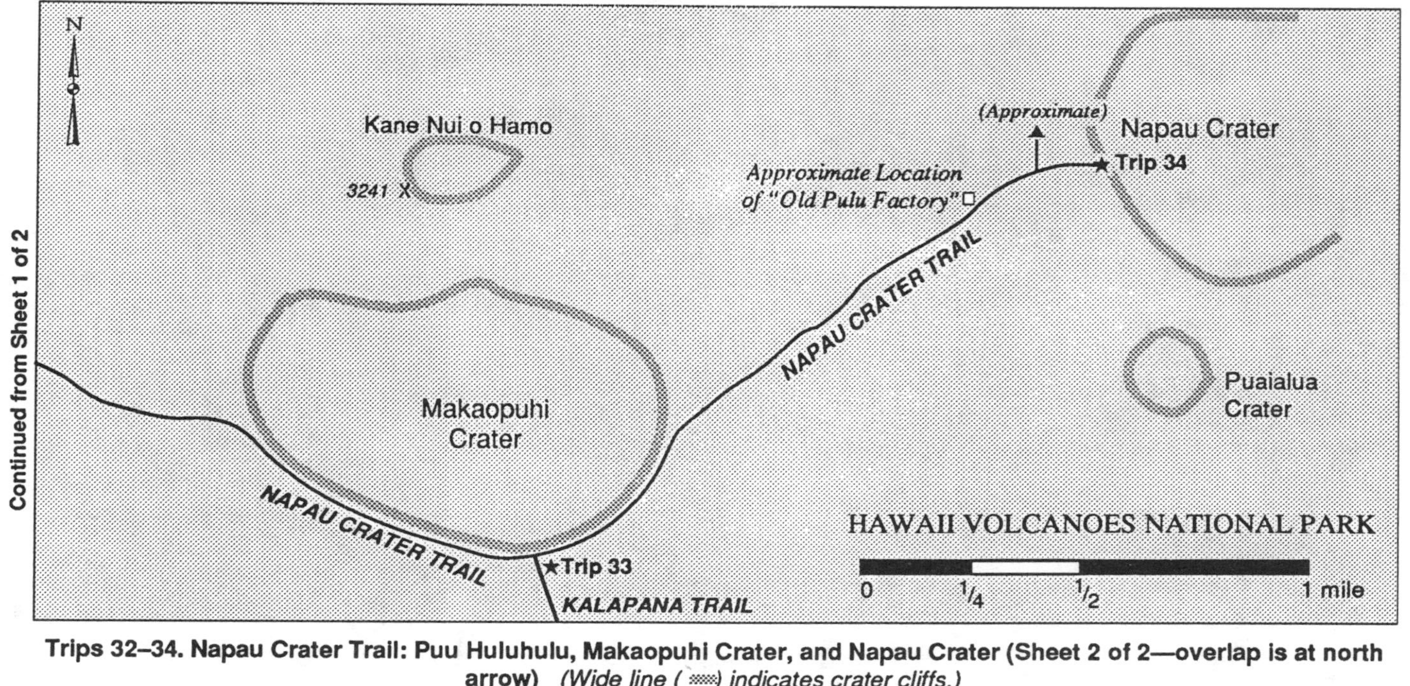

Trips 32–34. Napau Crater Trail: Puu Huluhulu, Makaopuhi Crater, and Napau Crater (Sheet 2 of 2—overlap is at north arrow) *(Wide line (▒) indicates crater cliffs.)*

Trip 33. Napau Crater Trail to Makaopuhi Crater

Distance: Just over 9 miles.

Elevation gain: 950' (includes spur up Puu Huluhulu).

Average hiking time: 4 2/3 hours.

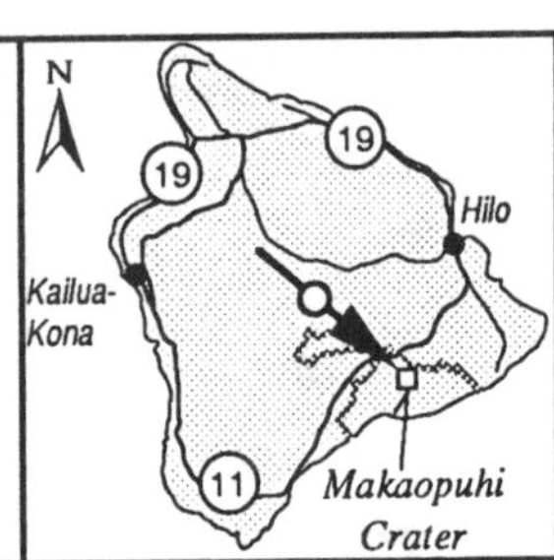

Topos: *Makaopuhi Crater, Volcano* 7½.

Trail map: At the end of Trip 32.

Highlights: Before the 1969–1974 eruption of Kilauea, the Chain of Craters Road swung east from Pauahi Crater as far as Makaopuhi Crater. That eruption not only obliterated that part of the road but also built a new shield volcano, Mauna Ulu; filled in Aloi and Alae craters, which had been attractions along that road segment; and sent lava cascading into huge Makaopuhi Crater. Fortunately, it did not succeed in obliterating Makaopuhi Crater as it did Aloi and Alae. Instead, it left a sort of dividing line through Makaopuhi Crater: the western part is in the lava-plastered landscape left by the eruption, while the eastern part blends into the old rainforest. You must walk to Makaopuhi now to enjoy these contrasts, and on the way, you have an close-up look at Mauna Ulu—maybe too close for comfort!

Driving instructions: Follow the driving instructions of Trip 32.

Permit/permission required: None.

Description: Follow Trip 32 to Puu Huluhulu. Be sure to take the time to enjoy the view from Puu Huluhulu!

Back at the bottom of Puu Huluhulu, you follow cairns northeast across the sloppy cake-batter landscape between Puu Huluhulu and the still-steaming hulk of Mauna Ulu. You make a long arc around the north side of Mauna Ulu and ascend a smaller hill that's full of steam vents. The *pahoehoe* lava is mostly gray-black, but here and there you'll find rainbow reflections and touches of browns and oranges. Golden-brown, glassy threads of Pele's hair have collected in some of the lava folds. Lava lies frozen around you in collapsed tubes, in sagging hills of dough, in draperies, ropes, and ribbons, and in plastered-on hunks like badly applied frosting.

(When this book gets to the excruciatingly long trips up Mauna Loa from its Kilauea side, I'm going to tell you to think twice before knocking yourself out to see the barren, sometimes-iridescent lava landscapes of Mauna Loa. I'm going to tell you that you can see plenty of barren, iridescent lava by dayhiking on Kilauea's slopes—or just by driving down the Chain of Craters Road. *This* hike is foremost in my mind when I utter those heretical thoughts.)

At last, you approach the edge of Makaopuhi Crater, skirt it, and get some good views down into its huge, partly scrub-covered floor. Makaopuhi Crater is the largest pit crater on Kilauea's east rift zone. Just as you seem fated to plunge into a terrible *aa* field, you veer off into—the rainforest! You cross a little more *pahoehoe* and are then in dense rainforest. *Ohia,* tree-size *aalii,* cayenne vervain, *uluhe, uki, pukiawe, hapuu, ohelo,* lycopodium, and grasses rise around you and entangle your feet. The growth is so dense you can't see into Makaopuhi Crater even though you're on its south rim. What a contrast it is to the bleak, stony acres around Mauna Ulu!

Soon you're at the junction with the Kalapana Trail. This is a good place to stop for a snack before you turn around and retrace your steps to your car.

Seeing the current eruption. . . . In June of 1991, we hiked over masses of brand-new Pele's hair in drifts so deep they hid the contours of the *pahoehoe* below them. (See Trip 32 for more on Pele's hair.) We were on our way to see the lava of the current eruption enter the sea, and we had almost reached that area. A volunteer ranger told us as we stepped carefully through the spun glass that only yesterday it had not been there. She directed us to an excellent, safe, upwind perch from which we watched as the wind occasionally blew the obscuring steam clouds away. When it did, we could see the glowing red lava oozing into the ocean from a tube, sometimes exploding into fine fragments from which came both the black-glass sand that was accumulating on beaches like Kamoamoa and the golden threads that we had just hiked over.

The eruption as we saw it was not a big show like the ones you see on the videotape at Kilauea Visitor Center. The ranger explained to us that we needed to spend some time watching *this* encounter of fire and water in order to get the most out of our visit. She was right. We sat there for over an hour, entranced; it seemed mere minutes.

We met other people who had also made the rather difficult 3-mile round-trip hike out there but who had stayed only a few minutes, or who had stood downwind and were unable to see through the steam, and who had left disappointed.

It really pays to get the latest information on where and how to see the current eruption from the authorities. The "show" conditions can change from day to day. The number for the latest recorded message on eruption activity is 808-967-7977. When you get to the area, ask the personnel on duty at the site about the best and safest vantage points. You want to both enjoy the show *and* get home safely with your memories and photos.

Fragile lava shapes on Napau Crater Trail

Trip 34. Napau Crater Trail to Napau Crater

34 (Napau Crater)

Distance: 12½ miles.

Elevation gain: 1220' (includes spur up Puu Huluhulu).

Average hiking time: 6¼ hours.

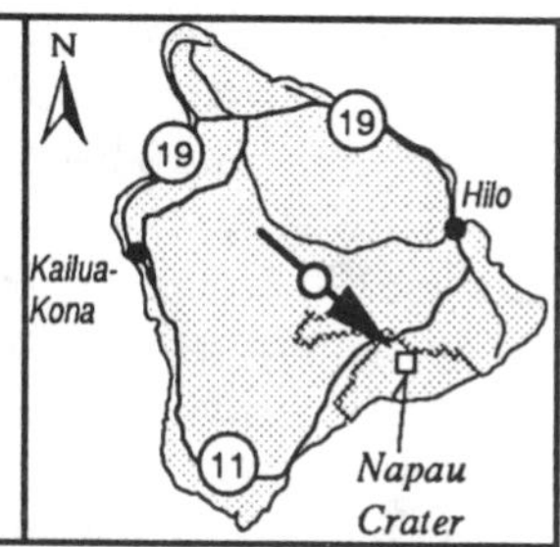

Topos: *Makaopuhi Crater, Volcano 7½.*

Trail map: At the end of Trip 32.

Highlights: This is a trip of enormous contrasts—miles of shiny, bare lava versus miles of green, sopping-wet rainforest. Near Napau Crater, you pass a historical site that will make you do a double-take.

Driving instructions: Follow the driving instructions of Trip 32.

Permit/permission required: None.

Description: Follow Trips 32 and 33 to the junction of the Napau Crater and Kalapana trails. After a rest here, continue east-northeast on the Napau Crater Trail toward Napau Crater. The rainforest continues to be very dense, but the trail is fairly well beaten. Look out for holes in the trail and for steep dropoffs beside it. Not far from the junction, you pass a spur trail to what looks like a rain gauge, perched on the edge of Makaopuhi Crater. There's a good crater view from here, but watch your step near the edge.

Your rainforest ramble continues with minor variations in the vegetation until, shortly before Napau Crater, you reach the marked ruins of The Old *Pulu* Factory. *The Old Pulu Factory?! With a name like that, it ought to be a trendy restaurant in Hilo. What's a factory doing out here? And what's "pulu," anyway?* you're thinking. There are some answers to these questions below. The Old *Pulu* Factory makes a nice spot for lunch.

Beyond The Old *Pulu* Factory, the rainforest opens up into a meadow of sedges and bamboo orchids. On your way toward Napau Crater, you brush the edges of two lava flows and cross a third one (the trail is poorly marked here, so look carefully for the cairns). You reach a junction where the left fork takes you north to an uninviting, very rainy, and very remote campsite (I cannot recommend it). On your way to this campsite, you pass a spur path to a pit toilet on your left. There's no outhouse, just the pit-toilet throne, hidden from the trail by shrubbery. A sign on your right proclaims HAZARDOUS AREA; there are steam vents and sulfurous fumes. This fork ends at an open area of cinders and *pahoehoe* on the crater's edge. Look around you for lava trees as well as steam vents.

Back at the junction, the other fork (left, as you return to the junction) leads east to an overlook down into Napau Crater. This fork is hard to follow and so overgrown with *uluhe* that you'll wish you had a machete. The first possible overlook is barricaded off because it's unsafe. At the next overlook, the cliff edge above Napau Crater is deeply undercut; be sure to stay safely back from the edge as you peer down to its desolate floor.

Return to the junction and then retrace your steps back to your car.

Pulu. . . . is the soft, reddish-brown down that covers the stems of *hapuu* ferns. In the mid-nineteenth century, a *pulu* industry flourished briefly. Dried *pulu*, it was reasoned, would make excellent pillow and mattress stuffing. So it was harvested and used as stuffing. The Old *Pulu* Factory operated between 1851 and 1854. As you see, it's certainly located at a good source of the raw material. It's hard to imagine the bustle of factory work in this utterly remote and tranquil spot. It's even harder to imagine that once upon a time, where these tumbledown walls enclose ferns and sprout lichens, someone gazed with pride upon a new *pulu* factory and dreamt of growing rich on fern fuzz.

The *pulu* market crumbled when the *pulu* did. *Pulu* holds up as stuffing for a few short years and then very suddenly crumbles into dust. That was not what people wanted from their pillows and mattresses. It was the end of the *pulu* industry and the end of The Old *Pulu* Factory.

Trip 35. Naulu and Kalapana Trails to Coast

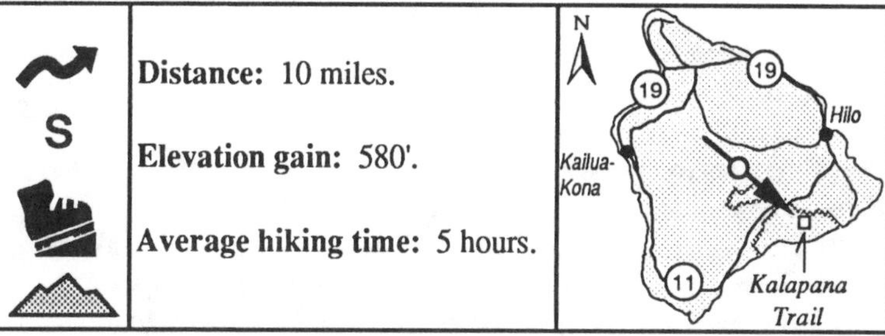

Topos: *Makaopuhi Crater, Kalapana* 7½. (Most of the Kalapana Trail that ought to be on the *Kalapana* topo isn't shown there. You can approximate it by drawing a line from the edge of the *Kalapana* topo at the point where the Kalapana Trail ought to continue from the *Makaopuhi* topo through the series of benchmarks (BM on the topo) that extends eastward to meet the southeast-trending remnant of the Kalapana Trail that *is* shown.)

Trail map (route approximated): At the end of this trip.

Highlights: You begin on the Naulu Trail in the nearly bare lavas of the 1969–1974 eruption. What a contrast this area is to the forested area through which the Kalapana Trail runs! When it's not overgrown, the Kalapana Trail offers a pleasant forest ramble down Kilauea's east slope to the seacoast, emerging opposite Lae Apuki (see Trip 40).

Caution: Check with the Park Service for the latest information on the Kalapana Trail's condition. If it has not been cleared recently, it will be hopelessly overgrown with dense *uluhe* and molasses grass. You should not waste your time on it if it is overgrown.

Driving instructions: Follow the driving instructions of Trip 20 but instead of turning right to go to Kilauea Visitor Center, turn left and follow Crater Rim Road downhill, soon making a mandatory left turn. You continue downhill to the junction with the Chain of Craters Road (opposite the Devastation Trail parking lot). Turn left onto the Chain of Craters Road and follow it downhill past the turnoff for Hilina Pali Road to the Ke Ala Komo Picnic Area (easily spotted by its prominent pavilion on the seaward side of the road) 13¼ miles from the Kilauea Visitor Center and 41¼ miles from

Hilo. This is where you start this hike, so have the shuttle driver drop the hikers off here. Or, if you're setting up a shuttle with two cars, note this spot and then continue to Lae Apuki.

To get to Lae Apuki, continue down the Chain of Craters Road for just over 12 more miles, past Puu Loa, and all the way to the coast, as given in the driving instructions for Trip 40. Either leave the second car here and return to Ke Ala Komo Picnic Area to start your hike, or have the shuttle driver pick you up here.

Permit/permission required: None.

Description: Once upon a time, the Kalapana Trail linked an upper segment of the Chain of Craters Road with its coastal segment. The upper segment of the road swung south from Makaopuhi Crater; it was overrun by lava during the 1969–1974 eruption. Now, the shorter way to the upper Kalapana Trail is from the Naulu Trail, which intersects it along the ruins of the old road.

(You can also pick up the Kalapana Trail from the Napau Crater Trail (see Trip 33), but this adds 3¼ miles and 200 feet of elevation gain to your trip, not including the optional climb up Puu Huluhulu. The segment of the Kalapana Trail between Makaopuhi Crater and the Naulu Trail is marginally passable but not particularly interesting.)

The Naulu Trail trailhead is across the Chain of Craters Road from Ke Ala Komo Picnic Area, by an inconspicuous marker in a weedy *aa* field. You begin by zigzagging up and down through the *aa,* on which *aalii, kupukupu* ferns, Indian pluchea, and lantana have found footholds. Soon you're out of the *aa* and onto gray-black *pahoehoe,* following cairns uphill and generally northward. *Amau* ferns and tiny *ohia* trees have found homes on this inhospitable, lava-plastered slope. Watch out for tree molds, which are deep holes left where lava engulfed and solidified around a tree that subsequently burnt away (see Trip 19). Pele's hair (Trip 32) gathers like golden needles in the cracks in the *pahoehoe*. You presently meet an old *kipuka* (an oasis of life spared by subsequent eruptions) right where a piece of the old Chain of Craters Road runs through it.

Pick up the old road, as indicated by a cairn, and follow it to its junction with the Kalapana Trail. The road is completely covered by lava in some places! Turn right (southeast) onto the Kalapana Trail toward Lae Apuki. Even when freshly cleared, this trail has plenty of encroaching plants: bamboo orchids, clover, grass, reeds, sedges, *pukiawe, ohelo, uluhe,* and firebush. Alien firebush is becoming a terrible pest plant in the park.

Soon you pass a fenced-off pit; be sure to keep a sharp lookout for holes and pits that *aren't* fenced off! *Uluhe* can conceal many hazards, so don't go wandering off into its dense thickets. The trail is also marked by plastic-ribbon tags and by colored metal tabs hammered into the occasional *ohia* tree. Keep your eyes and ears open for birds here, and have your spider stick handy.

The forest gradually becomes more open, but then huge hedges of *uluhe* close in around you again. Again and again, the forest draws back, only to close in again. Near the 5¾-mile point (4½ miles from the Naulu-Kalapana junction), the trail turns steeply downhill and the sea comes into view. The view vanishes as the trail levels out amid trees and shrubs draped with the orange threads of the parasitic vine *kaunaoa,* a native dodder. If you are alert, you will spot some of the old benchmarks embedded in the trail, although "BM 1250" on the topo is actually marked on the ground as being at 1251 feet.

By the time you reach benchmark 1251, the forest has thinned to the point of being a grassland where shrubs of white-flowered *ulei* and clumps of *laue* (the anise-scented sweet fern) grow. Suddenly, you enter a shady tunnel of Java plum trees, swamp mahogany, guava, and *kukui*; *ti* and *laue* appear in the undergrowth. On the inland side, an ancient stone wall parallels the trail (not, I believe, the one shown on the topo, which is a little too far south and west). Look closely at the trail: it is part of an ancient, built-up stone path. There's good guava-picking in season along here, for relatively few people visit the Kalapana Trail.

As the tunnel of trees opens up, you emerge into waist-high molasses grass. This grass grows in dense clumps, and its long, furry leaves tend to cling to each other and to you so that it can be quite an effort to push your way through them. Where molasses grass has grown over the trail, you'll feel like you're trying to swim through molasses instead of walk.

It's not long before you reach a trail sign pointing south. Now you begin switchbacking gently down toward the coast. At a low cliff, the trail—still on the old stone path—descends *very* steeply. There's a real sandalwood tree around here; see if you can spot it—but don't molest it!

Now the trail turns away from the old stone path, levels out, and presently deposits you on the inland side of the Chain of Craters Road opposite the site of the ancient village of Lae Apuki. You meet your ride, or find your second car, here.

Kalapana. . . . In *Pikoi and Other Legends of the Island of Hawaii,* Mary Kawena Pukui and Caroline Curtis retell the legend of Kalapana, an old man who paddled his canoe all the way from Kauai to the Puna coast of the Big Island to pay homage to Pele. It was his life's dream to see Pele; he had vowed that he would never cut his hair until he saw her.

But now Kalapana was aged, and he was very weary after his journey from Kauai. A man of Puna warned him that the way from the coast up to Pele's home in Kilauea was long and difficult. (You know this yourself, having just descended part of the way.) Kalapana insisted that he must see Pele, so the man of Puna befriended Kalapana, fed him, and gave him a place to sleep. It was warm and sunny in Puna but raining on Kilauea's upper slopes, so Kalapana waited for the weather to improve. When the weather got better, he set off. Up and up he climbed until, suddenly, a storm broke. He slipped and fell on the rocks; the rain blinded him, and the cold wind pushed him back. Exhausted, he turned around. He rested with his new friend and then tried to climb Kilauea again. Another storm forced him to retreat once more.

Kalapana's long, tangled hair, uncut because of his vow, had attracted the Puna villagers' attention. Two mischievous boys decided to cut it off. As Kalapana slept deeply, worn out by his second attempt to climb Kilauea, the boys crept into the house and burnt his hair short.

Kalapana awoke to see a beautiful woman standing by his mats. He knew she was Pele! She asked him why he had broken his vow and cut his hair. Kalapana, startled, would have denied it. But when he raised his hands to his head, he felt how short it was now. Pele realized that someone had cut Kalapana's hair without his consent. Still, she explained, there must be some punishment for the broken vow. He could never return to Kauai but must remain on the Big Island for the rest of his life. Kalapana didn't care, for he had seen Pele. Then she slowly disappeared.

Kalapana told his friend what had happened, and his friend invited him to stay. No matter what he was doing, Kalapana was always filled with joy. His life's dream had been fulfilled! In time, the villagers came to love the old man who had seen Pele. When he died at last, they named their district Kalapana in his honor. So it is known to this day.

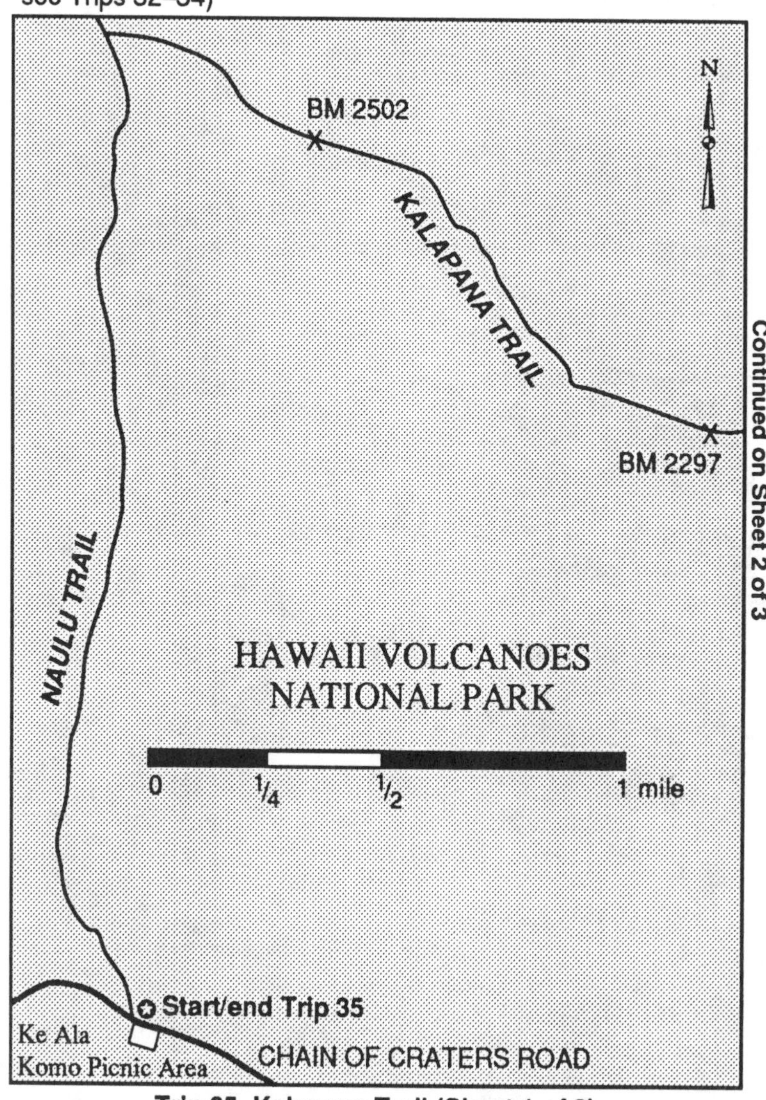

Trip 35. Kalapana Trail (Sheet 1 of 3)

Continued from Sheet 1 of 3

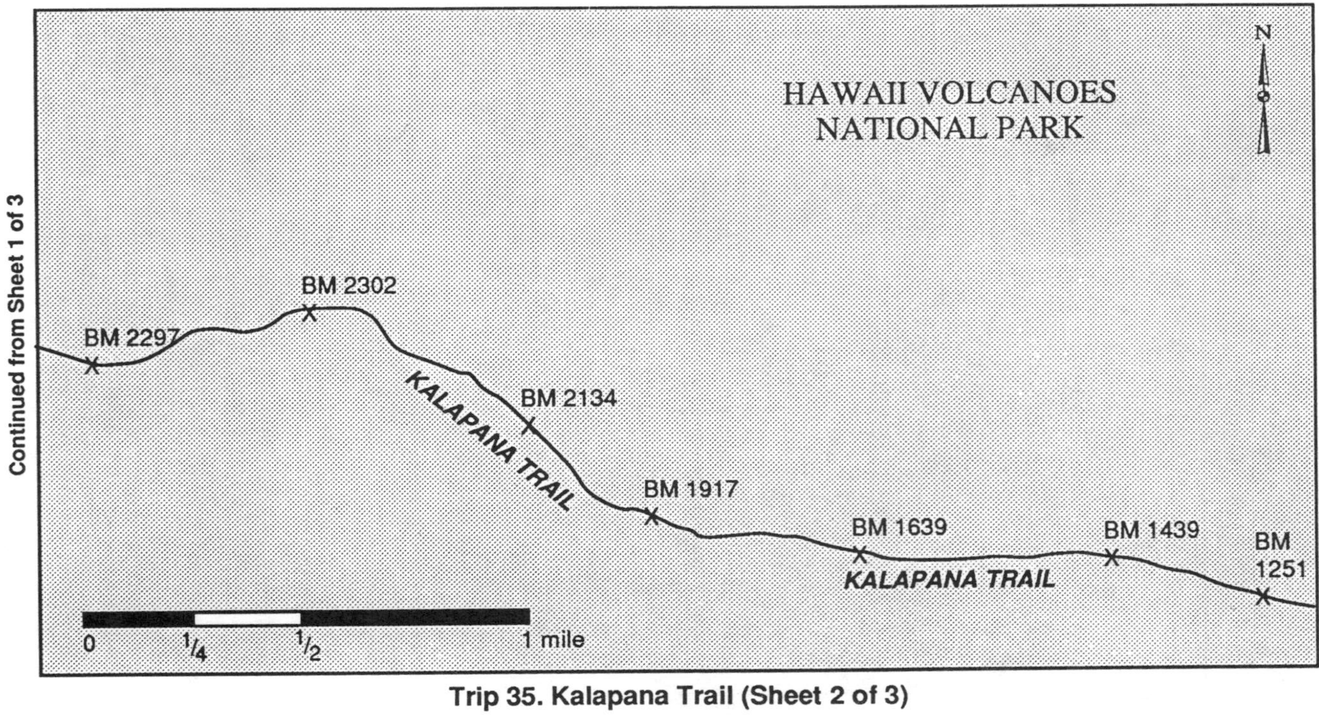

Trip 35. Kalapana Trail (Sheet 2 of 3)

Continued on Sheet 3 of 3

Continued from Sheet 2 of 3

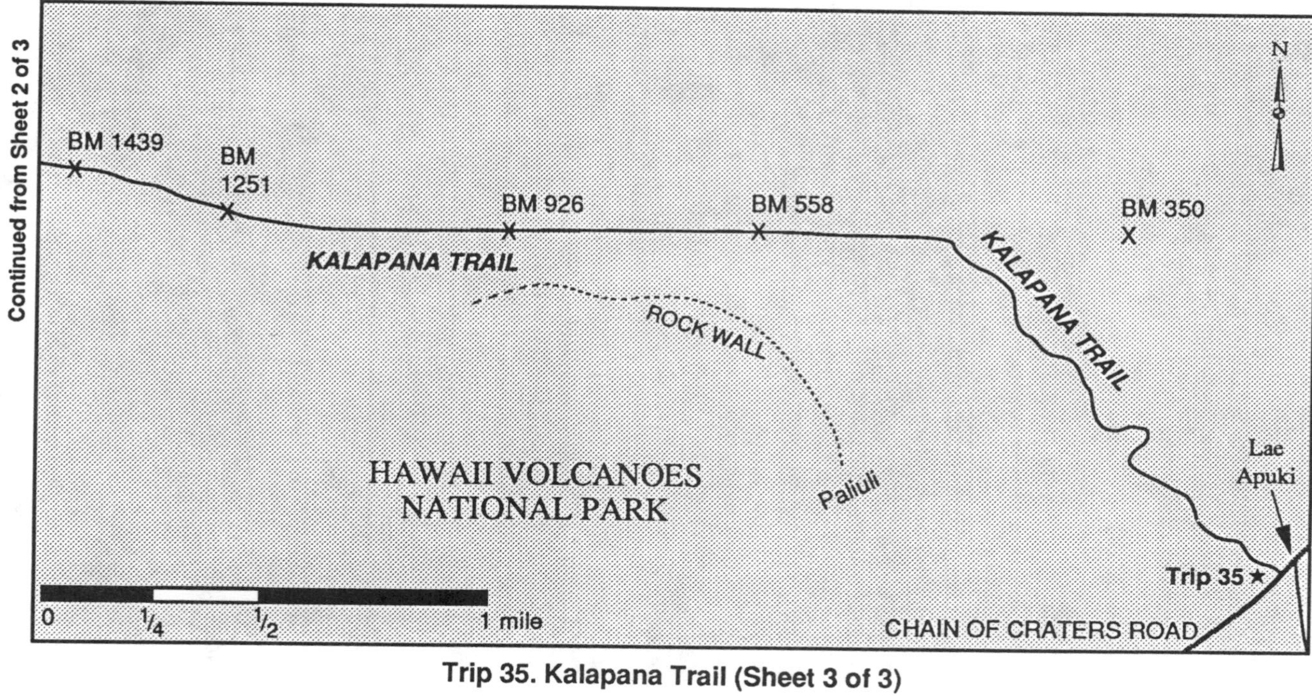

Trip 35. Kalapana Trail (Sheet 3 of 3)

Trip 36. Puu Loa Petroglyphs

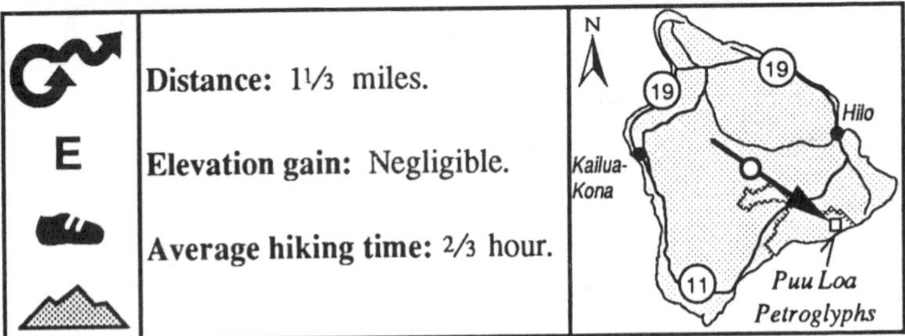

Topos: Optional: *Makaopuhi Crater, Kalapana* 7½.

Trail map: At the end of this trip.

Highlights: This short hike takes you to a concentration of petroglyphs, which are symbols chipped into stone. Preliterate societies often made petroglyphs to record their presence, commemorate important occasions, work charms, or ask for the help of guardian spirits. Sometimes petroglyph fields are hard to get to, but the Park Service has built a trail and a walkway to help you see these petroglyphs.

Driving instructions: Follow the driving instructions of Trip 20 but instead of turning right to go to Kilauea Visitor Center, turn left and follow Crater Rim Road downhill, soon making a mandatory left turn. You continue downhill to the junction with the Chain of Craters Road (opposite the Devastation Trail parking lot). Turn left onto the Chain of Craters Road and follow it downhill past the Ke Ala Komo Picnic Area (the prominent pavilion on the seaward side of the road). The road zigzags down the Holei Pali and then levels out. Shortly before it reaches the seacoast, look to your left (east-northeast) for the turnout for the Puu Loa petroglyphs, just under 20½ miles from Kilauea Visitor Center and just under 48½ miles from Hilo. Park here to start your hike.

Permit/permission required: None.

Description: You begin by bearing east-northeast through brown *pahoehoe* from the turnout/parking area. There are cairns to mark your way. The going, while easy, does involve some minor ups and downs over the lava, so watch your step.

In just over ½ mile, you reach the petroglyphs and the loop part of this hike. A boardwalk loops through the petroglyphs, inviting you to enjoy them without touching them. Petroglyphs occur outside the loop as well as inside it, so be sure to look on both sides of the boardwalk. An interpretive sign explains that the petroglyphs that consist of a simple hole in the rock, sometimes surrounded by one or more concentric circles, are the burial places of pieces of umbilical cords. The Hawaiians believed that Puu Loa ("Long Hill") had great power. In particular, the Long Hill's power could assure a child of long life if the child's umbilical cord was properly buried here.

There's a bench at the beginning/ending of the loop where you may wish to rest and reflect on these petroglyphs and their makers. Many kinds of petroglyphs occur here. While the hope expressed by the umbilical-cord burials is known, the meanings of some of the other petroglyphs are not as well known. Surely some of them are petitions for good luck in some undertaking. Before you chuckle at them as mere manifestations of superstition, throw away your lucky rabbit's foot or your religious medal or your prayer handkerchief or that four-leaved clover tucked into your wallet. . . . How alike we human beings are across the centuries in spite of our cultural and technological differences!

When you're ready, retrace your steps back to your car.

Hiding a child's umbilical cord. . . . was a common practice in old Hawaii. The cord could be buried or cast into a hole like Haleakala's Bottomless Pit. Or it could be shoved deep into a crevice like those around Kauai's birthstones. As noted above, burying the cord at Puu Loa was believed to secure long life. In some cases, it was believed that if the umbilical cord were found, the child would become a thief. In other cases, burying the cord at a powerful site was believed to ensure the child's safety and to help it grow strong.

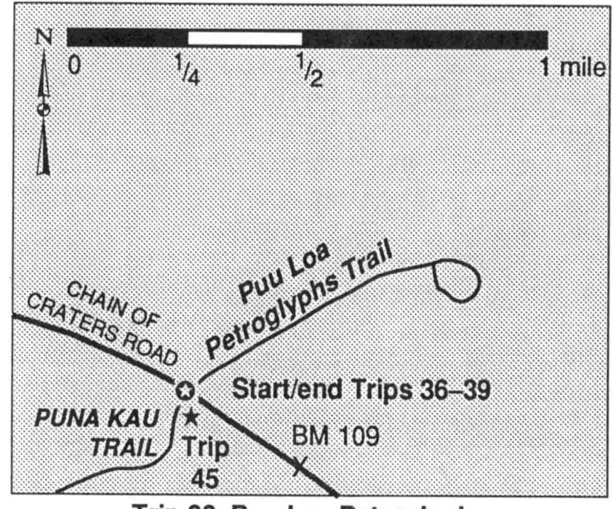

Trip 36. Puu Loa Petroglyphs

Trip 37. Puna Kau Trail to Apua Point

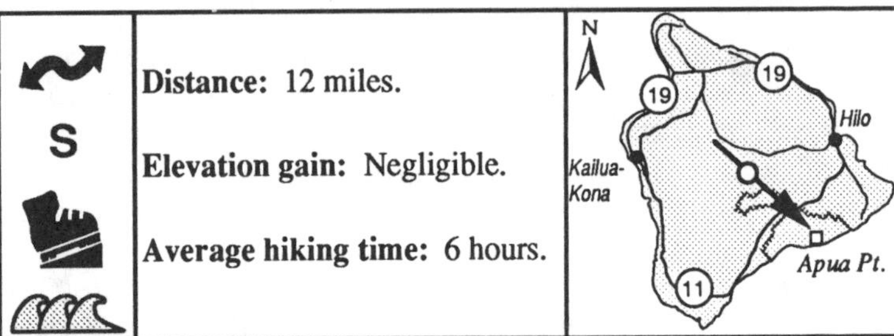

Topos: *Makaopuhi Crater* 7½.

Trail map: At the end of this trip.

Highlights: The Puna Kau (ka-oo) Trail leads past some interesting ruins to Apua Point, where you'll find a wild, picturesque bay and, inland, some intriguing petroglyphs.

Driving instructions: Follow the driving instructions of Trip 36 to the turnout for the Puu Loa petroglyphs. The Puna Kau Trail begins on the opposite side of the Chain of Craters Road from the Puu Loa turnout.

Permit/permission required: None.

Description: You leave the Chain of Craters Road behind and strike out generally southwest, sometimes on a beaten path and sometimes following cairns across *pahoehoe*. The route could use a few more cairns, especially on the newer lava, but otherwise the going is straightforward. It's not long before you see an arresting sight: a bulging lava dome from which a tree seems to be growing. At first, the *pahoehoe* is brown and weathered; around the 1-mile point, you encounter darker, less weathered lavas. The steep cliffs and rounded top of Puu Kapukapu rise in the distance, to the west. On this trip, you won't be going nearly that far, but Puu Kapukapu is a handy landmark.

You now pass through older, weedier lava full of Indian pluchea and beach *naupaka*, then through newer, more barren lava. It's not long before you reach the seacoast, though you are atop low cliffs rather than at the waterside. At a black-sand-and-cobblestone "beach" on the cliffs, you discover a large, two-chambered ruin. While it is possible to climb over its walls, it is probably safer to circumvent it. Shortly after you have done so, you find yourself crossing an *aa* field. Some people speculate that the name *aa* comes from the exclamations of the old Hawaiians as they walked over this stuff barefooted: "Ah! Ah!" (Or, as we'd say, "Ow! Ow!") Fortunately, you're soon back on *pahoehoe*.

Approaching Apua Point, you see a swath of greenery and some coconut palms. The little peninsula seems like an oasis in this *pahoehoe* desert. The green turns out to be not the prickly weeds so common elsewhere in this region but the shiny leaves of beach *naupaka*. Inland from Apua Point, some apparent ruins beckon you to go exploring. It's worth your while to poke around here, for there are some very special petroglyphs. You need to look patiently; the petroglyphs may be hard to see under some lighting conditions. As the Hawaiians were becoming literate, they sometimes pecked out not the usual symbolic petroglyphs like the ones on Puu Loa (Trip 36) but names and words in elegant capital letters carefully shaped to resemble those they saw in their textbooks. It is a strange feeling to stand at those petroglyphs, which so clearly represent the confluence—some would say the collision—of the Hawaiian and European cultures. Soon after that moment in history, the making of petroglyphs and the maintaining of Hawaiian oral traditions vanished, swept away in a European sea of paper and ink.

It's more work than you would have thought to pick your way through the beach *naupaka* to the shore at Apua Point, where there are patches of coarse gray sand fronting the wild ocean and strewn with chunks of black lava and white coral. Beach morning glory vines trail across the sand. A few coconut palms offer sparse shade. Signs advise you TURTLE NESTING AREA NO HORSES NO CAMPING NO FIRES OR LIGHTS. Swimming would be very hazardous here, but, along this coast, you can't beat the beach at Apua Point as a place to have your lunch and enjoy the scenery. (It was one of the few places where I was not overrun by cockroaches and ants when I sat down to rest and eat.) The endangered and beautiful *ohai* grows on Apua Point: look for a prostrate shrub with paired, oval leaves and pea-like, inch-and-a-half long orangey-red flowers.

There's much to enjoy here, but eventually you must return to your car.

Apua Point. . . . is one of the few remaining sea-turtle nesting sites along this coast. Volunteers come out here to monitor the turtles, their eggs, and their hatchlings in the hope of improving the turtles' chances of survival. Turtles used to nest at Halape, farther west along this coast. But Halape is also a very popular camping spot. Over the years, campfires and flashlights confused adult turtles attempting to nest, so that they failed to find a spot to lay their eggs or crawled inland and died. Turtles nest where they were hatched. As the numbers of hatchlings declined, so did the numbers of returning adults. At last there were none.

The camping area at Halape is now located where campers' activities supposedly will not interfere with the turtles' nesting, but the turtles have yet to return. It's hoped that there may be still be Halape-hatched turtles at sea who are just now maturing and who will soon return to nest for the first time, successfully. (Now you understand why, at Apua Point, the signs say NO HORSES NO CAMPING NO FIRES OR LIGHTS.)

Meanwhile, the sea turtles are now protected and seem to be making a modest comeback, particularly on French Frigate Shoals in the far northwestern part of the Hawaiian archipelago. These islets and atolls, from Nihoa to Kure, are sometimes called the Leeward Islands and are now in the Hawaiian Islands National Wildlife Refuge. In time it may be possible to re-establish the turtles in their former habitats by taking sea-turtle eggs to beaches from which the turtles have vanished and placing the eggs in human-dug nests. If the eggs hatch there, the surviving hatchlings should return there as adults.

Steam seeps up at edge of Kilauea Caldera

Hawaii Visitor Bureau

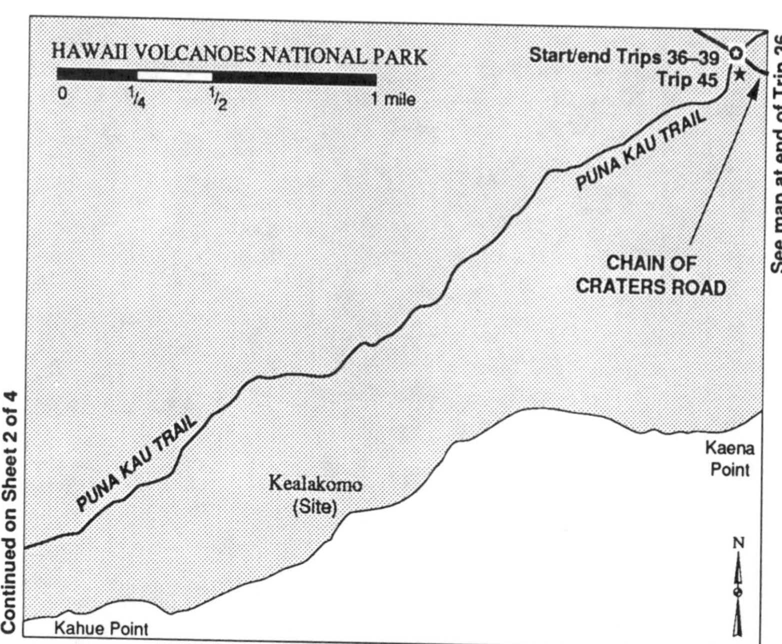

Trips 37–39. Puna Kau Coast—Apua Point, Keauhou, Halape (Sheet 1 of 4)

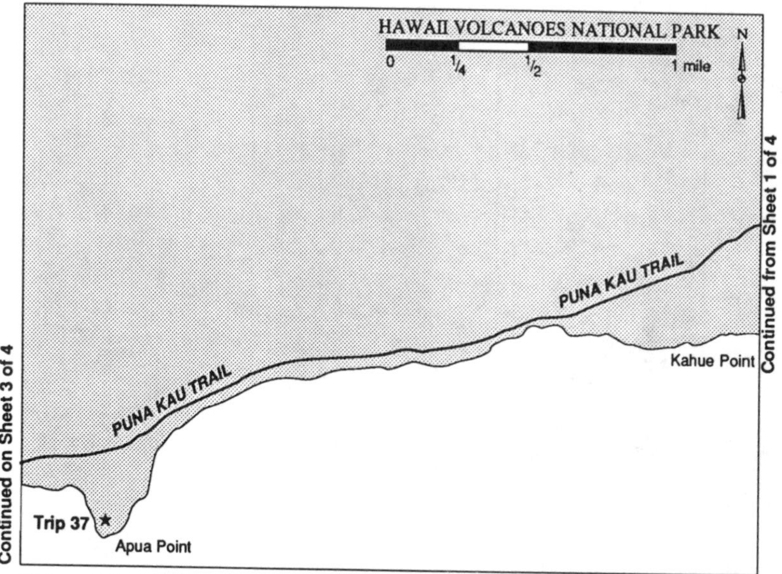

Trips 37–39. Puna Kau Coast—Apua Point, Keauhou, Halape (Sheet 2 of 4)

Continued on Sheet 4 of 4

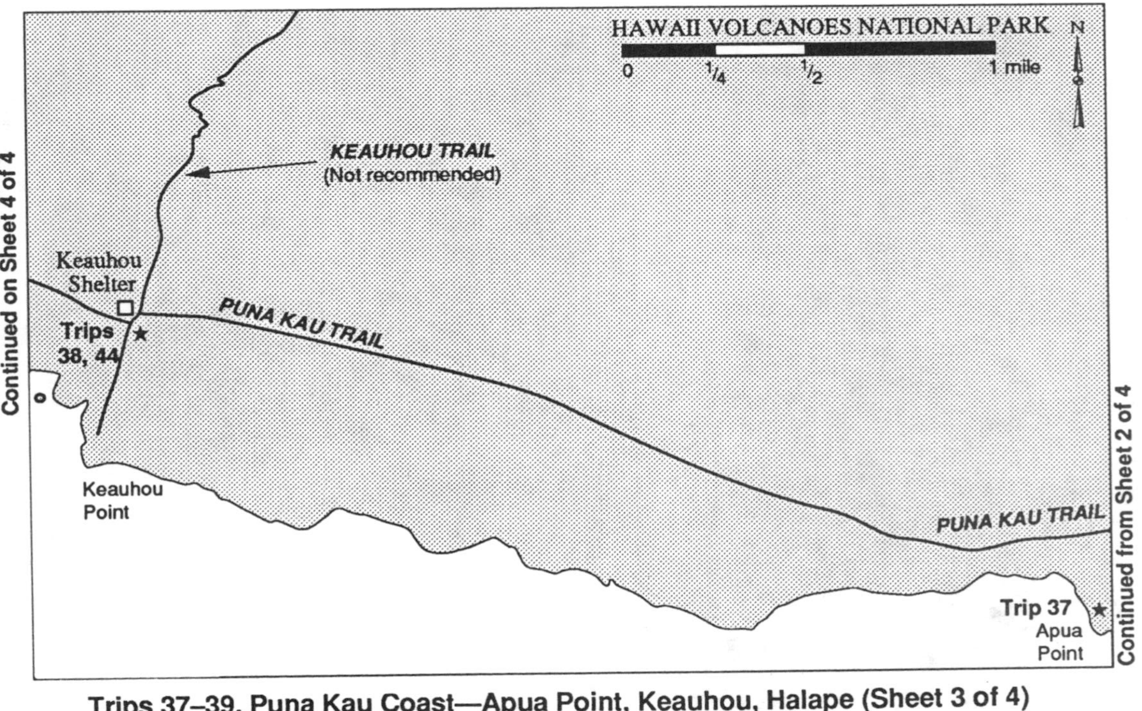

Continued from Sheet 2 of 4

Trips 37–39. Puna Kau Coast—Apua Point, Keauhou, Halape (Sheet 3 of 4)

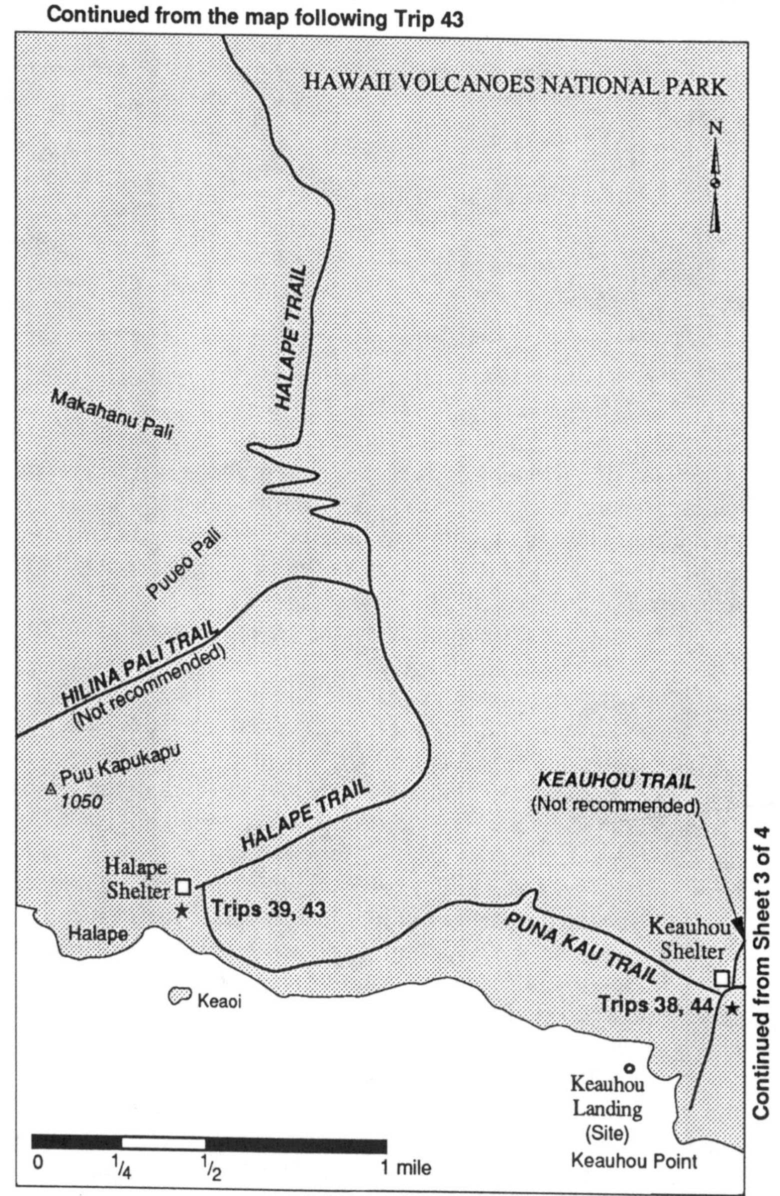

Trips 37–39. Puna Kau Coast—Apua Point, Keauhou, Halape (Sheet 4 of 4)

Trip 38. Puna Kau Trail to Keauhou Shelter

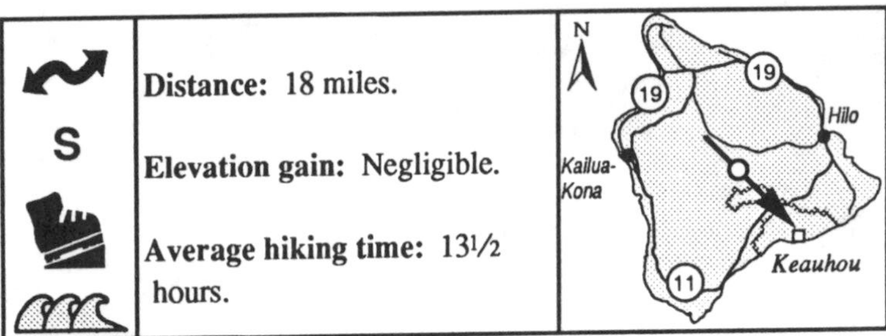

Topos: *Makaopuhi Crater, Kau Desert* 7½.

Trail map: At the end of Trip 37.

Highlights: Those with a yen to camp and sun at a wilderness beach may find Keauhou and the two other wilderness beach camping areas along this coast, Halape and Kaaha—formerly Kalue—to their liking. Then, again, they may not; see the Puna-Kau Coast cautions, below. The Puna Kau Trail is the best way to get to both Keauhou and Halape, I think.

Driving instructions: Follow the driving instructions of Trip 37.

Permit/permission required: You must have a valid permit from Hawaii Volcanoes National Park, available only by applying in person at the Kilauea Visitor Center, to stay overnight in the park's backcountry. This is true whether you stay in the cabins and shelters (which are on a first-come, first-served basis) or camp out near them. Unless you carry all your own water, you're going to have to stay near a cabin or a shelter: fresh water, if there is any, is available only at the cabins and the shelters. Their roofs catch dew and rain and funnel the water into an adjacent tank; you still have to purify it. When you get your permit at Kilauea Visitor Center, be sure to check on the water supply at the cabins and the shelters you'll visit on your trip.

For the Puna-Kau Coast, I strongly recommend that you take your own tent, etc., and *not* stay in the shelters or the cabin. See the Puna-Kau Coast cautions, below.

Description: Follow the description of Trip 37 to Apua Point. After a well-earned rest at Apua Point, find your way back to the cairn-marked Puna Kau Trail and continue west-northwest toward Puu Kapukapu. The lava presently gives way to weeds, and then the weeds give way to lava again. Look for places where apparently newer, black *pahoehoe* spreads around older, browner lava in octopus-tentacle-like patterns. As you approach lonely little Keauhou Shelter, 3 miles from Apua Point, the terrain becomes weedy again. Weeds like this are the bane of many coastal routes, rendering them unpleasant to almost impassable. You'll have your work cut out for you, picking their seeds off your boots and socks.

The shelter is about 100 yards inland from the junction where you meet the Keauhou (misspelt "Keaunou" on the topo) Trail. (See Appendix B for more on the Keauhou Trail.) Turn right (inland) at this junction and follow a rough path to the shelter, whose open side faces the sea. The water tank and its tap are outside the shelter, around the back. There is a pit toilet inside a low stone wall a few yards west of the shelter. What little level ground there is around the shelter on which to pitch a tent is on the path to the toilet.

Your other alternative for camping is on the palm-shaded beach. Turn left (seaward) at the Puna Kau Trail-Keauhou Trail junction and follow a rough path ⅓ mile through a sparse growth of *koa haole* and tall, dense grasses to the cove just west of Keauhou Point. (This additional distance is not included in the mileage given in the icon box.) Be sure the water is not too rough or the currents too strong for safe swimming before you venture into the sea here. A brackish-water pool is located near the next cove west and is accessible by scrambling over the lava of the short, blunt peninsula west of Keauhou Point. It's refreshing after you've been in the salt water. Smashed plants and occasional piles of rocks indicate the route. You will need to go back to Keauhou Shelter to get fresh water (treat before drinking) and to use the toilet.

To return, retrace your steps past Apua Point to the Chain of Craters Road.

Puna-Kau Coast cautions. . . . I've used the term "Puna-Kau Coast" to mean the coastal region of Hawaii Volcanoes National Park; the term has no official sanction.

The weather along the Puna-Kau Coast is often hot and muggy. Have plenty of drinking water in your canteens; you'll need it. Visitors from the mainland may find travel with a full backpack in the Puna-Kau Coast's heat and humidity very debilitating, perhaps to the point of heat exhaustion. It can also rain at any time. Be prepared for a wide range of weather conditions.

I think the Puna Kau Trail between the Chain of Craters Road and Halape is the best route to Keauhou and Halape, though high seas might make its waterside segments too dangerous to travel.

Unlike other trails in the area, most of it is *not* overgrown because it is largely on newer lavas; its elevation gain and loss are negligible; and the sea breezes will help to cool you off. Appendix B discusses other, less pleasant routes to and along the Puna-Kau Coast.

You should also be prepared to camp out with your own sleeping bag, rainproof and bugproof tent, and mattress. Don't plan on staying in the cabin or the shelters. There is a cabin with cots at Pepeiao, which is on the edge of the Kau Desert at about 1500 feet on one of the routes to Kaaha. There are three-sided shelters at Kaaha, Halape, and Keauhou, all of which are on the coast (actually, very slightly inland). Halape is considered by some to be the gem of the park's coastal backcountry and is an extremely popular destination among islanders. That's the good news.

The bad news is that Pepeiao Cabin and Kaaha, Halape, and Keauhou shelters are all thoroughly infested with ants, inside and outside, and with big cockroaches. Even when you camp in your own tent, you can expect to have roaches crawling over your tent at night. The ants seem attracted to human activity and will quickly swarm around when you are getting in or out of your tent, drawing water, preparing a meal, or just sitting around trying to rest, read, etc. Ants infest the trails. When you stop for that much needed rest on the trail, ants swarm over you within minutes. The occasional roach may lurch out of the trail weeds to join them in the scramble for your granola bar. The stone walls of the shelters are reported to be home to some other charmers: centipedes, black widow spiders, and scorpions. I found mud wasps at Keauhou; one built a nest on my backpack. A fellow backpacker reported losing some food to a mongoose at Halape. This same camper tried to tough it out at the beach without a tent but gave up: crickets were jumping on him every 20 seconds (he counted!).

The limited water supply at all four of these places is too precious to be wasted on bathing and washing clothes. Please use the water carefully and sparingly; be sure to purify it before drinking it. Pockets of undrinkable, brackish water just inland of the beaches at Halape and Keauhou provide a chance to rinse yourself off, but don't use any soap in them.

Carry some strong cord with which to hang your backpack, food, etc., out of the way of the ants, roaches, mongooses, etc. It won't keep the ants away indefinitely, but it postpones the invasion. It helps if you apply a little insect repellent to the cord and suspend your stuff away from the shelter walls.

Swimming can be dangerous along this coast, as it is nearly everywhere on the Big Island, because of the rough seas and strong currents. But it is also one of the principal attractions. Snorkeling is very popular and is reported to be best at Halape. Use your best judgment; at the very least, stay out of the water unless it is quite calm.

Visitors from the mainland may find the hot, shadeless, buggy Puna-Kau Coast backcountry less than idyllic. Consider carefully whether an overnight visit is worth your limited time on Hawaii. You may find that the dayhikes to Apua Point (Trip 36) or Pepeiao Cabin (Trip 46) will satisfy your curiosity about the Puna-Kau Coast and that the safer beaches on the Kona and Kohala coasts will satisfy your sunning, swimming, bodysurfing, and snorkling wishes—all with far fewer ants, roaches, crickets, etc.

People enjoying Liliuokalani Gardens in Hilo

Trip 39. Chain of Craters Road to Halape via Keauhou

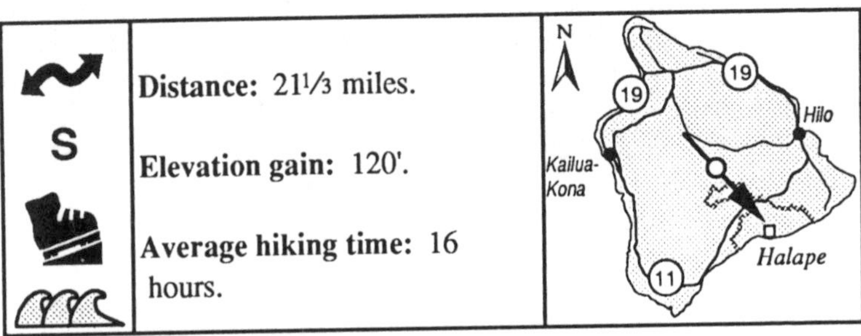

Distance: 21⅓ miles.

Elevation gain: 120'.

Average hiking time: 16 hours.

Topos: *Makaopuhi Crater, Kau Desert* 7½.

Trail map: At the end of Trip 37.

Highlights: Halape is an extremely popular coastal destination for backcountry hikers along the Puna-Kau Coast. The coves around Halape are the prettiest along the Puna-Kau Trail and reportedly offer the best snorkeling, though swimming is always risky along this coast because of the rough water. It's easiest to do this trip in four days, stopping at Keauhou on the way in and out. However, you may prefer to make it in two or three days.

Driving instructions: Follow the driving instructions of Trip 37.

Permit/permission required: As for Trip 38, you must have a valid permit from Hawaii Volcanoes National Park, available only by applying in person at the Kilauea Visitor Center, to stay overnight in the park's backcountry.

Description (easiest trip):

Day 1 (9 miles). Follow the descriptions of Trips 37 and 38 to Keauhou Shelter or to the beach (⅓ mile more).

Day 2 (1⅔ miles). Retrace your steps to the Keauhou Trail-Puna Kau Trail junction and turn right (west) toward Puu Kapukapu and Halape. (Halape is just below Puu Kapukapu.) You brush through weeds that include a little passionfruit vine called love-in-a-mist, distinguished by lacy bracts on its buds and flowers. Like all the passionfruits in Hawaii, this one was introduced from the Americas.

In ⅔ mile, you reach the foot of a fault scarp and climb somewhat steeply up its shattered, reddish-brown rock. Another mile brings you to Halape and to the junction of the Puna Kau and Halape trails. A trail-of-use leads away from the junction toward the camping area, which lies seaward of the trail—flat, sandy spots under coconut palms, hidden from sea-turtle view by a natural rock barrier (see Trip 37 for more on the turtles). Westward, blue-green waves splash onto white sand and black lava coves. A few dead coconut palms still stick out of the water (see below). You can follow the strand farther west around these coves and then over a lava peninsula to more coves. A fire here in 1991 left blackened shrubs and dead vines on scorched ground; watch your step as you pick your way over the dead plants as well as the new growth.

The Halape Trail leads inland toward Halape Shelter. As at Keauhou, the shelter's open side faces the ocean; the pit toilet, surrounded by a low wall, is a few yards east of the shelter. While the camping area is at the waterside, you must come up here to get water and use the toilet. Beware of the bugs, spiders, and mongooses here! What bugs, spiders, and mongooses, you ask? Check the information at the end of Trip 38 for some Puna-Kau Coast cautions.

Days 3 and 4 (10⅔miles). Return to the Chain of Craters Road by retracing your steps through Keauhou and past Apua Point.

The great earthquake of 1975. . . . Trip 15 discussed tsunamis (tidal waves) and mentioned that sometimes earthquakes on the Hawaiian Islands generate tsunamis. Most Hawaiian earthquakes are too small to be noticed. The largest recorded so far struck in 1868 and had an estimated magnitude of 7.5 on the Richter scale. It caused widespread damage and 79 deaths—46 by the tsunami it generated, 31 by a mudslide, and two by falling rocks.

In November of 1975, a predawn earthquake that registered about 7.2 on the Richter scale shocked the Kalapana coast. It was the second strongest recorded earthquake in Hawaiian history and caused heavy property damage. At Halape, the coastline dropped almost 12 feet, drowning a grove of coconut palms. A few minutes later, a tsunami spawned by the earthquake swept over Halape, killing two campers. According to *Volcanoes in the Sea,* "[The] earthquake destroyed many of the tsunami warning sirens along the Kalapana coast before they could ever be activated, and the sirens first sounded in Kona almost 30 minutes after the arrival of the first wave." One conclusion: "The best warning of a possible tsunami is the earthquake itself. If the quake appears severe, one should immediately vacate coastal areas and move to higher ground."

Remember that when you are camping on this coast! A tsunami consists of multiple waves that strike at intervals of 12 to 20 minutes; don't rush back after the first wave. Later waves can be more severe than earlier ones. If you feel an earthquake, abandon your campsite and gear—it's replaceable; you're not—and get *moving inland!* And stay there!

Trip 40. Lae Apuki Stroll

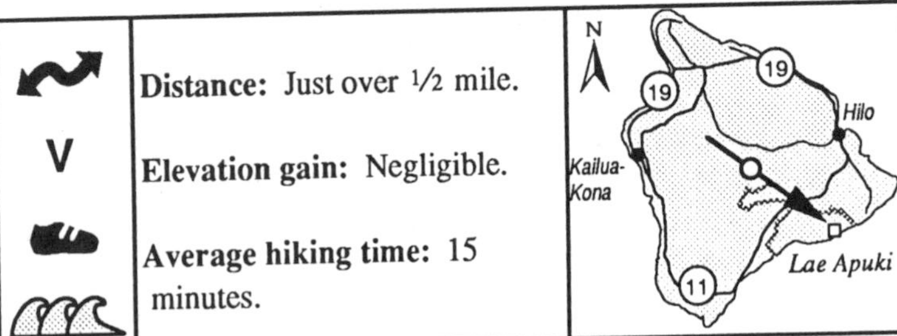

Topos: Optional: *Kalapana* 7½.

Trail map (route approximated): At the end of this trip.

Highlights: A fishing village once flourished at Lae Apuki (as it's spelled on the park's sign). It was abandoned early in this century; now, it has all but vanished in the scrub. Still, it is a protected archaeological site, and you must not disturb it. So why come here? Kilauea's current eruption has thrown up black sand to form a tiny beach at Lae Apuki—very pretty but very dangerous for swimming. Less than a mile farther down the road, at Kamoamoa, there's a much larger and more spectacular black-sand beach (but equally dangerous for swimming). Cars and buses unload scores of tourists daily at Kamoamoa. Almost no one visits Lae Apuki. If you want to have some quiet time at a black-sand beach, Lae Apuki may be just the spot for you.

By the way, Lae Apuki is spelled "Laeapuki" in two places on the topo. The Laeapuki you're visiting on this trip is the one opposite the lower end of the Kalapana Trail, just above the notation "Rock Walls."

Driving instructions: Follow the driving instructions of Trip 20 but instead of turning right to go to Kilauea Visitor Center, turn left and follow Crater Rim Road downhill, soon making a mandatory left turn. You continue downhill to the junction with the Chain of Craters Road (opposite the Devastation Trail parking lot). Turn left onto the Chain of Craters Road and follow it downhill past the Ke Ala Komo Picnic Area (the prominent pavilion on the seaward side of the road), down the Holei Pali and out to the coast. Now the road curves northeast. Keep your eyes open along the ocean side of the road for the interpretive sign marking the turnout for Lae

Apuki, just under 24¾ miles from Kilauea Visitor Center and just under 52¾ miles from Hilo. Park here to start your hike.

Permit/permission required: None.

Description: Wander seaward from the turnout on a worn *pahoehoe* path that curves through guava, *ulei,* lantana, and Indian pluchea. The ruins are mostly invisible in all this shrubbery, but a lone coconut palm sprouts bravely from a rock platform.

In just over ¼ mile, you emerge on a rocky point a few feet above the sapphire water. To the right of this point, there's a picturesque little black-sand cove with a sign that says SWIMMING PROHIBITED. As you can plainly see, the seas here are vicious. To the left are low bluffs dusted with glassy black sand. Black sand gets very hot, so keep those tennies on. Stroll to your left along the bluffs for a short distance to admire a sea arch, a natural bridge, and the powerful surf that carved them. The hot black sand holds back encroaching Christmas berry, lantana, and Indian pluchea. Raised mounds of rocks here may be shrines or raised burial sites; please treat them with respect.

Find a spot to rest and take in this marvelous scenery. As you leave, reluctantly retracing your steps, you'll notice that you have outstanding views inland, where the *pali*'s forest greenery has been repeatedly slashed by black cascades of lava in the long drama of the birth, death, and rebirth of these islands.

Black-sand beaches. . . . are rare anywhere in the world. Most beaches are of light-colored sand. In the tropics, that usually means that the sand is pulverized coral—a gift of the sea. Black-sand beaches are a gift of the land. Some form when hot lava flows enter the ocean, causing a steam explosion that blows the molten material into millions of glassy fragments. The prevailing current may sweep the fragments along the coast, depositing them to form beaches where the conditions are favorable. Lae Apuki's little beach is just such a beach; so are Kamoamoa's and, farther south on Highway 11, Punaluu's beaches. Walking on their coarse sand is like walking on tiny beads of jet. These beaches are short-lived, as there's no reliable source of new material to replace what the ocean and the winds carry away. The fragments are the result of a single episode of steam explosions. The chances of another flow occurring in exactly the same place and in the same way, yielding similar fragments to replenish the beach, are very remote. Most volcanic black-sand beaches succumb to erosion relatively soon, their glassy sands swept away or blown inland.

Other black-sand beaches are the products of erosion—particles of dark-colored material weathered from the rocks at the ocean's edge. That's the source, for example, of the black- (or, to my eyes, gray-) sand beaches at Waipio (Trip 1), Waimanu (Trip 2), and Pololu (Trip 60).

The once-famous black-sand beaches of Kalapana on the Big Island have suffered a triple whammy. Normal wind and wave erosion were of course reducing them gradually. However, they also suffered major damage when their section of coast abruptly sank several feet in the powerful earthquake of November 1975 (see Trip 39.) The death blow came in 1990, when lava from Kilauea's latest eruption overflowed them. Where there was once black sand, there is now black rock.

The loss was both a tragedy and a blessing. Many mourn the loss of these beaches as they once were. More recently, however, they had become grubby hangouts for people you wouldn't want as neighbors. A Hilo resident told me of standing in the company of a Hawaiian family—*kamaaina*—as they all watched the lava overrun Harry K. Brown Beach Park. The family's house, right by the park, was also in the path of the flow. They cried and laughed as they saw their home and the beach fall to the lava. They were sad to lose their home but glad that Pele had come to clean up the park.

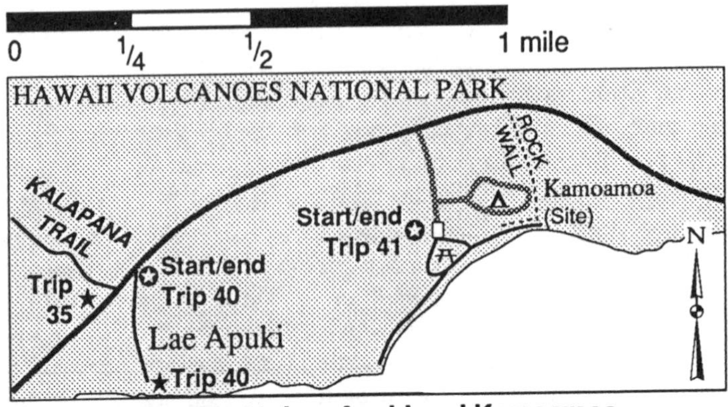

Trips 40–41. Lae Apuki and Kamoamoa

Trip 41. Kamoamoa Stroll

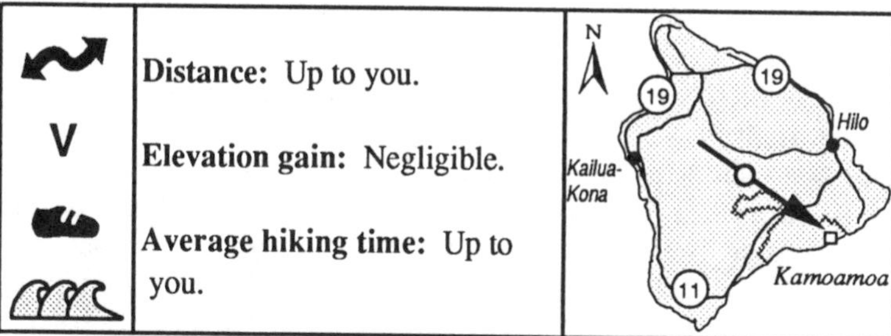

Topos: Optional: *Kalapana* 7½.

Trail map (route approximated): At the end of Trip 40.

Highlights: The big black-sand beach of Kamoamoa is a major tourist attraction, and there are also some interesting stone ruins here.

Driving instructions: Follow the driving instructions of Trip 20 but instead of turning right to go to Kilauea Visitor Center, turn left and follow Crater Rim Road downhill, soon making a mandatory left turn. You continue downhill to the junction with the Chain of Craters Road (opposite the Devastation Trail parking lot). Turn left onto the Chain of Craters Road and follow it downhill out to the coast. Going northeast, keep your eyes peeled for the turnoff to Kamoamoa beach and campground. The road forks shortly after the turnoff. Take the right fork to the beach, 25½ miles from Kilauea Visitor Center and 53½ miles from Hilo. Park here to start your hike. (The left fork goes to the campground.)

Permit/permission required: None.

Description: There's a pavilion near the parking lot, to your left as you face the sea, and a path runs by it. Pick up this path and follow it past the ruins of Kamoamoa village. Interpretive signs identify some of the ruins. You first pass some raised burial sites bracketing the path. Then, curving left to parallel the coastline, you pass the foundation of a canoe shed overgrown by morning glory vines. When in use, a canoe shed like this would have had a thatched roof in order to protect the canoes from the fierce sun. Now you begin passing through and along stone walls. An interpretive sign says the walls around these ruins are a mix of old Hawaiian work and of walls built in the 1880s, when this land was part of a ranch. Among the ruins are the remains of a place of worship, Moa *heiau*. Plants flourishing over and around these ruins include *laue, noni, ulei,* coconut palms, and Indian pluchea. Where the path along the ruins turns inland toward the road through the camping area, make your way seaward for a few feet through the weeds to the northeast end of Kamoamoa Beach. (The camping area is neither scenic nor interesting.)

You step out of the weeds and onto a huge, splendid black-sand beach, itself made of millions of tiny grains of black volcanic glass. This is a *big* beach, stretching northeast and southwest, recently built by Kilauea's steam eruptions when its lava exploded as it flowed into the seawater. Great mounds of new black sand are piled up here and there. Tiny, translucent, bubble-like seashells lie in little drifts in the hollows of the glittering sand, caught there like seafoam. It's hard to believe that before the currents swept the black sand up here, this was not a beach at all but a very rocky shore. Treat yourself to a leisurely stroll southwest to the far end of the beach, where it ends at some low lava cliffs. Black sand can get very hot, so it's best to keep your shoes on. Those with a yen to scramble up the rocks at the end of the beach will find a 1990 benchmark and a C-shaped stone shelter with its closed side to the fierce northeast winds. The bright blue water is extremely rough, and swimming is unsafe here—but what scenery!

Turning around, you make your way back northeast toward the coconut palms that fringe the grassy picnic area just seaward of the parking lot. Picnic tables, restrooms, and a water fountain invite you to stay and enjoy your lunch in this breezy setting. The beach is one of the newest and largest black-sand beaches on the Big Island, and it gets many visitors—often whole tour buses-ful—now that beaches like Kaimu and Harry K. Brown have been lost (see Trip 40). For this reason, Kamoamoa can be a fine people-watching spot, too.

A black-sand beach where you *can* swim. . . . is located at little Punaluu Beach County Park, roughly halfway between Hawaii Volcanoes National Park and South Point. The small bay here is generally safer than most along this coast, but you must still be alert for strong currents and rough seas. Stay close to shore; a nasty rip current reportedly occurs just outside the bay. A murky lagoon behind the beach is uninviting for swimming, but it attracts waterfowl who waddle along the beach like so many shoppers in a mall, looking for leftovers and nattering with one another in *quack-quack-quacky* voices. Camping is permitted on an adjacent grassy flat, while for non-campers, a resort just inland includes condominiums you can rent, a golf course, restaurants, and other amenities.

Trip 42. Hilina Pali Road to Pit Craters

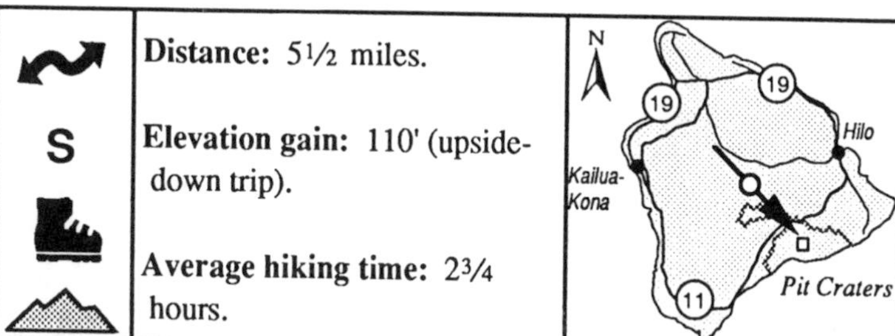

Topos: *Kau Desert* 7½.

Trail map: At the end of this trip.

Highlights: In the middle of the monotonous Kau Desert, there is a pair of colorful craters with some special inhabitants. Most of the Kau Desert is very uninteresting, I think; this hike is the exception.

Driving instructions: Follow the driving instructions of Trip 20 but instead of turning right to go to Kilauea Visitor Center, turn left and follow Crater Rim Road downhill, soon making a mandatory left turn. You continue downhill past Kilauea Iki Overlook and Thurston Lava Tube. At the junction with the Chain of Craters Road (opposite the Devastation Trail parking lot), turn left onto the Chain of Craters Road. Follow this road downhill to the turnoff for Hilina Pali Road on your right, just over 5½ miles from Kilauea Visitor Center. Be alert for this turnoff, as it comes up rather suddenly. Turn right onto Hilina Pali Road and follow it through an open *ohia* forest for 3¾ more miles to the Mauna Iki Trail trailhead, on the right side of the road at the top of a small rise. A rough turnout across the road offers a place to park, 9¼ miles from Kilauea Visitor Center and 34¼ miles from Hilo. Start your hike here.

Permit/permission required: None.

Description: From the marked trailhead, you bear west-southwest through a scrubby *ohia* forest. You follow cairns and lines of rocks in and out, up and down, over worn *pahoehoe*. The forest soon gives way to plain scrub, and the going is rather uninteresting for a time except for golden masses of Pele's hair (see Trip 32) trapped in the lee of *pahoehoe* ripples and of weeds.

But after a time, you approach some fierce-looking, squared-off rocky "teeth" that turn out to mark a low, weather-beaten scarp. You weave your way through the "teeth" and descend a couple of lazy switchbacks to a sandy plain. Soon you reach an area of newer, shiny black *pahoehoe*. The Kau Desert stretches around you, vast, dry, and lonely. Perhaps you are seeing things—mirages in the shimmering heat waves—for surely those cannot be white-tailed tropicbirds you see in the distance, spiralling along the updrafts! You shake your head to clear it and continue west-northwest toward the prominent cone called Puu Koae (not on the map; it's too far west).

As you approach a brownish-green cone crater, you can no longer deny that you *are* seeing a small flock of white-tailed tropicbirds soaring, chattering, and squabbling. Signs warn you DANGER OVER HANGING EDGE STAY BACK. You are at the Pit Craters, and here the birds make their homes—in almost as unlikely a spot as Halemaumau. What a contrast the colorful pit craters—dashed with pinks, golds, and grays—and the greenish cone crater make with the dull browns of the rest of the landscape! And what a contrast the lively tropicbirds make with the rest of the desert, which is nearly devoid of animal life. *Koae* means "tropicbird" in Hawaiian; now you know how nearby Puu Koae came by its name.

Enjoy the craters and the birds, and then retrace your steps to your car.

Kau Desert trails. . . . I have not included most of the miles of trails in the Kau Desert in trips in this book. This trip, Trip 46, and Trip 51 are the exceptions. *They* have interesting features. The rest of the miles are not bad trails. They're mostly cairn-marked routes across lava. They're safe as long as you keep a eye out for deep cracks and pits in the lava and follow the cairns. Unfortunately, they're very uninteresting compared to most of the other trails in Hawaii Volcanoes National Park. Perhaps there are times when it's raining everywhere else but in the Kau Desert, and it's sunny there. A Kau Desert hike might be appropriate then. On the other hand, when it's raining everywhere else, the Kau Desert may languish under heavy overcast and may even be foggy. You will have trouble following cairns in the fog.

So while it's safe for you to hike in the Kau Desert, I think it's not worth your time unless you've hiked everywhere else or unless the weather is bad everywhere else. There are brief descriptions of the other Kau Desert trails in Appendix B.

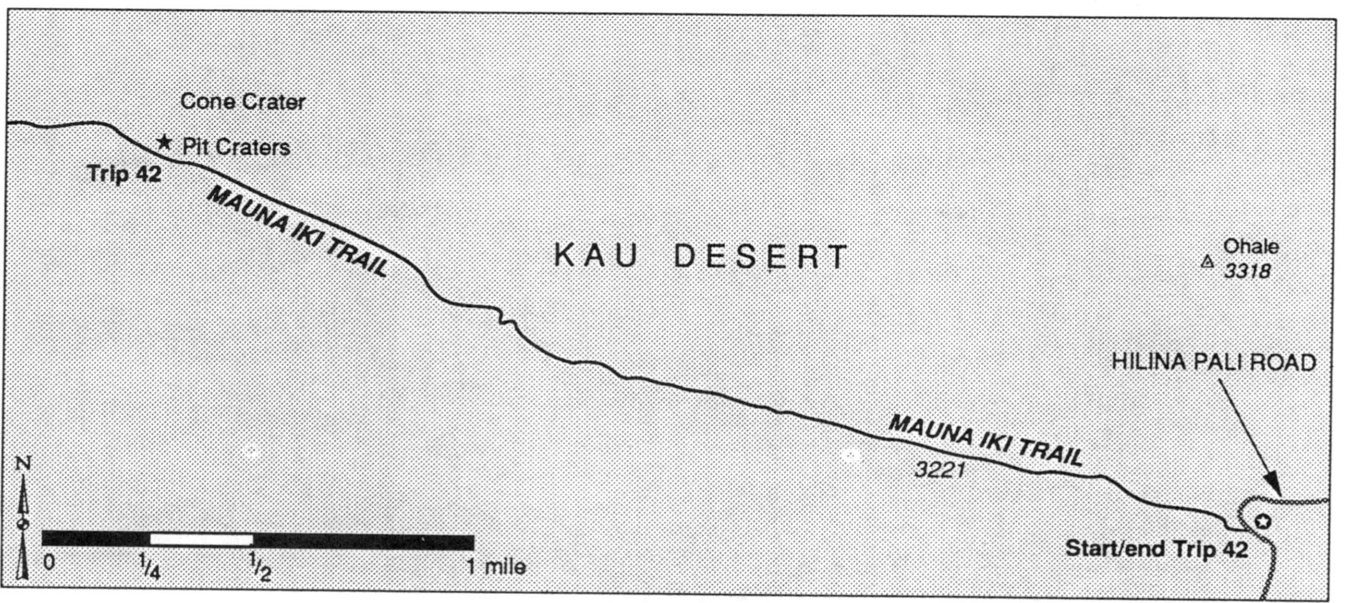

Trip 42. Pit Craters

Trip 43. Kipuka Nene Campground to Halape

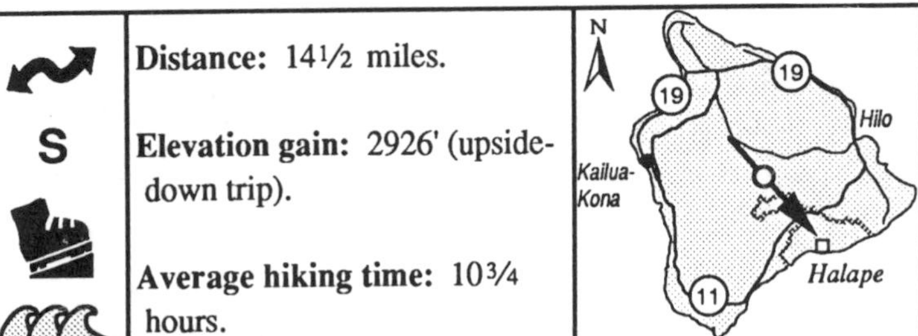

Distance: 14½ miles.

Elevation gain: 2926' (upside-down trip).

Average hiking time: 10¾ hours.

Topos: *Kau Desert, Makaopuhi Crater* 7½.

Trail map: Begins on the map at the end of this trip; ends on the map at the end of Trip 37.

Highlights: The coves at Halape are considered the best along Hawaii Volcanoes National Park's Puna-Kau coast for scenery and for snorkeling. Halape is an extremely popular destination!

Driving instructions: Follow the driving instructions of Trip 20 but instead of turning right to go to Kilauea Visitor Center, turn left and follow Crater Rim Road downhill, making the mandatory left turn. You continue downhill past Kilauea Iki Overlook and Thurston Lava Tube. At the junction with the Chain of Craters Road (opposite the Devastation Trail parking lot), you turn left onto the Chain of Craters Road. Follow the Chain of Craters Road downhill to the turnoff for Hilina Pali Road on your right, just over 5½ miles from Kilauea Visitor Center. Be alert for this turnoff, as it comes up rather suddenly. Turn right onto Hilina Pali Road and follow it through an open *ohia* forest past the Mauna Iki Trailhead to Kipuka Nene, a campground and picnic area on the left side of the road, 10½ miles from Kilauea Visitor Center and 38½ miles from Hilo. The warning sign of Kipuka Nene's being close is a yellow *nene*-crossing sign. For more about the *nene*, see below. There is parking on both sides of the road at Kipuka Nene. Start your trip here. (See Appendix A for information on staying at Kipuka Nene.)

Permit/permission required: As for Trip 38, you must have a valid permit from Hawaii Volcanoes National Park, available only by applying in person at the Kilauea Visitor Center, to stay overnight in the park's backcountry.

Description: (See also the Puna-Kau Coast cautions at the end of Trip 38.)

Day 1 (7¼ miles). A dirt road runs behind the picnic pavilion at Kipuka Nene. Say goodbye to the *nene* and head seaward (right as you face the front of the pavilion) on that road, which is the Halape Trail. You pass through a gate and bear east, then southwest. From here, the road generally runs east, with an occasional southward tack, through scrub: grasses, stubby guava trees, live *ohia* trees, and fire-killed *ohia* trees. These slopes are relatively dry, and forest fires are a problem here. Look out for holes in the road where lava tubes have caved in.

In 2 miles, you reach a marked junction where you turn south on a very faint old road that soon becomes a rocky foot trail. The footing is mediocre to poor, so be careful. For the next few miles, you alternately plunge steeply downward and then cross relatively level benches. A fence runs north-south on your left (east), roughly paralleling the trail almost to Puu Kapukapu. At last you reach a broad, sloping bench where the trail leads you to the edge of the cliffs called Puueo Pali overlooking Keauhou Shelter and Puu Kapukapu (you can't see Halape from here).

The trail plunges over Puueo Pali and descends steeply on switchbacks through *aa.* Just beyond the foot of Puueo Pali, you meet the Hilina Pali Trail (not recommended; see Appendix B). Continue downhill on this shoulder of Puu Kapukapu on the Halape Trail for a little over a mile more to Halape Shelter. See Trip 39 for a description of Halape's shelter, coves, and camping area.

Day 2 (7¼ miles). Retrace your steps to Kipuka Nene. The ascent can be excruciatingly hot at midday, so start as early as possible.

Nene. . . . This handsome, non-migratory goose is believed to have descended from the migratory Brant and Canada geese that occasionally winter over in the Hawaiian Islands. Unlike their ancestors, the *nene* aren't waterfowl. One of the *nene*'s adaptations to this dry habitat is feet that are only partially webbed.

There were once as many as 25,000 *nene* in the islands. But by the early 1950s, it was estimated that there were only 30 wild *nene* left. Their habitat had been destroyed by the deforestation that had left so much of Hawaii stripped of her native trees. Introduced animals, particularly mongooses and cats, had destroyed *nene* eggs, chicks, and nesting adults. Concerted efforts in Hawaii and in England have enabled the *nene* to survive in captivity. *Nene* have been reintroduced into the wild here on the Big Island at Hawaii Volcanoes National Park, on Maui at Haleakala National Park, and on Kauai in the lowlands around Lihue. It's not known whether they can successfully reestablish themselves in the wild, because the introduced animals that prey on them haven't been controlled.

Nene "honk" like other geese, but you're more likely to hear another of their calls, a cow-like "moo." Here, they are filling a sort of ecological niche, but in their own *nene* style. On the mainland, the campground beggars are typically ground squirrels, bluejays, and raccoons—the latter two are out-and-out thieves. Hawaii Volcanoes National Park's *nene* aren't thieves, but they're accomplished beggars. They come running, literally, when you drive up and open a car door, set out a picnic cooler, unzip a daypack, or pull some trail mix out of your pocket. You must be hardhearted and not feed them. (It's both the law and common sense, so they won't become dependent on people supplying food.) However, you will probably feel as guilty as I do when one of them stands there in front of you, eyeing your sandwich hopefully and mooing as if to say, "I'm endangered, I'm adorable, *feed me!*" Just hang onto your goodies. You'll be off the hook as soon as someone else drives up and opens a car door, sets out a picnic cooler, ...

I originally wrote the above about the *nene* at Haleakala National Park on Maui. Were the *nene* at Hawaii Volcanoes National Park a bunch of shameless and engaging moochers like the *nene* at Haleakala? Were they ever! At Kipuka Nene, seven *nene* hung around much of the time, looking for handouts. "Moo, something for me? *No?!* Too bad your parents didn't teach you any manners." Did I feel like Scrooge? Yes. But I was not alone at Kipuka Nene. There was also a class of local eighth-graders camped out. They had more food than they knew what to do with. Guess who helped them with the leftovers.

Nene (Hawaiian goose)

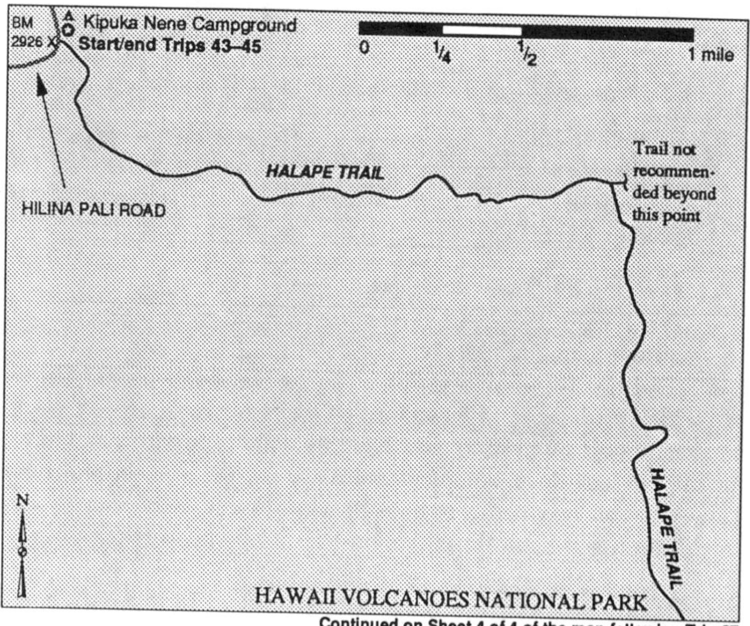

Continued on Sheet 4 of 4 of the map following Trip 37
(overlap is abreast of words HAWAII VOLCANOES NATIONAL PARK on both)

Trips 43–45. Kipuka Nene to Halape, Keauhou, and Chain of Craters Road

Trip 44. Kipuka Nene Campground to Keauhou via Halape

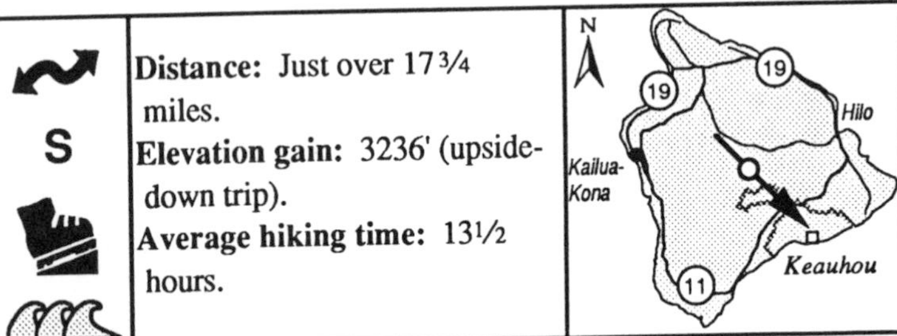

Topos: *Kau Desert, Makaopuhi Crater* 7½.

Trail map: Begins on the map at the end of Trip 43; ends on the map at the end of Trip 37.

Highlights: After enjoying a stay at Halape, you move on to the wide-open spaces of Keauhou, where there is another, though smaller, sunning and snorkeling area. As with Trip 39, it's easiest to do this in four days, stopping at Halape on the way in and out. However, you may prefer to do it in two or three days.

Driving instructions: Follow the driving instructions of Trip 43.

Permit/permission required: As for Trip 38, you must have a valid permit from Hawaii Volcanoes National Park, available only by applying in person at the Kilauea Visitor Center, to stay overnight in the park's backcountry.

Description (easiest trip). (See also the Puna-Kau Coast cautions at the end of Trip 38.)

Day 1 (7¼ miles). Follow Trip 43 to Halape.

Day 2 (1⅔ miles). From the junction of the Halape and Puna Kau trails, reverse the steps of Day 2 of Trip 39 to Keauhou Shelter. Camp either near Keauhou Shelter or down at the beach, as described in Trip 39.

Days 3 and 4 (Just over 8⅔ miles). Retrace the steps of Days 1 and 2 back to Kipuka Nene. As noted in Trip 43, the climb back up the pali to Kipuka Nene can be extraordinarily hot, so get as early a start as possible.

The Keauhou Trail. . . . As you look at the topos and the Park Service maps, you'll notice that you can get to Keauhou in at least four ways: from Kipuka Nene via Halape (this trip); from the Chain of Craters Road via the Puna Kau Trail (Trip 38); from Kipuka Nene via the Keauhou Trail (misspelled "Keaunou" on the topo; see Appendix B); and from the Chain of Craters Road also via the Keauhou Trail (see Appendix B). I haven't used the Keauhou Trail for any of the trips in this book. It is thoroughly overgrown (*talk about winding up covered with weed seeds!*) and very unpleasant to hike. Rangers have told me that they seldom brush out any of these Kipuka Nene-Hilina Pali trails except for the popular Halape Trail, used in this trip and Trip 43.

Fragrant hibiscus blossoms

Trip 45. Kipuka Nene Campground to the Chain of Craters Road via Halape and Keauhou

44 (Kipuka Nene-Chain of Craters Road)

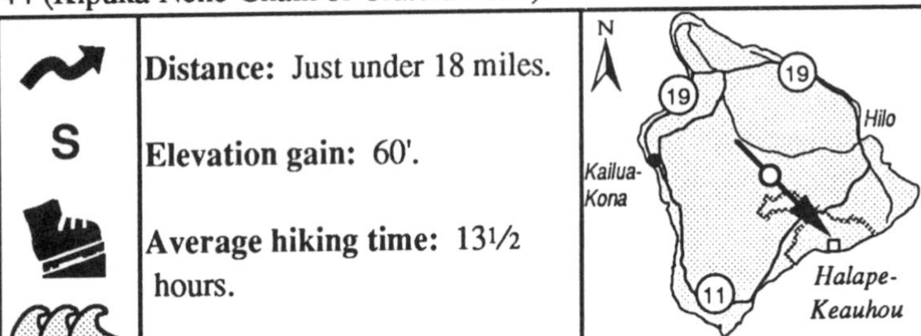

Topos: *Kau Desert, Makaopuhi Crater* 7½; continued on the map at the end of Trip 37.

Trail map: Begins on the map at the end of Trip 43; ends on the map at the end of Trip 37.

Highlights: Why not make a shuttle trip of your tour of Halape and Keauhou? No climbing back up the rocky, weedy *pali* on this trip! Instead, you walk out to the Chain of Craters Road on the Puna Kau Trail with an enjoyable break at Apua Point. This trip is easier if done in three days, with stops at both Halape and Keauhou, but you could do it in two days, stopping at either Halape or Keauhou, if you were in a hurry.

Driving instructions: Shuttle one car to the start of the Puna Kau Trail as described in the driving instructions for Trip 36; the Puna Kau Trail begins across the Chain of Craters Road from the Puu Loa Petroglyphs trail. Then, with the other car, follow the driving instructions of Trip 43 to get to the start of this trip.

Permit/permission required: As for Trip 43, you must have a valid permit from Hawaii Volcanoes National Park, available only by applying in person at the Kilauea Visitor Center, to stay overnight in the park's backcountry.

Description (easier trip).

Day 1 (7¼ miles). Follow Trip 43 to Halape.

Day 2 (1⅔ miles). From the junction of the Halape and Puna Kau trails, reverse the steps of Day 2 of Trip 39 to Keauhou Shelter. Camp either near Keauhou Shelter or down at the beach, as described in Trip 39.

Day 3 (9 miles). Reverse the steps of Trips 38 and 37 to your shuttle car on the Chain of Craters Road.

Trip 46. Hilina Pali Roadend to Pepeiao Cabin

46 (Hilina Pali Rdend to Pepeiao)

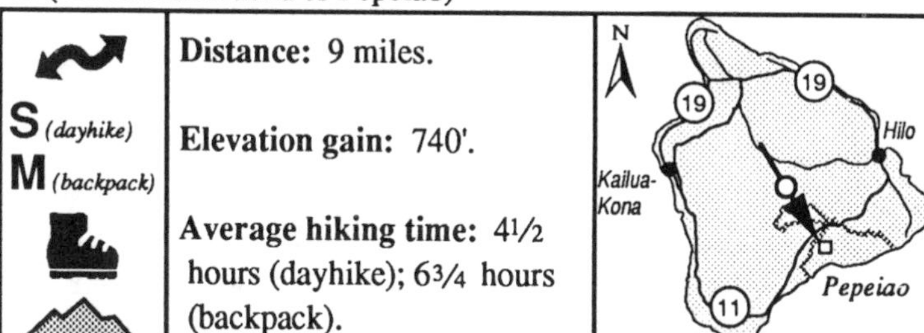

Topos: *Kau Desert* 7½.

Trail map: At the end of this trip.

Highlights: Pepeiao Cabin ("Pepeiau Shelter" on the topo), in a meadow of deep grasses on the edge of the Kau Desert, has a feeling of tranquility and remoteness, even a touch of melancholy, unmatched by the other backcountry shelters and cabins, even though all the others are in fact more remote in terms of mileage. You can visit Pepeiao as a dayhike or stay overnight.

If you are staying overnight, plan to camp out in your own tent in the vicinity of Pepeiao Cabin, because the cabin area is swarming with ants and, after nightfall, with cockroaches. The Puna-Kau coast cautions given at the end of Trip 38 apply to Pepeiao, too.

Driving instructions: Follow the driving instructions of Trip 43 to Kipuka Nene and continue to the end of the road, 14¼ miles from Kilauea Visitor Center and 42¼ miles from Hilo. On a clear day, there are outstanding coastal views from this roadend, which is 2280 feet above sea level on the edge of Hilina Pali. There's a picnic shelter here and a pit toilet but no water. Park here to start your hike.

Permit/permission required: Not required for a dayhike. As for Trip 38, you must have a valid permit from Hawaii Volcanoes National Park, available only by applying in person at the Kilauea Visitor Center, to stay overnight in the park's backcountry.

Description (as a backpack).

Day 1 (4½ miles). Two trails lead away from the roadend (see below). Neither is marked by name. You take the one that leads south-southwest (to the right as you stand in front of the picnic shelter, facing the ocean). It's the Kau Desert Trail.

You stroll through tall grasses occasionally punctuated by *ohia* and *pukiawe*. Clover and bamboo orchids grow along with the grasses. The clover, which has spikes of little pale pink to cherry-pink pea-shaped flowers, is the villain that leaves strings of tiny, sticky, flattened oval seeds all over your boots, socks, shorts, etc., and gear. Cairns help keep you on the trail, which wanders over old *pahoehoe* now and then, but the grasses are so tall that they may hide the shorter cairns. Still, as long as the path is fairly well-beaten, it's not a problem.

Your descent is very gentle, and you cross a number of runoff channels. Around the 2-mile point, you begin crossing good-sized lava-floored gullies which require a little climbing down and up. A pattern is established: a lonely meadow, a scant *ohia* wood, a gully, another lonely meadow, ...

The little cabin, which seems sunken up to its roof in the tall meadow grass, comes into view before you reach the junction with the Kaaha (Kalue) Trail. At the junction, you turn left onto the Kaaha Trail and descend a little to the cabin, which is less than ¼ mile from the junction. A sign over the door says it's at 1500 feet elevation, but it's at almost 1700 feet. Sharp-eyed campers will notice petroglyphs in the lava in front of the cabin. The cabin has three cots, a bookcase, a table, a metal cabinet, and a water tank (the tap is outside). Purify the water before drinking it. There is a second table outside and a rickety bench by the cabin door. There's an outhouse a few yards west of the cabin. Don't plan on staying *inside* the cabin unless you love cockroaches.

Day 2 (4½ miles). Return the way you came.

Trails from Hilina Pali Roadend. . . . The Kau Desert Trail, which goes southwest from Hilina Pali roadend, is the one used in this trip. It's reasonably clear and leads to Pepeiao Cabin and the Kaaha Trail. Beyond there, it swings north into the Kau Desert and is just another dull segment of the Kau Desert trail (see Appendix B).

Another trail, the Hilina Pali Trail, goes roughly south from the roadend and soon plunges—I do mean *plunges*—steeply over Hilina Pali in rocky, weedy, loose switchbacks. Its condition as it goes down the *pali* is poor. Its condition as it curves southeast and east to meet the Halape Trail is appalling; I am surprised that this part of it still appears as a trail on so many maps. I strongly recommend you avoid the Hilina Pali Trail. See Appendix B for more details.

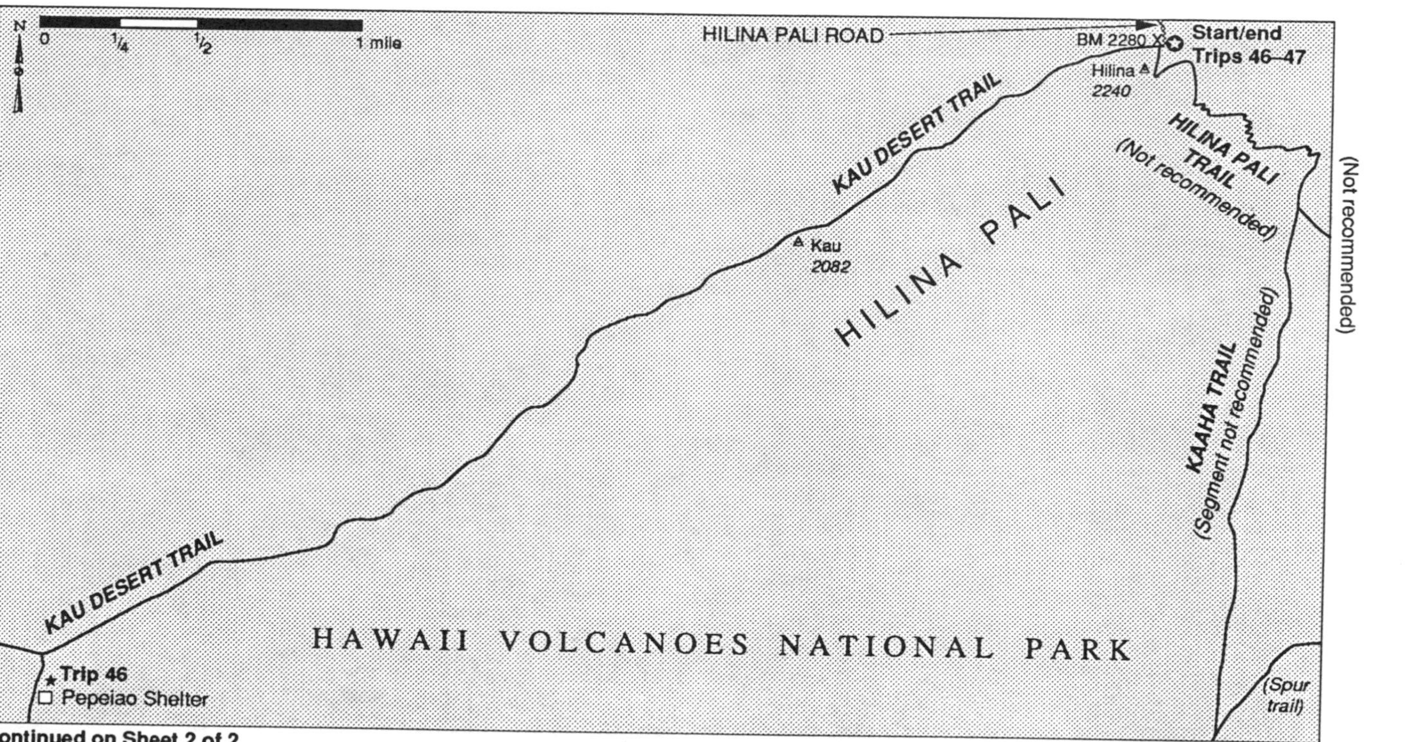

Continued on Sheet 2 of 2

Trips 46–47. Pepeiao Shelter and Kaaha Shelter (Sheet 1 of 2)

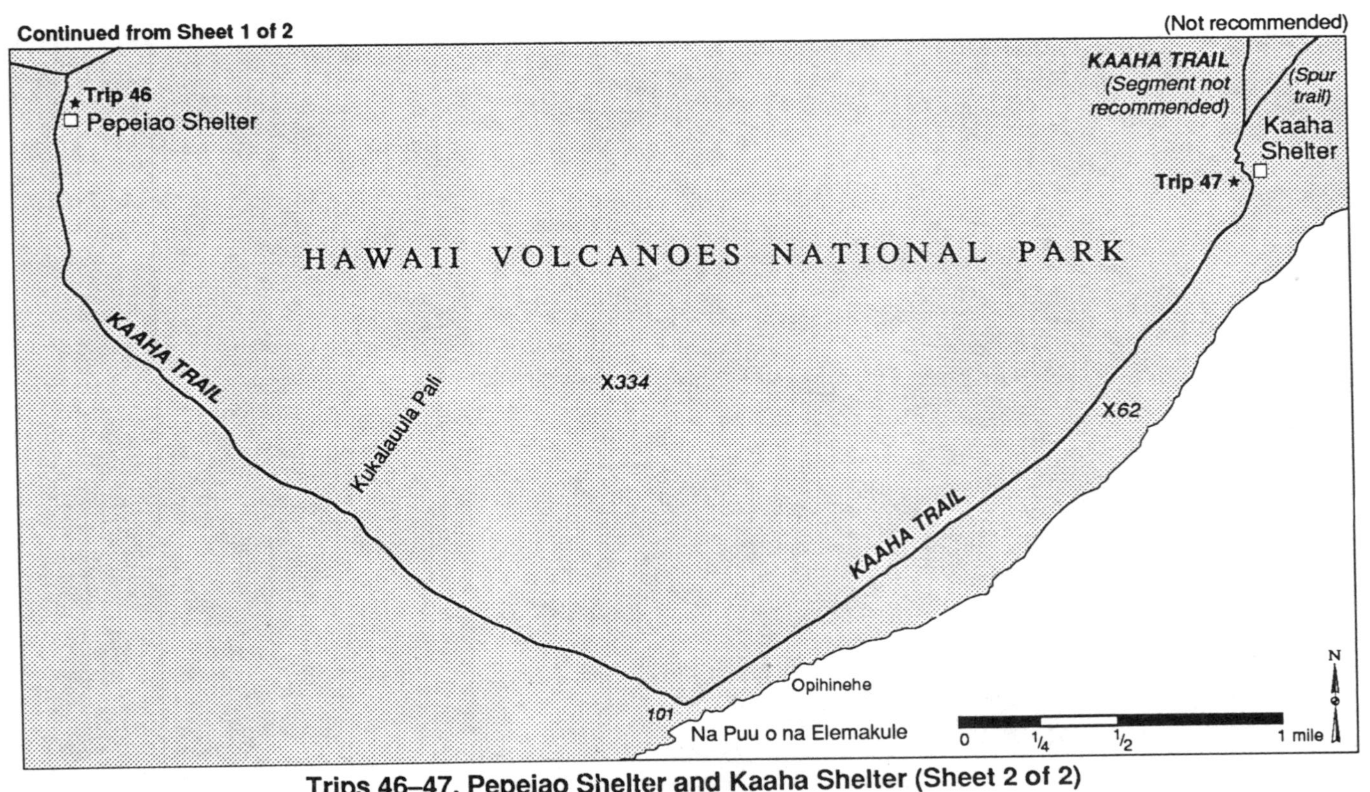

Trips 46–47. Pepeiao Shelter and Kaaha Shelter (Sheet 2 of 2)

Trip 47. Hilina Pali to Kaaha Shelter via Pepeiao Cabin

47 (Hilina Pali Rdend to Kaaha via Pepeiao)

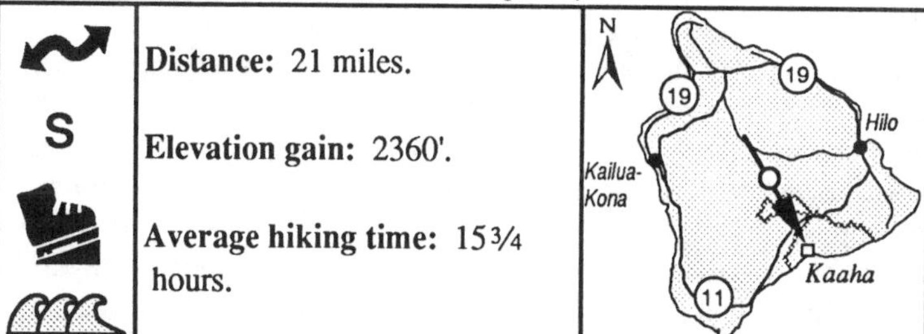

Topos: *Kau Desert, Naliikakani Point* 7½.

Trail map: At the end of Trip 46.

Highlights: After your visit to Pepeiao Cabin, you descend to Kaaha Shelter on the coast. This trip is easiest if done in four days, but you could do it in two or three days if you were in a hurry.

Driving instructions: Follow the driving instructions of Trip 46.

Permit/permission required: As for Trip 38, you must have a valid permit from Hawaii Volcanoes National Park, available only by applying in person at the Kilauea Visitor Center, to stay overnight in the park's backcountry.

Description (easiest trip). (The Puna-Kau Coast cautions of Trip 38 apply to this trip.)

Day 1 (4½ miles). Follow Trip 46 to Pepeiao Cabin.

Day 2 (6 miles). Leave Pepeiao Cabin heading generally southeast, at first over terrain that is much the same as the terrain you traversed to get to Pepeiao Cabin from Hilina Pali roadend. Soon, however, the vegetation becomes more sparse, the sections of lava longer. The ocean looms ahead, while Puu Kaone rises to the east (Puu Kaone is off the map to the east-northeast of Kaaha Shelter).

The descent becomes steeper and, as you pass through an *aa* field, it's hard to tell the cairns from the other volcanic debris. You come abreast of Puu Kaone, and the route veers briefly toward that hill before resuming its downhill course. At the edge of Kukalauula Pali, you turn toward Puu Kaone as you descend the cliffs. It's a steep descent over loose rubble, so be careful!

At the bottom of the *pali,* you bear east-southeast through a sandy wash into a field of *aa,* heading for some shiny *pahoehoe* ahead.

Route-finding is difficult through the spiky *aa* because most of the rocks look like cairns. Fortunately, the cairns soon become more distinct. The green slopes of Na Puu o na Elemakule come into view ahead, and a salt breeze soon tickles your nose.

Just behind Na Puu o na Elemakule, you turn east-northeast along the coast, toward Puu Kaone. Here, waves have battered an arch through the black lava cliffs. Black cairns lead you across a hot, shiny, black landscape inland of the pounding sea. Just as you're about to venture onto a broad plain of brown-black sand, your route veers inland toward the grassy slopes leading up to Puu Kaone. At the top of a small rise, the route may be indistinct because the cairns are hard to spot. But you continue in the same general direction you've been going in and presently climb into an area of deeply cracked lava domes. You pick your way carefully around the cracks and enter a trackless area of cairns and weeds. There's a bad section of *aa* where the weeds are quite deep and you'll need to watch where you step.

You veer toward the base of the cliffs behind Kaaha Shelter and soon reach it. Here, you'll find a three-sided shelter whose open side faces the sea. The water tank is behind it, and the tap is accessible from there. There's a pit toilet along the trail beyond the shelter, nearer the cliffs. A rock-walled shelter just uphill of Kaaha Shelter may offer a good tent site. Like all the shelters along this coast, and like Pepeiao Cabin, Kaaha Shelter is home to plenty of creepy-crawlies. Kaaha's cove is ¼ mile away, looking from the shelter like a lagoon. Remember that the seas are rough and treacherous on this coast, so exercise caution if you swim or snorkel here.

Day 3 (6 miles). Retrace your steps to Pepeiao Cabin.

Day 4 (4½ miles). Retrace your steps to Hilina Pali roadend.

Continuing to Halape and Keauhou: don't do it. . . . The Kaaha Trail continues up the cliff behind the shelter to a **Y** junction. The left (north) branch meets the Hilina Pali Trail at the base of Hilina Pali. The right (northeast) is the spur that meets the Hilina Pali Trail behind Puu Kaone and, as the Hilina Pali Trail, eventually meets the Halape Trail. It is tempting to continue to Halape on this route—I had originally intended to do so—but I cannot recommend it. As described at the end of Trip 46 and in Appendix B, this route is in extremely poor condition and very hard to follow. Until the trails are considerably improved, if they ever are, I think the better choice is to visit Pepeiao-Kaaha and Halape-Keauhou as two separate trips.

Trip 48. Bird Park (Kipuka Puaulu)

E

Distance: Just over 1 mile.

Elevation gain: 170'.

Average hiking time: 35 minutes.

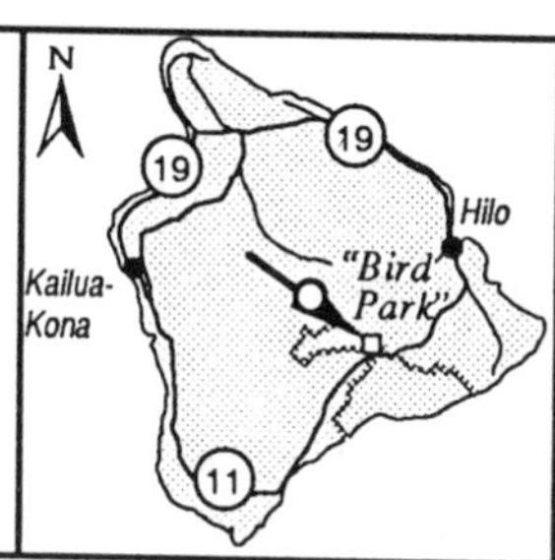

Topos: Optional: *Kilauea Crater* 7½.

Trail map: At the end of this trip.

Highlights: Kipuka Puaulu is perhaps the second most delightful hike in Hawaii Volcanoes National Park. I rate it a close second to Kilauea Iki (Trip 28) for sheer enjoyment. If you have time for only one other hike besides Kilauea Iki in the park, this should be it. And what a contrast it is! On almost every other hike in the park, you are sooner or later confronted by the alien barrenness of a lava landscape. Here, at Kipuka Puaulu, you escape from that barrenness entirely and enter a woodland soft, green, and alive with birds—hence its other name, the Bird Park.

Driving instructions: You need not stop at Kilauea Visitor Center in order to visit Kipuka Puaulu, but you will probably enjoy your visit more if you do stop there and pick up an interpretive guidebook to the Bird Park. (Sometimes there are guidebooks available at the trailhead, but getting one at Kilauea Visitor Center can spare you disappointment in case the trailhead guidebooks are all gone. It cost only 50¢ when I bought mine.)

Drive southwest from Hilo on Highway 11 past the turnoff to Hawaii Volcanoes National Park's Kilauea Visitor Center and continue just over 2 miles more on Highway 11, past the turnoff to the golf course. At the next turnoff on your right (inland), turn right and follow the Mauna Loa Road 1½ miles uphill, past the turnoff to the Tree Molds to the parking area for Kipuka Puaulu, 31½ miles from Hilo (3½ miles from Kilauea Visitor Center).

(The Mauna Loa Road has a turnaround just beyond Kipuka Puaulu and becomes a one-lane road after that. It ends at the parking lot and picnic shelter at the Mauna Loa Trail.)

Permit/permission required: None.

Description: Pause to read the interpretive sign at the trailhead and then go north into the *kipuka*. A *kipuka* is an area of vegetation spared by later lava flows. Over time, an isolated *kipuka* may come to harbor unique animals and plants—animals and plants that have followed their own evolutionary course since the *kipuka* was largely cut off from the ecosystem that once surrounded it.

Almost immediately, you pass a box that may have trail guidebooks in it. If you didn't get the better one at Kilauea Visitor Center, see if there's a guidebook here. The guidebook's entries are numbered, keyed to numbered sites along the trail. To follow the numbered sites in order, bear left at the trail junction just after you pass through a fence. The trail ascends gently, but the occasional rest bench is welcome. I will not attempt to repeat the guidebook's contents but will let you discover the pleasures of this trail with your own guidebook.

The forest has a wonderful fragrance, and the *kipuka* rings with birdsong. However, because most of the forest is so dense, it's much harder to see the birds than it is to hear them. Birding, as always, requires patience. (Here, I must take a minor exception to something in the guidebook. The green bird shown on the inside of the back cover and labeled "elepaio" is not an *elepaio.* I think it's an *amakihi.*)

Near the ½-mile mark, halfway through this stroll, a sign invites you to take a short detour (five minutes) to a giant *koa* tree. It looked like two giant *koa* trees to me, one with lots of ephiphytes growing on it. You may notice a smell here that is to me the scent most uniquely Hawaiian: a rich, garlicky, oniony smell around *koa* trees when the soil is damp. This scent can betray the presence of *koa* trees to your nose even before your eyes spot them. In *Hawaii: A Natural History,* Sherwin Carlquist describes the scent as "sharp ozone-like or perhaps faintly skunk-like," which correctly captures one of its qualities: it is not entirely pleasant.

Soon you're curving downhill and back toward the road. Too soon, you're back at the fence and then your car. Reluctant to leave? It's a short hike; you *could* go around the loop again! Or, instead of rushing off, stay for a picnic at the adjacent picnic area.

Tree Molds. . . . Back down the Mauna Loa Road, at a loop at the end of a short (⅓ mile) spur road to the northeast, you'll find several tree molds. They're deep, narrow holes in a *pahoehoe* flow where trees once stood. Railings keep you from stepping into the larger tree-mold holes; watch out for smaller ones that lack railings.

As explained in Trip 19, tree molds are formed by a process similar to the one that forms lava trees. A lava tree forms when still-fluid lava flows away, leaving a free-standing shell composed of lava that solidifed in contact with a tree. A tree mold forms when a lava flow solidifies in place around a tree. The interpretive sign says the trees that burnt away here were *ohia* trees. One advantage of tree molds over lava trees for the visitor is that it's much easier to look down into a tree-mold hole to see the imprint of the long-gone bark than it is to see into the tall shell of a lava tree.

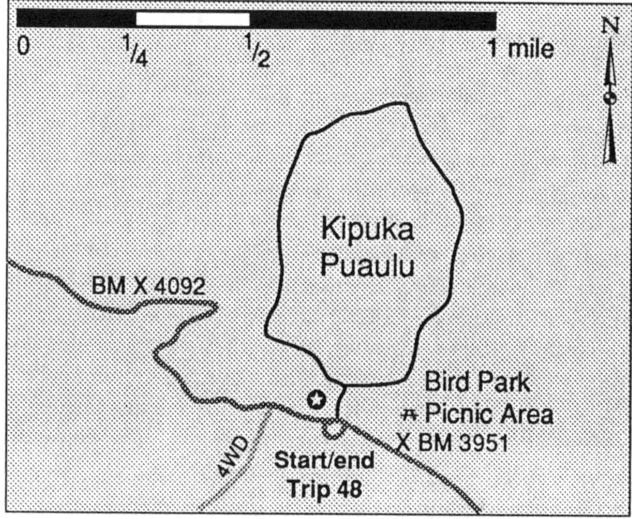

Trip 48. Bird Park (Kipuka Puaulu)

Trip 49. Mauna Loa Trail to Red Hill

Distance: 15 miles.

Elevation gain: 3373'.

Average hiking time: 11-12 hours.

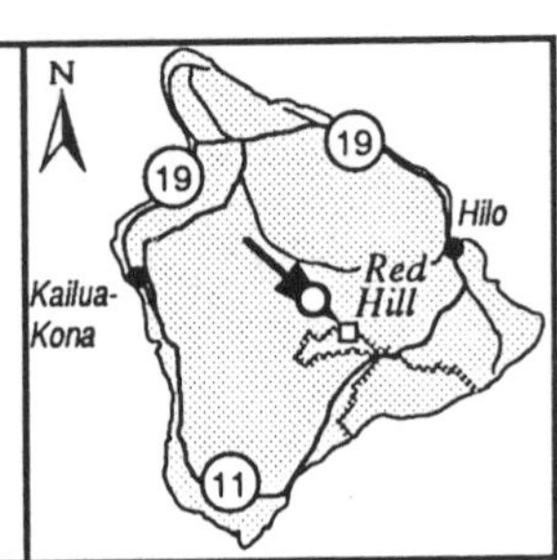

Topos: *Kipuka Pakekake, Puu Ulaula* 7½.

Trail map: At the end of this trip.

Highlights: Those who yearn to hike on Mauna Loa but who fear they may suffer altitude sickness if they risk going all the way to the summit or if they attempt the Observatory Trail hikes (Trips 11 through 13) may enjoy going partway, to the Red Hill Cabin at 10,035 feet.

Driving instructions: You must have a permit in order to stay at or near the cabin (see below), so follow the driving instructions of Trip 20 to Kilauea Visitor Center to get your permit. Then return to Highway 11 and turn left onto the highway. Continue just over 2 miles on Highway 11, past the turnoff to the golf course. At the next turnoff on your right (inland), turn right onto the Mauna Loa Road and follow it past the parking area for Kipuka Puaulu. The Mauna Loa Road has a turnaround just beyond Kipuka Puaulu. From the top of the turnaround, bear right on the now-one-lane road and follow it uphill to the parking lot and picnic shelter at the Mauna Loa Trail, 13½ miles from Kilauea Visitor Center and 41½ miles from Hilo. The last, one-lane part of the drive is very slow going, and you must be alert for oncoming traffic on this winding, narrow road. Park here to start your hike.

Permit/permission required: As for Trip 38, you must have a valid permit from Hawaii Volcanoes National Park, available only by applying in person at the Kilauea Visitor Center, to stay overnight in the park's backcountry.

Description: (*Please* review the special hiking hints at the end of Trip 11. Mauna Loa must not be taken lightly just because it's in the tropics.)

Day 1 (7½ miles). You begin in a pleasant, open forest but soon curve around the mountain, descend a little, and emerge into a lava-and-scrub landscape of *pukiawe, aalii, oheo,* a few *mamane, ohia, kukaenene,* and bracken fern. The trail is generally very rough, and you need to watch your footing. On a clear morning, it's not long before you can make out Kilauea far below to the south and southeast.

You pass through a gate in the summit's protective fence. Please be sure to close it behind you! Now you head northwest and uphill. Stretches of smooth *pahoehoe* and dirt are a welcome relief from the rougher *aa.* Your rest stops, probably taken frequently, offer wonderful views (until the clouds move in), complete with background music by the many birds on these slopes.

The trail soon becomes indistinct, and you must follow cairns. Some of them are fine examples of the cairn-builder's art. Your route is increasingly over lava, and the going is so rough at times that it's less like hiking and more like boulder hopping. At times, the trodden path appears on the light, reddish-brown *pahoehoe* as a discernable dark stain. Elevation markers at the 7000-, 8000-, 9000-, and 10,000-foot levels help you track your vertical progress, something not easily gauged on this immense, gently sloping mountain. You wind in and out through lava blisters, avoiding the worst of the *aa* flows. The vegetation grows scrubbier and more sparse.

Around 8400 feet, the trail becomes somewhat easier, but the desolation is almost complete. Only a few battered *pukiawe* and *ohelo* cling to life up here. Greenish crystals of olivine have weathered out of the rock here and have collected like coarse, olive-drab sand in the tread. Broken lava tubes, burst lava bubbles, and collapsed lava domes lie all around the trail. It's not a safe area for wandering off-trail! The landscape is a solemn, gray-brown near-monotone, sometimes dusted by white lichens.

Nearing Red Hill, you may notice a spot where concentric rings of dark red, olive, and black spread out below a dusty brown rock. A closer look at the broken rocks here reveals a touch of orange, a dash of red or purple, and a miniature world of intricate bubble holes. It is a landscape full of hidden charms, which it hides very well.

The Red Hill Cabin is hidden inside a red cinder cone named Puu Ulaula, which (surprise!) means "red hill." You'll find bunks, a table, benches, a counter, a water tank (tap outside), and a pair of pit toilets here—no bedding, no lanterns (bring candles), no stoves, no cooking or eating utensils. Weather permitting, there are splendid views from the edge of the cone, high above and behind the cabin, where a marker points out Mauna Kea, Haleakala, and other sights. An extremely steep trail-of-use leads up there. Very early morning is the best time for a clear view.

Day 2 (7½ miles). After your night at the Red Hill Cabin, retrace your steps to the trailhead.

Is hiking Mauna Loa worth your time and trouble? . . . I said in Trip 33 that I would utter heresy by telling you that hiking up Mauna Loa may not be worth your time and trouble. Your time on Hawaii is probably limited, and a backpack all the way to the summit of Mauna Loa will take you five precious days—four at the very least. That's two days up, two days down, and a layover day at the summit cabin on which you dayhike to the true summit, which is on the other side of Mauna Loa's caldera, Mokuaweoweo. You may be able to descend in a single day, shortening your trip to four days.

If your goal is to see a caldera or to see miles of iridescent lava, you can see those things on dayhikes in the Kilauea area. Try Trips 20 through 23, 31 through 35, and 37 through 39. Or drive around Crater Rim Road and then down the Chain of Craters Road.

If your goal is to enjoy traditional alpine scenery, sorry: Mauna Loa hasn't got any—no sharp peaks, no shimmering lakes, no rushing streams, no wooded valleys. Mauna Loa's scenery is very special in its own way, of course, and Hawaii residents appreciate it. You may, too.

Four thousand meters equals just over 13,123 feet. If your goal is to bag a 4000-meter peak and you are from the mainland, there are plenty of 13,123-plus peaks out West in areas which are far more scenic in the traditional sense and which give you more opportunities to move at your own pace. The absence of water on Mauna Loa pretty much limits you to Red Hill Cabin and Mauna Loa Cabin. And your access is limited to the two public routes, the Mauna Loa Trail and the Observatory Trail. These factors limit everyone else, too, so you may find yourself moving along in a small crowd on Mauna Loa. (On the other hand, it can't possibly be as bad as the crowd on Mt. Whitney on a summer day.)

Finally, if you are in extremely good shape and think you will not be felled by the altitude, Trips 11 through 13, which use the Observatory Trail, may let you see Mauna Loa more quickly.

Or you can bag taller Mauna Kea instead (Trip 10) if you are in shape to do so. Note that bagging Mauna Kea, which is possible only as a dayhike, is even more arduous than bagging Mauna Loa as a dayhike from the Observatory Trail.

The bottom line: there are lots of places and lots of ways to see and enjoy volcanic landscapes on the Big Island. Think carefully about your abilities, your interests, and the total time available to you on the Big Island before committing yourself to hiking Mauna Loa.

Mauna Loa: cairns stretch across the flat black lava of North Pit; walls of Mokuaweoweo rise in the background; Mauna Loa cabin is atop the walls on the left (east)

Continued on Sheet 2 of 5

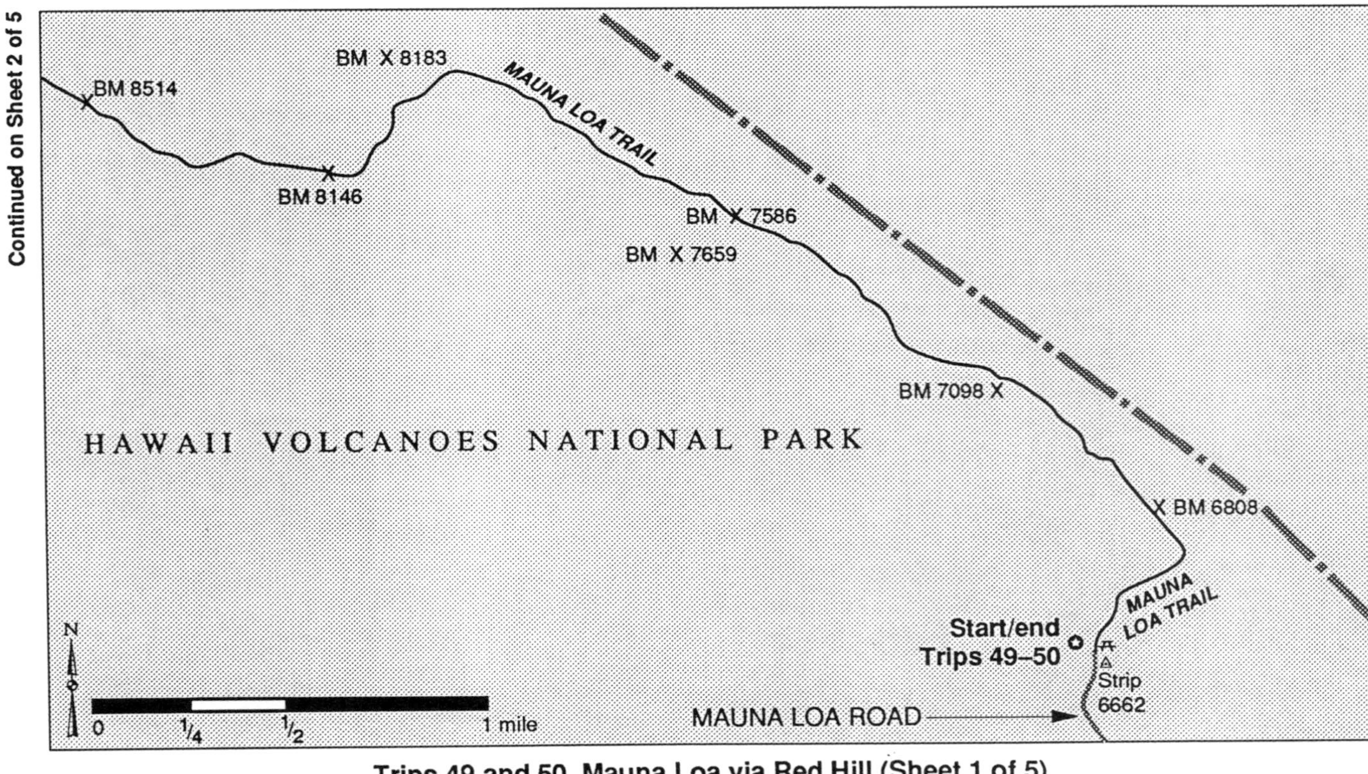

Trips 49 and 50. Mauna Loa via Red Hill (Sheet 1 of 5)

Continued on Sheet 3 of 5

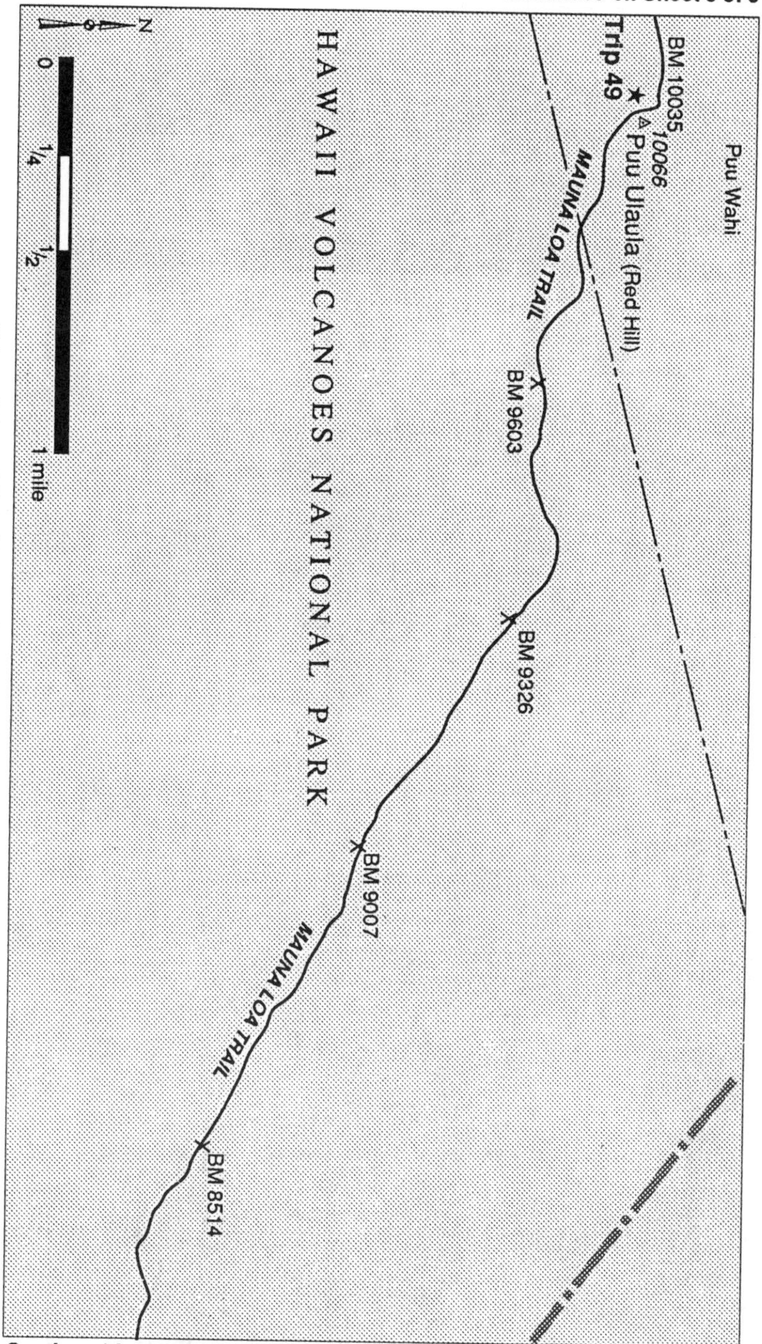

Continued from Sheet 1 of 5

Trips 49 and 50. Mauna Loa via Red Hill (Sheet 2 of 5)

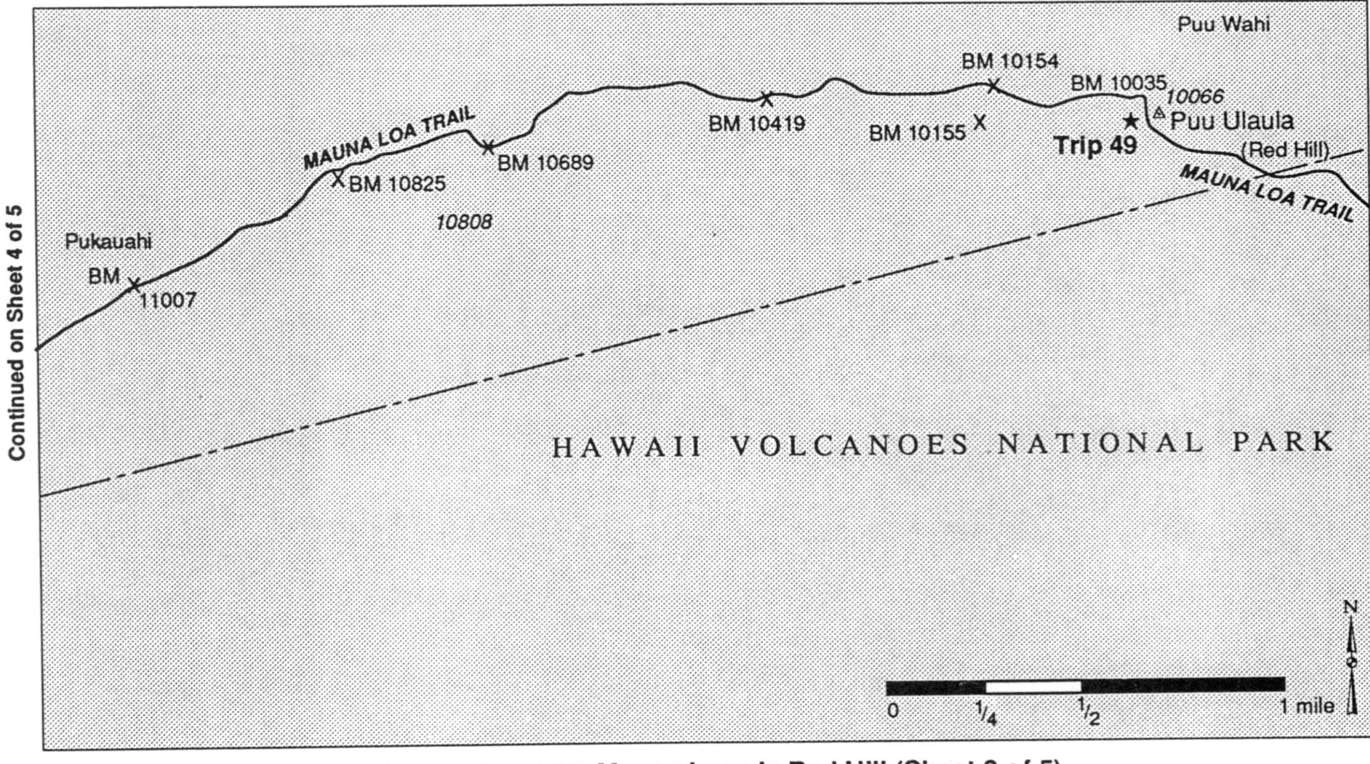

Trips 49 and 50. Mauna Loa via Red Hill (Sheet 3 of 5)

Continued on Sheet 5 of 5

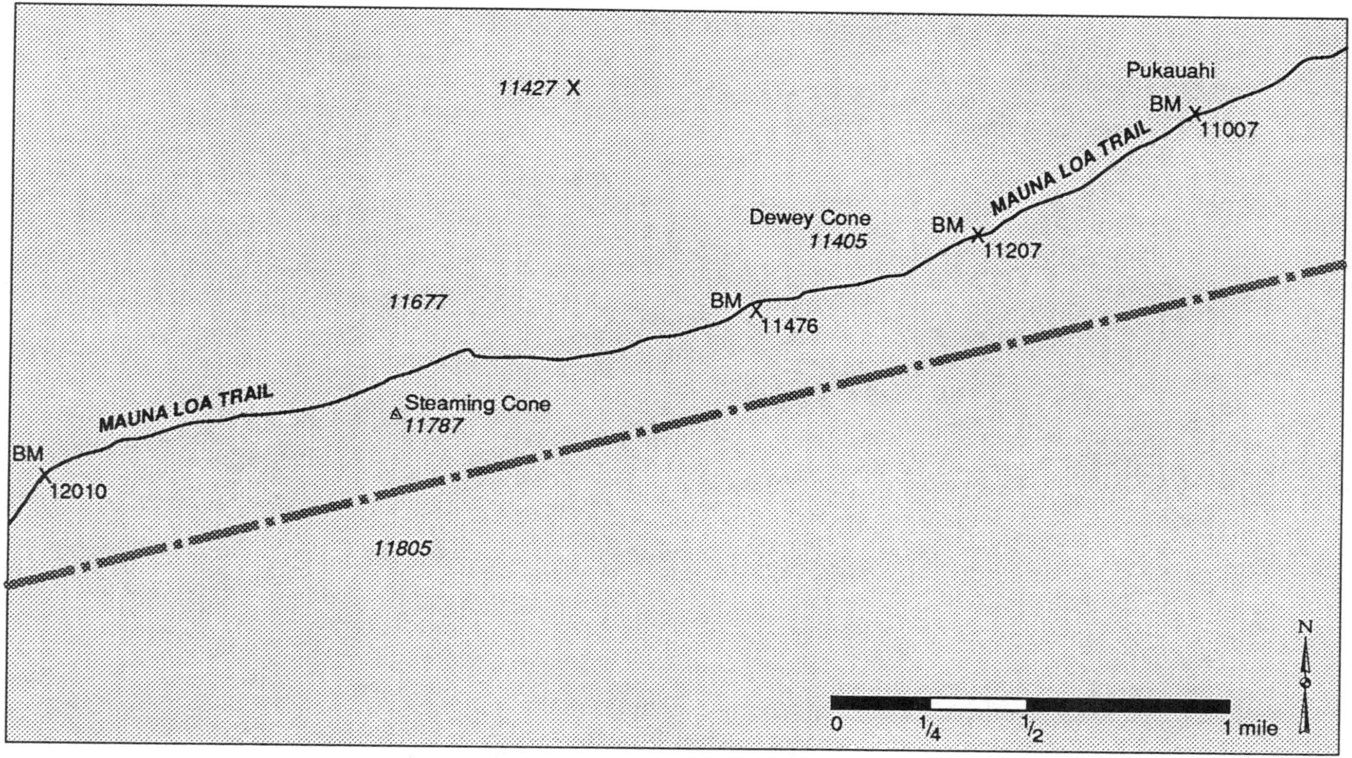

Trips 49 and 50. Mauna Loa via Red Hill (Sheet 4 of 5)

Continued from Sheet 3 of 5

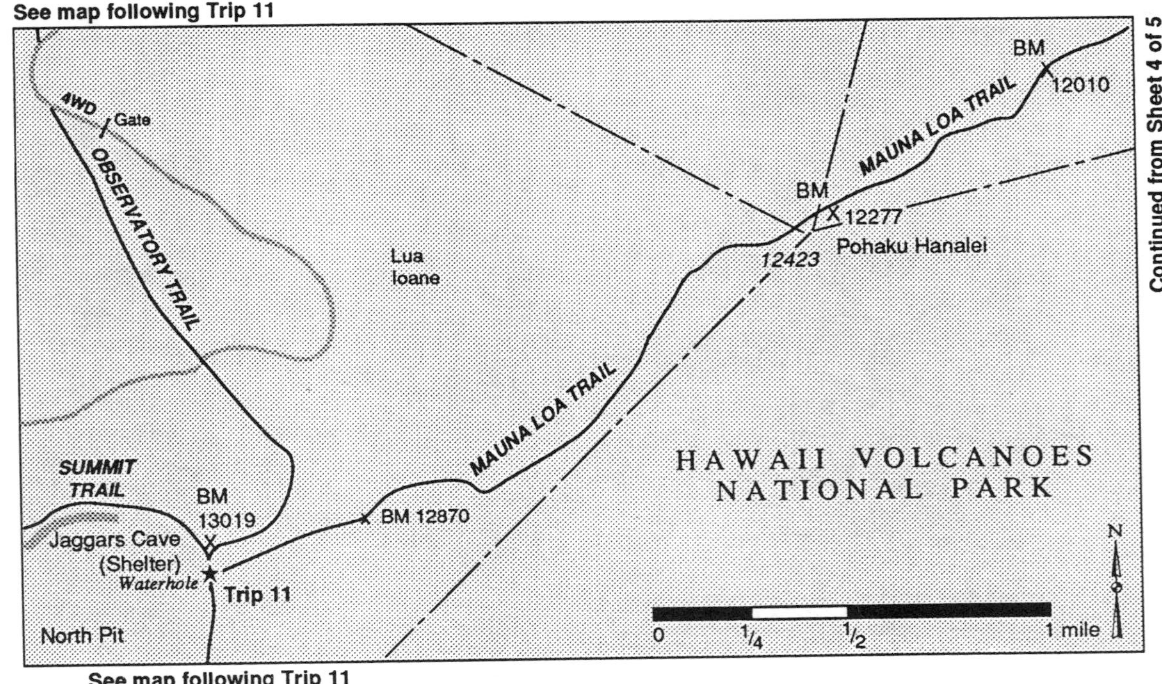

Trips 49 and 50. Mauna Loa via Red Hill (Sheet 5 of 5)

Trip 50. Mauna Loa Trail to Mauna Loa Cabin

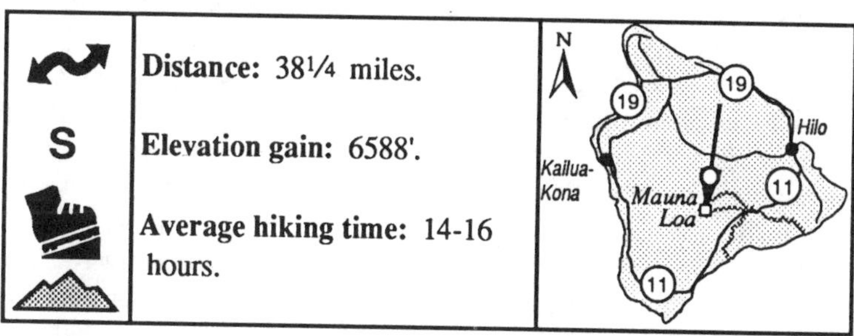

Topos: *Kipuka Pakekake, Puu Ulaula, Kokoolau, Mauna Loa* 7½.

Trail map: At the end of Trip 49.

Highlights: Some of you will find it an irresistible temptation to climb to the top of a mountain that's the world's most massive volcano and also one of its most active volcanoes. You can do this trip more easily in four days (allowing five days if you want to take a layover day at the cabin in order to dayhike to the true summit). Or, more difficult, you can hike up in two days and hike down in one monumental day. (For other alternatives, see the end of Trip 49.)

Driving instructions: Follow the driving instructions of Trip 49.

Permit/permission required: As for Trip 38, you must have a valid permit from Hawaii Volcanoes National Park, available only by applying in person at the Kilauea Visitor Center, to stay overnight in the park's backcountry.

Description ("easier" trip—but still a very strenuous one).

Day 1 (7½ miles). Follow Trip 49 to Red Hill Cabin.

Day 2 (11⅔ miles). You leave the west side of Red Hill as you head toward Mauna Loa Cabin. Dead and dull though these acres may seem under cloudy skies, they take on a strange liveliness under the full sun—usually in the early morning. The broken surfaces show tormented reds, purples, and ochres. Smoother black surfaces glitter with mineral flecks; caves—broken-in lava tubes—pock the lumpy landscape.

Here, on this gray-black *pahoehoe,* the trail is sometimes discernable as a reddish stain. Cairns are essential, though; don't lose sight of them. The ragged lips of the occasional spatter cones display a splendid range of reds, oranges, yellows, and creams. The going is slow, partly because of the altitude and partly because of the very gentle rise of these slopes. It's made more interesting than the stretch from the trailhead to Red Hill by more-vivid touches of volcanic color. Pukauahi cone is worth a photo stop: a golden-brown taffy of glassy lava drapes itself across the other rocks hereabouts.

Continuing, you pass by Dewey Cone and presently approach red-capped Steaming Cone, from which a slender feather of steam may be rising. Brown-gold cinders around Steaming Cone make for pleasant going, though *aa* poking through the cinders looks deceptively like the cairns. The route passes to the north-northwest of Steaming Cone and is soon back in the rocks. Trudging onward, you reach a marked waterhole, where there may be only ice—or nothing. Don't count on finding water here. The waterhole is roughly halfway to the cabin.

The footing deteriorates after the waterhole, and you are soon twisting your way across *aa* more often than *pahoehoe*. After a very long 1½ miles more, you approach the prominent cone called Pohaku Hanalei. Surprisingly, Pohaku Hanalei isn't marked, though Dewey Cone and Steaming Cone are.

Beyond Pohaku Hanalei, you gradually approach what you hope will be the caldera rim (it is). A barricade forces you to curve to your right, away from the rim. In a hundred or so rough yards, you reach the 13,000-foot marker. Just beyond it, you curve left toward the signed trail to the cabin, and then follow the description of Day 1 of Trip 12 from this trail junction to Mauna Loa Cabin.

Days 3 and 4 (just over 19 miles). Retrace the steps of Days 1 and 2 to the trailhead.

Side trip to the true summit. . . . A layover day at Mauna Loa Cabin will let you take Trip 13, the side trip from Mauna Loa Cabin to Mauna Loa's true summit. According to a park Pervice Brochure, Mauna Loa, with a total volume of 10,000 cubic miles, is actually greater in volume than California's entire Sierra Nevada!

Trip 51. Footprints

E

	Distance: Just under 1¾ miles.
	Elevation gain: 100' (upside-down trip).
	Average hiking time: Just over ¾ hour.

Distance: Just under 1¾ miles.
Elevation gain: 100' (upside-down trip).
Average hiking time: Just over ¾ hour.

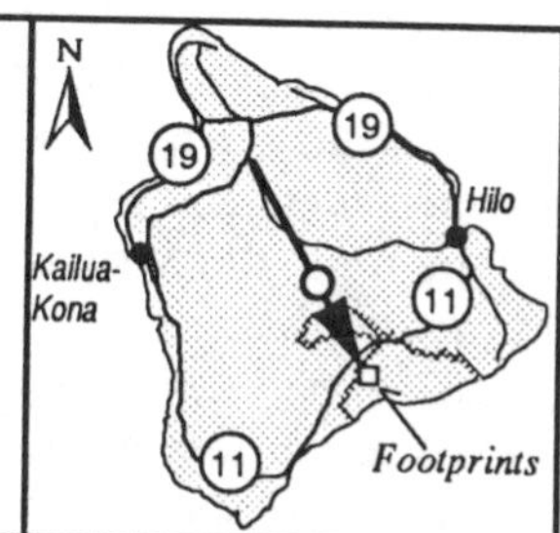

Topos: *Kau Desert* 7½.

Trail map: At the end of this trip.

Highlights: A shelter at the end of this trip protects human footprints left perhaps 200 years ago in a kind of volcanic mud that turned to rock. No one really knows for sure how old these particular footprints are or who made them. But many like to think they were left behind when Keoua's army crossed the Kau Desert in three groups, and the third group found everyone in the second group dead in the middle of the desert—more below.

Driving instructions: From Hilo, drive south and southwest on Highway 11 past the entrance to Hawaii Volcanoes National Park. Continue down Highway 11 past the turnoffs to the golf course, the Mauna Loa Road, and Namakani Paio Campground and cabins. Six and a third miles past Namakani Paio, you'll see a sign for the Footprints on the left (seaward) side of the road. There's a small turnout/parking area at the sign. Park here to start your hike, just over 37 miles from Hilo.

Permit/permission required: None.

Description: A path that's partly paved, partly graveled, and partly over sand leads southeast away from the parking area into the Kau Desert through a giant jumble of *aa.* The path is flanked by a scrubby cover of *ohia, pukiawe,* and *aalii.* Emerging from the scrub, you dip down into a broad gully, and the *aa* presently gives way to *pahoehoe* and sand.

In just over ¾ mile, you reach a lonely shelter, partly open-sided. Here, slightly protected from the elements and from vandals, you'll see depressions in the rock—depressions that are vaguely human-foot-shaped. Interpretive signs around the shelter explain the depressions. Or you can get a head start on the interpretive signs by reading the discussion below. Are these depressions really human footprints? Were they really left by Keoua's army?

After you've studied these depressions, retrace your steps to your car.

Keoua . . . , Keawemauhili, and Kamehameha strove against each other for domination of the Big Island throughout most of the 1780s. Things ended in a stalemate. Then, in 1790, Keoua slew Keawemauhili and began ravaging Kamehameha's Big Island lands. At the time, Kamehameha was trying to conquer Maui. When he learned of Keoua's depredations, Kamehameha returned to the Big Island to wage war on Keoua.

Their armies met on the east side of the island at Puna and fought two ferocious but indecisive battles. After that, Kamehameha withdrew. Keoua decided to go home to the south end of the island, Kau, past Kilauea and across the Kau Desert. Keoua divided his army—the warriors, their families, and their livestock—into three groups for the journey. They were to cross at two-hour intervals. The first group crossed the Kau Desert without trouble. As the third group started across, Kilauea erupted with hot, suffocating smoke and cinders that rained down, burning the travelers' backs. Fortunately, no one in the third group was seriously hurt. They hurried on, giving thanks for their escape. Coming upon the second group, the third group at first thought that the second group was taking a rest, for many were lying down. Others were sitting up, clutching their loved ones and touching noses with them in what must have been a final, desperate, loving farewell. Upon reaching the second group, the third group discovered that everyone in the second group was dead. The bodies appeared to be unharmed, but in fact, only a few pigs were left alive.

No one knows exactly which product of the eruption actually killed the second group, though Kilauea's eruption certainly caused their deaths. In *Volcanoes in the Sea,* the authors conjecture that the second group was "caught in a cloud of poisonous gas liberated from vents along the rift zone. Perhaps the pigs had greater resistance to the poison, or perhaps they simply breathed a pocket of fresh air closer to the ground."

There are a number of places in the Kau Desert where there are human footprints impressed in what is now stone-like material. Popular lore says that some of those footprints, like the ones at the shelter, were left by Keoua's army as they sought to flee the eruption. It was apparently a violent steam eruption, very rare at Kilauea and similar to the 1924 eruption of Kilauea that ended Halemaumau's lava lake (see Trip 31). Such an explosion would produce great quantities of ash. Volcanic ash particles tend to "cement" together to form tuff, a stony material. Ash particles that remain unconsolidated may later cement together when a little water is added, as by rain. A person walking across unconsolidated ash may leave footprints that are preserved when the ash turns to tuff.

And, indeed, the footprints you see here at the shelter are impressed into solidified ash. However, as *Volcanoes in the Sea* points out, "[S]ince footprints can be found in several different layers in the ash they certainly cannot all have been made at that one time. The route was a common one, followed frequently by travelers between Kau and Puna."

The footprints at the shelter are badly blurred by weathering and by vandalism. I found it difficult to see them as footprints rather than as mere depressions in the rock. But farther out in the Kau Desert, you may find clearer footprints in unexpected places. I shan't say where I found some, partly to protect them and partly to leave the thrill of discovering them for you. As the desert's sands shift, they uncover some footprints and bury others. So the ones you find may be different from the footprints I found. See Trip 46 and Appendix B for more on the Kau Desert trails.

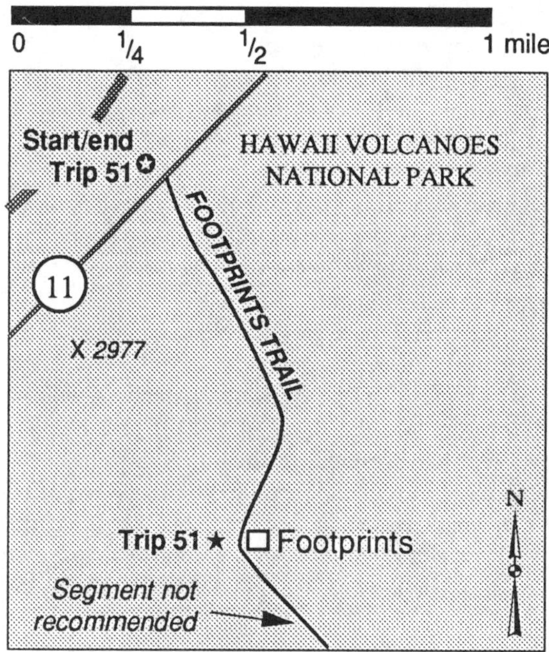

Trip 51. Footprints

Trip 52. Manuka Nature Trail

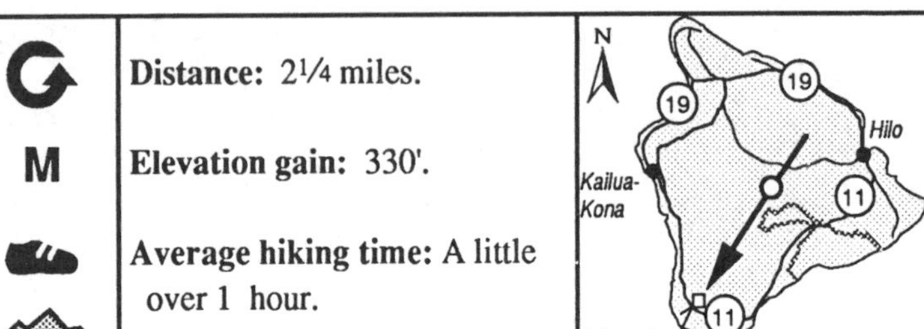

Topos: Optional: *Pohue Bay* 7½.

Trail map (route approximated): At the end of this trip.

Highlights: If you have other reasons for visiting the south end of the Big Island, complement your trip there with a visit to Manuka State Wayside and its pretty, pleasant nature trail.

Driving instructions: If possible, take this hike as a side trip from the village of Naalehu or its smaller neighbor, Waiohinu. However, most of you will pass Manuka State Wayside only on your way from Hilo (or Hawaii Volcanoes National Park) to Kona.

From Hilo, drive south and southwest on Highway 11 past all the turnoffs for Hawaii Volcanoes National Park, through Naalehu (64 miles from Hilo) and Waiohinu, and past the turnoff for the South Point Road. Continue to Manuka State Wayside, which is just west of the 81-mile marker on Highway 11 and, therefore, 81 miles from Hilo. The wayside is not marked in advance along the highway, so keep your eyes peeled for its marker. It is on the inland (north) side of the highway. Turn right and go up a short driveway to the parking lot. Park here to start your hike.

Permit/permission required: None.

Description: The beginning and end of this trail are currently unmarked and obscure. Orient yourself by standing with your back to the picnic pavilion (on the south side of the parking lot) with the restrooms on your left (west side of the lot). You want to start out to your left, crossing the lawn and passing the restrooms (which will be on your left as you go by) and a shed. As you near the corner where the manicured lawn ends and the forest gathers darkly around, you'll see a path made of small *aa* rocks and bordered by mossy *aa*. This is your trail.

The path almost immediately curves left and climbs into the forest. Native *ohia,* ferns, and *pukiawe* share the forest here with Polynesian-introduced *kukui* and *ti* and recent introductions like coffee shrubs and strawberry guava. The trail climbs gently, generally northward, and then descends a little as it curves left. Look for that fascinating native climber *ieie* as you climb again and curve right into a fern-lined lane. It almost looks like a climbing *hala.* Handsome tree ferns grow here, too, and the path gets much less rocky. Native *moa,* the low, clumping plant whose naked green stems end in yellow knobs, is a welcome sight. An unwelcome sight is that aggressive invader the thimbleberry.

Curving east now, you encounter thickets of guava, and the path is more overgrown. The rustling of birds in the understory may have you down on your hands and knees, peering into the dimness of the thickets to see if you can identify them. Muddy-kneed now, you ascend into a stand of *kukui.* You stroll for quite a while under their spreading branches and maple-like leaves. Then, at an unmarked but obvious fork (not shown on the map), you can detour left for a few yards to an overlook of a huge vertical cave now filled with tropical greenery—a novel and beautiful sight, but watch that you don't step off the edge. Returning to the junction, you turn left onto the main trail and head west.

The trail curves southwest as you duck under a low-hanging limb of a huge *kukui.* You descend as you pass through strawberry guava and tall scheffleras. At a junction with an old road, you bear right to return to Manuka's broad lawns and to your car. A picnic under the large pavilion here can be delightful, even if it's rainy, so why not stay awhile to enjoy those goodies you bought as you passed through Naalehu?

Sights around South Point. . . . are, in my opinion, very few and not worth a special trip to the South Point (Ka Lae) area if you have no other reason to go there. One good reason to swing through there would be to make it part of a multi-day trip around the Big Island on the Belt Road (Highways 19 and 11). Highway 11 is so slow at some places between Kona and Naalehu that it will take you at least 1½ hours to cover the 60 miles between them. South Point itself is a long, slow detour on a paved one-lane road (the South Point Road) from Highway 11. Many car-rental contracts forbid you to drive the South Point Road, though it's really not *that* bad. Those who remember World War II in the Pacific are in for a shock when they pass the windmill farm along the South Point Road: the windmills with their whirling propellers, reminiscent of World War II-vintage planes, were built by Mitsubishi—*Zeroes!* But South Point itself is uninteresting—flat, raked by strong cold winds, and constantly pounded by fierce seas. The word is that if you decide to go swimming at South Point, you should tell your next of kin to look for your body on the frozen shores of Antarctica.

This trip—the nature trail at Manuka State Wayside—is the only hike I think is worth your time down in the South Point area. More on this in Appendix B.

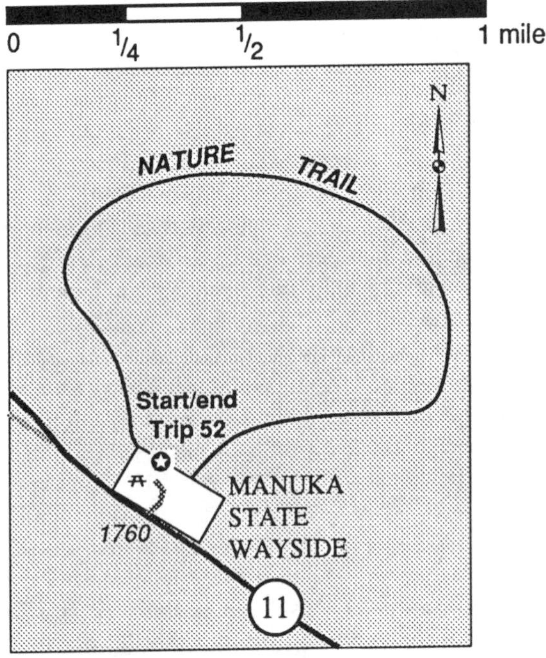

Trip 52. Manuka Nature Trail

Trip 53. Puuhonua o Honaunau (City of Refuge) Side Trip from Kailua-Kona

53 (Puuhonua o Honaunau)

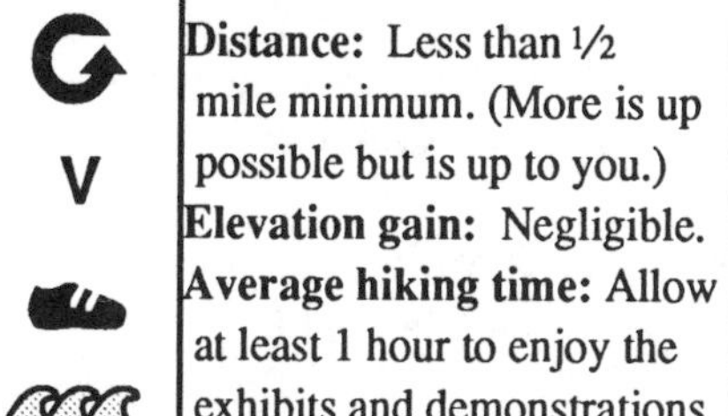

Distance: Less than ½ mile minimum. (More is up possible but is up to you.)
Elevation gain: Negligible.
Average hiking time: Allow at least 1 hour to enjoy the exhibits and demonstrations.

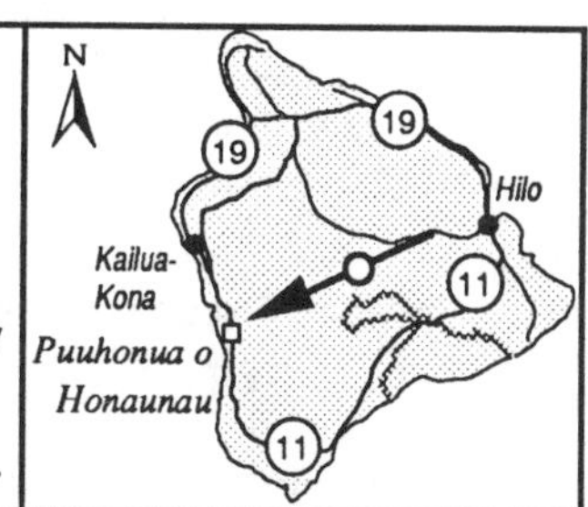

Topos: *Honaunau* 7½.

Trail map (route approximated): At the end of this trip.

Highlights: This fascinating re-creation of a Hawaiian royal compound and its adjacent city of refuge also offers pleasant, easy walking, beautiful scenery, snorkeling, and picnicking at Puuhonua o Honaunau, formerly known as the City of Refuge. An option not covered in the distance and time figures above is a visit to a "modernized" segment of an old Hawaiian trail. This National Historical Park is open from 7:30 A.M. to 5:30 P.M. daily.

Driving instructions: It is simply not practical to see Puuhonua o Honaunau from Hilo, so plan on staying on the Kona or the Kohala coast while enjoying this and the next 7 hikes (Trips 53 through 60). (Or, for Trips 57 through 60, you can stay in Waimea.) Kailua town on the Kona coast ("Kailua-Kona") is convenient for these hikes and is one of the Big Island's most popular destinations for visitors. I'll describe the driving instructions for these trips in terms of driving from Kailua-Kona. But first, you have to get to Kailua-Kona:

To get to Kailua-Kona from Hilo. From the east-side intersection of Highways 11 and 19 in Hilo, take Highway 19 northwest and then west through Waimea to Kawaihae. At Kawaihae, turn south toward Kailua-Kona, still on Highway 19, and go past Ke-Ahole Airport to the intersection with Palani Road (Highway 190) at Kailua-Kona, 97 miles from Hilo. This also is the west-side intersection of Highways 11 and 19. Some of the Big Island's finest beaches are located off this stretch of Highway 11 between Kawaihae and Kailua-Kona.

Alternatively, you may prefer to take the mountain route from Waimea by turning onto Highway 190 and following it southwest toward Kailua-Kona. Highway 190 becomes Palani Road and brings you to the west-side intersection of Highways 11 and 19, 94 miles from Hilo.

Yet another alternative—long, slow, and winding—is to drive south from Hilo past Hawaii Volcanoes National Park, through Naalehu, past South Point, and then north to Kailua-Kona, 124 miles. This route would offer you a chance to stop at Manuka State Wayside (Trip 52).

Under no circumstances should you waste your time taking the Saddle Road (Highway 220) as if it were a shortcut between Hilo and Kailua-Kona. It's no shortcut. It's a "longcut." The Saddle Road runs through a world that you should explore for its own treasures, if your rental-car contract does not forbid it. See Trips 7 through 13.

To get to Puuhonua o Honaunau from Kailua-Kona. From the junction of Highways 11 and 19 in Kailua-Kona, take Highway 11 south through Kealakekua and Captain Cook. In Keokea, turn right on well-marked Highway 160, follow it down to a spur road to the park entrance, turn left onto the spur road, and follow it to the large parking lot at Puuhonua o Honaunau National Historical Park. Park here, just over 22 miles from Kailua-Kona, and go over to the visitor center, where you pay the fee, or present your Golden Eagle or Golden Age pass, to start your trip.

Permit/permission required: None.

Description: Your admission to Puuhonua o Honaunau includes an excellent brochure keyed to numbered sites on the park's grounds. Before you start, however, I encourage you to stop at the display just by the visitor center to hear the taped messages. *Hearing* these chants and stories will give you an emotional sense of who the ancient Hawaiians were in a way that profoundly complements seeing how they lived.

I cannot improve upon the brochure's map and interpretive information for the path through the park and the exhibits of old Hawaiian life. Use it to guide your visit. You don't have to follow the sites exactly as they are numbered in order to enjoy the park, though. Be sure to stop and watch the demonstrations of old Hawaiian crafts. For example, I watched women making *ti*-leaf rain capes. I would never have guessed that the *ti* leaves had to be carefully dried before being fastened to a woven foundation to make the capes!

Snorkeling and swimming are permitted in the coves here, but the park asks you not to sunbathe on their beaches "because of the area's historical importance." You can readily appreciate that the sight of modern sunbathers here would clash with the park's attempt to re-create the spirit of old Hawaii. If the sea is not too rough or the tide too high—never turn your back on the ocean!—you will enjoy tidepooling around here, too. This complicated lava coastline offers hundreds of large and small pools to explore. Remember that you cannot take anything from the park's grounds, so put that cowrie shell back.

At the south end of the Great Wall that runs through the park, you'll find a track that leads out to an area where there are picnic tables under the coconut palms. After enjoying your picnic lunch or snack here, you can optionally wander farther along this sandy path, curving inland, until it connects with what appears to be a segment of an old Hawaiian trail, built up with rocks. (This additional distance and time are not included in the icon box above.) If you've seen these old Hawaiian trails elsewhere, you'll notice that this one seems almost twice as wide as the others. Most such trails were used only as footpaths. *This* old Hawaiian trail was widened in the nineteenth century to allow for horse travel. You can follow it along the coast, eventually climbing a ramp past some barred-off caves, and into the coastal scrub above beautiful but inaccessible Alahaka Bay. The trail becomes very overgrown beyond Ahinahina Point on the south side of the bay, and you will want to turn around. If you follow the old trail on your return, as opposed to swinging seaward through the picnic area, the trail will lead you directly back to the visitor center.

"[W]hat do you think it would be like to live here?" . . . asks the park's brochure of the refuge area, which is east (seaward) of the Great Wall. *Miserable,* I thought. The refuge area is mostly low, tide-swept, barren, lumpy *pahoehoe*. The brochure says that refugees got food from the tidepools. I asked a ranger where people would get drinking water; she pointed out some pools of brackish water. There is nothing here to encourage a long stay, and, indeed, most refugees stayed no longer than a few hours to a few days.

In *Feathered Gods and Fishhooks,* Kirch calls Puuhonua o Honaunau "one of the most significant archaeological and historical complexes in the entire archipelago. . . ." A little radiocarbon dating has been done, but it has yielded "spurious results" so far. From oral traditions, anthropologists estimate that the complex was established around A.D. 1475. The area around Puuhonua o Honaunau was densely settled and should yield fascinating information if and when archaeologists can thoroughly survey it.

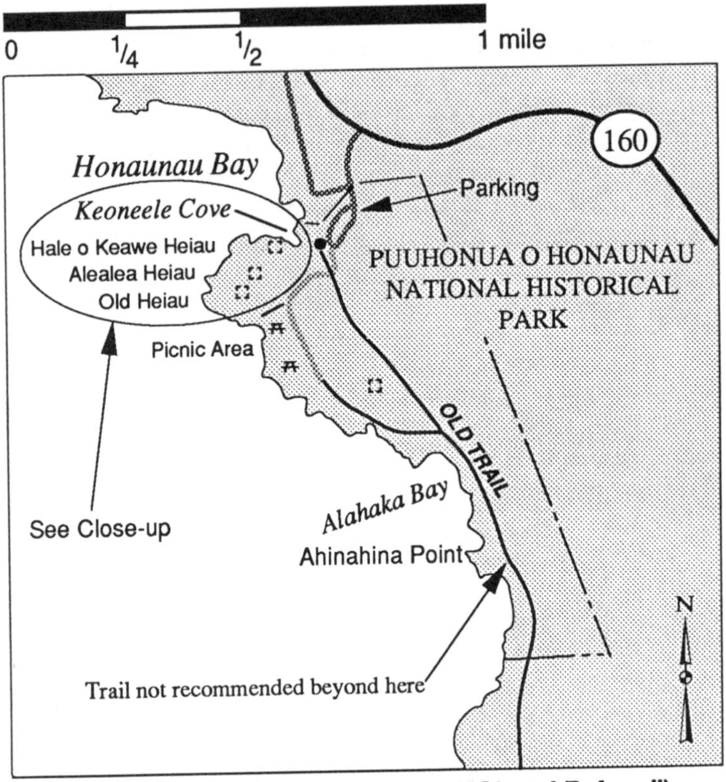

0
1/4
1/2
1 mile
160
Honaunau Bay
Keoneele Cove
Hale o Keawe Heiau
Alealea Heiau
Old Heiau
Parking
PUUHONUA O HONAUNAU
NATIONAL HISTORICAL
PARK
Picnic Area
OLD TRAIL
See Close-up
Alahaka Bay
Ahinahina Point
Trail not recommended beyond here
N

Trip 53. Puuhonua o Honaunau ("City of Refuge")

Keoneele Cove
Great Wall
Hale o Keawe
Heiau
Visitor Center
Alealea Heiau
PATH
Old Heiau
Refuge area
Palace grounds
Not to scale
To Picnic Area

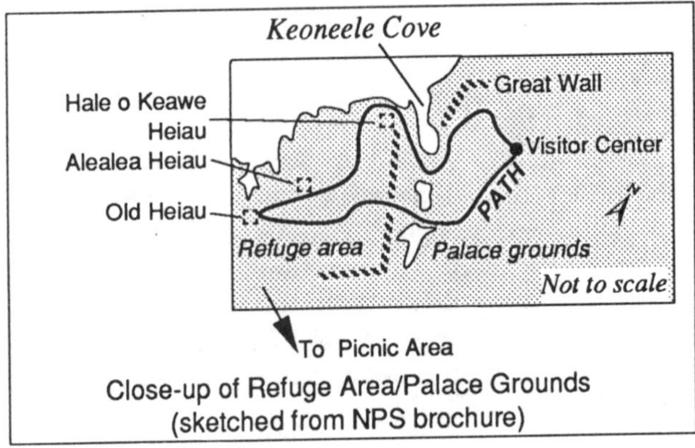

Close-up of Refuge Area/Palace Grounds
(sketched from NPS brochure)

Trip 54. Captain Cook's Monument Side Trip from Kailua-Kona

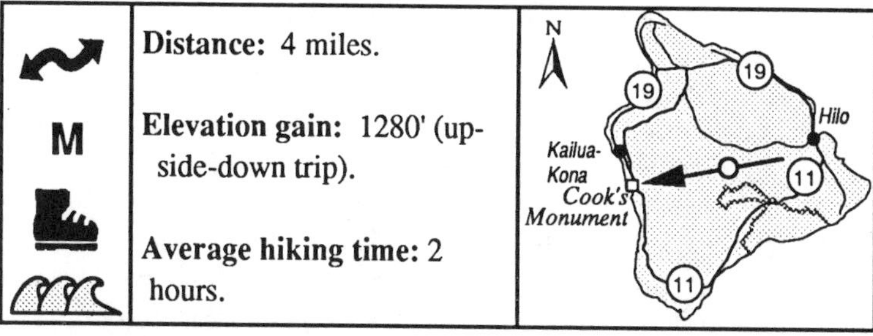

Topos: *Honaunau* 7½.

Trail map: At the end of this trip.

Highlights: A white obelisk on the north side of Kealakekua Bay marks the approximate site where Captain James Cook died in 1779 in a skirmish with Hawaiian natives over their theft of one of his auxiliary boats (see the chapter "Geology and History, Natural and Human" in this book). The spot is both beautiful and thought-provoking. It's inaccessible except to those who hike down to or boat over to this lonely, rocky shore.

Caution: The old 4WD road used as a trail down to the monument can become completely overgrown by very tall grasses. Do not take this hike if it is overgrown. See also under "Permit/permission required," below.

Driving instructions: To get from Hilo to Kailua-Kona, see the driving instructions of Trip 53. From Kailua-Kona, take Highway 11 south through Kealakekua and into Captain Cook to the turnoff to Kealakekua Bay and Napoopoo, just under 12 miles. Turn right onto the road to Kealakekua Bay and Napoopoo. In barely a tenth of a mile, an old 4WD road leads steeply seaward from the righthand side of the road. A wide space at the top of this old road affords steep, rocky parking for a very few cars. Park here to start your hike.

Permit/permission required: None as of this writing, but it's always possible that between the time I write this and the time you try to hike it, someone may have bought the property this 4WD road runs through, developed it, and closed it to hikers. If that has happened, please do not trespass—and please let me know about it.

Rampant development all along the Kona and Kohala ccasts is making hiking here an increasingly rare and "iffy" experience.

Description: You leave the parking area, such as it is, and bear west-southwest down the steep old road. In just a few steps, you reach a fork; go left here. You continue to descend steeply to moderately between veritable walls of tall, dense grasses, past avocado, mango, *koa haole* festooned with morning glory vines, tamarind, monkeypod, and papaya trees. Your route is paralleled on the left by a wire fence and a stone wall, half-lost in the dense growth.

In a little over ½ mile, you begin to have tantalizing glimpses of the coast far, far below. As you near 1 mile, views of the ocean really open up, the *koa haole* becomes increasingly sparse and scrubby, and the understory dwindles to shorter grasses and air plants. The road swings west-northwest, then west, atop some low cliffs and through some old lava flows. In these lower, drier regions, the road becomes much steeper and rockier at times—watch your footing!

Near a switchback turn, the ruggedly scenic coastline from Cook Point to Kaweakaheka Point spreads out below you. You curve southeast at the turn as you descend the extreme west end of the Pali Kapu o Keoua, the cliffs that provide such a stark backdrop to Kealakekua Bay. Near the bottom, you pass through a ruined stock gate in the shade of *kiawe* trees. Another 4WD road comes in from the right (west); you continue southeast (ahead) in the welcome shade of *kiawe* trees. A wall of lichen-splattered black stones lines your route on both sides as the grade eases and the going becomes easier. Soon, substantial ruins stretch away from you on all sides under the thorny *kiawe*. The road ends at the water's edge, where black *pahoehoe* fingers reach out into the bay to make tiny coves. There's no sandy beach here (there's an extremely small, often crowded beach on the other side of the bay at Napoopoo). However, snorkeling is extremely popular at Kealakekua Bay, which is a State Underwater Park. People snorkel from these black rocks and from commercial and private vessels out in the bay. Note that sharks occasionally visit Kealakekua Bay, too.

One thing you won't see at the end of the road is Cook's monument. It's farther north along the curving coast of the bay. You can thrash through the *kiawe* to get to it, or you can try this easier route. Turn around and walk about 60 yards back up the road you just came down, looking on what is now your right (north) for a broken place in the stone wall where an old track as wide as a road wanders northeast through the ruins to meet a path to the monument. Turn left onto this path, ignoring the evidence that this part of the thicket is

Puuhonua o Honaunau: pond on palace grounds

used as a casual bathroom by people picnicking and snorkeling on the shore. In a few more steps, you're at the monument, where a tiny jetty juts out into the blue water. The steep cliffs cupping the bay curve away from you toward the Napoopoo side. Retrace your steps to the 4WD road when you're ready.

If you feel like doing a little more exploring, retrace your steps to the 4WD road you came down on, go back to the end of the road at the bay's edge, and bear right to pick up a trail-of-use. You can follow it a short way to more tiny coves and tidepools.

At last, you must retrace your steps to your car. Take your time; it's apt to be extremely hot and muggy on your uphill return.

Cook's death. . . . Scholars have long wondered why the Hawaiians killed Cook when, apparently, they considered him a god. In *Shoal of Time,* Gavan Daws explains that during the long *Makahiki* season (roughly from October to February) Lono, the god of harvest, and his priests ruled Hawaii. During the rest of the year, Ku, the god of war, and his followers, the chiefs and their warriors, were supreme. By the end of the *Makahiki* season, Ku's followers were itching to wrest authority from Lono's followers. On the Big Island, *Makahiki* traditionally ended with a symbolic combat between the forces of Lono and of Ku at Kealakekua. There, the warriors of Ku symbolically defended the ruling chief against the priests of Lono.

Cook's initial visit in 1778 and his return in 1779 fell within *Makahiki*. It was the priests of Lono who mistook Cook for Lono and accordingly "deified" him. By the time Cook returned to Kealakekua Bay for the second time in 1779 (after the *Resolution*'s foremast broke), the chiefs and warriors were fairly sure that he and his crew were not gods but mortals. And by pure bad luck, Cook blundered back that second time at the end of *Makahiki*—just when Lono's followers ought to have been handing power back to Ku's followers. When the Hawaiians stole one of Cook's auxiliary boats, Cook led a small punitive expedition ashore to take Kalaniopuu, the ruling chief, hostage until the boat was returned. It was a strategy Cook had successfully used before, and he meant no harm to Kalaniopuu. But the timing was such that Cook-as-Lono was perceived as literally, not just symbolically, attacking the ruling chief. Cook had no idea what he had stumbled into. The chiefs and warriors, as followers of Ku and protectors of their ruling chief, Kalaniopuu, staged a real, not a symbolic, defense of Kalaniopuu in which Cook-as-Lono "died in a distorted realization of the symbolic conflict that marked the close of the makahiki season."

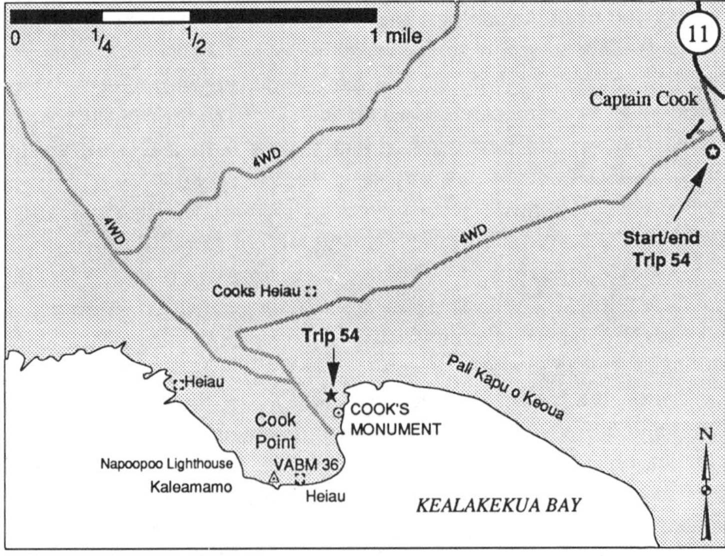

Trip 54. Cook's Monument

Trip 55. Kalahuipuaa Historical Park (Mauna Lani) Side Trip from Kailua-Kona

Distance: 1 mile or less, depending on how you meander.

Elevation gain: Negligible.

Average hiking time: Allow 1 hour to fully enjoy the ponds.

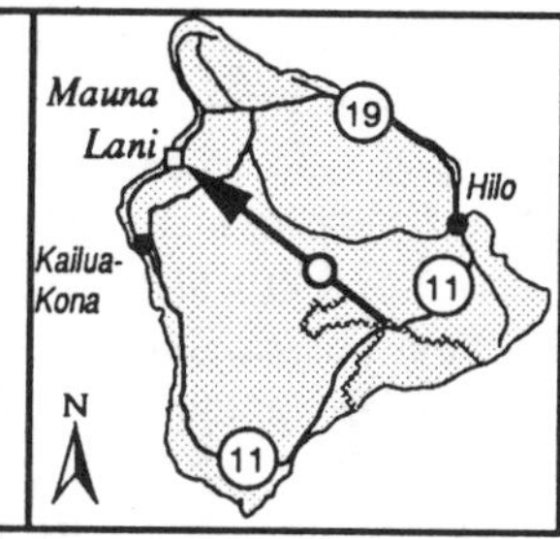

Topos: Optional: *Anaehoomalu, Puu Hinai* 7½.

Trail map (route approximated): At the end of this trip. Note: Please rely on the Mauna Lani's road and trail signs for directions and not on the map. The map is based on the topos, but development has completely changed the area—roads, paths, buildings—since the topos were drafted. And the changes continue! My sketches of the trails therefore correspond only loosely to the topo features.

Highlights: You say you wouldn't go for a hike if you were paid to do so? Well, consider this: The builders of the Mauna Lani resort complex have preserved a number of sites of historical and archaeological interest on the resort grounds as Kalahuipuaa Historical Park. In this civilized setting and on a paved path, visitors can easily stroll through a lava field, cross a segment of an old paved Hawaiian footpath, and visit wonderfully scenic tropical fishponds that are still in use.

My sister Christina, a devout non-hiker, loved this walk. We began by picking up hiking chow (soft drinks and potato chips) at the mini-market across from the trailhead parking lot. We finished by flicking the trail dust from our aerobics shoes and going shopping at the Mauna Lani Bay Hotel. A truly macho hike.

Driving instructions: From the intersection of Highways 11 and 19 in Kailua-Kona, drive north past Ke-Ahole Airport on Highway 19 to the marked turnoff for the Mauna Lani. Turn left into the Mauna Lani, drive down the access road to the multiple junction of the roads to the hotel and terrace, to the golf course and historical park, and to the petroglyphs. Bear left toward the golf course/historical park and then right into the small, shady parking and picnic area for the historical park, 30 miles from Kailua-Kona. Park here to start your hike. The mini-market is just across the road.

Permit/permission required: None as of this writing. However, this hike is on private property. To be sure it is open, call ahead (Mauna Lani Bay Hotel and Bungalows, 808-885-6622).

Description: Begin your walk near the restrooms, where an interpretive sign shows the general layout of the park. Now you walk uphill a few feet on the paved path that leads away from here—not on the spur that leads to a metal pedestal (whatever it supported is gone). You immediately find yourself in a field of reddish-brown *pahoehoe* that's sparsely shaded by *kiawe* trees. You may see wild goats out on the lava and game birds in the *kiawe* thickets, but they will flee as you approach. Interpretive signs along the path invite you to pause and consider the origin of this lava field and the uses to which some of its features were put. Most interesting is a large cave, just to the left of the paved path on a short spur. The cave was formed by a lava tube, and the old Hawaiians used it as a cool, roomy home.

You soon dip down to intersect a rocky trail. This is the old Hawaiian footpath I mentioned in the Highlights. Look at it here and follow it for a short distance if you wish, but I can't recommend it for hiking. Why not? See below.

Beyond this intersection, you climb a little, cross a paved road, and reach the first of the fishponds. They are shining tropical lagoons, surrounded by coconut palms and providing a marvelously romantic setting for the condominiums and cottages that front on them. It's especially enchanting near sunset. Stay out of the condo complex. Instead, explore the scenic paths, some of them dead ends, that wander in and out among the ponds. Some ponds are tiny and hold fish the size of minnows; larger ponds hold good-sized food fish—yes, they're destined for the restaurants around here. Pause to enjoy watching the fish. It's a real thrill to see a school of the larger fish suddenly arc out of the water all at once!

The main path eventually leads you out to the edge of a sparkling little cove. Before you actually get to the cove, you bear right, pass a boathouse, and walk across an inlet on a walkway atop the barriers and gates that maintain and nourish these fishponds. (Don't attempt this unless the ocean is calm enough for you to cross safely. If it's not, turn around and retrace your steps now.) Watch your step on the walkway; it can be slippery here. Interpretive signs explain how the ponds work. On the other side of the inlet, you walk over a lawn, pass an old home, and pick up a paved path. There's a thatched canoe shed a few steps from here that you may want to take a look at. Back at the path, you follow it as it curves inland, back around the fishponds and past the landscaped grounds of the condominiums, to the point where you first reached the fishponds.

From here, retrace your steps across the road and through the lava field to your car.

The old Hawaiian footpath. . . . Let's suppose you do follow it. The old footpath, surfaced with loose bits of *aa*, climbs steeply to the golf course clubhouse grounds and then shoots off straight southwest toward the next luxury hotel down the coast. You stumble over its *aa* surface. Inland, you see the desolate, lava-streaked slopes of Hualalai—very authentic, very Hawaiian. (The highway is too far away to intrude.) Seaward, you see a modern dirt road, an exposed pipeline, telephone poles and lines, and a manicured emerald golf course—very unauthentic, very mainland-like. Looking far down the footpath, you see a construction crane beckoning. (Or, by the time you read this, whatever is under construction here may have been completed and something even less authentic may have sprung up.)

You pass a driving range on the inland side. Around here, crevices in the *aa* hold fluorescent yellow golf balls. One thing you're sure of: the ancient Hawaiians did not play golf. Golf balls and old Hawaiian trails are just too strange a mixture. Why are you wrecking your shoes and possibly your ankles by walking on *aa* in the midst of this un-Hawaiian scenery, anyway? Especially when there's a perfectly good dirt road on your seaward side? You take a couple of steps seaward over the low wall separating the trail from the dirt road and turn back to the historical park on the road.

My hiking hat is off to the Mauna Lani's developers for having preserved this trail and the many other important sites on their grounds. I hope they continue to do so. But I hope they will excuse me if I find this footpath's present setting too unsettling to think that hiking it is worthwhile.

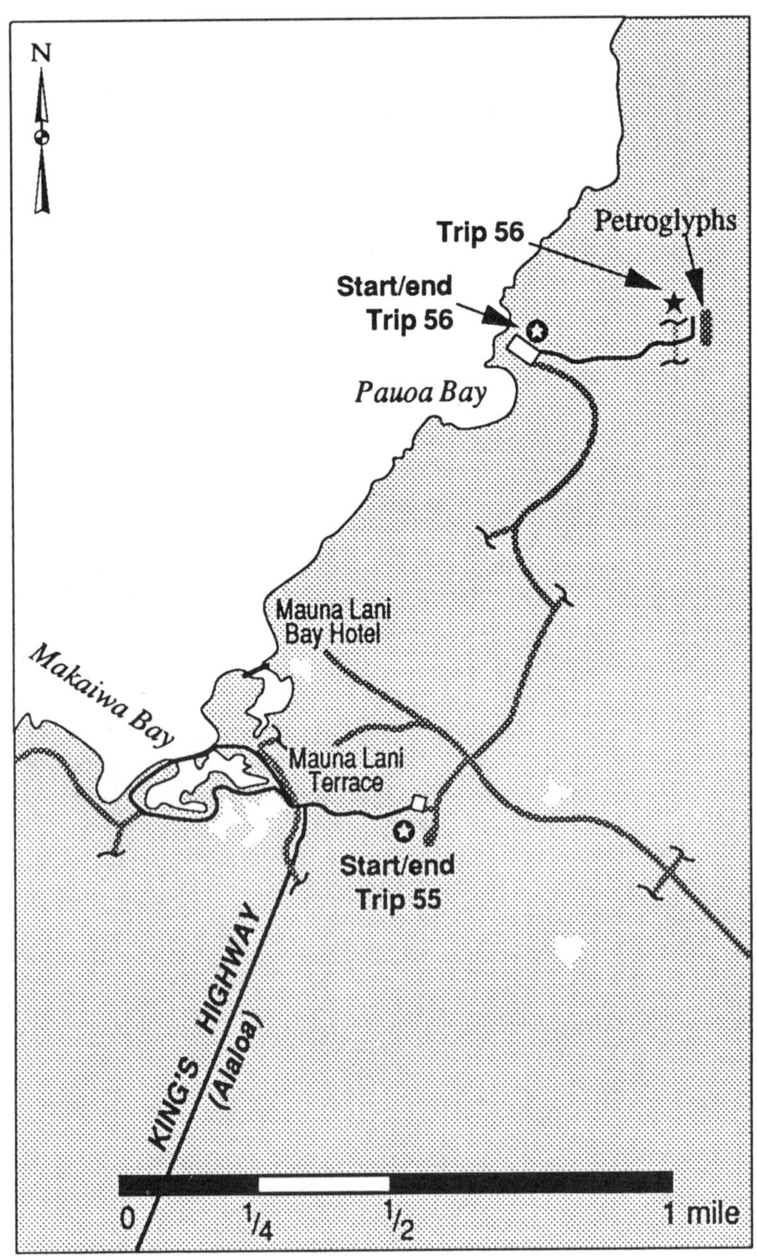

Trips 55–56. Kalahuipuaa and Puako Petroglyphs

Trip 56. Puako Petroglyphs (Mauna Lani) Side Trip from Kailua-Kona

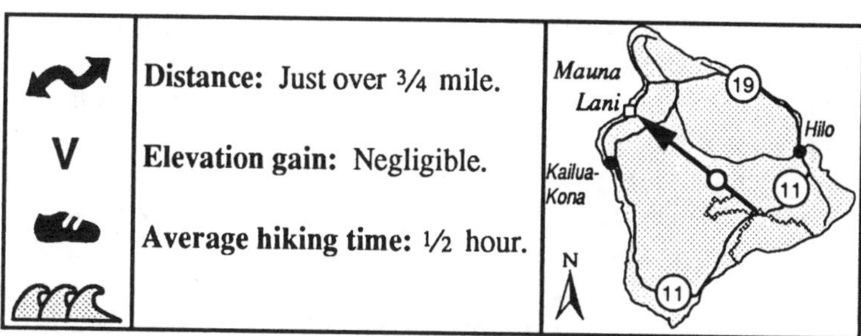

Distance: Just over 3/4 mile.

Elevation gain: Negligible.

Average hiking time: 1/2 hour.

Topos: Optional: *Anaehoomalu, Puu Hinai* 7½.

Trail map (route approximated): At the end of Trip 55 (please take the *Note* in Trip 55 into account).

Highlights: A large group of petroglyphs lies at the end of a short trail under *kiawe* trees; it's part of one of the most extensive petroglyph fields in the archipelago. The trail, though short, is uneven and rocky. A few petroglyphs have been set up near the start of the trail for the enjoyment of those who cannot walk the entire trail. Just a few steps away, and thus also near the start, other petroglyphs have been especially set up so that you can make rubbings of them (according to the sign).

Driving instructions: Follow the driving instructions of Trip 55 except that, at the junction where the access roads diverge to the golf course/historical park, hotel/terrace, and petroglyphs, you bear right to the petroglyphs. This spur road takes you to a parking lot on the ocean. Park here to start your hike. The petroglyph trail leads away from the inland end of the parking lot.

Permit/permission required: None as of this writing. However, this hike is on private property. To be sure it is open, call ahead (Mauna Lani Bay Hotel and Bungalows, 808-885-6622).

Description: The first segment of your short trail is paved, and in a few steps you'll find the petroglyph viewing area set up for the enjoyment of those who cannot walk the whole trail. Because the petroglyphs are raised for easy viewing and are widely separated, perhaps to let people whose mobility is limited get around them, they are ideally placed for photograph-taking. This is the place to get your camera out and start snapping away!

It's only another step or two to a small area on your left where, as the sign here says, a few petroglyphs have been set up especially so you can make rubbings of them. Making a single rubbing minutely but irreparably damages a petroglyph. Walking over one petroglyph to get to another so you can make a rubbing would cause still more damage. The sheer numbers of people who visit here and who might want to walk out into the petroglyph field to make rubbings would soon destroy work that had endured for hundreds of pre-rubbing years. It's important to the survival of the other petroglyphs that you make your rubbings only here.

Beyond this second special viewing area, the trail becomes rock and dirt through *kiawe* thickets. You wander generally northeast, climbing over *kiawe* roots and irregularities in the lava. You cross a dusty old jeep road and in another few hundred yards emerge at a large, pebble-paved viewing area. The viewing area overlooks a large bare area of reddish *pahoehoe* where the old Hawaiians have chipped hundreds of petroglyphs (the entire Puako field includes more than 3,000 individual glyphs, according to *Feathered Gods and Fishhooks*). Please stay in the viewing area and don't wander out into the petroglyph field or make rubbings.

An interpretive sign here asks questions that must tantalize archaeologists and visitors alike:

> What brought [the old Hawaiians] here, to this particular spot? What made them work so hard with primitive tools, to carve the symbols you see? And why are most of the petroglyphs oriented toward the mountain?

"The mountain" is apparently Mauna Kea. But that yields no answers to those questions, answers which are hidden forever in the long-vanished hearts of those who made these petroglyphs. These were people with a long and proud cultural and artistic tradition. If only we could wake to a morning when time was as transparent as the early morning skies around Mauna Kea, and we could see and talk with the petroglyphs' makers for a few brief hours before the obscuring clouds of the centuries gathered around them once more. . . .

With these interesting thoughts in mind, you retrace your steps to the parking lot. Seaward, you'll find Holoholokai Beach Park, where there is a rough black lava-white coral beach with pleasant picnic sites under *kiawe* and tree heliotrope. You may see local people fishing from the rocks around here. It's a great place to enjoy your lunch and to mull over the questions the petroglyphs have raised.

Puako petroglyphs. . . . The famous Puako petroglyph fields are far more extensive than you can see from this viewing area. At one time, the petroglyphs were accessible from Puako village by way of a path that went inland, starting about 100 yards before the turnaround at the end of the road that goes down through Puako. Unfortunately, that access is currently fenced off by the Mauna Lani, and you are forbidden to trespass. Please respect that barrier. Let us hope that the Mauna Lani's developers will preserve these irreplaceable artifacts and provide a new access to them when they are through building around them.

Puako: petroglyph set up for easy viewing near the trailhead

Trip 57. Puukohola *Heiau* National Historical Site Side Trip from Kailua-Kona

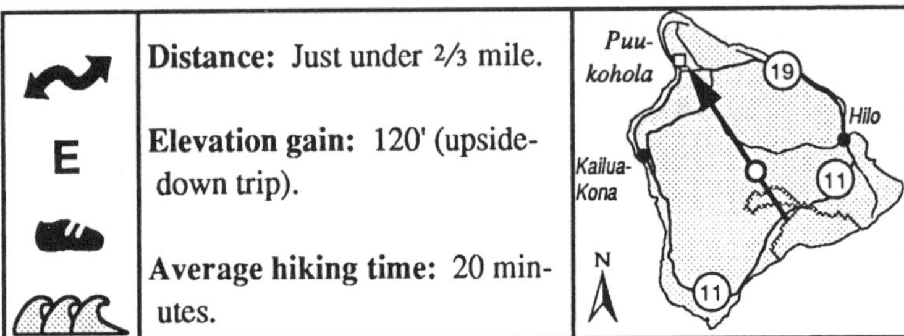

Topos: Optional: *Kawaihae* 7½.

Trail map (route approximated): At the end of this trip.

Highlights: The massive ruins of Puukohola *Heiau* are an impressive sight even if you have no idea of their historical significance. But their historical significance is enormous, as you'll read below. Puukohola *Heiau* is a must-see site for those interested in Hawaiian history.

Driving instructions: From the intersection of Highways 11 and 19 in Kailua-Kona, drive north on Highway 19 past Ke-Ahole Airport and the Mauna Lani complex to the junction of Highways 19 and 270. Turn left onto Highway 270 here and follow it for just under ½ mile to the marked turnoff for Puukohola *Heiau* National Historical Site. Turn left here and follow the access road a short distance to the parking lot and visitor center. Park here and stop at the visitor center to get your pamphlet, which contains a map and fascinating information about the site. The park's hours are 7:30 A.M. to 4:00 p.m daily; there is no admission fee.

Permit/permission required: None.

Description: Before you begin your walk, look inland from the visitor center. If the day is clear (as it usually is early in the morning), there is a spectacular view of four of the Big Island's volcanoes: Kohala, Mauna Kea, Mauna Loa, and Hualalai. The central attraction of the park is the massive remains of Puukohola *Heiau,* which you can see by following the path that leads seaward past *milo, kiawe, ilima,* and gourd vines. As you descend this paved trail and curve gently to the right, the ruins of Puukohola rise above you. Its precincts are *kapu,* and you are not permitted to enter them. There's another reason you're not permitted to enter the *heiau*: its outer walls are beginning to collapse after having stood for over 200 years. Frankly, I cannot imagine that Puukohola could be any more impressive from the inside than it is from the many vantage points along this trail. It is immense and awe-inspiring. What months of wearisome toil were required of thousands of workers to carry, lift, and place these huge reddish stones on these fiery hot, bone-dry slopes!

You descend to the spur road to Spencer Beach Park and cross it to continue your exploration of this historical site. The paved trail picks up on the other side of the road, and you pass Mailekini *Heiau,* which is much more ancient. It, too, is unsafe to enter because of loose rocks. Just beyond Mailekini *Heiau,* a paved spur leads out to an overlook of the Leaning Post and the cove where offerings were made at a sunken *heiau* to the shark god. The brochure says that a high chief used to lean on this post as he watched the sharks circle the *heiau* "before devouring the offerings he had placed there." This cove is unsafe to swim in. Some say it's because sharks still come here looking for offerings; others cite pollution. In any case, you should visit adjacent Spencer Beach Park in order to picnic and swim.

Returning to the main trail, you wander down into the shade of coconut palms, *kiawe* and *milo* trees, and tree heliotrope on the beach fronting the sharks' cove. This area was the site of the royal residence at Kawaihae. Succulent *akulikulikai,* beach morning glory, and beach *naupaka* share the site of the royal compound. The exact location and extent of the sunken *heiau* aren't known, so exciting archaeological discoveries are waiting for future investigators in this picturesque area. Relax, cool off, and catch your breath here before turning around and tackling the hot climb back up to the visitor center and your car.

Why Kamehameha built Puukohola. . . . Kamehameha built this temple in 1790–1791 in response to a prophecy. In the 1780s, Kamehameha, the high chief Keoua (Keoua Kuahuula), and a third chief were rivals for control of the Big Island. Their struggles had ended in a stalemate, and Kamehameha had gone off to try to conquer the rest of the islands. In 1790, Keoua killed the third chief and began plundering Kamehameha's Big Island lands.

Kamehameha sent his aunt to seek the advice of a famous prophet. The prophet told Kamehameha that if he built a temple to his family war god, Kukailimoku, on Puukohola hill at Kawaihae, he would go on to conquer all the islands. Kamehameha returned to the Big Island to fight Keoua, but their battles were indecisive.

Kamehameha withdrew. Keoua and his army set out for home; the journey required them to pass Kilauea and cross the Kau Desert. As related at the end of Trip 51, a third of Keoua's army were found dead in the Kau Desert after an eruption at nearby Kilauea; astonishingly, the corpses bore no traces of harm.

With the prophet acting as the architect, Kamehameha set about building the new temple, even joining the thousands of workers in its construction. Upon its successful completion in 1791, Kamehameha invited Keoua to the temple's dedication. The dedication of Puukohola would require human sacrifice.

Here is one of Hawaiian history's great puzzles: Keoua came. No one knows why. Surely he must have known that he risked death by doing so. Something seems to have inclined Keoua, whom Kamehameha had not defeated militarily, to nevertheless accept Kamehameha as the victor. Many speculate that Keoua interpreted the strange deaths of his army in the Kau Desert as proof that the gods had turned against him. Others judge that Keoua had come to believe in the power of the prophecy: the gods had willed that Kamehameha should triumph and unite the islands. To resist the will of the gods was useless.

Keoua made a ceremonial journey around his part of the island—from Kau, around South Point, and then up the Kona coast—by canoe. At each stop, the people came out to pay a last farewell to their high chief. His next-to-last stop was just down the coast from Puukohola at Luahinewai, a sacred pool. (You can see the area of Luahinewai from the "Scenic Turnout" on Highway 19 south of Kawaihae.) At Luahinewai, Keoua ritually prepared his own body for sacrifice. Then he set out for Kawaihae. He landed at the beach below Puukohola—the sharks' cove. Keoua and his companions were met by the high chief Keeaumoku, an ally of Kamehameha. Keeaumoku slew Keoua and ten of his companions there on the beach. Keoua's body became the principal sacrifice that evening as Puukohola was dedicated to Kukailimoku.[1] Surely there could be no sacrifice more perfect than the sacred person of a high chief. If Keoua knowingly came to be that sacrifice, it was an act of great courage and one which helped to unite the Hawaiian people.

But the manner of his death has left another puzzle: did Kamehameha allow Keeaumoku to kill Keoua? Keeaumoku always maintained that he had acted on his own without Kamehameha's permission. Some scholars believe Keeaumoku; others think Kame-

[1]The gods hated visible blood. Ritual dictated that a sacrificial victim be slain and his blood washed away *before* he was placed on the altar.

hameha had a hand in the assassination. Of one thing there could be no doubt: Kamehameha was now the undisputed ruler of the Big Island. Soon, he would rule all the islands, fulfilling the prophecy.

Bicentenary celebrations, rededication of Puukohola, and re-enactments of Keoua's journey and its consequences were held on the Big Island in the summer of 1991—bloodless, of course. It is more than just the passage of 200 years that inspired the rededication, as the *Pu'ukohola Heiau Bicentenary Celebration Fact Sheet* notes:

> In Hawaiian tradition, spiritual completion occurs when the seventh generation hands down their knowledge of all things ancient and sacred to their children. It is now the seventh generation since the *heiau* was built and this bicentenary re-dedication offers a unique and fitting opportunity for the new generations of Hawaiians to learn, understand and preserve their cultural heritage, thus unifying the past with the present and the future.

John Young and his house site. . . . When Kamehameha acquired European armaments, he needed Europeans to manage them. A terrible tragedy at Olowalu on Maui led to two Englishmen falling into Kamehameha's hands: Isaac Davis and John Young. Both were uneducated, but both had a great deal of common sense and integrity. Kamehameha eventually persuaded them to serve him, and they became his most trusted European advisors. John Young became a full Hawaiian chief and the governor of the Big Island. He outlived Kamehameha I, and his granddaughter Emma became the queen of Kamehameha IV.

John Young's lands included those now in this historical site, and the site of his Kawaihae residence lies inland from the sharks' cove. Queen Emma inherited these lands, and eventually they passed to a charity she had founded. The charitable foundation donated them to the Federal government, and Congress designated Puukohola a National Historic Site in 1972.

There is little to see at the house site now, but you may want to pay your respects to John Young by visiting it. It is not a pleasant trail, and the additional distance (a little less than ⅔ mile round trip, doubling the length of your hike), elevation gain (about 20 feet), and time (20 minutes) are not included in the icon box for this trip. Look for a dirt-and-rock path leading inland, away from the sharks' cove. It follows the banks of the brackish lagoon that's in back of the cove and then of the nearly dry stream that feeds the lagoon. It crosses the stream bed, ducks under *kiawe,* crosses a jeep road, and finally climbs up to the highway on an old log pathway. You must cross the highway near here; be very careful!

Walk northwest on the highway shoulder, cross the bridge over

Makeahua Gulch, and, about 25 paces beyond the bridge, look up the highway bank to your right for a faint path and (possibly) a National Park Service "don't touch the artifacts" sign. Follow this path up through weeds to a flat area, where a sort of shed protects some of the remains at the house site.

Retrace your steps from here.

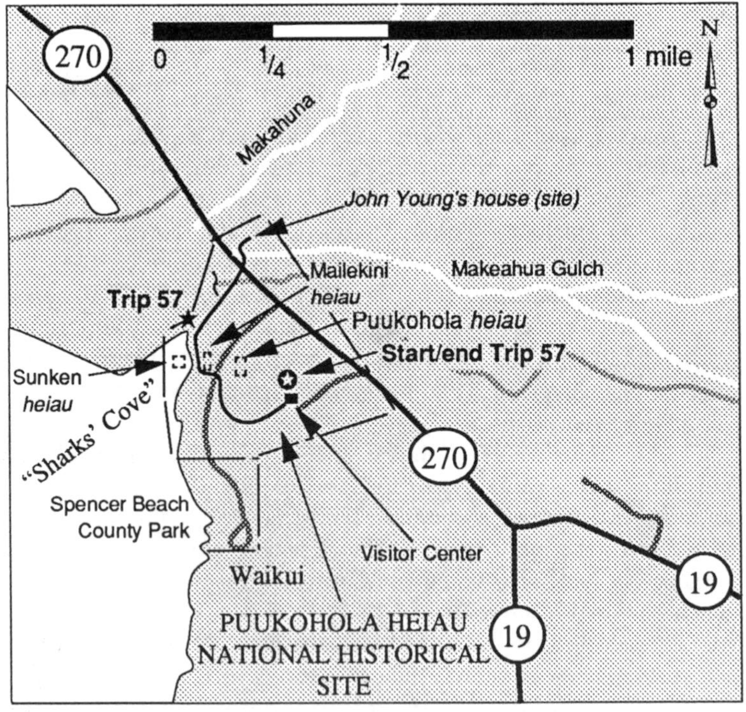

Trip 57. Puukohola *Heiau*
(Trail sketched from NPS brochure; not to scale)

Trip 58. Lapakahi State Historical Park Side Trip from Kailua-Kona

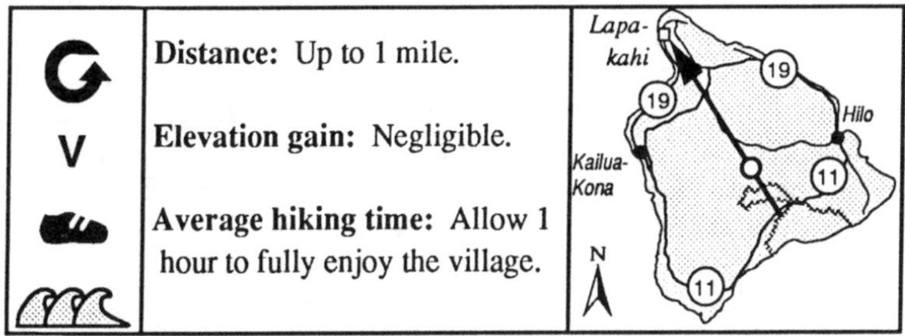

Topos: Optional: *Keawanui Bay* 7½.

Trail map (route approximated): At the end of this trip.

Highlights: Thanks to the brochure provided at the park's entrance, you can enter an old Hawaiian village established some 600 years ago, walk through it, and, in your imagination, see its inhabitants going about their daily lives before Captain Cook arrived in 1778.

Caution: Lapakahi State Historical Park is supposedly open daily from 8:00 A.M. to 4:00 P.M. and staff are supposed to be on duty to explain the exhibits. However, it may be open but unstaffed and with no brochures available, or it may be closed for no apparent reason. Call ahead to be sure it's open (808-889-5566) and staffed in order to get the most out of your visit.

Driving instructions: From the intersection of Highways 11 and 19 in Kailua-Kona, drive north on Highway 19 past Ke-Ahole Airport and the Mauna Lani complex to the junction of Highways 19 and 270. Turn left onto Highway 270 here and follow it past Puukohola to the turnoff for Lapakahi State Historical Park. Turn left onto its access road and follow it to the gate. Check the brochure box here and pick up a brochure now in case none are available inside the park. Now continue through the gate to the parking lot. Park here to begin your hike, just over 45 miles from Kailua-Kona.

Permit/permission required: None.

Description: A thatch-roofed information counter just below the parking lot may offer brochures if you did not pick one up at the gate. Or you may find a staffer there to answer your questions. With brochure in hand, bear to your left as you face the sea to pick up a stone-bordered path that is feature number one in the brochure.

From here, you can follow the path approximately clockwise in a loop around the village complex. Paths across the loop offer ways to cut your explorations short or to extend them; it's up to you.

Here, as at Puuhonua o Honaunau, the brochure speaks of the place and to your imagination in a way I cannot hope to better in this book. How would *you,* it asks, go about solving the challenges of surviving here solely on what the land, the sea, and your labor could provide? Then, on your circuit of the village, it attempts to answer these questions. And by thus drawing you into the everyday life of the village, it makes you, in a way, a part of the village for a while.

Useful and edible plants grow here as they did long ago; the brochure explains their uses. Artifacts such as fishermen's tools and game boards are provided for you to touch, perhaps even play with. The brochure includes the rules for *konane,* the game often called "Hawaiian checkers," and you may try your hand at playing it if you wish.

As the brochure points out, wresting a living from these dry lands was much harder than making a living in luxuriant wetland valleys like Waipio (Trip 1). Studies of prehistoric Hawaiian agriculture have concentrated on wetland agriculture, particularly on irrigated taro. Dryland agriculture was overlooked. Yet, as *Feathered Gods and Fishhooks* reports, early European explorers had described intensive dryland agriculture in Hawaii. More recently, archaeologists have begun investigating prehistoric dryland agriculture and have identified three extensive dryland field systems on the leeward (west) side of the Big Island. You won't be surprised to learn that Lapakahi is part of one of those dryland field systems. Radiocarbon dating and other dating techniques show that these Lapakahi fields were developed over the period A.D. 1450 to 1800. In dryland agriculture, the sweet potato was more important than taro.

How productive were these dryland systems? Very, according to *Feathered Gods and Fishhooks.* For example, these Big Island dryland field systems provided the economic base for the line of chiefs from which Kamehameha eventually rose to unite all the islands.

It's a lot to ponder as you close this loop and return to your car.

The sweet potato. . . . Anthropological studies have established that the Polynesian stock originated in Southeast Asia, spreading eastward into the Pacific over thousands of years. The plants and animals they took along on their voyages all have tropical Southeast Asian origins, too—taro, yam, breadfruit, banana, sugar-cane; pigs, dogs, chickens; and so on. All but one, the sweet potato. There is no question that the sweet potato is from South America. Here at Lapakahi, archaeologists have unearthed carbonized sweet potatoes, proving beyond a doubt that the sweet potato was cultivated in Hawaii in prehistoric (pre-European) times.

How did the sweet potato get to East Polynesia before the arrival of Europeans? It cannot have dispersed on its own or with the inadvertent help of birds. (Can you picture a bird in flight with a sweet potato stuck in its feathers?) People had to bring it, but who were they? Voyagers from South America? As far as is known, there was no South American group skilled in long-distance seafaring. Kirch points out in *Feathered Gods and Fishhooks* that the Polynesians were skilled long-distance navigators who deliberately set out on long voyages of discovery. Thus, it's more likely that Polynesian seafarers reached South America on one of their long voyages. They would have recognized the common sweet potato as a root crop similar to the familiar yam, capable of lasting in storage over a long voyage. They stocked sweet potatoes for their return trip and, when they returned, planted those potatoes they hadn't eaten. Sweet potatoes can tolerate arid conditions, have high yields, and can be propagated by tubers or cuttings. They became the dominant dryland crop, introduced "relatively early after initial settlement" of central East Polynesia and from there dispersing "to the marginal areas of East Polynesia"—Hawaii, Easter Island, and New Zealand. (Interestingly, sweet potatoes hadn't reached West Polynesia by the time of European contact.)

Are you wondering, as I am, whether the Polynesians beat Christopher Columbus and even the Norsemen to the Americas?

***Konane* ("Hawaiian checkers") board at Lapakahi**

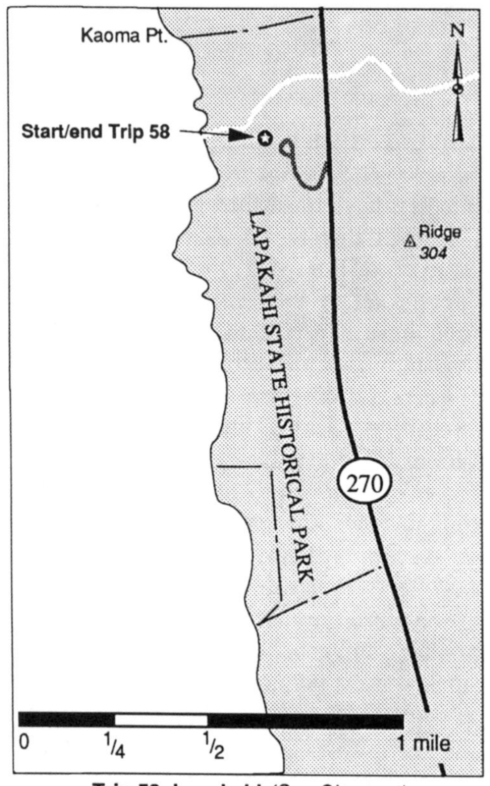

Trip 58. Lapakahi *(See Close-up)*

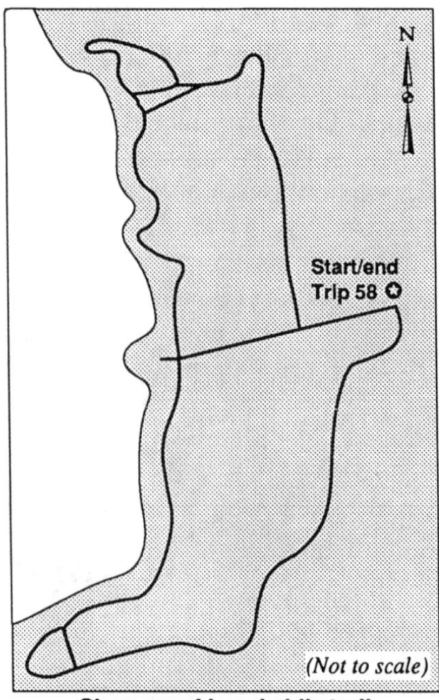

Close-up of Lapakahi's trail
(Sketched from DNLR brochure)

Trip 59. Mookini *Heiau* and Kamehameha Birthplace Side Trip from Kailua-Kona

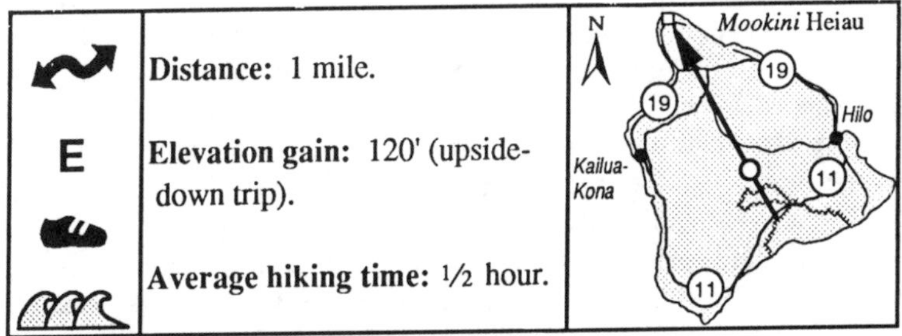

Topos: Optional: *Mahukona* 7½.

Trail map: At the end of this trip.

Highlights: Two remote, lonely, and awe-inspiring spots await you on the far north end of the Big Island: Mookini *Heiau,* one of the oldest, largest, and most sacred sites in old Hawaii; and the birthplace of Kamehameha at an even lonelier spot ⅓ mile away.

Driving instructions: From Kailua-Kona, follow Highway 19 north past Ke-Ahole Airport to its junction with Highway 270 near Kawaihae. Turn left onto Highway 270 and follow it past Puukohola and Lapakahi almost, but not quite, to Hawi. Just before Hawi, a sign directs you seaward to Upolu Airport. Turn left here; take this little road seaward (north) to the boundary of Upolu Airport, where you meet a road paralleling the boundary. Turn left onto the dusty road paralleling the airport boundary and follow it west to the marked turnoff for Mookini Heiau. Here, you turn left again, climb a low hill, and drive into the parking lot. Park here to start your hike, 53¾ miles from Kailua-Kona.

Permit/permission required: None.

Description: Brochures describing Mookini *Heiau* are available at a brochure box next to the parking lot. Be sure to pick one up and use it to guide your visit—although the temple walls as seen from here are intimidating enough to make you think twice about entering the temple precincts. Your first view of Mookini *Heiau* from the parking lot is as an impressive mound of lichen-covered rock rising on the west side of the lot. Tradition says these waterworn basalt boulders came from Pololu Valley (Trip 60), many miles away, and were all transported here by being passed from hand to hand down a living chain of men in a single night. It is clear that you must enter only with the greatest respect.

The people of Kohala built the low wall surrounding the site in 1981 to protect and define the site. A gate in the modern wall bars vehicle access at one end of the parking lot; you'll end your loop around the temple grounds there. Start by entering the temple grounds through the opening in the wall at the other end of the parking lot—the end where you drove in—in order to tour the grounds as shown in the brochure. Mookini was a *luakini heiau*—a temple of human sacrifice—and one of the first artifacts you will see is the large, dish-like rock "used by the ancient priests to prepare sacrificial victims for offering at the altar."

The high priest uses the thatched hut at the south-southeast corner of the temple grounds when he or she is there. (Yes, there is still a high priest for Mookini *Heiau*, and it is still a sacred place; see below.) These temple grounds were not closed to the people, but the temple proper, whose massive walls still rise almost 30 feet in places, was *kapu* to all but the high chiefs and kings (*alii nui*). That *kapu* has been lifted; you may now enter with a respectful spirit. Most of the interior, however, is roped off; please do not go beyond those boundaries.

After having visited the interior of the temple, you can close the loop by walking around the other end of the temple proper and exiting through the gate in the modern wall at the other end of the parking lot.

Kamehameha's birthplace is so close that there is no point driving to it. Instead, cross the parking lot and walk down on the spur road you drove up on. At the bottom of it, turn left onto the dirt road and follow it along the coast for ⅓ mile. The ocean is a vivid blue against the gray and black rock; the road is a ribbon of red dust flanked by dry grasses that continually rustle in the wind. Maui may be visible to the northwest across Alenuihaha Channel. Walking between Mookini *Heiau* and Kamehameha's birthplace, you may see, as I did, windsurfers with their colorful sails skimming over the choppy sea—a lighthearted note in this solemn place.

The low stone walls enclosing Kamehameha's birthplace are on the inland side of the road. You can't get inside the inner wall (don't climb over it), but you can walk around it. Mookini is visible to the east from here, especially the thatched hut. There's not much else to see, but you can feel the eerie loneliness of the place. It is fitting that "Kamehameha" means "the lonely one." Tradition says that he was taken from here to Mookini *Heiau* for his birth rituals.

Retrace your steps to Mookini *Heiau* and to your car.

The Mookini family. . . . The Mookini family has provided the high priest (*kahuna nui*) for Mookini *Heiau* ever since it was built in what we would call A.D. 480, according to the family's oral tradition. Down the generations, "a single family member was trained in temple ritual and tradition and was responsible for providing guidance and direction." This family member was chosen by the current *kahuna nui* and eventually became the *kahuna nui* in his or her turn. The responsibility was generally reserved for men, and you will read in other sources that only men were permitted to enter and serve at such a *heiau*. However, seven women have served as *kahuna nui* at Mookini, including the present *kahuna nui,* Leimomi Mookini Lum. This unbroken line of priestly responsibility in one family is now perhaps unique in Hawaii and is a precious cultural inheritance and resource.

Many *kapu* lie upon Mookini *Heiau,* and you can sense their weight as you walk around it. For example, Mookini *Heiau* was once reserved exclusively for the *alii nui* for fasting, prayer, and human sacrifice. Leimomi Mookini Lum has lifted that one *kapu* so that Mookini *Heiau* might come alive again, particularly by having Hawaii's children visit: there is an annual Children's Day at Mookini *Heiau.* The *heiau,* through the children of Hawaii, will in turn bring new life to Hawaii.

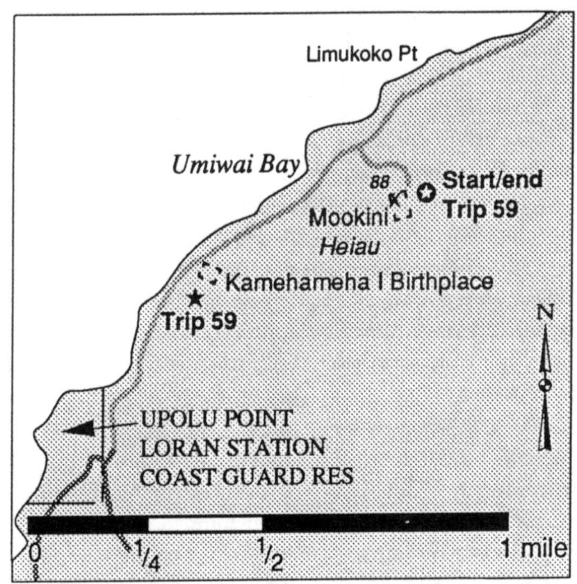

Trip 59. Mookini *Heiau* and Kamehameha Birthplace

Trip 60. Pololu Valley Side Trip from Kailua-Kona

M

Distance: Just over 1½ miles.

Elevation gain: 400' (upside-down trip).

Average hiking time: ¾ hour.

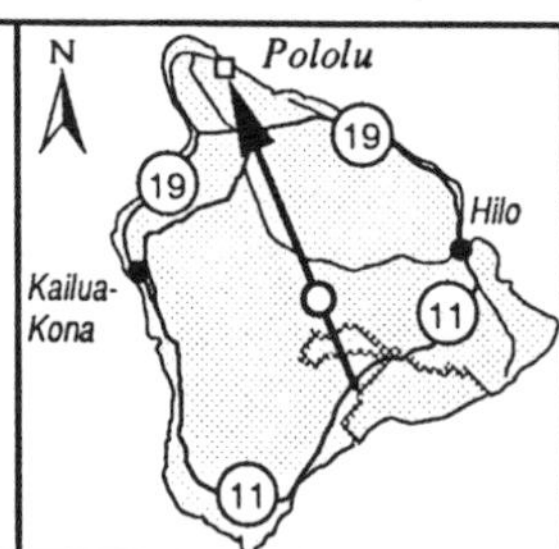

Topos: *Honokane* 7½.

Trail map: At the end of this trip.

Highlights: Waipio is the southeasternmost of the Hamakua coast's dramatic stream valleys (see Trip 1). Pololu is the northerwesternmost of those valleys. It is drier than Waipio and lacks waterfalls, but it is lovely in its own way. You can descend into Pololu only on foot or horseback, and chances are you won't have to ford its stream. Like Waipio, Pololu boasts a gray-sand beach (some call it a black-sand beach) which offers pleasant sunning but not swimming—the ocean is too dangerous. Come early: by midmorning, the little parking area at the roadend, Pololu Valley Lookout, is jammed. However, relatively few of those people actually make it down to the beach, as the descent is quite steep.

Driving instructions: From Kailua-Kona, follow Highway 19 north past Ke-Ahole Airport to its junction with Highway 270 near Kawaihae. Turn left onto Highway 270 and follow it past Puukohola and Lapakahi, through Hawi, and to its end at Pololu Valley Lookout, 59½ miles from Kailua-Kona.

Permit/permission required: None as of this writing. However, most of Pololu Valley is privately owned; public access is restricted to the trail down the cliff and to the beachfront.

Description: Pause to take in the marvelous view at the parking area; the green valley to the southeast is Pololu. Now head south-southeast, away from the roadend and slightly inland, to pick up the trail into Pololu Valley. You descend under Christmas berry, guava, ironwood, *hala,* and *hau,* and alongside air plant, morning glory, *ulei, ilima,* white shrimp plant, and cayenne vervain. The trail is very steep at times—you descend 400 feet in less than ½ mile!—

and is muddy and slippery in some places, rocky in others. You have occasional excellent views out over the valley on your descent, and soon you pass through a stock gate (be sure to close it behind you).

Shortly after the stock gate, you reach the bottom, pick up a sandy track, and follow it out toward the driftwood-strewn beach and the stream. NO HUNTING OR TRESPASSING signs are hung on many of the ironwood trees backing the beach; please respect them, even though you are tempted to explore beyond them. The pond is off-limits, too. Pololu Valley's small stream, which looked badly polluted to me, may be low enough that you can circumvent it altogether by sticking to the beach. Otherwise, test its depth and swiftness to determine if it's safe to ford.

On either side of the stream, you're likely to find a big piece of driftwood to lean against while you enjoy the sun, watch the surf, and have a picnic. You can walk along the sand and then over the cobbles to the far end, where a deeply eroded, unmaintained trail zigzags up the valley's southeast wall. I recommend you avoid this unsafe old track. Instead, relax and enjoy the charming beach.

Retrace your steps to your car when you're ready, thankful that the trail is quite shady!

The dynamic Hawaiian culture.... I envision Pololu Valley, when it was inhabited, as full of gleaming taro ponds—a miniature version of Waipio Valley (Trip 1). I imagine that that Eden-like scene has been typical of old Hawaii for the more than 1500 years that it's been colonized. And I assume that the highly stratified Hawaiian social structure with its complete separation of chiefs from commoners has also been typical for those 1500 years. The Hawaii that Cook found in 1778, I thought, was the Hawaii that had always been.

I was wrong. As Kirch shows in *Feathered Gods and Fishhooks*, intensive irrigated farming as represented by acres of taro ponds began perhaps as late as 1500 A.D. Intensive dryland farming as found at Lapakahi (Trip 58), aquaculture (fishponds) as preserved at Kalahuipuaa (Trip 55), and the rigid social structure as exemplified at Puuhonua o Honaunau (Trip 53) are also late developments. There is archaeological evidence that these late developments were linked to one another and to fundamental changes beginning perhaps around A.D. 1200, nearly a thousand years after colonization. In fact, the Hawaii that Cook found in 1778 was at just the latest stage of a dynamic social evolution from its ancestral Polynesian roots. In these next few paragraphs, I'll try to briefly summarize a few of the conclusions that Kirch skillfully develops over whole chapters of

Feathered Gods and Fishhooks.

The ancestral Polynesian society had some kind of *kapu* system; it was stratified to some extent into chiefs and commoners. The chiefs linked the commoners with the gods. Land was held by groups organized on the basis of their descent from the same revered ancestors. At the head of a large descent group was a hereditary chief. Chiefs and commoners shared land ownership and genealogy: they belonged to the same clan. The commoners paid tribute to the chiefs, who interceded with the gods and who were supposed to "assure the peace and security of the land."

On Hawaii, by the time Cook arrived, only the chiefs owned land. Only the chiefs could reckon descent from deified ancestors through elaborate genealogies. Commoners worked land they could not own; they had no deified ancestors and kept no genealogies. In social fact, though certainly not in genetic fact, chiefs and commoners had ceased to belong to the same clan. The *kapu* system had become very rigid and elaborate.

What had happened to change Hawaiian society? The change may have been related to population growth. Archaeological evidence, though sketchy, suggests that around 1200 A.D., the Hawaiian population, which had grown gradually till then, began to grow explosively. By about 1650 A.D., the size of the population may have been ten times what it had been around A.D. 1200—all in an isolated setting with inherently limited resources. Then it abruptly declined. Kirch observes that this kind of growth-decline pattern is often found in population cycles in limited environments like islands.

Material evidence further suggests that around the time the population exploded, agricultural practices evolved from a simple slash-and-burn style, compatible with few people and relatively plentiful resources, to an intensive style, required when many people compete for limited resources. Farming and fishing became highly organized in order to increase yields through labor-intensive projects like large-scale taro ponds and fishponds. To further increase yields, people expanded into previously unfarmed areas.

Paralleling this, other material evidence points to an increase in the differences between chiefs and commoners, such as elaborate ornamentation unique to the chiefly class. The evidence suggests that commoners were increasingly obliged to overproduce in order to support a growing chiefly class of non-producers. A chief's prestige and holiness rested on his ability to command the labor and the products of the commoners. The more he could command, the greater were his political and spiritual powers. With a rapidly

Pond in Polulu Valley

expanding population, there was a tendency for chiefs to want more and more, as long as the resources held out.

The expansion of people into previously unoccupied land probably led to conflicts between groups. War became more frequent. War allowed a victorious chief to greatly increase his material wealth, his power, and thus his prestige and sanctity. A victorious chief would parcel out land he had won and the commoners that worked it to his junior chiefs, ensuring the junior chiefs' loyalty but dispossessing the commoners. A warrior cult led by the chiefly class developed around the god Ku, further distancing the chiefs from the commoners. Rituals and *kapu* were elaborated in ways that justified and increased this distance. Eventually, the chiefs and the commoners no longer recognized their common ancestry.

Growth has its limits, and an abrupt population decline apparently began around 1650 A.D. Kahoolawe's fate may show what happened elsewhere. It's the smallest of the eight major Hawaiian islands and the one with the most severe environment—it's extremely arid. Kahoolawe was settled late, around 1000 A.D., and then only along its coast. But around 1300 A.D., perhaps in response to population pressures, people moved to the inland plateau and cleared it for dryland agriculture. Stripped of its cover, the inland plateau eroded, and its fragile soil was soon exhausted. The population on Kahoolawe began to decline rapidly around 1550 A.D.; the inland plateau was abandoned by 1750 A.D. Today, the interior is barren, stripped of its soil down to the hardpan.

There is evidence elsewhere in Hawaii that marginal lands that had been intensely cultivated lost their productivity and that this loss was associated with the general population decline. Competition intensified between the chiefs for the services of a diminishing number of commoners and for ownership of the remaining productive lands, culminating in Kamehameha's domination of all the islands. What might have happened then? We'll never know.

The Hawaii that was a tranquil Eden unchanged for a thousand years, that was an innocent world of shimmering taro ponds, of happy farmers and fishermen, and of wise chiefs ensuring the peaceful continuance of this paradise—that Hawaii never existed, not here in Pololu Valley and not anywhere else. Are modern Hawaii's elaborate, luxurious, self-contained resorts an attempt to carve that Hawaii-of-the-imagination out of the difficult but far more interesting Hawaii-of-reality?

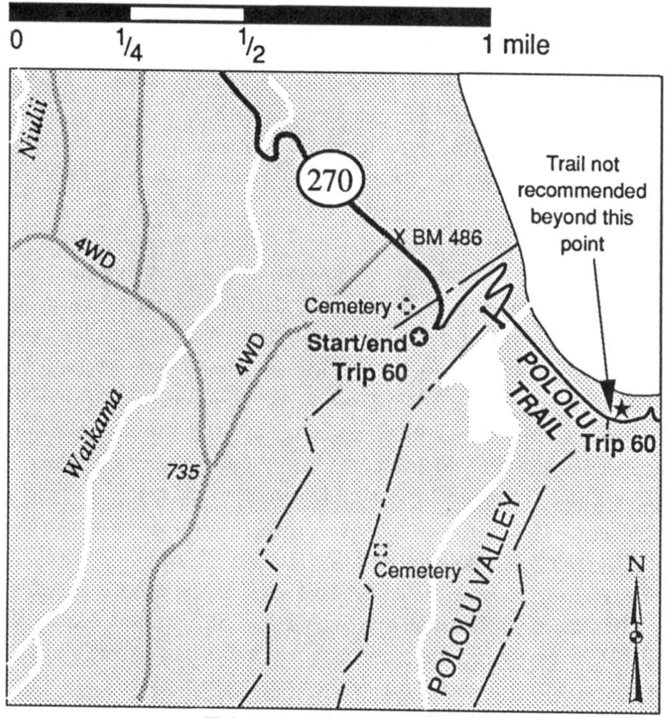

Trip 60. Pololu Valley

Bibliography

Beckwith, Martha. *Hawaiian Mythology.* New Haven: Yale University Press (for the Folklore Foundation of Vassar College), 1940. Reprint. Honolulu: University of Hawaii Press, 1970, 1976.

Bisignani, J.D. *Hawaii Handbook.* 2nd ed. Chico, California: Moon Publications, Inc., 1989.

Carlquist, Sherwin. *Hawaii, A Natural History.* 2nd ed., 2nd printing. Lawai, Kauai: National [formerly Pacific] Tropical Botanical Garden, 1980, 1985.

Chisholm, Craig. *Hawaiian Hiking Trails.* 3rd ed. Lake Oswego, Oregon: The Fernglen Press, 1989.

Clark, John. *Hawaii's Secret Beaches, A Guide to Twenty-Four Hawaiian Beaches.* Honolulu: Tongg Publishing.

Cruikshank, Dale P. *Mauna Kea: A Guide to the Upper Slopes and Observatories.* Honolulu: University of Hawaii, Institute for Astronomy, 1986.

Day, A. Grove, and Carl Stroven, Eds. *A Hawaiian Reader.* Appleton-Century-Crofts, 1959. Reprint. Honolulu: Mutual Publishing Company, 1984.

Day, A. Grove. *Hawaii and Its People.* New York: Duell, Sloan and Pearce, 1955.

Epidemiology Branch, State Department of Health, State of Hawaii. "Leptospirosis in Hawaii." October 1, 1987.

Hargreaves, Dorothy, and Bob Hargreaves. *Hawaii Blossoms.* Japan: Dorothy and Bob Hargreaves, 1958. Reprint. Lahaina: Ross-Hargreaves.

______. *Tropical Trees of Hawaii.* Kailua: Hargreaves Company.

Hawai'i Audubon Society. *Hawaii's Birds.* 4th ed. Honolulu: Hawai'i Audubon Society, 1989.

Hazlett, Richard W. "Kipuka Puaulu Trail." Hawaii Natural History Association, 1978.

Joesting, Edward. *Hawaii, An Uncommon History.* New York: W.W. Norton & Company Inc., 1972.

Kaye, Glen. *Hawaii Volcanoes: the Story Behind the Scenery.* Las Vegas, Nevada: KC Publications, Inc., 1976.

Kirch, Patrick Vinton. *Feathered Gods and Fishhooks: An Introduction to Hawaiian Archaeology and Prehistory.* Honolulu: University of Hawaii Press, 1985.

Levi, Herbert W., and Lorna R. Levi. *Spiders and their Kin.* New York: Golden Press, 1987.

Macdonald, Gordon A., Agatin T. Abbott, and Frank L. Peterson. *Volcanoes in the Sea, the Geology of Hawaii.* 2nd ed. Honolulu: University of Hawaii Press, 1986.

McPhee, John. *The Control of Nature.* New York: Farrar, Straus and Giroux, 1989. Republished in New York by The Noonday Press, 1990.

Merlin, Mark David. *Hawaiian Coastal Plants and Scenic Shorelines.* 3rd printing. Honolulu: Oriental Publishing Co., 1986.

———. *Hawaiian Forest Plants.* 3rd ed. Honolulu: The Oriental Publishing Co., 1980.

Penisten, John. *Hawaii: The Big Island: A Paradise Guide.* 2nd ed. Portland, Oregon: Paradise Publications, 1991.

Pukui, Mary Kawena, Samuel H. Elbert, and Esther T. Mookini. *The Pocket Hawaiian Dictionary.* Honolulu: University of Hawaii Press, 1975.

Pukui, Mary Kawena, and Caroline Curtis. *Pikoi and Other Legends of the Island of Hawaii.* 3rd printing. Honolulu: The Kamehameha Schools Press, 1949.

Reed, Frances. *Hilo Legends.* 2nd printing. Hilo, Hawaii: The Petroglyph Press, Ltd., 1987.

Richardson, Jim, Ed. *The Honolulu Advertiser's Wildlife of Hawaii.* Honolulu: The Honolulu Advertiser, 1986.

Sohmer, S.H., and R. Gustafson. *Plants and Flowers of Hawai'i.* Honolulu: University of Hawaii Press, 1987.

Westervelt, W.D. *Myths and Legends of Hawaii.* (Selected and edited by A. Grove Day.) Honolulu: Mutual Publishing Company, 1987.

Winnett, Thomas, and Melanie Findling. *Backpacking Basics.* 3rd ed. Berkeley: Wilderness Press, 1988.

Woolliams, Keith. *A Guide to Hawaii's Popular Trees.* 2nd ed. Aiea, Hawaii: Island Heritage Publishing, 1988.

Zurick, David. *Hawaii, Naturally.* Berkeley: Wilderness Press, 1990.

Appendix A. Camping on Hawaii

Backcountry camping (accessible only on foot.) I have stayed at most of, and visited all of, the following places.

Hawaii Volcanoes National Park. This is the Big Island's prime backpacking area. You *must* have a permit to stay overnight in the backcountry of Hawaii Volcanoes National Park. Permits are available only by applying in person at Kilauea Visitor Center and are issued on a first come, first served basis. Because water is usually available only at the shelters and the cabins, they are where you will stay. Space *in* the cabins and shelters is on a first come, first served basis, and you will share that space with whoever (and whatever) else shows up.

Hawaii Volcanoes National Park—Mauna Loa (Trips 12–13 and 49–50). There are two cabins on Mauna Loa: the Red Hill Cabin (10,035 feet) on the Mauna Loa Trail and the Mauna Loa Cabin (13,250 feet) on the edge of the summit caldera and accessible by both the Mauna Loa and Observatory trails. Each cabin offers bunks (eight at Red Hill, eleven at Mauna Loa), a table or tables, benches or chairs, counters on which to cook, water collected from the roof and kept in a tank (treat before drinking), and a pit toilet. There is no bedding, no lanterns (bring candles), no stoves, and no cooking or eating utensils. There are also a few flat spots outside those cabins where you may pitch a tent.

Hawaii Volcanoes National Park—Puna Kau coast (Trips 38–39, 43–45, and 46–47). Along the Puna Kau coast, you will share your living space with cockroaches, ants, black widow spiders, scorpions, mongooses, crickets, etc. I strongly recommend you bring your own bugproof, rainproof tent, a sleeping pad, and a lightweight sleeping bag. There is one cabin (at Pepeiao) with three bunks, an inside table (no benches or chairs), an outside table, and a couple of ant-infested benches by the door. There are three three-sided shelters (at Kaaha, Halape, and Keauhou). The cabin and the shelters have tanks for water collected from the roofs (treat before drinking) and pit toilets. There is no bedding, no lanterns (bring candles), no stoves, and no cooking or eating utensils. The fire hazard is extreme along this dry coast, so please be very careful with any stoves, candles, etc. There are a few flat areas outside the shelters and the cabin, and more flat areas at the beaches seaward of the shelters, where you can camp. You will have plenty of creepy-crawly company there, too.

Hang your food away from the creepy-crawlies and the mongooses.

Hawaii Volcanoes National Park—Napau Crater (Trip 34). There is a campsite of sorts near Napau Crater, as evinced by the presence of a pit toilet. No water, shelter, or other amenities; very rainy. Not recommended.

Waipio Valley. What little camping is available in Waipio Valley is really car camping, even though you and I have to hoof it down that awful road. See Car camping on private property, below.

Waimanu Valley. The Division of Forestry and Wildlife, Hawaii District, of the Division of Land and Natural Resources strictly controls camping in Waimanu Valley (Waimanu National Estuarine Research Reserve). Camping is restricted to a few sites along the beach at the valley mouth. Each site has a maximum number of campers. Each site has a grill. You will be assigned a site and given a map showing the site's location when you get your permit. The site number is not marked at all of the sites, but you can figure it out from the map. Your stay is limited to a maximum of four days and three nights. There are two elevated composting toilets in the camping area. Water is available from spring-fed streams on the west side of the valley; purify it before drinking it.

You may apply for your permit by telephone or in person no earlier than one month in advance of your intended stay from:

Division of Forestry and Wildlife, Hawaii District, DNLR
1643 Kilauea Avenue
Hilo, Hawaii 96720
808-933-4221

Their office is near the corner of Kilauea and Kawili in Hilo and is co-located with Hilo Arboretum (Trip 16). It is *not* co-located with the office of the Division of State Parks (which is in the State Office Building in downtown Hilo).

Car camping on public property. The Big Island offers a lot of opportunities for car camping—the kind of camping where you drive up, pay your bucks, pick a space, park your car, and pitch your tent there and live out of it (or live out of your parked vehicle). For those who enjoy car camping, there is a list below of the places you can car camp on the Big Island. This information is largely from other sources, especially *Hawaii, Naturally.* I've verified the information for few of these places. The table at the end of this section summarizes these data. Note that a number of campgrounds are *not recommended for tourists!* Places I have seen are asterisked (*); I stayed only at Kipuka Nene.

Car camping in Hawaii Volcanoes National Park is possible at three sites: Namakani Paio,* just off Highway 11 a few miles past the turnoff to Kilauea Visitor Center; Kipuka Nene,* which is on Hilina Pali Road (itself off the Chain of Craters Road); and Kamoamoa,* at the end of the Chain of Craters Road and next to Kamoamoa Black Sand Beach. There are picnic shelters and fireplaces at each but no wood (you can buy wood in Volcano). Each also has toilets. Namakani Paio and Kipuka Nene have drinking water, but you must bring your own water down to Kamoamoa. Neither fees nor reservations are required for any of these campgrounds, but permits are required for Namakani Paio and Kipuka Nene. Your stay is limited to seven days per campground per year. For more information, write or call:

Hawaii Volcanoes National Park
P.O. Box 52
Hawaii 96718-0052
808-967-7311

Car camping at the state parks is by permit only and for a maximum of 5 consecutive nights in any 30-day period. Permits are free. They are issued Monday through Friday, 8 A.M. to 4 P.M., at the Division of State Parks office in Hilo. The person appearing to apply for the permit must provide proper identification for each person in the party who is 18 years old or older. "Proper identification" means a driver's license or a passport. You may also apply by mail at least seven days in advance of your proposed trip by writing to the Division of State Parks. When applying by mail, include a copy of the proper identification for each person in the party who is 18 years old or older. Trailers and RVs are not permitted in Hawaii's state parks. For the state parks, write or call:

Department of Land and Natural Resources
Division of State Parks, Hawaii District
P.O. Box 936
Hilo, Hawaii, HI 96721-0936
808-961-7200

Car camping on Division of Forestry and Wildlife lands. At present, there are no car campgrounds in areas managed by the Division of Forestry and Wildlife.

Car camping at Hawaii County's parks. Permits are required for Hawaii County's car campgrounds (see the end of the table below). There is a fee per night: $1.00 per adult and 50¢ per child. I don't know what amenities, if any, you will find. Obtain permits by mail from:

Department of Parks and Recreation, County of Hawaii
25 Apuni Street
Hilo, Hawaii HI 96720
808-961-8311

Public car-camping summary table. The following table summarizes the *public* car-camping opportunities on the Big Island. Note that Harry K. Brown Beach Park, long a favorite spot but one that had lately deteriorated badly, no longer exists: Pele reclaimed it in 1990. There is no car camping (or any other kind of camping) at either Mauna Kea State Park or Kilauea State Recreation Area (see below, under **Cabins**).

Name	**Type**	**Nearest Town**	**Amenities; Restrictions**
Namakani Paio*	National Park	Volcano	Picnic shelter, grills, water, restrooms. Tents only. Very rainy and cold. Free. Permit required. Stays limited to 7 consecutive days. At 4000′.
Kipuka Nene*	National Park	Volcano	Picnic shelter, grills, water, pit toilets. Tents only. Occasional rain. Free. Permit required. Stays limited to 7 consecutive days. At 2926′.
Kamoamoa*	National Park	Volcano	Picnic shelter, griils, restrooms. No water. Free. No permit required. At sea level.
Kalopa*	State Park	Honokaa	Picnic shelter, grills, restrooms. Tents only. Very rainy. Free. Permit required. Looked unpleasant and dirty to me. 5-day maximum stay. At 2000′.
Manuka*	State Wayside	Naalehu	Picnic shelter, grill, restrooms. No tents allowed: sleeping area consists of concrete slabs under a roof, just downhill from the picnic shelter. Free. Permit required. 5-day maximum stay. At 1700′.
MacKenzie*	State Recreation Area	Pahoa	Picnic pavilions; restrooms; no drinking water. Tents only. Women's restroom so filthy that people were using the area behind the restroom building instead of the restroom proper. Not recommended! Free. Permit required. 5-day maximum stay. Sea level.

Keokea	County	Hawi	Fee. Permit required. Tents and trailers okay. Sea level.
Kapaa	County	Hawi	Fee. Permit required. Tents and trailers okay. Sea level.
Kolekole	County	Honomu	Fee. Permit required. Tents and trailers okay. Sea level.
Laupahoehoe	County	Laupahoehoe	Fee. Permit required. Tents and trailers okay. Sea level.
Mahukona	County	Hawi	Fee. Permit required. Tents and trailers okay. Sea level. *Hawaii, Naturally* recommends *against* a stay here.
Milolii	County	Milolii	Fee. Permit required. Tents and trailers okay. Sea level. *Hawaii, Naturally* recommends *against* a stay here.
Onekahakaha	County	Hilo	Fee. Permit required. Tents and trailers okay. Sea level. *Hawaii, Naturally* recommends *against* a stay here.
Punaluu*	County	Naalehu, Pahala	Fee. Permit required. Tents and trailers okay. Sea level. Heavily used by local people on weekends.
Samuel M. Spencer*	County	Kawaihae, Waimea	Fee. Permit required. Tents and trailers okay. Sea level. *Hawaii, Naturally* recommends *against* a stay here.
Whittington	County	Naalehu	Fee. Permit required. Tents and trailers okay. Sea level.

Car camping on private property.

*Waipio Valley (Trip 1).** Camping in Waipio Valley is essentially car camping by people who have 4WD vehicles capable of negotiating the dreadful road down into Waipio Valley. I found it unappealing. On one occasion, I stayed at the hotel; see the fourth paragraph below.

You must get a permit *in person* from the Hamakua Sugar Company, 808-776-1211, in order to camp in Waipio Valley. The Hamakua Sugar Company offices are located in Paauilo (locally pronounced "pau-ee-lo") just inland of Highway 19 on the Hamakua coast. Paauilo is 35 miles northwest of the junction of Highways 19 and 11 in Hilo. Look for a pedestrian overpass across the highway and a turnoff inland and slightly uphill to a post office, a general store, and a snack bar. The sugar company's offices are in the same building as the post office, on the other side from the store and the snack bar.

Camping is restricted to an area behind the beach and on the east side of the stream draining Waipio Valley. It is reported to be marked by Hamakua Sugar Company signs on the trees; I did not spot them. There is neither drinking water nor toilets nor trash service, so be prepared to purify stream water, to dig a hole to bury your body wastes and tissues, and to pack out everything else.

The road down into Waipio Valley is extremely steep and rough, suitable for 4WD vehicles only. You will probably need to backpack down into Waipio. There is a parking lot for passenger cars at the end of the highway that leads to the edge of Waipio Valley (Highway 240) and just before the black-diamond descent into Waipio. It really is marked with a black diamond, which for skiing runs means "most difficult." You cannot leave a car parked at the roadend for more than 24 hours. If you plan on being gone more than 24 hours, you may be able to find a place to park on the side of the highway (not appreciated by the local people), or you may find, as I did, a local homeowner who will let you park in his back yard for a reasonable fee.

*Hotel in Waipio.** I normally do not mention hotels or other lodgings in these books, but I shall make an exception for Waipio Valley. Mr. Tetsuo ("Tom") Araki runs a five-room hotel on his property in Waipio Valley. Guests must bring their own food and prepare it in a kitchen that is below the rooms. Guests share a toilet, cold-water shower, and cold-water tub. There is no electricity; illumination is by kerosene lamps. The rooms are plain, clean, and comfortable. Payment is in cash only. To get there, turn left (away from the beach) at the foot of the descent into Waipio Valley. Follow the 4WD road over a stream and past a junction to the Arakis' big silver mailbox. ("Biggest mailbox in the valley," someone told me.) For reservations, you can write to Mr. Araki at 25 Malama Place, Hilo, HI 96720, or telephone him in Waipio Valley at 808-775-0368. Reservations are necessary: the space is very limited, and the tiny hotel attracts guests from all over the world. It is possible that at some time in the future, the hotel will no longer be in operation, Mr. and Mrs. Araki being well on in years.

Kona area. Kona Lodge and Hostel* will let you pitch a tent in their back yard for a fee. The lodge has a communal kitchen, toilets, and showers. Get in touch with them at P.O. Box 645, Kealakekua, HI 96750, 808-322-9056.

Puna area. Kalani Honua Culture Center and Retreat is reported to permit camping on their grounds in Pahoa. Get in touch with them at R.R. 2, Box 4500, Pahoa, HI 96778, 808-965-7828.

Cabins. The following areas offer cabins, which you should reserve well in advance. Asterisks (*) mark places I have stayed or have at least seen.

Hawaii Volcanoes National Park. Most of the cabins in Hawaii Volcanoes National Park are accessible only on foot; see above under **Backcountry camping (accessible only on foot).** There are also cabins at Namakani Paio,* which you can rent through Volcano House (Volcano House, Hawaii Volcanoes National Park, HI 96718, 808-967-7321 or 800-325-3535). The cabins sleep four in one double bed and two bunk beds. There are also shelves and a rod from which you can hang things. Renters share centrally located toilets and showers. Each cabin has indoor and outdoor light bulbs (but no electrical outlets), an outdoor picnic table, and an outdoor grill (wood is not provided). Use your backpacker's stove only outside on the picnic table; even out there, fumes from it may be enough to set off the unshielded smoke alarm inside the cabin. As of this writing, your rental fee includes a bag of linens from Volcano House, but the single blanket is inadequate against Namakani Paio's penetrating dampness and chill. Plan to bring a warm sleeping bag.

State parks. The rules for getting permission to use the cabins at the state parks are the same as for getting permission to car-camp as described above. This applies at Hapuna, too, even though it is run by a concessionaire. There are rental fees for the cabins, and you may need to make arrangements to pick up the keys. State parks with rental cabins are:

> *Mauna Kea State Park* (Trip 10)* on the Saddle Road offers housekeeping cabins with electric heat, hot and cold running water, flush toilets and showers in each cabin, electricity, refrigerators, gas ranges, linens, furniture, and a strange assortment of cooking and eating utensils. There are group as well as individual cabins. Popular with local people. Crowded and noisy on weekends.
>
> *Kilauea State Recreation Area.* There is also a single housekeeping cabin off Highway 11 near Hawaii Volcanoes National Park at Kilauea State Recreation Area. Reported to have furnished bedrooms, electric heat, kitchen. Available only Wednesday through Monday nights.
>
> *Kalopa State Park* (Trips 4 and 5).* Group cabins (up to 32 persons each). Reported to have beds, bedding, toilet, hot showers, kitchen facilities, and electric heating. Popular, especially with local youth groups.

*Hapuna State Park.** A-frame cabins located just inland of Hapuna Beach. Each cabin reportedly accommodates four persons on sleeping platforms and has electric outlets and a cold-water shower. Toilets (separate). Shared kitchen (range, refrigerator) in central pavilion. Very popular! These cabins are run by a concessionaire, whom you should write or call instead of the Division of State Parks (Hawaii Untouched Parks and Recreation, Inc., 74-5543 H Kaiwi Street, Kailua-Kona, HI 96740, 808-329-2944).

Division of Forestry and Wildlife. The Division of Forestry and Wildlife has five cabins on the 4WD roads that arc around Mauna Kea from the Saddle Road. They are used primarily by hunters. I know nothing more about those cabins. The roads are said to be very bad, but I have not ventured onto them myself. A Hilo resident told me of finding a passenger car abandoned on the main 4WD road and buried in mud up to its doors. For more information, write or call the Division of Forestry and Wildlife; the address and telephone number are under "Waimanu Valley" in this appendix.

Appendix B. Hikes You Won't Find Here and Why

You may have read articles on the following hikes, seen them mentioned in other books, or noticed them on topos. Some of them are in this book but under different names. Some of these routes are closed because landowners no longer give permission to hike them. Development has interfered with access to some routes. Other trails have become unsafe; I firmly believe that a vacation is not enhanced by a trip to the emergency room that you could have missed by avoiding a dangerous route. Finally, I judge that some are just too remote and too boring to be worth your time.

Back in Waipio Valley. Most of Waipio Valley is privately owned. You are not welcome to go exploring back in the valley (unless, of course, people who live down there invite you to do so or you need to get to the hotel). Stick to the 4WD road, the camping area, the beach, and the trail to Waimanu Valley.

Muliwai Trail. This is the official name for the trail that connects Waipio and Waimanu valleys; see Trip 2.

Kalopa State Park. The Gulch Rim Trail, Robusta Lane, Bluegum Lane, Silkoak Lane, Ironwood Lane, and the Perimeter Horse Trail are badly overgrown and poorly tagged. Bluegum Lane and Silkoak Lane were indistinguishable from the rest of the forest. All of these routes were also uninteresting.

Kaumana Trail. Not to be confused with Kaumana Caves County Park. This was once a loop off the Saddle Road. It is unmarked, very difficult to find, badly overgrown, and virtually untagged.

Puu Huluhulu (off the Saddle Road). The "trail" is a confusing, unsigned, largely untagged mess of crisscrossing tracks. The hill is dominated by uninteresting, non-native vegetation. A cinder quarry chomped out of its west slope doesn't add much its "beauty." A July 1989 brochure from the Department of Land and Natural Resources (DNLR) calls it "Puuhuluhulu" and recommends it for children, but I think it is no longer worthwhile for anyone.

Cape Kumakahi (1960 eruption; easternmost point of the Big Island). A decent road goes all the way out to the uninteresting automated lighthouse now. Beyond there, the area is rugged, dull, and full of trash. Not worth your time.

Kaimu Beach and Harry K. Brown Beach parks (Kalapana coast). Overrun by lava in 1990.

Hawaii Volcanoes National Park.

Naulu Trail between Napau and Kalapana trails. There's nothing of interest on this short trail segment that you couldn't see as well or better elsewhere.

Kau Desert trails. These trails are well-marked, mostly by cairns. Some of the cairns are quite admirable examples of the art of cairn-building. But the trails themselves are monotonous. They are not worth your time unless you have seen everything else in the park. Trips 42, 46, and 51 are exceptions. For your information:

—The Kau Desert Trail leaves the Crater Rim Trail after the latter has passed the observatory and the museum and has crossed Crater Rim Road. It extends south-southwest into the Kau Desert and passes a small shield volcano named Mauna Iki, formed in 1919. Near Mauna Iki, it meets trails from Hilina Pali Road (the Mauna Iki Trail, Trip 42) and from Highway 11 (the Footprints Trail, Trip 51). From Mauna Iki, it continues south-southwest almost to Hilina Pali and then curves east-northeast past Pepeiao Cabin and the Kaaha Trail (Trip 46) to the end of Hilina Pali Road. It is largely marked by cairns as it crosses older and newer lava flows. Its total one-way length is just under 19 miles.

—The Mauna Iki Trail, which you follow for Trip 42, continues from the Pit Craters past Puu Koae to meet the Kau Desert Trail a little north of Mauna Iki. It's 6⅓ miles one way to the junction with the Kau Desert Trail. From that junction, it's just under ¾ mile one way down the Kau Desert Trail to the junction with the Footprints Trail (below).

—The Footprints Trail, which you follow for Trip 51, continues beyond the shelter for the footprints to meet the Kau Desert Trail at Mauna Iki. Some sources consider this to be part of the Mauna Iki Trail. It's just over 1¾ miles one way from Highway 11 to the junction with the Kau Desert Trail.

Spur trail to Keauhou Trail from the Chain of Craters Road. See below in connection with "The Keauhou Trail" under Trails from Kipuka Nene. It has no particular merit of its own; 2 miles one way.

Trails from Kipuka Nene: the Halape and Keauhou trails. An old 4WD road runs generally east from Kipuka Nene. The topo considers it to be part of the Halape Trail as far as the point where the

Halape Trail turns south and descends the cliffs. After the Halape Trail turns south, the old 4WD road continues east to a junction with the Keauhou Trail. The spur trail mentioned above meets the old 4WD road and the Keauhou Trail at this junction:

—The rest of the Halape Trail. After turning south from the old 4WD road, this trail descends to Halape on the the Puna Kau coast. It's an important and popular, though not particularly pleasant or scenic, route. Rangers told me it's maintained fairly often because of its popularity. Trips 43 through 45 use the Halape Trail.

—The Keauhou Trail. Three miserable miles and *road* junctions beyond the point where the Halape Trail turns south, the old 4WD road reaches an obscure *trail* junction with the Keauhou Trail. The 4¾ miles (one way) of the Keauhou Trail itself are very overgrown and unpleasant. Rangers told me they maintain the Keauhou Trail infrequently, as it's not popular. I can see why. The same obscure *trail* junction may be reached by the spur trail mentioned above; it runs southwest from the Mauna Ulu o Mauna Loa turnout on the Chain of Craters Road (2 miles one way). Either way you don't get to it, the Keauhou Trail is a must-miss. And both the Halape and Keauhou trails can be ordeals on a hot day—wretched going down, unspeakable on the way back up. As I said earlier, I think the Puna Kau Trail is a better way to get to Keauhou *and* Halape (see Trips 38, 39, and 45).

Kaaha Trail. Okay between Pepeiao Cabin and Kaaha Shelter; see Trip 47. Overgrown and should be avoided between Kaaha Shelter and the Hilina Pali Trail (see below).

Trails from Hilina Pali roadend.

—The Kau Desert Trail. This trail is okay as far as its junction with the Kaaha Trail near Pepeiao Cabin; see Trips 46 and 47. After that, it's not bad, just dull (also see above, in this appendix).

—The Hilina Pali Trail. I recommend you avoid the Hilina Pali Trail itself. It dives over Hilina Pali and plunges just under 2¼ miles one way to a small plateau a thousand feet below. This segment of the Hilina Pali Trail is extremely steep, and the footing is very poor in many places. On the plateau, it meets an overgrown segment of the Kaaha Trail, which curves away south to Kaaha Shelter. The Hilina Pali Trail itself curves southeast from this junction and becomes extraordinarily overgrown and difficult to follow. You are expected to follow cairns across lava, but the lava itself is so overgrown with tall, dense weeds that it's hard to plow through the weeds and hard to see the cairns. Worse yet, unseen morning glory vines snake through the dense weeds and are ready to wrap around your ankles and trip you. The Hilina Pali Trail nearly vanishes in the overgrowth as you ascend behind Puu Kaone, thrashing through *koa haole* thickets draped in morning glory vines. Then you go skidding steeply down into a gully filled with another vine-draped *koa haole* thicket. Across the gully, cairns reappear and the trail becomes a little more apparent You climb to a shoulder behind Puu Kapukapu before you at last descend to meet the Halape Trail. You do all of this in the glare, heat, and humidity typical of this coast. It's a must-miss. One backpacker I met, who had struggled with a full pack across that weary, waterless route, said, "I was sure I was going to collapse of heat exhaustion." Three others, also toting full packs, just shook their heads. I found it very unpleasant even as a dayhike.

—Spur trail from Hilina Pali Trail to Kaaha Trail. A spur trail across the seaward end of the plateau connects the Kaaha and Hilina Pali trails (just under 1½ miles one way). It, too, is terribly overgrown and booby-trapped with morning glory vines.

—Kaaha Trail from Hilina Pali Trail to Kaaha Shelter. As noted above, this segment (1⅔ miles one way) should be avoided because it, too, is overgrown, though not as badly as the Hilina Pali Trail and the spur trail.

Ainapo Trail. This trail appears on some maps as leading to the summit area of Mauna Loa. *Hawaii, Naturally* says, ". . . the Ainapo Trail is not recommended unless you go with someone familiar with the trail."

Green Sand Beach. I think this geological oddity, near South Point, is not worth your time. It is extremely remote, and many rental-car contracts forbid driving on the South Point Road. The fabled "green" sand—crystals of olivine weathered out of the surrounding cliffs—is more the faded olive drab of an Army vehicle left out in the sun. The beach is very narrow, and the South Point waters are extremely rough and treacherous. It's reported to be very difficult to get down to the beach; I didn't bother to climb down to it. It's a four-mile round trip by Ankle Express down the 4WD road that runs northeast from South Point's tiny harbor to and from a good overlook of the Green Sand Beach, if you really must see it. Otherwise, you can see olivines weathered out in small quantities along the Mauna Loa and Puna Kau trails. "Once upon a time," I've heard oldtimers tell newcomers, "the green sand was emerald green and the beach was much, much wider. . . ."

Kaheawai Trail. This hard-to-find trail near Manuka State Wayside is in very poor condition—overgrown, poorly marked, and treacherous. At first it runs mostly near the edge of a steep-sided gulch, where a misstep could have disastrous consequences. The tags and cairns, always inadequate, peter out at an *aa* field about halfway to the coast. It's boring, too.

Kaloko-Honokohau National Historical Park. This park has been under development for years and is still not finished or fully open to the public. Its entrance is not marked on the highway, making it nearly impossible to find. I suggest you wait until it's really ready for business, though goodness knows when that will be in the present political and economic climate.

Keolonahihi State Historical Park. Land for it was purchased years ago, but nothing more has been done, I'm told. It remains an unmarked patch of scrub on the Kona coast in spite of being listed in the July 1989 DNLR brochure. Its "existence" was news to most of the people I talked to at the DNLR on the Big Island.

Kiholo Bay. Development along the Ko*hala* coast is proceeding at a frantic pace. The number of private residences down at Kiholo Bay has grown, and the owners are very protective of their turf. The 4WD road that once connected Highway 19 with Kiholo Bay has been deliberately obliterated where it once met the highway. The built-up coastal area bristles with private property and no trespassing signs. One imposing palace boasts a TV security system. The state has acquired and plans to develop public access to Luahinewai, the sacred pool where Keoua bathed before his death at Puukohola (see Trip 57). However, until that public access is secured and marked, I suggest you avoid this area altogether.

Puako petroglyphs. This important petroglyph field is currently accessible only through the grounds of the Mauna Lani resort (Trip 56). Only a small portion of the field may be seen from the viewing area. The former access from Puako village has been fenced off and posted, forbidding entry. Perhaps when the developers are through, they will re-open the access from Puako village.

Trail out of Pololu Valley southeastward. Deeply eroded, unmaintained, and dangerous. Avoid this one.

Appendix C. How I Got Distances, Elevations, Times, and Trail Maps

I estimated distances primarily by time, knowing that I hike 2 miles/hour and backpack at 1⅓ miles/hour. I compared the distances I got by time with distance values supplied by the agencies in charge of the trails. In a few cases, I also had distance data from plots I'd made from the topos. When those distances were close, I felt satisfied with the distance I'd estimated by time. I rounded the distances off to the nearest ¼ or ⅓ mile.

I got most driving distances by rental-car odometer, which was consistent to within 1/10 mile over routes I drove repeatedly. When I had not started from Hilo, I added or subtracted the distance from my starting point to Hilo. I found that in a some cases I did not get usable odometer data; in those cases, I used data from the University of Hawaii Press map of Hawaii or calculated the mileage from the topos.

I determined elevation from topos and with an altimeter. Where I had altimeter data, I looked for close correspondence between those values, topo values, and any values supplied by the agency in charge of the trail.

Trail times are based on the time I actually spent in motion on the trail.

I made the trail maps by first scanning relevant pieces of the USGS topos into a computer. I put the resulting digitized topo information that applied to a trip or a set of trips into the bottom layer of a multiple-layer electronic drawing. I then traced selected topo information from the bottom layer onto a transparent electronic top layer. I hid the bottom layer containing the scanned data when I printed out the finished maps for this book. I left out the elevation contours because the resolution of the scanned data is too coarse to show the elevation contours and they would have taken me too long to draw. I added, deleted, or modified topo information that I knew had changed. My choices of conventions for trails, roads, boundaries, etc., primarily reflect the software's capabilities.

Many trails on Hawaii do not appear at all on the topos or in usable form on any official agency map. For them, I approximated the route based on field notes and sketches and any agency or landowner information I could find.

Index

Acknowledgements

For their encouragement, help, advice, and endless patience: alphabetically, Barbara Dallavo, Christina O'Keefe, and Thomas Winnett. Tom, who *is* Wilderness Press, has provided some of his own photographs for this series of books and has not always given himself proper credit. He has been a patient and thorough editor and has also provided me with many helpful books and articles about Hawaii.

For sending useful information to and answering questions from a total stranger, I thank the people at Hawaii Volcanoes National Park; the Division of Forestry and Wildlife, Hawaii District; the Division of State Parks, Hawaii District; and the Hawaii Visitors Bureau, Los Angeles office. Ray Brouillard shared the longer Mauna Loa summit trail and his insights on it with me. Rangers and volunteer rangers at Hawaii Volcanoes National Park were helpful in more ways than I can enumerate.

I am very much indebted to Jerry Schad. His use of icons to help summarize hikes in his outstanding *Afoot and Afield . . .* series of guides for Southern California (available from Wilderness Press) inspired me to create and use icons in this book and in its predecessors, *Kauai Trails* and *Maui Trails.*

I hope I have accurately and adequately reflected the information these people, and many others, provided directly or indirectly. Any misunderstanding or errors are my responsibility.

K.M.

More Hawaiian Guidebooks

If you enjoyed **Hawaii Trails**, and want to do more exploring in the Hawaiian Islands, be sure to look for these other Wilderness Press books:

Maui Trails: Walks, Strolls and Treks on the Valley Isle, by Kathy Morey. Describing 54 walking tours, this guidebook leads you to the beaches, waterfalls and mountains that make up the dramatically beautiful tropical landscapes of Maui.

Kauai Trails: Walks, Strolls and Treks on the Garden Isle, by Kathy Morey. Kauai may seem like a little island from the air, but from the trail it becomes like a faceted diamond, revealing a new face to you at every step. The 62 trips described in this book will be your key to this lush treasure.

Oahu Trails: Walks, Strolls and Treks on the Capital Isle, by Kathy Morey. If images of Oahu bring to mind only high-rise hotels, then you haven't trekked far from Waikiki. Oahu has beautiful mountains, spectacular beaches and dramatic cliffs that can offer any hiker an exciting expedition far from the tourists and traffic. *Available late 1992*

Hawaii, Naturally: An Environmentally Oriented Guide to the Wonders and Pleasures of the Islands, by David Zurick. If you're interested in experiencing the natural and cultural beauty, not the commercial amusements, of Hawaii, this guidebook is for you. Hawaii, Naturally is a comprehensive guide to attractions and activities on all four major islands, plus Molokai and Lanai. Parks, natural- and cultural-history areas, hiking trails—even health food sources—are included.

Check your local bookstore or hiking supply dealer for these books or write for our free mail order catalog: